Imperialist Canada

TODD GORDON

IMPERIALIST CANADA.

ARBEITER RING PUBLISHING · WINNIPEG

Arbeiter Ring Publishing
201E-121 Osborne Street
Winnipeg, Manitoba
Canada R3L 1Y4
www.arbeiterring.com

Cover design by Robyn Taylor
Typeset by Relish Design Studio, Ltd.
Printed in Canada by Hignell Printing

With assistance of the Manitoba Arts Council/Conseil des Arts du Manitoba.

We acknowledge the support of the Canada Council for our publishing program.

ARP acknowledges the financial support to our publishing activities of the Manitoba
Arts Council/Conseil des Arts du Manitoba, Manitoba Culture, Heritage and Tourism,
and the Government of Canada through the Canada Book Fund.

Arbeiter Ring Publishing acknowledges the support of the Province of Manitoba
through the Book Publishing Tax Credit and the Book Publisher Marketing Assistance Program.

Printed on 100% recycled paper.

LIBRARY AND ARCHIVES CANADA CATALOGUING IN PUBLICATION

Gordon, Todd, 1973-
    Imperialist Canada / Todd Gordon.

Includes bibliographical references and index.
ISBN 978-1-894037-45-7

    1. Canada--Foreign relations. 2. Canada--Foreign economic
relations. I. Title.

FC242.G67 2010   327.71   C2010-905696-5

CONTENTS

Acknowledgements

A number of people have made important contributions to *Imperialist Canada*. Jeff Webber offered many thoughtful comments on an earlier draft of chapter one, while our frequent political discussions and writing partnership have helped me to develop many of the ideas expressed throughout the book. The part on Colombia in the mining section of chapter four is drawn from our article "Imperialism and Resistance" in *Third World Quarterly* (vol. 29, n. 1, 2008). Murray Cooke provided me with a number of opportunities to try out my ideas-in-progress on the several panels he organized on Canadian imperialism at the annual Socialist Studies conferences. The title of the book is borrowed from one of those panels. Regular attendees at these panels who contributed to the discussions include Bill Burgess, Bill Carroll, Paul Kellogg and Abbie Bakan. The Latin American Solidarity Network in Toronto has also been an important space in developing an analysis of Canadian imperialism. Carlos Torchia, Ilian Burbano and Greg Albo, among others, have been committed to insuring that Canadian foreign policy is part of our discussion on Latin America. Deb Simmons and Shiri Pasternak, meanwhile, kindly gave their time and knowledge as I tried to clarify my thoughts on colonialism in Canada. Special thanks is also owed to Esyllt Jones for her comments on a draft of the manuscript and to everyone else at Arbeiter Ring Publishing for supporting this project and helping to make the book a reality. As always, Jackie Esmonde has been an immeasurable source of love, friendship and support.

My father Bob and my sister Leslie both passed away during the course of writing *Imperialist Canada*. I dedicate it to their memories.

INTRODUCTION:
Rethinking Canada's Role in the World

The time is long overdue for a serious reconsideration of Canada's role in global affairs. This book is a contribution to that much-needed rethinking.

It argues that Canada is an imperialist country—not a super-power, but a power that nevertheless benefits from and actively participates in the global system of domination in which the wealth and resources of the Third World are systematically plundered by capital of the Global North.

The old ideas that effectively portrayed Canada as a subordinate nation with little or no imperial ambition of its own and dominated first by Britain and then the United States, which have in fact been a mainstay of much of the Canadian left as much as other parts of the Canadian political spectrum, are simply not relevant to understanding its role in the contemporary world order (if they were even relevant in their heyday thirty years ago). While there have always been dissidents on the Canadian left who have eschewed nationalism, they have been going against the grain.[1] Nationalism has been a dominant ideological force on the Canadian left since the new left of the 1960s and 70s, though its roots go back at least to the pre-Second World War Communist Party. While some left nationalists have occasionally identified some of the problematic actions of the Canadian state and capital in the Third World, they have failed to develop a systematic analysis of

Canadian imperialism. Just like the other major capitalist powers, Canadian capital is driven by a logic of expansion. The insatiable drive to seek out new markets and territories in which to accumulate wealth in the capitalist game of survival of the fittest drives it deeper into sovereign indigenous lands within its borders and increasingly beyond its own borders. This expansionary process is made possible by the aggressive policies of the Canadian state.

Canada's stature as a sub-superpower nation, in other words, does not gainsay the fact that it faces pressures to search out new markets and has the ability to project its power in its own political and economic self-interest, regardless of the cost to indigenous communities at home or to the people of the Third World. Indeed, this is precisely what it does. Driving Canadian foreign policy, for instance, is the goal of creating the conditions for the successful international expansion of Canadian corporations, at the heart of which is forcibly opening up the markets and resources of the Global South. The list of options in its imperialist toolkit is varied, as I will show, and includes both bilateral and multilateral (with its imperial partners) policies. Canada actively pursues one-sided trade and investment agreements with poor countries, forcibly liberalizes markets in the South through International Monetary Fund-imposed structural adjustment policies, ignores flagrant human rights violations committed in defence of Canadian investments and is pouring increasingly large sums of money into the development of a military with the capability to project its power abroad.

Canadian capital, especially in the mining and financial services sectors, has always had an international orientation, and Canadian diplomacy has always sought to support its interests and reinforce the subordination of the Third World. Banks like Scotia and Royal have long histories in the Caribbean, while the presence of Canadian mining companies in Latin America, Asia-Pacific and Africa goes back many decades. But the last twenty years, following the emergence of neoliberal globalization, has seen a major intensification of the outward expansion of Canadian capital. The period of neoliberalism, which began roughly in the late 1970s and early 1980s (its adoption and the aggressiveness of the adoption having differed from country to country), has been witness to a major offensive by Canadian capital and the state against indigenous and working people both at home and abroad. The goal has been the restoration of profitability in the wake of the global economic downturn of the 1970s through the unleashing of free market forces and increasing the rights of corporations. At home it has involved an attack on working-class living standards through workplace restructuring, the rollback of labour rights and severe cuts to the welfare state. It has also entailed in Canada a greater push into First Nation territories, in search of natural resources and more generally to facilitate the domestic expansion of Canadian capitalism. The net result of neoliberalism in Canada has been a massive transfer of wealth from the bottom of the economic pyramid to its very top.[2]

But just as important to the success and profitability of Canadian capital during this period has been its aggressive penetration of the Third World. The fact is, as I will demonstrate, Canada has become a major foreign investor in the South, facilitated no doubt by the state's active support in providing Canadian companies access to this region. Canada has become a significant player in the Third World, especially in its own backyard—Latin America and the Caribbean. And thus we find that in 1980 profits from Canadian Third World investments were $3.7 billion, while by 2007 they were $23.6 billion after tax—an increase of 535 percent, which is greater than the increase in profits earned at home over the same period of time.[3]

There is no bright side to Canadian investment in the South. It is accomplished by displacing indigenous people and poor peasants from their land (to get at mineral and oil deposits, for example), destroying ecosystems and ruthlessly exploiting the sweat labour of typically poor women in the region's export processing zones, where workers' rights are minimal if they exist at all. We can also add to this the steep burden of debt obligations Third World governments are forced to pay Canadian banks, money which otherwise could go to social programs for their own citizens. The significant increase in corporate earnings in the Third World, in other words, is happening on the backs of some of the world's most vulnerable people; it is matched by a corresponding increase in displacement and misery. And thus the neoliberal domestic transfer of wealth up the economic ladder is matched by an international one even more grotesque in its scale.

Another important indicator of the nature of Canada's role in the Global South comes from the communities directly affected by Canadian investment. Canadian companies and policies are increasingly met by a fierce resistance—people fighting for their indigenous rights, their land, and their dignity in the workplace. The struggles against Canadian companies and policies in the Third World are a loud and forceful—and perhaps the most important—reminder that Canada's role in the world is in serious need of a profound rethinking. The notion of Canada as either a benevolent, neutral or subordinated international actor that does not put its own self-interests first is badly misleading. As I detail in the fourth chapter, it is not benevolence or neutrality that Third World activists are resisting, and in some cases losing their lives over. It is the predatory nature of Canadian capital they are fighting: the mining and oil and gas companies stealing and destroying their land, the sweatshop manufacturers who go to all lengths to keep unions out and maintain poverty-level wages, and the banks that finance these investments and cater to the whims of local elites.

But resistance does not deter Canada from its global mission of free market fundamentalism. It simply inspires it to build up its capacity to engage in violence. The ability to more assertively and efficiently throw its weight around in the world is held in very high regard by military, political and business leaders. The $18 billion increase in military spending between 2005–2010 alone, and the projected increase of $50 billion over the next two decades, is not for peacekeeping. It is for a combat-capable military that will be taken seriously by both friend and foe. Peacekeeping is in fact another piece of Canadian history that desperately needs to be deconstructed. Not only is the actual practice of peacekeeping far more problematic than its proponents across the political spectrum acknowledge, as I argue in the fifth chapter, but peacekeeping claims simply do not resonate with indigenous peoples in Canada facing military and paramilitary assaults on their land reclamations, Haitians opposed to the Canadian-supported 2004 coup d'état against Jean-Bertrand Aristide, or Afghans who have been living under violent occupation since 2001. On this score, the right's analysis of Canada's military role in the world is more accurate than much of the left's, when the former—often in response to the claims made by the likes of the New Democratic Party that

Canada is at heart a peacekeeper—asserts that Canada is not a peacekeeping nation but one that engages in war. The right's justification of Canada's military missions may be wrong and very misleading, but their basic understanding of the military's history and its role in foreign policy is not.

Canadian security doctrine, like that of its allies, is being developed in response to the resistance to and instabilities facing neoliberal globalization in the South. As a complement to foreign economic policy, it is about maintaining the security of free markets and capital: making the South a safe place to do business. This requires a stability, order and transparency for foreign investors that cannot always be obtained by trade and investment agreements or structural adjustment policies. Instabilities caused by poverty, the long historical legacy of colonial violence (expressed, for instance, in internecine violence) and anti-neoliberal political mobilization are all threats to the sanctity of free markets, upon which the order of neoliberal globalization rests, and militarism is viewed as a perfectly legitimate option by the nations of the imperialist centre.

But in the mobilization of the defence of free markets, whether through military or economic policy, the racist nature of imperialism is unmasked. Divorced from any meaningful historical context (including the history of colonialism itself), people in the Third World are presented starkly as culturally backward and uncivilized people who need to be saved from themselves by the imperialist powers, including Canada. Free markets, imposed by the rich world, and the foundation of neoliberal civilization, are countenanced as the ticket out of poverty. All the scientific advice of the North's best-trained economic minds is marshalled to promote unhindered market forces. People's failure to embrace neoliberal dogma or to lift themselves up out of poverty is thus surely a sign of their irrationality. But how else can this cruel economic medicine be defended in the face of increased poverty and misery, except for the old racist tropes that somehow the Third World's poor, primarily people of colour, are responsible for their own situation or simply do not know—cannot know—what's best for them? They cannot win in an imperialist game that is stacked against them from the start: they accept free markets but their situation declines, it is a sign of their own civilizational failures; they opt for an alternative, it is just another sign of their incapacity to look after themselves.

How else can the treatment of indigenous peoples, violently forced off their land, and workers of colour, labouring in conditions that rival the Industrial Revolution of the First World, be justified, except through an implicit, and sometimes explicit, characterization of them as somehow less than fully human? As I discuss in the third chapter, Canada has steadfastly refused to pass human rights legislation governing the practices of its corporations abroad, in spite of all the evidence that such laws are desperately needed. The implication is clear: peoples of colour in the Third World aren't deserving of such human rights. But when they refuse to be expendable, when they are so bold as to challenge the diktats of neoliberal order, their threat level rises exponentially in the eyes of the managers of global imperialism. As was the case with Jean-Bertrand Aristide's Haiti, they become a "failed" state necessitating intervention. Canada, for example, funded far right-wing forces that led the coup and its military played a lead role in violently pacifying the poor neighbourhoods where Aristide's support was the strongest. Never mind that Aristide was democratically supported, that living conditions for many people in the poorest country in the hemisphere improved modestly under his leadership, and that the situation in Haiti worsened dramatically after the coup; the country is now, once again in alignment with the interests of Canada, the U.S. and France, responsible and on the right path toward development. As I show in the sixth chapter, the same logic underlies Canada's relations with anti-neoliberal movements and governments in the Andes and its rapprochement with that human rights disaster, Colombia.

Some defenders of the traditional view of Canada as either a benevolent, neutral or subordinate force in global affairs may try to comfort themselves in the notion that whatever belligerent turns Canadian foreign policy has taken in recent years, it is the result of pressures from the Americans and an increased integration with them. But this is a dangerously misleading position. Whatever influence the U.S. may have on Canadian foreign policy, Canadians will achieve little by convincing themselves that Canadian imperial practice is strictly reducible to American demands. Continental integration has occurred over the last two decades, but Canada is far from fully integrated with the U.S. Canadian capital is still an independent force, however much its interests often coincide with its American counterpart. At the same time, the interests of Canadian capital are global. It has as much stake in the maintenance of the imperialist system as do the Americans, even if Canada is not a superpower and does not therefore lead that system. Canada was not pulled into it against its own will, in other words; it is an active and willing participant. And if those of us committed to a more socially just world are going to mount a challenge to Canada's role in the global order, we need to understand what is driving it. Blaming Canadian imperialism on the U.S. simply does not get us very far.

Who Owns Canada?

A few comments on the status of Canadian capital are in order here, given that we are often told by mainstream commentators and left nationalists that Canada is dominated by foreign capital and that it is more akin in some respects to an industrially underdeveloped country. Despite being challenged by critics in the past, this idea has been fairly pervasive on the left for several decades now.

The supposed underdevelopment of Canadian capitalism is typically traced back to the days of the exploitation of the fur trade by the British, and the dominant role played by financial capital (such as banks), often in rivalry with a weak industrial capital, in capitalist development. While there are different twists on the historical argument about exactly why Canada did not develop properly, they all stress that the end result is that Canada has a weak domestic industrial base, and therefore bourgeoisie, and has been dominated by foreign—mainly American—capital. Drawing on studies by the dependency school in the 1960s and 70s on Third World countries' relations with the imperialist core, but putting their own unique spin on it, some observers describe Canada as a rich dependency. Unlike poor countries in the Global South, Canada is a rich nation due in no small part to its geographic proximity to the United States and its abundant natural resources, but like the Global South, Canada, lacking a strong industrial bourgeoisie of its own, is dependent on its economic ties to rich countries like the United States—and in particular their foreign investment—for its economic growth and prosperity.[4]

The consequence of this analysis is that left nationalists have failed to develop a systematic theory of Canadian imperialism and the global ambitions of the Canadian ruling class, and focus instead on the need for stronger protection from foreign ownership and control in the Canadian economy in order to promote an independent Canada. This analysis can potentially obscure the different class interests shaping Canadian society and misdirect working-class Canadians' political energies, if the main problem facing Canadians is seen as America's dominance of Canada rather than the power of the Canadian capitalist class whose objective (that is, class) interests are to exploit both Canadian and Global South workers and their surrounding environments as much as possible. It also mistakenly suggests the Canadian state can be a progressive space and play a central role in this struggle for sovereignty from American influence, when, as I argue in this book, the state has itself been imperialist since its formation.

One measure the left nationalists have used to advance their claim that Canada never developed a dominant capitalist class that has significant control over its domestic economy, like that of other imperial powers, is foreign ownership of Canadian assets. But the extent of foreign ownership in the Canadian economy is not so clear cut, on the one hand, nor is Canada as distinctive from other advanced capitalist countries when it comes to inward foreign investment, on the other.

Data on foreign ownership of all industries combined in Canada only goes back to 1988. Prior to that, ownership figures were only presented as divided between financial and non-financial industries. A break in the data occurs in 1988, when the government refined its definition of foreign ownership for financial corporations.[5] The series for all industries combined from 1988 onwards uses the refined definition for finance and insurance. The only data that accurately covers both pre- and post-1988 data, then, is for non-financial corporations. This data goes back to 1965. What we find for non-financial corporations is that foreign control of non-financial corporate assets is still lower today (averaging 27.8 percent for 2000–05) than it was in the 1960s (thirty-one percent for 1965–69). It reached its lowest ebb in the mid-80s (averaging 22.8 percent for 1980–89) and has since then been creeping back up again, though it still remains lower for the 2000–05 period than it did for the 1965–69 period, and it in fact declined modestly from 2001 to 2005 (28.8 to 27.2 percent).[6] The decline in foreign ownership from the late 1960s to the mid-1980s corresponds to the tightening of restrictions on foreign ownership of corporate assets associated with the establishment of the Foreign Investment Review Agency (FIRA) in the early 1970s; the renewed increase corresponds in turn to the subsequent reversing of the FIRA-associated restrictions (and the transformation of FIRA into Investment Canada) in the context of neoliberal restructuring.[7]

When we consider all industries (financial and non-financial), however, we find that over the eighteen years from 1988 to 2005, foreign ownership increased by a mere 0.7 percent—hardly a significant margin.[8]

FOREIGN CONTROL OF ASSETS, ALL INDUSTRIES, 1988-2005

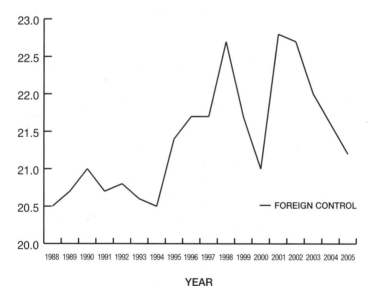

YEAR

And, the data for financial corporations prior to 1988 shows a low ebb for foreign control in the early 1980s with a gradual increase following that, while as I have just noted the data for the pre-1988 years for non-financial corporations shows foreign ownership was at its lowest in the mid-1980s. This suggests that there was not a significant jump in foreign ownership for all industries combined predating 1988 (when the official record on foreign ownership in all industries began), and that therefore the rate has held fairly steady with a only a modest increase since the early 1980s. To the extent there has been an increase in foreign ownership (however slight for all industries combined), though, this phenomenon is not isolated to Canada; it is part of a broader trend affecting most advanced capitalist countries.

Other advanced capitalist countries do not collect foreign ownership data in the way that Canada does through its Corporations Returns Act (CRA) (formerly the Corporations and Labour Unions Returns Act), which makes cross-country foreign ownership comparisons difficult. Inward Foreign Direct Investment (FDI) stock as a percentage of Gross Domestic Product (GDP) can, however, give us a comparative view of the trend of foreign ownership among advanced capitalist countries. FDI constitutes ten percent or more of equity in an asset, which is considered to give the investor some degree of managerial control in their investment. So FDI gives us a limited sense of the long-term managerial control of economic wealth in an economy by foreigners; and by measuring it in relation to GDP we can control for differences in the size of economies. When we do this, we find that Canada's inward FDI-GDP ratio, at 36.5 percent in 2007, is considerably higher than that of G8 countries like Japan (3 percent), the U.S. (15.1 percent), Italy (17.3 percent) and Germany (19 percent). It is also higher than Russia's, which stands at 25.1 percent. But it is quite a bit lower than that of the U.K. (48.6 percent) and is not as high as France (40.1 percent), both countries that are obviously considered advanced capitalist powers and not underdeveloped dependencies. Canada's ratio is also considerably lower than other rich nations like Belgium (165.2 percent), Netherlands (87.9 percent), Switzerland (65.7 percent), Sweden (56 percent) and Denmark (47.1 percent). Furthermore, among G8 countries, Canada has by far the lowest rate of increase of inward FDI stock as a percentage of GDP from 1980 to 2007 (81.6 percent), with Russia (3037 percent, from 1990 onwards) and Japan (900 percent) having the highest rate of increase. What this suggests is that the differences in inward FDI stock to GDP ratio between Canada and other G8 countries is decreasing, if slowly.[9]

William Carroll's study of corporate elite networks in Canada, which are expressed in the overlapping of directorships of different companies, also helps to clarify left nationalist misperceptions surrounding Canadian capital. Not only is foreign ownership not as extensive as they presume, but Carroll finds that there is a strong, interlocked Canadian capitalist ruling class. In other words, Canadian capital is strongly concentrated (measured in terms of board of directorships) and internally linked. There are actually fewer than 500 individuals who sit on the boards of the top 250 corporations. The most powerful positions within this corporate elite network are the majority and minority shareholders—people with a controlling influence, through share ownership, in a company. Canada actually has, according to Carroll, a much higher level of concentrated shareholding than the United States. Carroll cites economic geographer Bill Burgess's study on corporate ownership in Canada, which notes that "the Canadian corporate network is characterized by the large degree of majority or strong minority control, and by the incorporation of many firms within larger corporate groups [i.e., enterprises]." By 1996, less than one-fifth of the top 250 firms did not have an identifiable controlling shareholder. This suggests that corporate power in Canada is strongly concentrated among a fairly small number of Canadians.[10]

Both Burgess and Carroll also find that foreign ownership of the largest and most powerful companies across all sectors of the economy declined through the 1980s and 90s. Thus Canadians have greater control today of the largest Canadian companies than in previous periods, while the web of interlocking Canadian corporate elites has grown denser. Burgess's more recent research on patterns of economic control of Canada's largest enterprises confirms his and Carroll's earlier work, and finds that there are few ownership linkages between foreign-controlled and Canadian-controlled enterprises that interfere with the overall trend of strong Canadian ownership patterns within and across economic sectors.[11] At the same time as Canadian control of Canadian-based companies has become more centralized, the transnationalization of Canadian corporations has increased, and among the largest Canadian companies the number of transnationals—companies Carroll defines as having operations in at least five countries—overtook the number of national companies. More broadly, there are roughly 1,400 transnational corporations based in Canada, which have approximately 3,700 foreign affiliates and employ more than one million workers.[12]

The University of Toronto-based Institute for Competitiveness and Prosperity's study "Canada's Global Leaders" challenges, from a pro-business perspective, the idea that Canada does not have a strong or internationally competitive corporate base. It argues that instead of concerning themselves with defending Canada against a hollowing-out process that is not really occurring, policy-makers should instead be doing more to promote the growing global ambitions of Canadian multinationals. The study argues that Canada's "global leaders" have increased over the last two decades. To be included in its list of global leaders, a Canadian-controlled company must be in the *Report on Business* Top 1000 or *Financial Post* 500 lists, have revenues exceeding $100 million in 2005 (which is equivalent to $50 million in 1985) and be one of the five largest by revenue globally in a specific market segment. By the Institute's calculations, Canada had thirty-three corporate global leaders in 1985. This figure jumped to seventy-two in 2006. These global leaders can be found in various sectors, and not just in natural resources: mining, high-tech machinery, chemicals, telecommunications, food and beverage, auto parts, financial services and aerospace and arms, among other sectors. Canada's corporate sector has a strong multinational presence that cannot be ignored.[13]

Canadian nationalists also commonly suggest that Canadian industry is being hollowed out by foreign takeovers. In the fall of 2006, for instance, nationalists publicly raised concern about a couple of high-profile takeovers of Canadian mining companies.[14] The implication was that this was but another example of Canada being effectively colonized by foreign capital. The data on share-holding and corporate directorships above suggest this claim is overblown. What the nationalists also fail to acknowledge, however, is that behind these high-profile foreign takeovers is the longer-term trend whereby Canadian companies conduct cross-border acquisitions of foreign assets at approximately the same rate that foreigners acquire Canadian assets.[15]

As part of a broader worldwide trend, the value of Canadian mergers and acquisitions grew through the late 1990s and early 2000s. In the late 1990s, mergers and acquisitions activity was eight times greater than a decade earlier, and most of the Canadian cross-border takeovers took place in the U.S. and Global South countries. Between 1992 and June 2009, the value of Canadian acquisitions of foreign assets actually matched the value of foreign purchases of Canadian assets. For eleven and a half of those years, Canadian companies were net acquirers of foreign assets, and on the whole over this period the number of Canada's foreign acquisitions was considerably higher than the number of foreign takeovers of Canadian assets. It is really three particular years—2000, 2006 and 2007—in which foreign takeovers of Canadian companies are heavily concentrated and outpace Canadian acquisitions by a big margin. But even in these years, the numbers of Canadian foreign takeovers are still higher than that of foreigners' takeovers of Canadian firms. The increase in foreign takeovers in those years are actually accounted for by a few rather large (in terms of value) purchases. In 2000, for example, the difference between outward and inward acquisitions was due to one notable and very expensive foreign takeover: Vivendi of France's $41.6 billion purchase of Seagram's. It is also worth noting that four G8 nations (the U.S., Germany, Italy and Russia) weren't net acquirers of foreign assets over this period.[16]

In the late 1990s and early 2000s, Canadian companies acquired $85 billion worth of American assets, which accounted for sixty-eight percent of its cross-border mergers and acquisitions activity. Furthermore, like Canadian foreign direct investment more generally, Canadian cross-border acquisitions were concentrated among Canada's biggest multinational corporations which were engaged in quite large purchases. Over seventy percent of cross-border takeovers were of a value of more than $1 billion, and more than a third were greater than $5 billion. In 2004, Canada had four cross-border acquisitions, worth a combined US$18 billion, in the top twenty-five of all acquisitions in the world, and for the years 2002–2004, Canada was fourth in the world in the value of cross-border purchases.[17] The aggressive foreign takeover posture of Canadian capital in recent years, combined with the devastation in the American banking sector in the wake of the 2008 financial collapse, in fact led to Canada's first ever surplus in bilateral foreign direct investment with the United States in 2008. Despite Canada's economy being less than a tenth the size of the United States', Canadian companies invested $17.1 billion more in the U.S. than American companies invested in Canada.[18]

Beyond Left Nationalism

In short, Canada has a strong and coherent capitalist class that cannot be said to be dominated by foreign interests. To the extent Canadian capital has ties to international capital, or there is a growth in foreign ownership in Canada, these trends are part of broader developments in the global economy affecting other major powers. They are by no means exclusive to Canada.

By extension, any assumptions that Canadian capital is unable to project its power and influence are misplaced, as are those that treat Canada as a benign presence in the world. As a coherent social force with clear class interests (the unyielding accumulation of wealth), Canadian capital is quite capable, with the abiding support of the state, of exercising power beyond its borders, and does so. Simply because Canada is not as big as the U.S. does not mean it is not as imperialist. Quantitative difference does not imply a qualitative one. Canada is no more or less imperialist than its other major power counterparts. The struggles against Canadian political and economic intervention in the Third World, from Afghanistan to Haiti, and from Guatemala to Tanzania, confirm this.

And so it is time for a fresh look at Canada's role in the world. The following chapters will explore the different facets of Canadian imperialism, both at home, where it begins and where Canadian capital has built itself up to become a major force on the world stage. The efforts at the domestic dispossession of indigenous communities are explored, different bilateral and multilateral strategies for penetrating foreign markets are examined, the growth of Canadian investment in the South is detailed, case studies on human rights and ecological abuses committed by Canadian capital and the resistance they generate are presented, and the pronounced increase in militarism is considered. While by no means intended as the last word on the subject, I hope *Imperialist Canada* will at least contribute to an ongoing effort to rethink the role Canada plays in the world today.

1   Important criticisms of the left nationalist thesis include J. Niosi, *Canadian Multinationals* (Toronto: Between the Lines, 1985); W. Carroll, *Corporate Power and Canadian Capitalism* (Vancouver: University of British Columbia Press, 1986); D. McNally, "Staples Theory as Commodity Fetishism," *Studies in Political Economy* (n. 6, 1981), 35-63; B. Burgess, *Canada's Location in the World System: Reworking the Debate in Canadian Political Economy*, Ph.D. Dissertation, Geography Dept., University of British Columbia, 2002. Burgess's dissertation also includes discussion the development of left nationalism within the Communist Party.

2   This has been documented by a number of studies written by the Canadian Centre for Policy Alternatives, Centre for Social Justice, Statistics Canada and the Organization for Economic Cooperation and Development.

3   Developing country profits are from Cansim Table 376-0001, "investment income," which includes direct, portfolio and "other" earnings, for non-OECD and non-EU countries. Canadian-based profits are from Cansim Table 187-0001, operating profits "total all industries, after tax." Third World earnings are after tax as well. The comparison is imperfect, as the operating profit methodology includes some writedowns, such as for inventory, while the foreign investment profits, collected on a Gross Domestic Product (GDP) basis, do not. Canadian-based profits collected on a GDP-basis aren't after tax.

4   Classic left nationalist accounts include K. Levitt, *Silent Surrender: The Multinational Corporation in Canada* (Toronto: Macmillan, 1970); G. Teeple, ed., *Capital and the National Question in Canada* (Toronto: University of Toronto Press, 1972); R. T. Naylor, *The History of Canadian Business* (Toronto: J.L. Lorimer, 1975); W. Clement and D. Drache, *A Practical Guide to Canadian Political Economy* (Toronto: J. L. Lorimer, 1978).

5   The refinement for defining foreign ownership in the finance industry involved a change from publishing worldwide assets of corporations pre-1988 to "booked-in-Canada" assets after 1988. Also, holding and investment company data is now excluded in order to minimize the effect of double counting. There was a break in 1988 for the non-financial series, though it was less pronounced and government data analysts have been able to adjust the pre-1988 series to correspond to the post-1988 series using the same definition.

6   Data from 1999-2005 is from Statistics Canada, *Corporations Returns Act* (2005), <www.statcan.gc.ca/pub/61-220-x/61-220-x2005000-eng.pdf>, retrieved November 2008. Pre-1999 data is from Statistics Canada, *Global Links: Long-Term Trends in Foreign Investment and Foreign Control in Canada, 1960-2000*, Canadian Economy in Transition Series, n. 8 (2005), 18.

7   Statistics Canada, *Global Links.*

8   Statistics Canada, *Corporations Returns Act* (2005), 55 and Statistics Canada, *Corporation Returns Act* (1998), 99.

9   This data is drawn from the United Nations Conference on Trade and Development, World Investment Directory Online, "Key Data," <www.unctad.org>, retrieved October 2009.

10   W. Carroll, *Corporate Power in a Globalizing World: A Study in Elite Social Organization* (Toronto: Oxford). Burgess's quote is taken from Carroll, 44.

11   B. Burgess, "Inter-corporate ownership and finance capital in Canada," paper presented to "Beyond Dependency, Beyond Borders: Canadian Capitalism in the 21st Century," session of the Society for Socialist Studies, University of British Columbia (May 7, 2008), 1-20.

12   J. Klassen, "Canada and the New Imperialism: the Economics of a Secondary Power," *Studies in Political Economy* (n. 83, 2009), 163-190.

13   Institute for Competitiveness and Prosperity, "Canada's Global Leaders, 1985-2005," (2006) <www.competeprosper.ca/research/index.php>, retrieved November 2006. As I show in the third chapter, foreign investment is particularly strong in the mining industry. But this should not be taken as confirmation of the staples thesis—that is, that Canadian capital is relegated to producing staples (raw materials) for export to manufacturers in more industrially developed countries. For one thing, the international strength of Canadian capitalism is not exclusive to mining. Leaving aside the fact that, as Marx argued, investors will go to where they can find a strong rate of return, regardless of whether that is in the natural resources or other industries, it is also simply the case that mining is not the staples industry of 100 years ago. Mining is in fact one of the most capital-intensive sectors, with one of the highest rates of productivity increases, in the economy today. The long-standing left nationalist staples thesis has been thoroughly refuted most recently by Burgess, *Canada's Location in the World System: Reworking the Debate in Canadian Political Economy*, and J. Klassen, "Canada and the New Imperialism."

14   The mining companies are Falconbridge and Inco. See C. Gonick, "Is Canada an Imperialist State?" *Canadian Dimension* (November/December 2006). The *Globe and Mail* also ran a series of articles on whether or not Canada was being hollowed out following the takeover of Inco.

15   Since the "foreign" takeover of the Canadian economy feared by nationalists is usually referring to American takeover, it is worth noting that from 1997 to 2002, Europe actually was a larger acquirer of Canadian assets than the U.S. Statistics Canada, "Cross-border Acquisitions: A Canadian Perspective, 1997-2002," (www.statscan.ca, 2004), retrieved August 2006.

16   Canadian mergers and acquisitions data is from Crosbie & Company Investment Firm, which has the benefit of providing figures on the

numbers of acquisitions and breaks the data down into the largest acquisitions, including participating companies, <www.crosbieco.com/ma/index>, retrieved November 2009. Comparative G8 figures are from UNCTAD, World Investment Directory Online, "Key Data," tables four and eight, retrieved October 2008.

17   Statistics Canada, "Cross-border Acquisitions: A Canadian Perspective, 1997-2002" and UNCTAD, *World Investment Report, 2005: Transnational Corporations and the Internationalization of Research and Development* (New York: UNCTAD, 2005).

18   G. Quinn, "Canada tops U.S. in direct investing," *Globe and Mail* (April 9, 2009), B4.

CHAPTER 1:
The Contemporary Imperialist Order

Although the major powers are no longer actively seeking to directly colonize territories, the global order is still largely defined by imperialism. Imperialist relations are as much a part of the world today as they were a century ago, when the European powers (and to a lesser degree the United States) exercised direct control over countries of the Global South.

This assertion may seem counterintuitive to some observers, given that most Third World nations have won their formal independence—often through long and bitter struggles—from the colonizers of the North. But to reduce imperialism to the direct control of a people and their territory is to ignore the relations of power and privilege that dominate international affairs today, and unnecessarily narrow our understanding of the political-economic logic that drives it. David McNally offers us a helpful definition of imperialism, one that allows us to see how its form may change over different historical periods while its basic presuppositions remain constant. He suggests that " *[i]mperialism is a system of global inequalities and domination—embodied in regimes of property, military power and global institutions—through which wealth is drained from the labour and resources of people in the Global South to the systematic advantage of capital in the North.*"[1]

The means by which that domination is maintained may shift over time, but the basic fact persists that countries of the North use their power to subordinate countries of the South for their own advantage. Thus we can see how direct territorial conquest is only one form that imperialism can take, and that the shift away from it (although not total) on the global landscape today does not imply the absence of relations of domination and subordination between nations. We can also see, furthermore, that imperialist power is not simply the dominion of a superpower, such as the U.S., even though the latter obviously plays the leading role today. Countries of the Global North that are less powerful than the U.S. can nonetheless exercise and benefit from imperial control over Third World nations.

It is also worth noting that McNally's definition obviously highlights the relationship between Global North and South, which is the focus of this chapter. But imperialism also refers to the colonizer-indigenous dynamic of settler states such as Canada, which I take up in the second chapter. Various forms of power, including military and paramilitary, economic and political, have been used to dominate indigenous communities and drain them of their wealth to the systematic benefit of mostly Canadian capital.

Imperialism and Capitalist Market Imperatives

One of the most important contributions to our understanding of contemporary imperialism comes from Ellen Meiksins Wood's *Empire of Capital*. Wood argues that not only is the contemporary global order shaped by imperialism despite the fact that the major powers aren't actively pursuing direct territorial conquest, but what we are seeing today is in fact the most fully developed form of capitalist imperialism the world has thus far witnessed.

A fully capitalist imperialism, she argues, is a relatively recent phenomenon. During the period of so-called classical imperialism, from roughly 1875 to the postwar period, the major imperial powers circled the globe in a mad and murderous scramble of territorial conquest. Peoples the world over were occupied by the imperialist countries. However, capitalism was far from a global system during this period; and thus access to the wealth of the Third World (through its labour and natural resources) involved a very blunt form of exploitation. Direct political control, backed by military violence, was employed to pillage their wealth and impose capitalist market relations—including the privatization of property and resources and the establishment of a labour market by dispossessing people from their traditional forms of subsistence—on the colonies.[2]

Modern imperialism really only emerges following the Second World War and the breakdown of the classical system of imperialism in the face of anti-colonial movements and the push by the U.S. as the world's new superpower toward a more stable means of subordinating the Third World.[3] But if the system of territorial conquest led to instability (as the colonized did not simply accept the sovereignty of the colonizers over them and the great powers fought one another for access to these territories) and was a drain on the treasuries of the imperial powers (spending large sums on the administrative and military ends of running colonies), it did help to spread capitalist market imperatives beyond Europe. The globalization of capital in the late nineteenth and first half of the twentieth centuries was done as much by violence as it was by the mere operations of the free market itself.

Thus the classical age of imperialism set the stage for contemporary imperialism. "The new imperialism that would eventually emerge from the wreckage of the old," Wood argues, "would no longer be a relation between imperial master and colonial subjects but a complex interaction between more-or-less sovereign states."[4] In place of the blunt force of direct territorial conquest and exploitation, Wood stresses, is the more subtle exploitation advanced through the universality of capitalist imperatives now framing the relations between nominally free and equal nation-states. After decades of colonial subordination and the destruction of non-capitalist livelihoods for many, formal freedom from the direct tutelage of the imperial powers did not bring the people of the Third World freedom from the imperatives of the capitalist market; and this dependence on the capitalist market enabled the countries of the rich world, led by the United States, to maintain their dominance over the Global South as the old empires fell in the postwar period. Working with the other core capitalist nations in a sometimes discordant alliance, the U.S. established an international economic regime through the Bretton Woods institutions (the International Monetary Fund [IMF] and World Bank) and the General Agreement on Tariffs and Trade (GATT—the forerunner to the World Trade Organization [WTO]). The aim was to open the economies, labour markets and resources of the former colonies, now independent states, to the more competitive capital from the North.[5]

None of this is to suggest that the capitalist state lost its relevance with the shift away from the classic form of imperialism toward capitalist market imperatives in the postwar period. If anything, Wood contends, imperialism is more dependent today than it has ever been on a system of multiple states to administer it. For one thing, multinational corporations are still typically based in and usually have a dominant group of shareholders within a particular nation-state; and they rely on those states to actively facilitate their penetration of foreign markets. At the same time, the ability of capital to expand beyond the territory of a single nation-state (expressed for Wood in the separation of economic from extra-economic—political, juridical, military—power) means that a system of multiple states (in tandem with multilateral international institutions such as the IMF or WTO) is necessary to administer the global economy. These states are responsible for insuring the conditions necessary for capital's expansion—strong private property laws and predictability, transparency and certainty (such are the buzzwords) in trade and investment rules—are met.[6]

Imperialism and the Logic of Capitalism

The analysis presented thus far begs the question, however, of why capital from the North is compelled to expand into the South. This is an important question. It is a wrong though common assumption among many observers to reduce imperialism to the misguided and ill-conceived actions of a particular leader and his or her advisers—such as a reckless presidential regime and its insatiable thirst for oil, or an ideologue prime minister (take your pick which one) who cravenly seeks to please the American president. It is also wrong to assume that imperialism can be reduced to the way in which an imperialist country's state has been institutionally configured that makes it more amenable to imperialism. While a given set of actors, such as the so-called "neo-cons" in the U.S., no doubt shape imperialist policy according to their predilections (or the predilections of the section of the ruling class they represent), imperialism is a dynamic, the roots of which lie at the heart of contradictory capitalist social relations, and the imperialist practices pursued by the state are an expression of those relations. Imperialism, in other words, will not disappear with the disappearance of George W. Bush and company or with an institutional rearrangement of the capitalist state.

Imperialism's form may change in different historical periods, of course, but it is nonetheless rooted in the way in which wealth is produced and accumulated in capitalist societies. Labour is the source of new wealth in capitalist economies. Thus capitalists constantly seek to increase labour productivity: the amount workers produce for them in a given amount of time relative to, and in fact beyond what, they are in turn paid for their labour over that same period (Marx referred to this as exploitation). There are different strategies for increasing labour productivity and exploitation, including the deployment of new sophisticated technologies, the intensification of the pace of work, the extension of the workday, and depressing wages or at least maintaining them below the rate of inflation. Often a combination of these strategies is employed.

The capitalist exploitation of labour is unique from other forms of exploitation (such as, for example, under feudalism) in that it is done through market means rather than through direct political or juridical coercion. A defining feature of capitalist societies is that the majority of people are systematically dispossessed from the means of producing wealth—from the land and its resources, mines, factories and so on. This is often done through conscious effort by the state and capital, in order to gain access to what was previously collectively or publicly controlled resources and to create a market in wage labour. In turn, in order to survive people must then enter the labour market and sell their ability to work to the people who have secured ownership over the means of producing wealth. The dispossession of the majority from their land and the private ownership over the means of producing wealth confers a great deal of power to capitalists, including the ability to control the conditions of work and thus maintain (from their perspective) a healthy degree of exploitation and profits.[7]

At the same time, the exploitation of labour takes place in the context of the competitive and unplanned pursuit of profit by capital. The ongoing attempt by rival corporations to outdo one another by increasing their productivity (and thus profitability) and securing a greater share of the marketplace is built into the logic of capitalism. "Accumulate or perish" is the law governing a corporation's success in the capitalist game of the survival of the fittest. Those companies that fail to constantly revolutionize the process of production, increase the exploitation of labour and keep pace with their rivals risk extinction.

While this revolutionary dynamic may lead to significant advances in wealth creation and technology, the flip side is the systematic tendency toward the overaccumulation of capital (sometimes referred to as overcapacity) and overproduction of commodities. Too many factories, mines, big box stores and so on are created to be deployed profitably, and too many goods, whether for consumers or capital (such as machinery, parts and technology) are produced for the market—not to mention the environment—to absorb. As corporations sit on overcapacity, their profitability declines, investments shrink, factories and stores shut down, and workers are laid off. This is the recessionary tendency of capitalism's cycle of boom and bust. As what now appear as surplus factories, stores, labour and investment capital sit idle (as investors, scared by the economic instability and weak returns awaiting their investments, become more reserved), the risk of system-wide devaluations, and with it the significant loss of wealth, increases.

Employers will certainly try to avoid recessions in the first place or escape their difficulties by intensifying the exploitation of labour, restoring their rates of profit (that is, the return on each input they make in the production process) at the expense of their workers. As the economic downturn grows, unemployment increases and the balance of power between capital and labour shifts further in favour of the former. However, while gains may be made here, it is not a simple or uncontested strategy. Working people do not simply acquiesce to the intensification of their exploitation, and capital always risks increasing class conflict by engaging in such manoeuvres. This is what Werner Bonefeld describes as the contradiction of capitalism, the existence of labour in-and-against capital: labour is the source of new wealth, but its struggles for better conditions of employment are impediments to the efficient creation of wealth from the capitalist's perspective.

There are a few other options available to deal with crises of overaccumulation, including for financial investors the search for new markets to—speculatively—invest their surplus capital, such as real estate markets (as they did in the 1980s and 2000s) or large infrastructure projects in the Third World (as they did in the 1970s). States of the Global North also have the option of borrowing excess capital (helping its owners avoid devaluation) to spend on things like local infrastructure development or social programs (the latter option being rarely taken). But, as geographer David Harvey notes, "geographical expansion is one of the most potent paths for surplus absorption."[8]

Harvey argues that in a context of overaccumulation, "[i]f system-wide devaluations (and even destruction) of capital and of labour power are not to follow, then ways must be found to absorb these surpluses. Geographical expansion and spatial reorganization provide one such option."[9] Capital pursues what he refers to as a spatial fix to resolve the systematic crisis of overaccumulation. New geographical regions are sought to absorb the existing surpluses of capital and avoid their devaluation, for instance, while flagging profitability can be improved by accessing cheap labour, raw materials and natural resources in these areas. In effect, fresh spaces of wealth accumulation are established as capitalism penetrates new territories, creating "a world after its own image," or as older colonial spaces are radically transformed in the interests of a new imperial strategy.[10] Capitalism, then, has a self-expanding geographical logic internal to it, and this is at the root of imperialism.

Imperialism and the State

The capitalist state plays a central role in imperialist expansion. Capitalist states developed historically out of the struggles surrounding the reproduction of capitalist social relations. Contrary to the fantasies of classical economists, capitalist social relations—the exploitative relations between workers alienated from control over the means of producing wealth and the small percentage of people who own those means—aren't an intrinsic part of the human condition and do not reproduce themselves automatically. These relations have always been contested, as capital's efforts to subordinate labour to its interests comes up against the latter's struggle for better wages, more control over the conditions of work, and occasionally against the wage labour relation itself. As noted above, capitalist social relations, and thus the capitalist accumulation of wealth, are at heart contradictory: the stability of the system is contingent upon the ability of employers to effectively exploit their workforce, while labour has an obvious interest in resisting exploitation.

The capitalist state—with its laws defending such things as the sanctity of private property and individual over collective rights, its administrative mechanisms designed to manage class struggle such as policing, labour law and welfare systems, and its privileged role in printing money and influencing the financial system—emerged as a means of containing that contradiction, and thus of producing stable market relations by ensuring that social struggles and any other threats to market relations are safely defused or, as is sometimes the case, repressed. (It is worth reminding ourselves too that once capitalism emerges as the dominant means for the production and distribution of wealth in a country that the state becomes dependent on capitalism as its source of revenue for its own survival, and so has an interest in ensuring the system's reproduction). The contradictions at the heart of capitalist relations, expressed in the struggle between classes over the conditions of the production and distribution of wealth, have therefore shaped the development of the state, while the state has in turn shaped those contradictions and the struggles surrounding them as it seeks to manage or contain them in ways that maintain the integrity of market relations. In the case of union rights in Canada, for example, working-class struggles that threatened to go beyond and potentially undermine market relations were absorbed by the state in the postwar period and subsequently managed through the adoption of a bureaucratic labour relations regime that sets out rights not just for workers but capital as well. Workers won concessions from the state and employers (the right to collective bargaining and a broad welfare state, for example), and thus transformed the state in important ways, but the state in the process secured private property relations and won an acknowledgement from workers of employers' right to govern the workplace. Thus the fundamental relation between capital and labour, in which the latter is alienated from control over the means of producing wealth, was left intact.

In this respect, the state should be considered as internally related to market relations. That is to say, the state and market relations do not exist, and have not developed historically, independently of one another: they in fact constitute each other. There is a relational, or dialectical, dynamic between them. They both develop out of their interaction with one another, and in fact only exist through that interaction with one another. You cannot properly understand the state, for instance, without being alive to the way in which market relations, and the class struggles at the heart of those relations, have shaped it, and vice versa.[11]

But the state does not operate simply within the domestic context to ensure the reproduction of capitalist social relations. If a country's capital expands geographically in search of new spaces of accumulation as a way of dealing with its crisis tendencies, it is the state that makes this possible. State policies of rich nations toward the Third World (and sometimes toward one another)—whether through bilateral or multilateral trade and investment laws, aid policy, militarism and so on—are designed to facilitate the imperialist domination of foreign territories. Imperialist power, in other words, is a feature of the state's effort to contain the contradictions of the capitalist accumulation of wealth, and can therefore be understood as a product of the internal (or dialectical) relationship between the state and market relations. In order to ensure the maintenance of capitalist relations, the state must exercise its power not only domestically, but externally as well, subordinating foreign regions to the interests of the capitalist accumulation of wealth as led by the imperial centres (and thus in turn shaping market relations abroad). That multilateral organizations such as the IMF and World Bank play an important role here offers us an example of the coordinated mobilization of state power by the Western nations, and does not obviate the continued importance of the states of rich countries, whether acting bilaterally or multilaterally, in the global order today.[12]

In any case, it was the desire of the states of Europe to manage the contradictions of capitalism that led to their competitive race around the world in the classical age of imperialism. In this period, as I discussed above, the various imperialist states worked to impose capitalist market relations in parts of the world where they previously did not exist. The exploitation of the colonies was therefore primarily facilitated through direct political coercion. In the present period, as Wood points out, states of the rich world facilitate the geographic expansion of capital of the North in general and their domestic capital in particular largely through the exploitation of capitalist market imperatives on the South.

We should be cautious, though, not to see the more violent features of imperialism, including even territorial conquest, as simply a thing of the past. Wood herself acknowledges that "more traditional forms of coercive colonization" aren't necessarily ruled out today.[13] However, while very insightful for our understanding of the current global order, the stress on the shift from classical to contemporary market-based imperialism, whereby the latter is presented as the most fully developed form of capitalist imperialism, can potentially tempt us into treating the two types of imperialism as mutually exclusive stages rather than as different strategies that, while responding to different material conditions, nevertheless exist on a continuum of imperialist state power.

Thus while the strategy of territorial conquest may fit more easily into an earlier historical moment of imperialism, it is by no means exclusive to that period. State power, we need to recall, is constituted in part by the social relations—including struggles over the conditions by which wealth is produced and distributed—in those spaces in which it is being mobilized (again, it is internally related to those social relations). Where market relations exist, imperial state power tends to be more focused on exploiting people's dependence on them (manipulating debt burdens, forcing open economies to capital from the North, and so on). Where they do not exist, where people have not been fully absorbed into them, where people are threatening them (or at least threatening the imperialists' preferred form of market relations, such as neoliberalism), or where broader geo-political interests demand it, imperial state power is often mobilized in more violent ways, including territorial conquest. Iraq and Afghanistan are presently subject to a foreign occupation, which may continue well into the future. Perhaps the best example of continued territorial conquest and occupation, though, is that of colonial settler states such as Canada, Australia, New Zealand, the U.S. and Israel. As I will discuss in the next chapter with respect to Canada, direct conquest is still a key strategy in these states for dominating colonized populations. It is clearly not a strategy of the past alone.

Accumulation By Dispossession and Neoliberalism

David Harvey's theory of accumulation by dispossession captures the predatory nature of the geographic expansion pursued by imperialist states, even when not done through direct territorial conquest. The creation of new spaces for the accumulation of wealth is after all not an innocuous process; the spaces are only new to capital of the North. Thus geographic expansion inevitably involves the dispossession of people from their wealth, whether that wealth is in the form of natural resources and land (in the case of indigenous peoples, peasants and small farmers, for instance), publicly owned assets (such as utilities) and government finances. Either way, it amounts to a dramatic reorganization of people's lives as they are subordinated to the fancy of imperial capital.

Accumulation by dispossession is in fact the process Marx refers to as "primitive accumulation" in his description of the violent and bloody emergence of capitalist social relations in seventeenth- and eighteenth-century England in *Capital*, where the state was used to force peasants off of the land and into the new labour market. Nascent British capital gained access to the land and its resources while a new labour force, dependent on market relations, was created. But, as Harvey argues, Marx incorrectly "relegate[s] accumulation based upon predation, fraud, and violence to an 'original stage' that is considered no longer relevant."[14] Because, however, all the features Marx describes are still actually a central part of the capitalist accumulation of wealth, "[a] general re-evaluation of the continuous role and persistence of the predatory practices of 'primitive' or 'original' accumulation within the long historical geography of capital accumulation is ... very much in order."[15] This "primitive accumulation," or accumulation by dispossession, is a key *modus operandi* of imperialism, and as such is "omnipresent in no matter what historical period and picks up strongly when crises of overaccumulation occur ... when there seems to be no other exit except devaluation."[16]

The period of neoliberalism has witnessed an intensification of both the geographic expansion of capital from the North and accumulation by dispossession. Neoliberalism is a ruling class response to the crisis of overaccumulation in the advanced capitalist economies of the 1970s. It is aimed at the restoration of profitability through the aggressive restructuring of social relations:

social spending was dramatically cut, labour rights weakened, wages attacked, public utilities privatized, etc. The effect has been the imposition of greater reliance on market relations upon people.[17] At the same time, the advanced capitalist states, with the U.S. providing leadership, have successfully sought out new spaces of accumulation, targeting regions that have not been fully absorbed into capitalist relations (often indigenous communities) or dramatically reorganizing others in their neoliberal interests, to absorb the North's surpluses and boost flagging profitability.

The debt crisis of the early 1980s was seized on by the imperialist nations as an opportunity to submit the Third World to their aggressive agenda of neoliberalism and dispossession. Third World debt grew sharply in the 1970s when financial institutions in the North found themselves with excess American dollars but without a profitable place for investment in the stagnating economies of North America and Europe. These excess American dollars were a product of the rise in gas prices resulting from the Organization of Petroleum Exporting Countries (OPEC) embargo in the early 1970s (the dollar serves as currency of choice in oil markets) and the American government's profligate spending in support of the Vietnam War and growing trade deficits (covered by simply printing more dollars). These dollars eventually found their way into the Third World to sponsor large and often ill-advised development projects and the extravagant personal spending of corrupt dictators. But despite having benefited little from the tremendous (and speculative) inflow of financial capital in the 1970s, the poor in the Third World would be made to pay severely for the debts their governments amassed. When countries of the North raised their interest rates to double-digit figures in the early 1980s as a way of creating domestic unemployment to weaken their working class's ability to resist neoliberal restructuring, the massive and unsustainable debt burden of the South was exposed. The problem was compounded by the recession of the early 1980s, as the export markets in the North that the South depended on for a sizable portion of its income shrank.

The ruling classes of the North, led by the U.S. Treasury Department and Wall Street financiers, used the IMF and World Bank to open up the economies of, and impose drastic bouts of neoliberal restructuring on, Third World nations through debt management practices. Market imperatives would be used to exploit the vulnerabilities of the Third World and dispossess it of its wealth. Strapped for cash and at risk of defaulting, Third World countries were offered much-needed bailouts by the Bretton Woods institutions—but with a major catch. In order to receive the loans, indebted countries had to agree to extremely strict conditions known as structural adjustment policies. Structural adjustment entails the removal of trade and investment barriers for capital from the North; slashing of public services and government jobs; cuts to subsidies to local producers and consumers; privatization of communal land, natural resources and public utilities; and deflationary fiscal policies, which are aimed at providing stability in financial markets for foreign investors and keeping governments from paying off foreign debt by simply printing off more money. It is Thatcherism, Reaganomics and Mike Harris's Common Sense Revolution ramped up several more notches. Since the early 1980s, over 100 countries have been subjected to structural adjustment, as rich countries, through the IMF and World Bank, replaced protectionist development strategies adopted by Third World nations following decolonization in the postwar period with liberalized economic policies that benefit capital from the North. As McNally trenchantly observes, these structural adjustment policies "effectively constitute a process of 'recolonisation'" as "[t]hey utterly subordinate the Third World debtor nation to the dictates of global capital."[18] Structural adjustment has in fact become a key feature of Canadian aid policy.

One of the most significant ways capital from the North has seized the new opportunities in the South provided by structural adjustment policies is the massive increase in foreign direct investment (FDI). Despite the rhetoric of free trade heard from neoliberal globalization's advocates, what really "defines the era of globalization" is not trade, McNally argues, but "large-scale foreign direct investment (FDI)."[19] This trend is important to our understanding of the global economy, since FDI represents the long-term investment by corporations in foreign economies and managerial control over those assets they are investing in, and thus, potentially, increasing influence over these economies. In the last two decades, FDI has increased at a phenomenal pace, growing by over 200 percent from the late 1980s to the mid-1990s alone. It has involved long-term investments in factories, mines, financial systems, and privatized natural resources, communication systems and public services. By the 2000s, total outward foreign direct investment is estimated to have reached the $1 trillion mark.[20]

While much of this investment takes place between rich nations, FDI from the Global North into the South has grown significantly since the 1990s and makes up an increasing percentage of the international total. It is this economic trend, McNally stresses, that lies behind international economic pacts like the failed Multilateral Agreement on Investment, the North American Free Trade Agreement (NAFTA), and the proposed Free Trade Area of the Americas; international bodies like the World Trade Organization; and the structural adjustment policies pursued by the IMF and World Bank. These agreements and policies codify investor rights, locking the Global South into neoliberalism (I discuss them in more detail in chapter three).[21]

Another aspect of contemporary global capitalism that has wreaked havoc in poor countries has been the deregulation of financial markets and the shifting of currencies in the 1970s from fixed exchange rates (exchangeable with U.S. dollars at a guaranteed price) to fluctuating (or floating) rates based on market conditions. This process is sometimes referred to as part of the so-called "financialization" trend of the neoliberal era.[22] The move to floating exchange rates followed the Nixon administration's decision in 1971 to take the dollar off of the gold standard. Previously, the dollar's value was tied to gold, and dollars could be exchanged for gold at a guaranteed price (one dollar for one-thirty-fifth of an ounce of gold). But as trade deficits and excessive borrowing to fuel the Vietnam War increased steadily, foreign trading partners and investors became weary of holding U.S. dollars (fearing a loss of value) and began to exchange them for gold. Facing a potential run on gold but unable, or unwilling, to address its trade deficit or international borrowing, the U.S. simply went off gold and turned to a floating exchange rate instead.

Detached from gold, but still operating as world money (that is, the preferred means for international transactions) American dollars flooded onto world markets. This was exacerbated by the oil price spike following the 1973 OPEC embargo (the dollar is, again, the major means of payment in oil markets). Foreign governments and investors found themselves with surplus American dollars and went looking for places to invest them. As noted above, one of those places was the Third World, and a period of questionable speculative investments, designed to earn investors of the North a quick and handsome reward, contributed to the Third World debt crisis of the early 1980s, and the eventual IMF attack on poor economies.

Meanwhile, the floating of exchange rates made currencies, especially those of poorer indebted countries, susceptible to speculative attacks and volatile swings in value. For example, a rapid decline in the value of a Third World country's currency, which could result from the more easy movement of unregulated foreign financial investment flows out of a country because of concerns around the state of its economy (including government deficits, a drop in the price of its raw material exports or too high tax rates on investors) or from the selling of the currency on the world market (i.e., a decline in demand for the currency) because of the country's mounting trade deficits, could mean a significant real increase in the price of its foreign debt. At the same time, the turn to floating exchange rates has led to the proliferation of financial instruments, such as derivatives, that are designed to provide insurance against currency fluctuations for investors and firms engaging in international transactions. Contracts are purchased to cover potential losses that might result from the future movement in the price of a currency. What happens, though, is that speculators who have no plans to purchase the currency in the future for their own international transactions buy up these derivatives in the hopes that the currency declines in value, so that they can cash in their insurance claims, the payout of which is greater than the original price of the derivative. In other words, they are speculating, or betting, against the currency.[23]

In response to the volatility of currency values, some Global South countries have responded, under encouragement from the imperial centre, by pegging their currencies to the U.S. dollar. Despite the pressures on the dollar with the unravelling of the postwar era discussed above, it remains a fairly stable form of money and is still considered the main form of world money. Pegging your currency to the dollar, then, sends a signal to rich world investors that you are serious about stabilizing your economy. But it comes with a considerable cost. To peg its currency to the dollar, a country has to be able to guarantee investors and trading partners the ability to exchange its currency with the dollar at a guaranteed price. This means the country has to raise money to purchase dollars in order to keep its currency at the proper exchange rate (if trading partners demand dollars, for instance, the country has to restore its dollar reserves). It also means the country effectively gives up meaningful control over its fiscal policy, as control over the printing of dollars and their injection into foreign markets (where the country will purchase them) belongs to the U.S. Treasury. It is harder for poor countries that have pegged to the dollar, in other words, to pursue inflationary policies such as increasing government spending, keeping interest rates low to encourage borrowing to keep the economy growing, and printing money to cover foreign debts. Indeed, this is one of the main reasons imperialist countries encouraged dollarization in the Third World; it is a means of imposing neoliberal fiscal austerity. The cost to Third World countries, as I discuss in the fourth chapter with respect to Argentina, has been high.

The Tragedy of Neoliberal Globalization
Rich nations, of course, present neoliberal globalization with the shiniest of glosses. It involves, the mantra goes, tough but necessary measures to help Third World countries to help themselves and become internationally competitive (establish "macro-economic stability" is a common refrain). They never take responsibility for neoliberalism's clear failures. If things do not work out for the poor in the Global South, well there is always more red tape and more government to cut, and more market liberalization to be undertaken. But the direct impact of neoliberalism on the economies and people of the South has been nothing short of tragic. Despite hundreds of billions of dollars in debt having been paid to rich countries, because of the extraordinarily high interest rates of the 1980s, the Third World's debt burden has actually increased from US$580 billion in 1980 to US$2.4 trillion in 2002. Third World countries are today more than four times more indebted than they were in 1980, and thus countries of the North can continue to basically rob them blind. But because of the sheer size of the debt burden and the impoverished status of developing nations, their debt payments only cover the interest—the principal re-

mains untouched. At the same time, the neoliberal shock therapy to which they were subjected wreaked havoc on the countries of the South. With local industry unable to compete against the large multinational corporations from the North that won unfettered access to their domestic markets through structural adjustment and trade agreements, and with consumers and small farmers cut off from subsidies (while rich countries still subsidize their own agro-industries) and government spending curtailed, Third World economies have stagnated, reinforcing their dependence on the First World.[24]

The governments of rich countries try to cover up the grotesque nature of this massive transfer of wealth from the South with stately announcements (sometimes with Irish rock stars at their sides) of supposedly generous aid packages for the world's poor, but the proof is in the pudding. In the 1990s, donor aid to Africa, the world's poorest continent, actually declined forty percent. While aid to poor countries increased in the 2000s, it did so only marginally and has not made up for the cuts of the 1990s in real terms (i.e., adjusted for inflation). In fact, aid inflows to the South from the North are but a fraction of debt payments going the other way. In 2004, US$370 billion in debt service payments went from the South to the North, while only US$80 billion in development aid from the donor countries went the other way. Aid spending projections for the next several years do not come close to the Third World's debt service levels.[25] Moreover, the amount of real aid is actually considerably lower than the official figures suggest. When we factor in costs associated with things like aid bureaucracy, tied aid (where aid has to be spent by the recipients on companies or products from the donor countries) and debt relief (when rich countries write down debt they count it toward their aid budget; I discuss debt relief in chapter three), the actual amount of real aid received by poor countries, according to Action Aid, declines by more than half.[26]

Debt bondage and structural adjustment represent nothing less than a plundering of the wealth of Third World countries by the North. Billions of dollars a year in much-needed funds that could otherwise go to things like health services and nutrition programs are drained away by governments and banks of the First World. And while this happens, the economies of the South are being pried open. Public utilities, the banking system, much-coveted subsurface riches, plant life and other forms of biodiversity, even water—nothing is off the table now for capital of the North. People are being systematically dispossessed of their livelihoods, their land, their ways of life and the basic resources necessary for their survival. Transformed into commodities (goods produced to be sold on the market), everything from seeds to public services is increasingly now only available for purchase from multinational corporations. This is the contemporary face of accumulation by dispossession: capital from the North grows richer by dispossessing the South of its wealth by exploiting the latter's poverty and economic vulnerabilities. This is not to suggest, mind you, that dispossession is done only through market imperatives; it also has a violent side, where paramilitaries, both local and private security forces, and militaries are deployed to ensure the South's resources come under control of multinational corporations (I discuss this in more detail in chapters four and six).

Predictably, the imperialists' claims that the new *laissez faire* would ultimately lift the South out of the Third World has not materialized. A staggering billion people have been dispossessed of their land and resources and separated from their subsistence livelihoods in the last two decades as a result of structural adjustment policies. In turn they have flooded into rapidly growing urban slums in desperate search of work in a Third World labour market that cannot possibly keep pace with the growth of proletarianization.[27] All the while government services have been hollowed out. And so we find, not surprisingly, that not only has income inequality between the rich world and Third Worlds increased markedly since the 1980s—with the share of world income received by the richest twenty percent of the world's countries relative to the share received by the poorest twenty percent rising from 60:1 in 1990 to 74:1 in 1997[28]—but so too has poverty. The Economic Commission on Latin America and the Caribbean (ECLAC) reports that the rate of poverty in Latin America increased from thirty-five percent to forty-one percent of the population in the 1980s as one country after another was structurally adjusted, and according to Petras and Veltmeyer the rate of poverty continued to climb through the 1990s.[29] It is only with the commodities boom and the election of centre-left regimes that have increased social spending that poverty rates declined modestly in Latin America between 2003 and 2008, though this may turn around again as a result of the 2008 financial meltdown.

The region hardest hit by neoliberalism, though, is Africa. Patrick Bond points out that "[t]oday, Africa is still getting progressively poorer, with per capita incomes in many countries below those of the 1950s-60s era of independence. If we consider even the most banal measures of poverty, most sub-Saharan African countries suffered an increase in the percentage of people with income of less than US$1/day during the 1980s and 1990s, the World Bank itself concedes."[30]

There is simply no basis to the claim, then, made by the right and some observers on the centre, that more than two decades of free market fundamentalism has rendered obsolete the profound geographic hierarchies that previously divided the world order. Without trivializing the increase of inequality within countries of the North, the conclusion that neoliberal globalization has exacerbated the divisions between the North and South is unavoidable.[31] Nor should this be surprising, as capital is driven by the pursuit of profit and thus it is drawn to those regions that offer an optimum rate of return on its investments.[32] Removing barriers to its accumulation of profits, which are mechanisms by which human rights and socially just living standards are defended (such as market regulations, programs for wealth redistribution, legislation protecting workers, indigenous people and their environment), is a premise upon which capital expands to new spaces. In other words, an increased standard of living is far from an inevitable outcome of capitalist investment. Indeed, as noted earlier, it is the restraint on market forces by governments and the strong mobilization from below that has led to an improvement in living conditions for the world's poor, whether in the North or South. The theory of the trickle-down of wealth is a fiction.

Even in those countries cited by apologists for global neoliberalism as examples of the transformation from Third World backwater to emerging power, such as China and India, the reality for the majority is far from the rosy picture it is often made out to be. The simple truth is, the lives of the majority of people in both these countries have since worsened, not improved. The benefits of economic growth have been extremely unevenly distributed. In

China, for instance, the rapid economic growth of the last twenty years has been based on a massive displacement of people in rural areas (in the order of hundreds of millions of people) and incredibly high rates of exploitation. Flooding into rapidly growing urban centres, internal migrant workers, often without the limited labour protections provided to documented city residents, have formed an extremely cheap and inexhaustible labour supply for China's new robber barons, many of whom were managers of state-operated enterprises and became rich via the nepotism of state leaders in the privatization process. As Harvey suggests, work conditions in the new industrial centres of Chinese capitalism—from the systematic non-payment of wages, to the extreme dangers represented by a lack of meaningful health and safety regulations, to the absence of organizing rights—are grim compared even to those described by Marx and Engels during England's Industrial Revolution. News reports of deadly mining accidents and rising health problems due to extreme air pollution in industrial towns are not rare. China now has one of the highest rates of income inequality in the world. At the same time, it is worth noting that the growth that China has experienced has in fact been based on state intervention in the economy to direct that growth in specific regions and industries, and not on the strict reliance on free market forces.[33]

In India, the gains from neoliberal restructuring and the invasion of foreign investment capital have been heavily concentrated among a largely urban affluent elite. The absolute number of people living in poverty rose through the 1990s, as did malnourishment, which affected 47% of children four years old and younger and 48.5% of adults. Much of this increase in poverty has occurred as a result of IMF-supported agricultural reform, where subsistence farming is being replaced by larger export-oriented commercial farming, and large development projects, such as dam building that diverts much-needed water supplies from small farmers to power the large commercial farms and other development projects. Millions of poor Indians have been pushed off the land as a result, and seen their living standards plummet.[34] In Brazil, which is now the eighth largest economy in the world, the situation is the same. Despite its economic growth, it still suffers from staggering poverty and grotesque levels of inequality.

Race and Empire

It should come as little surprise that while the working class in the rich world has not escaped the wreckage wrought by neoliberal globalization, it is the Third World, the majority of whose inhabitants are people of colour, that has suffered its most deleterious effects.

The history of imperialism is infused with racism as both motivation and justification for the plunder of peoples in the Third World. In the classical period it was up to the imperialist powers to bring civilization to people of colour in the Global South (as Kipling wrote, it was the white man's burden), while civilizing missions that entailed shocking levels of violence and cruelty would be defended on the basis of the racial inferiority of the victims. While racist ideology, based on pseudo-scientific pronouncements about white supremacy, developed before the classical age of imperialism, it nonetheless "became a centrepiece of the new age of empire," McNally observes.[35] People in the Third World were systematically racialized as inferior to Europeans and North Americans, and as savage, dangerous and licentious, driven by passions rather than by reason. It was, therefore, not only the right of Europeans to dominate the Third World, but their responsibility. "As 40 million black Africans were brought under British domination," McNally notes, "Cecil Rhodes could console himself that 'the British were the best race to rule the world.'"[36] So too would the French, Belgians, Germans, Portuguese, Italians and Americans console themselves in those regions of the world they came to dominate. A profound belief in their racial superiority, and in the colonizing process's ability to lift the colonized out of savagery, allowed the imperialists to countenance the ruthless exploitation of the labour and environment of the Third World. The capitalists of the empire might become wealthy, but the savages would learn the values of industriousness, discipline and morality.

Notions of white supremacy were more than an ideological tool for justifying the barbarism of imperialism, however. Ideas of white supremacy would become deeply absorbed in the culture of the imperialist centres and in the consciousness of the people living there. And it was not simply the ruling elites that absorbed racist ideology and a profound belief in white supremacy. Whiteness came to shape the worldviews of large segments of the European and North American working class in important ways. In this way racist ideology contributed to divisions within the world's working class, as many European and North American workers came to identify as much with their perceived whiteness as they do with their class. So ingrained did these ideas become that racist notions of the civilized North versus the uncivilized South are still quite pervasive today.[37]

Contemporary imperialism may not be commonly justified through recourse to such explicitly racist or crude formulations as those of the classical age (though such formulations certainly have not completely disappeared), but presentations of the Third World today are often not that far removed from the stereotypical depictions of the past. Notions of biological difference between races have lost much of their lustre, but race, often couched in terms of immutable cultural differences, still frames international relations, as well as domestic realities in countries of the North. Razack makes a very important observation when she argues that "imperialism is not just about accumulation but about the *idea* of empire ... Empire is a structure of feeling, a deeply held belief in the need to and the right to dominate others *for their own good*, others who are expected to be grateful."[38] The idea of empire is rooted in the commonsense view of people in the Global South as unable to care for themselves, and thus as responsible for their own poverty and seemingly endless internecine violence. They are culturally backward. Such a view can only be sustained by racializing them as inferior, helpless, irrational and potentially dangerous. Such racist stereotypes require divorcing the region from any historical, political or economic context, including certainly its relations with the rich world, that might help explain its wretched situation. The Third World is thus left with no one to blame for its suffering except itself, making foreign intervention by the Global North—whether by economic, political or military means—both justifiable and necessary.

Contemporary imperialism, then, is transformed into an ostensibly positive force in the world, an expression of the First World's benevolence, which echoes the justifications mobilized in the classical period. Debt management and structural adjustment aren't about exploitation, they are about providing economic stability; war is not about domination, it is about democracy and security. The rich nations are carrying the burden of lifting the world's poor out of their self-imposed misery. But as Razack stresses, when the Global North speaks of its responsibility to save the South from itself, "the underlying logic is the same as nineteenth-century colonialism and imperialism's notion of a civilizing mission."[39] As in the past, some individuals in the First World might get rich from their intervention in the Third World, but the latter will be the better for it.

The War on Terror, with the apocalyptic rhetoric employed by politicians and media ideologues surrounding it, has intensified the racialization of the Third World as inferior and dangerous. This is at its most virulent, particularly in the first few years following 9/11, for people of Arab, South Asian and Muslim background. Not only are the backward peoples of the South a danger to themselves, but they have shown that they are also a danger to Western civilization. The War on Terror has thus been presented as a *defence* of civilization against the uncivilized, against the "barbarians" at the gates of the Global North. Concepts like that of the "failed" state and corresponding doctrine, couched in humanitarian terms, advocating preemptive military intervention both to help the uncivilized and protect the North from such dangerous places have gained considerable prominence in this period (for a detailed discussion of this doctrine, see chapter five). In Canada (as well as the U.S. and Western Europe), Arat-Koc argues, it has led to a campaign by the right to define Canada along "civilizational lines." This has involved a "re-whitening of Canadian identity," the flip side of which is the intensified marginalization of non-white populations. Immigrants, especially those from outside Europe, are viewed with increased suspicion; their Canadianness is more explicitly questioned than previously, their potential threat to Canada is more regularly and openly invoked. They are the subject of new, far-reaching anti-terror legislation and security certificates, which run roughshod over much-vaunted liberal rights.[40]

As I have noted, the stark reality of the Third World does not match the lofty rhetoric of the imperialists today any more than it did a century or more ago. The Global North's "civilizing" mission has bled the South dry, leaving abject poverty, dislocation and growing anti-imperialist mobilizations in its wake. One of the groups hardest hit by the new round of accumulation by dispossession is the Third World's indigenous nations (they are also targets of dispossession in the North, which I discuss in the next chapter). Living off of lands rich in natural resources, indigenous peoples have been the principal targets of the predatory practices of capital and governments from the rich world. Their lands and resources have been systematically privatized as a result of structural adjustment and trade and investment agreements, while militaries, paramilitaries and private security forces have been employed to violently dispossess those communities that do not blithely accept the new neoliberal world order.[41]

The displacement of indigenous peoples is predicated on profoundly racist attitudes toward them. Often colonizers do not even offer any form of defence for their actions and proceed as if indigenous peoples either do not exist or could not possibly have any rights (as inferior or uncivilized peoples) to be respected. When justified, it is typically presented as a benevolent act designed to aid a backwards people by facilitating their entry into market relations. But even the World Bank's own study of indigenous people in Latin America acknowledges that since the 1990s they saw few gains in poverty reduction, in several countries are worse off today than they were a decade ago, face systemic discrimination by employers, and fare much worse on basic health indicators than do non-indigenous people.[42] Pushed from their land, many indigenous people are forced to migrate to the Third World's growing slums and join the burgeoning ranks of the under- or unemployed. It is not surprising that in regions like Latin America indigenous peoples are on the cutting edge of resistance to contemporary imperialism.[43]

Racist imperialism also has a strong gendered character. As indigenous peoples and small farmers are driven from their lands, it is typically the women from these communities who, in order to survive and feed their families, have filled the ranks of the Global South's growing sweated labour force as multinational corporations from the North have actively sought out their cheap labour. Much of this sweated labour is found in the Export Processing Zones (EPZs) of the Third World. The last twenty years has witnessed an incredible growth of EPZs, as they are tax-free manufacturing havens with limited labour rights and environmental standards. There are now an estimated 1,000 EPZs in seventy different countries with a twenty-seven-million-strong labour force. Multinational corporations exploit the dirt-cheap and largely female workers in these zones and export the products, free of charge, back to the consumer markets in the North. In a Honduran EPZ, investigators have found women working for as little as 20 cents an hour, which is still higher than what some women workers make in China's EPZs. Working conditions have been found to be extremely dangerous, with workers regularly exposed to carcinogens, poor ventilation and fire hazards. But, as I will discuss in the case of Montreal's Gildan ActiveWear in chapter four, if the women try to organize to defend their rights the corporation may simply move somewhere where the workers aren't organizing. Gildan shut down one such plant in Honduras and shifted its focus to El Salvador and Haiti. Given the extremely high rates of exploitation of the cheap female labour found in them, EPZs have been key to the restoration of profitability in the imperialist centres.[44]

The massive human displacement caused by neoliberal restructuring in the South has led to migration not only to urban centres in the region, but to a historically unprecedented wave of migration to the First World. An estimated 1.5 billion people crossed national borders in the 1990s, many of them into Europe and North America, and this number is expected to double by the end of 2010.[45] Forced from their land, facing an economy where jobs cannot grow as fast as the labour market, and unable to get any support from a state whose budget has been slashed by IMF conditionalities, people in the Third World are increasingly moving to countries like Canada in order to eke out an existence.

Third World labour has become increasingly important to domestic Canadian capitalism. If this labour supply were to be cut off, construction in many major cities, the agricultural industry, janitorial services, such as those cleaning the towers of Toronto's Bay Street, domestic care giving and even the Alberta Tar Sands would shut down. Despite this, the state has made it increasingly difficult for Third World workers to live in Canada permanently or legally. If in 1973, fifty-seven percent of immigrants classified as workers had permanent residency status (a probationary status that provides the same rights of citizens with the possibility for citizenship), by 1993 only thirty-percent of workers admitted to Canada had this status. Increasing numbers of migrants come with temporary permits or illegally. Illegals have no rights, despite their importance to the Canadian economy, while the conditions of temporary workers can be quite onerous: many, such as agro-workers, have no chance of becoming citizens, they can only stay for the length of the contract, they do not have the right to unionize in some parts of the country, they pay taxes but cannot access many social services, they have no right to vote and they cannot leave their job. Not surprisingly, immigrant workers of colour have wages far below the rest of the Canadian population and poverty rates much higher. Thus, as Canada becomes increasingly dependent on migrant labour from the Global South, it is systematically making it harder for these workers to work here with the same rights as citizens. The Canadian labour market is taking on an increasingly apartheid-like structure. It is hard to imagine the state trying to impose such conditions on those Canadian workers defined as white without risk of backlash.[46]

The Return of Inter-Imperial Rivalry?

One question that is getting increasing attention in discussions on contemporary imperialism is whether or not there will be a return of inter-imperial rivalry between the major powers. There are those observers who argue that a new great game between imperialist nations is unlikely. Some, such as William Robinson, argue that there has been increased integration between capital from different regions of the world in multinational corporations in the last three decades, and thus their shared interests are stronger than they have ever been. In line with this integration, it is suggested, is a tendency toward the gradual consolidation of international state institutions to manage global capitalism (such as the WTO and Bretton Woods institutions).[47] Panitch and Gindin argue that imperialism needs the state system, but, emerging at the end of the Second World War as the unrivalled dominant power, the U.S. successfully subordinated the other advanced capitalist nations in its establishment of a coordinated and integrated system of liberalized global trade with it playing the leading role. It strengthened its hegemony further following the debt crisis with the reordering of the world economy in the last two decades under the international dominance of finance capital based on Wall Street.[48]

    While there may have been some economic and political integration over the last couple of decades, and while the U.S. remains the leading global power, we should be cautious not to overstate either the degree of political and economic integration or the U.S.'s dominance. Most multinational corporations are still headquartered in a specific country, have a network of minority or majority shareholders situated there, and rely on their particular state to facilitate their global expansion. Canadian-owned multinationals, for example, still rely on the financial support and varied bilateral and multilateral practices of the Canadian state in their pursuit of new markets. As Wood notes, furthermore, at present "[n]o conceivable form of 'global governance' could provide the kind of daily order or the conditions of accumulation that capital requires."[49] It is certainly true that institutions like the IMF and WTO play important roles in the global economy today (if more modest in recent years than in the past), but they are made up of and led by individual states, and neither is anywhere near being able to take on the many domestic and international responsibilities of those states. The multiple state system may be an inheritance of the European pre-capitalist network of feudal and absolutist states, and thus not inherent to any logic of capitalism, as Hannes Lacher argues, but the anarchic conditions of the global order, the persistence of the national organization of capital, and the uneven nature of development between states make any transnationalization process a difficult one.[50]

While this certainly does not mean that inter-imperial rivalry necessarily exists, there are signs of growing tensions between the U.S. and emerging great powers like Russia and China. Whether or not these tensions become full-blown rivalries is impossible to say at this point, but clearly the U.S. ruling class is cognizant of the growing ambitions of both Russia and China (and the economic power of the latter), and its foreign policy is definitely shaped in part by a desire to thwart any claims for global hegemony the ruling classes of these two nations might have. A number of U.S. reports have stressed the importance of preventing the emergence of new great power rivals, warned of China's military growth and its potential for upsetting the balance of power (i.e., American influence) in Asia-Pacific, and call for a beefed-up military presence in the Middle East through to Central Asia and East Asia, forming a half-ring around Russia and China. Examples of these reports include "The Defence Planning Guidance," written by Paul Wolfowitz and I. Lewis Libby in 1990 for then defence secretary Dick Cheney in the wake of the collapse of the Soviet Union; "Rebuilding America's Defenses," written in 2000 by the Project for a New American Century (which includes the likes of Donald Rumsfeld, Paul Wolfowitz, I. Lewis Libby and Zalmay Khalilzad; the latter would become the U.S.'s special envoy to Afghanistan after the overthrow of the Taliban); the National Security Strategy of 2002; and various security assessments of China conducted by Congressional committees and the Pentagon in the last several years.

The U.S. is also trying to isolate Russia by maintaining and enlarging its transatlantic alliance with Canada and Western European nations. This has been most visible in its push to enlarge the North Atlantic Treaty Organization (NATO) by including former Soviet satellite countries (the Defense Planning Guidance calls for using NATO to maintain American security hegemony over Europe). The U.S.'s rapprochement with a number of countries in the Soviet/Russian sphere of influence is clearly what lay behind Russia's war with Georgia in the summer of 2008, as Russia took the opportunity provided it by Georgian President Mikhail Saakashvili's ill-conceived invasion of the independent region of South Ossetia to send a clear warning to countries on its periphery whose leaders are shifting their allegiances toward the U.S.[51] The superpower is trying to maintain a North American-European imperialist axis with smaller powers (established during the Cold War), whereby the latter throw their lot in with a U.S.-led transatlantic alliance as a way of insuring both their own particular imperialist interests and the collective interests of the West in its dominance over the Third World and in the face of the emergence of potential non-Western rivals for global hegemony. But it is an uneasy relationship. On top of ongoing trade disputes between a number of European countries and the U.S., France, Germany and Belgium have also pushed for a more independent European Union (EU) security and foreign policy to the chagrin of the Americans. Indeed, the American push for the inclusion of former Soviet satellites in NATO and the EU is also motivated in part by these countries' friendly relations with the U.S., which could water down the more independent streak in the EU. Tensions between France and Germany, on the one hand, and the U.S., on the other, peaked in 2003 when the former refused to support the invasion of Iraq.[52]

Many of those who do argue that intensified rivalry is likely base their position on the assumption that the U.S.'s hegemony in the world is threatened with unravelling, as it never fully recovered from the economic downturn of the 1970s and its economy continues to move from bad to worse in the face of unsustainable trade and budget deficits. Its increasing belligerence, including wars in Iraq and Afghanistan, is then a proactive effort to head off potential rivals. Part of the strategy involves maintaining the dominance of the dollar as the means of global payment. The international demand for the greenback allows the U.S. to continue printing large volumes of dollars despite its weak economy and therefore to cover its increasingly large foreign debt. Linked to this is the goal of maintaining control over the global oil and gas markets (or at least limiting Russian and Chinese influence in them), in which the dollar serves as means of payment.[53]

However, the predictions of America's economic decline may be overstated, as some observers argue with reference to the rebound of its productivity and profitability rates in the 1990s.[54] They suggest that the U.S. did indeed recover from the crisis of the 1980s and 90s, largely through its massive assault on its working class and its successful penetration of foreign markets. Even considering the impact of the 2008 financial meltdown on the American economy, it is unlikely the U.S.'s leadership status will be completely forsaken. A rebalancing of the global order between the Americans and the EU or Russia or China, in which the U.S. still remains dominant, may be more likely in at least the medium term than the outright replacement of American hegemony. But a crisis in American hegemony is not a necessary prerequisite for a return of great power rivalry. Global capitalism is shaped by international competition between what are still largely nationally based capitals who are forced, with the aid of their respective states, to expand geographically in the search for new spaces of accumulation. Competition, and tensions surrounding that competition, for new markets and wealth are a key part of the global capitalist order. Thus while the different powers may have parallel interests in insuring the necessary conditions for the global accumulation of wealth, those interests do not necessarily entail a complete unity between them. There will likely always be tensions of one form or another between the dominant centres of global capitalism. Whether this leads to a return of serious inter-imperial rivalry, involving deeper political disputes, economic isolationism and direct or indirect military conflict, rather than mere ongoing frictions and a rebalancing of power between the dominant nations remains to be seen.[55]

Sub-superpower Imperialism

Most writing on contemporary imperialism focuses exclusively on either the U.S. or the U.S.'s relations with the likes of Russia or China. Unfortunately there is very little written on sub-superpower, or junior, imperialism. This represents a considerable gap, as a number of smaller non-superpower countries, including Canada, engage in and benefit from imperialist practices. Simply because they do not have the global influence of a superpower is no reason to ignore the role they play in the international order today. As Tom O'Lincoln, writing about Australia, notes: "[t]he Australian state lacks a global reach, but it does project power."[56] Canada, while by no means a superpower, actually has a fairly global reach, and does project power. Some observers identify the way in which smaller powers like Canada benefit from imperialism or work closely with the U.S., but suggest that the smaller power in question was forced to do as it did to placate the superpower and that it does not have imperialist interests of its own—it is an enabler, perhaps, but not imperialist in its own right.[57] This analysis, however, obscures the imperialist nature of these practices and the states that engage in them, incorrectly reduces the responsibility of imperialism to the superpower alone and ignores imperialist actions taken by countries like Canada independent of the U.S., including those taken in the domestic context.

The goal of this book is to move toward a more serious consideration of Canadian imperialism. An understanding of the contradictory nature of the capitalist accumulation of wealth and its inherent tendencies toward geographic expansion, and the ability of countries of the North to systematically drain the wealth and resources of the South, suggests that imperialism is not the preserve of a single superpower. It underlies the dynamics of other advanced capitalist economies as well, and perhaps even some economies outside the capitalist core (Brazil in South America, for instance), though richer nations are obviously in a much better position to engage in imperial practices than poorer ones.[58] And so when I use adjectives like "sub-superpower" or "junior" for Canada (or other smaller powers), I do so to differentiate the power of Canadian imperialism from that of the superpower. It is not meant to imply that Canada is any less imperialist in nature or intention than the U.S., or that it only does the bidding of the Americans; rather, it speaks to Canada's size and relative influence in the world. Some sub-superpowers are of course larger and more influential than others politically, economically and militarily. Britain carries more weight than Canada on the world stage, for instance. But Canada and Britain have in common a stake and an important role in an imperialist order that they clearly do not lead.

There are a few characteristics that can typically be identified with many of the sub-superpower imperialists from the North, though some are more representative of some nations than others. For instance, while they do not have the economic clout of a country the size of the U.S., the junior imperialists nevertheless have an agenda of penetrating and exploiting the markets of the Third World. That is to say, they have their own independent capitalist interest in securing the wealth of the South. Sub-superpowers such as Canada are no doubt integrated to a degree with American capital, and draw on Wall Street, which is an important source of international investment capital. But this does not gainsay the interests of capital from sub-superpower nations in the Third World, which cannot be strictly reduced to American interests. The smaller powers pursue their interests bilaterally via trade and investment agreements, and through multilateral institutions designed and led by the countries of the rich world, such as the IMF, World Bank and WTO. Some also deploy military force when necessary to ensure stability in the imperial order. This is true of Western European countries, Japan, Canada and Australia.

Some of the sub-superpower nations also have their own regional niche in which much of their imperialist influence is concentrated. Many of the former European colonial powers still retain economic and political influence in their old colonies in Africa, the Middle East, Asia-Pacific and the Caribbean. Australia, meanwhile, has considerable political and economic influence, going back to the nineteenth century, in the South Pacific region, including in Fiji, Samoa, Tonga, East Timor, Indonesia and Papua New Guinea. The Australian state has pushed neoliberal restructuring on these nations through its aid policies, intervened in them militarily and dominated them economically through its trade and investment practices. Australia, to be sure, cannot dominate in the region in the same way that the U.S. can, and solicits U.S. support for maintaining the status quo in the Pacific. But it works with the superpower, as O'Lincoln stresses, precisely because it has its own specific interests in the region and requires American power to help ensure them.[59]

While Canada's foreign economic interests actually extend as far as central Asia, Africa and the Asia-Pacific, they are nevertheless most pronounced in Latin America and the Caribbean. Canada is the third largest investor in the region and it has sought under both Liberal and Tory governments to strengthen its political and economic influence through its pursuit of the Free Trade Area of the Americas and bilateral trade and investment agreements, its military intervention in Haiti in 2004 (deposing a democratically elected government) and its political rapprochement with human-rights troubled Colombia. Although the U.S. is obviously the dominant power with long-standing influence in the Americas, and Canada certainly benefits from America's role as lead imperial power, Canada is positioning itself as a major player in the region, which is resource-rich and whose markets have been aggressively liberalized since the 1980s.

Although they have imperialist interests independent of the superpower, sub-superpowers also play an important supporting role for the former when necessary. Despite its size and influence, the U.S. is not powerful enough to ensure the stability of the global order alone. The smaller powers may add their support for the pursuit of neoliberalism in the South in organizations like the IMF or WTO. Canada, for instance, has promoted the Poverty Reduction Strategy Papers process in the IMF, in which structural adjustment is presented with a new democratic and pro-development veneer by giving poor countries the opportunity to plan their own restructuring programs. Canada and other rich nations also supported the U.S.'s successful push for, among other things, patent protections for pharmaceutical companies at the WTO, to the detriment of the people of the Third World who cannot afford name-brand medicines. The sub-superpower countries also provide important support for U.S.-led military adventures, as Britain has in Iraq and

Canada and other NATO nations have in Afghanistan. Given the resistance in both Iraq and Afghanistan, such wars would be difficult
to prosecute without the assistance of America's allies.

In some cases the smaller powers may even play a leading role
in a given action or policy, such as Australia did in the military intervention in East Timor in 1999 in the face of violence surrounding the Pacific nation's independence, or as Canada did in the imposition of debt restructuring on Guyana in the 1980s or in some
stages of the planning to remove Jean-Bertrand Aristide from the
Haitian presidency in 2004.[60] In the Canadian cases I have cited
here, Canada's role has also been to provide cover for the imperialist actions undertaken, as it, as a non-superpower, does not have
the baggage of the U.S. (and nor does it have a history of territorial
conquest in the Third World). Its participation is intended to put
a friendlier face (for some anyways) on an otherwise unfriendly
policy given Canada's more positive global image than the U.S.'s
(that image, though, is certainly fading). This was a key reason
why Canada was selected to lead donor country initiatives to re-
structure Guyana's economy in the 19080s. Support from allies is
not always forthcoming for the U.S., of course. I noted above the
tensions between the U.S., on the one hand, and France and Germany, on the other, over the Iraq War in 2003. But the tensions between these countries do not obviate the fact that France and Germany (at least for now) still offer important support to the U.S.-led
imperialist order, if not every aspect of it.

An Imperialist Context
Globalization, Harvey argues, "is nothing more than a massive resort to geographical displacement and restructuring, the systematic breakdown of all spatial barriers and the 'battering down' of
the closed doors of recalcitrant nations."[61] With some important
exceptions noted above, the imperialist powers do not employ
direct territorial conquest as their principal means of dominating the Global South. Conquest is instead pursued through market means, exploiting the poverty and vulnerabilities of the Third
World to systematically dispossess it of its wealth. This is of course
always backed up by the possibility of force in the case of those
countries or communities that do not fall into line.

This is the context for understanding Canada's role in the global
order today. As a rich nation of the North, Canada has a privileged

position in a system that systematically exploits the countries of the South; and it has embraced that system. It is not a reluctant player in imperialist relations, it is an eager and often quite aggressive participant. As I will demonstrate in the chapters that follow, it is heavily invested in the Third World, it is active in organizations like the IMF and WTO, it is pursuing one-sided trade and investment agreements with poor countries and it is seeking to rebuild its military strength as a means of defending its global interests. Canada has its own imperialist interests and a stake in the system more broadly, which it pursues both multilaterally in those organizations led by the U.S. and bilaterally where possible. It follows, then, that you simply cannot understand Canada's role in the world today if you do not situate it within the patterns and dynamics of imperial power discussed in this chapter.

Canadian imperial power begins at home, however. And it is to Canada's domestic empire that we turn our attention in the next chapter.

1   D. McNally, "Canada and Empire," *New Socialist* (n. 54, 2005/06), 5. Emphasis in original.

2   Some world systems theorists, such as Immanuel Wallerstein, incorrectly date the world capitalist system back to the sixteenth century. This is based on a flawed analysis of capitalism as a means of market exchange, when the latter can and has existed without being capitalist. Capitalism entails the emergence of a specific form of property relations between the owner of capital and propertyless labourers, where the former is driven by market forces to engage in productive improvement, exploiting the labour of the latter, as the primary means of wealth accumulation. For an excellent history of the emergence of capitalism, see E. Meiksins Wood, *The Origin of Capitalism* (New York: Monthly Review, 1999).

3   E. Meiksins Wood, *Empire of Capital* (London: Verso, 2003), 128.

4   Wood, *Empire of Capital*, 129.

5   Wood, *Empire of Capital*, 132.

6   Wood, *Empire of Capital*, 141.

7   Exploitation is discussed by Marx in *Capital*. In Part Eight he discusses the history of dispossession, which he calls "primitive accumulation," in England. E.P. Thompson also provides a history of dispossession in England in, among many places, his classic *The Making of the English Working Class* (Penguin: 1991). I discuss this history in Canada and its impact on indigenous peoples in the next chapter.

8   D. Harvey, "In What Ways Is the 'New Imperialism' Really New?" *Historical Materialism* (15, 2007), 62. Harvey discusses other strategies for addressing overaccumulation on p. 62, as well as in his book *The New Imperialism* (London: Oxford, 2005). I've chosen to focus on the one that he highlights as key to imperialist strategy and which also helps to illuminate Canadian practices discussed in the following chapters. Harvey discusses the conscious decision actually made by the British bourgeoisie in the late nineteenth century to engage in imperialist expansion. When faced with the option of absorbing overaccumulation through domestic social reform, capitalists opted to maintain their class privileges and were forced to look externally for solutions.

9   D. Harvey, "The 'New' Imperialism: Accumulation by Dispossession," in L. Panitch and C. Leys, eds., *Socialist Register: The New Imperial Challenge* (Halifax: Fernwood, 2003), 64.

10   K. Marx and F. Engels, *The Communist Manifesto* (New York: International, 1995), 13.

11   My theory of the capitalist state draws on the work of what I refer to as the Open Marxists, such as W. Bonefeld, *The Recomposition of the British State During the 1980s* (Aldershot: Dartmouth, 1993), S. Clarke, "State, Class Struggle and the Reproduction of Capital," *Kapitalstate* (10, 1983). See also the three volume series Open Marxism (London: Pluto).

12   The IMF's role declined somewhat since the late 1990s with fewer governments seeking loans. In Latin America, the decline of the IMF was in part a product of Venezuela's strategy of using its revenues to offer cheaper loans to its neighbours without IMF conditionalities. However, in the wake of the 2008 financial crisis, the IMF is poised for a comeback as a number of countries have already gone to it for assistance.

13   Wood, *Empire of Capital*, 4.

14   Harvey, "The 'New' Imperialism," 74.

15   Harvey, "The 'New' Imperialism," 74.

16   Harvey, "The 'New' Imperialism," 76.

17   For neoliberalism in Canada, see chapter three of my *Cops, Crime and Capitalism: The Law-and-Order Agenda in Canada* (Halifax: Fernwood, 2006).

18   D. McNally, *Another World is Possible: Globalization and Anti-Capitalism* (Winnipeg: Arbeiter Ring, 2006), 228.

19   D. McNally, *Another World is Possible: Globalization and Anti-Capitalism* (Winnipeg: Arbeiter Ring, 2002), 238.

20   McNally, *Another World is Possible* (2002), 38.

21   McNally, *Another World is Possible* (2002), 39–40.

22   There has been a lot written on financializaton on the Left. However, as McNally argues, much of this analysis has been "highly misleading." Many commentators imply that finance capital (banks, investment firms, insurance companies, etc.) dominates capitalism today, and/or that capitalism is now driven by the circulation of commodities rather than their production. In fact, the circulation of goods obviously presupposes their production, while their production, including the expansion of manufacturing facilities and the production of raw materials to fuel manufacturing, requires financial investment. Finance and industrial capital exist in a symbiotic relationship; they necessitate one another (this point is well stressed by Bonefeld in *The Recomposition of the British State*). Moreover, neoliberalism, as noted earlier in the chapter, has entailed an aggressive bout of restructuring—at the centre of which is an assault on workers' rights and incomes—by industrial capital that led to a rise in productivity and profitability levels in the 1990s. It is really only after the downturn of 2001–02 that financialization sustained economic growth in place of increased industrial productivity. At the same time, large industrial capital has increasingly developed banking roles in response to increased profitability in the financial sector in the last couple of decades (the financing of auto sales by GM and Ford being a good example of this).

Financialization, McNally argues, is the process by which "interest-paying financial transactions" have played an increasingly important role in the relations both between different capitals and between capital and wage labour. It involves the shift of currencies in the 1970s to fluctuating rates based on market conditions, which has in turn led to the proliferation of various financial instruments such as derivatives that were designed as means of insurance against currency fluctuations for investors engaging in international transactions, but which have also become sources of speculative activity; the increasing resort to debt (particuarly via credit cards) by workers, especially in the U.S., as a means of maintaining living standards in the wake of the neoliberal assault on their livelihoods; and the massive growth of the U.S. current account deficit leading to the flooding of the world economy of U.S. dollars. See D. McNally, "From Financial Crisis to World Slump: Accumulation, Financialisation, and the Global Slowdown," *Historical Materialism* (17.2, 2009), 35–83.

23   This speculative activity, and its massive rise under neoliberalism, is explained well by McNally, "From Financial Crisis to World Slump," 6-8.

24   P. Bond, *Looting Africa: The Economics of Exploitation* (London: Zed Books, 2006), 25–26.

25   Committee for the Cancellation of Third World Debt, "The debt in figures," (2005), <www.cadtm.org/spip.php?article876>, retrieved October 2008; Organization for Economic Cooperation and Development Observer, "Development aid record," (September, 2005), <www.oecdobserver.org/news/fullstory.php/aid/1689/Development_aid_record.html>, retrieved October 2008.

26   Bond, *Looting Africa*, 32-34.

27   On the startling growth of slums see M. Davis, *Planet of Slums* (London: Verso, 2006).

28   McNally, *Another World is Possible* (2006), 130. When considering this statistic, we should also bear in mind the growth in inequality in the First World. If we take the richest ten percent from the North, for instance, that ratio would increase considerably. McNally suggests that the income of the average American CEO would be two and half million times greater than that of the average Ethiopian.

29   J. Petras and H. Veltmeyer, *Globalization Unmasked: Imperialism in the 21st Century* (Halifax: Fernwood, 2001), 86.

30   Bond, *Looting Africa*, 2. Obviously the one-dollar-a-day measure of poverty, which is what ECLAC used to determine poverty in Latin America, is extremely arbitrary and likely lowers the rate, particularly if one considers that inflation will cut into the already meager value of one dollar.

31   For a discussion on the continued relevance of categories such as North/South, see J. Saul, *Development After Globalization: Theory and Practice for the Embattled South in a New Imperial Age* (London: Zed, 2006), 21–25.

32   It should of course be noted that the investments in traditional regions of accumulation in built infrastructure, such as factories and other productive assets, and transportation and communication networks, and a desire to be close to wealthy and large consumer markets, also influences capital's investment decisions, and can act as a restraint on expansion.

33   D. Harvey, *A Brief History of Neoliberalism* (London: Oxford University Press, 2007), 142–148; M. Hart-Landsberg and P. Burkett, "China and the Dynamics of Transnational Accumulation: Causes and Consequences of Global Restructuring," *Historical Materialism* (14.3, 2006), 3–43.

34   McNally, *Another World Is Possible* (2006), 101–104.

35   McNally, *Another World Is Possible* (2006), 163. McNally provides an excellent summary of the emergence of modern racism and its ties to capitalism in his chapter, "The Colour of Money."

36   McNally, *Another World Is Possible* (2006), 164.

37   D. Roediger offers a good history of the emergence of whiteness as an important identity amongst American workers in *Wages of Whiteness: Race and the Making of the American Working Class* (London: Verso, 1991) and *Working Toward Whiteness: How America's Immigrants*

Became White (New York: Basic Books, 2005). For a first-hand account of the impact of white supremacy on an indigenous person in Canada, see H. Adams, *Prison of Grass: Canada from a Native Point of View* (Saskatoon: Fifth House Publishers, 1989), especially section three.

38 S. Razack, *Dark Threats and White Knights: The Somalia Affair, Peacekeeping, and the New Imperialism* (Toronto: University of Toronto Press, 2004), 9-10. Emphasis in original.

39 Razack, *Dark Threats and White Knights*, 9.

40 For a good discussion on racism and the "War on Terror" see, for example, S. Thobani, "White wars: Western Feminisms and the 'War on Terror,'" *Feminist Theory* (vol. 8, n. 2, 2007), 169–185 and S. Arat-Koc, "The Disciplinary Boundaries of Canadian Identity After September 11: Civilizational Identity, Multiculturalism, And the Challenge of Anti-Imperialist Feminism," *Social Justice* (vol. 32, n. 4, 2005), 32-49. The Arat-Koc quotes are from p. 32. "Barbarians" is the term regularly invoked by Michael Ignatieff, pro-imperialist intellectual and now Liberal Party politician, in *Empire Lite*. For a sharp critique of Ignatieff's defense of imperialism, see D. McNally, "Imperial Narcissism: Michael Ignatieff's Apologies for Empire," in C. Mooers, ed. *the new imperialists: Ideologies of Empire* (Oxford: One World Press, 2006), 87–109. McNally notes that Ignatieff uses the term "barbarian" or "barbarians" eight times in the first twenty-one pages of *Empire Lite*.

41 In chapter four I discuss the often violent dispossession of indigenous peoples in Latin America and Africa as a result Canadian investment.

42 World Bank, *Indigenous peoples, Poverty and Human Development in Latin America: 1994-2004*, (Washington: World Bank, 2005).

43 McNally offers a good survey of indigenous organizing in chapter six (both editions) of *Another World Is Possible*. Some of the most exciting organizing has occurred in Bolivia. See J. Webber, "Rebellion to Reform in Bolivia (Part 1): Domestic Class Structure, Latin-American Trends, and Capitalist Imperialism," *Historical Materialism* (n. 16.2, 2008), 23-58. Webber's articles can also be found on Znet, Counterpunch and in *New Socialist*.

44 McNally, *Another World Is Possible* (2006), 183–187.

45 N. Sharma, "Travel Agency: A Critique of Anti-Trafficking Campaigns," Refuge (vol. 21, n. 3, 2003), 56.

46 See T. Basok, *Tortillas and Tomatoes: transmigrant Mexican harvesters in Canada* (Montreal: McGill-Queen's University Press, 2002), N. Sharma, *Home Economics: nationalism and the making of 'migrant' workers in Canada* (Toronto: University of Toronto Press, 2006), and chapter five of my *Cops, Crime and Capitalism: The Law-and-Order Agenda in Canada* (Halifax: Fernwood, 2006).

47   W. I. Robinson, *A Theory of Global Capitalism: Production, Class, and State in a Transnational World* (Baltimore: Johns Hopkins University Press, 2004).

48   L. Panitch and S. Gindin, "Global Capitalism and American Empire," in Panitch and Leys, eds., *Socialist Register*, 1–42; L. Panitch and S. Gindin, "Finance and American Empire," in L. Panitch and C. Leys, eds., *Socialist Register: Empire Reloaded* (Halifax: Fernwood, 2004).

49   Wood, *Empire of Capital*, 141.

50   H. Lacher, *Beyond Globalization: Capitalism, territoriality and the international relations of modernity* (London: Routledge, 2006). See also B. Teschke and H. Lacher, "The changing 'logics' of capitalist competition," *Cambridge Review of International Affairs* (vol. 20, n. 4, 2007), 565–580.

51   As an example of the NATO/Canadian solidarity against Russia, following the latter's war with Georgia, Canadian Secretary of State (Foreign Affairs and International Trade), Helena Guergis, visited Georgia as well as the Ukraine and Poland (both of which are being courted into the NATO/TransAtlantic orbit), and declared her solidarity with Georgia against Russia. Foreign Affairs and International Trade, "Secretary of State Guergis to Visit Georgia, Ukrain and Poland," (August 28, 2008), <w01. international.gc.ca/MinPub/Publication.asp?Language=E&publication_id=386479&docnumber=187>, retrieved August 2008.

52   A good analysis of the U.S.'s strategy toward Europe can be found in P. Gowan, *The Global Gamble: Washington's Faustian Bid for World Dominance* (London: Verso, 1999). K. van der Pijl also discusses the development of the transatlantic axis and its rivalries against new contender powers. While insights are offered, he reduces the transatlantic axis in my opinion largely to its leader, the U.S., and fails to consider the roles and interest of smaller imperial partners. He also has what for lack of a better term one might call a liberal determinism, whereby he implies that if contender states such as China can be pushed toward liberalism their contender status will decline and they can work more in concert with the transatlantic alliance. The implication is that what drive rivalries and tensions is liberalism and or the lack thereof, rather than the pressures of capitalist accumulation that drive geographic expansion and the search for markets. He has a number of books taking the issue up, but the argument is summarized in K. van der Pijl, "Capital and the state system: a class act," *Cambridge Review of International Affairs* (vol. 20, n. 4, 2007), 619–637.

53   Those arguing that declining American hegemony is leading to a potential return of inter-imperial rivalry include Harvey (see references above) and A. Callinocos—for example: "Imperialism and global political economy," *International Socialism Journal* (n. 108, 2005), <www.isj.org/uk/index.php4?id=140&issue=108>.

54 For discussion on the increase of productivity and profitability under neo-liberal restructuring, see, for example, D. McNally, "From Financial Crisis to World Slump," 47–55; F. Moseley, "The United States Economy at the Turn of the Century: Entering a New Era of Prosperity?" *Capital and Class* (n. 67, 1999); L. Panitch and S. Gindin, "American Imperialism and Euro-Capitalism: The Making of Neoliberal Globalization," *Studies in Political Economy* (71/72, 2004), 7–38; and E. Wolff, "What's Behind the Recent Rise in Profitability in the U.S.?" *Cambridge Journal of Economics* (vol. 27, n. 4, 2003), 479–499. On Canada, see F. Baragar, "The Canadian Economy in the 1990s: The Character of Accumulation," in Akram-Lodhi etal., eds., *Globalization, neo-conservative policies and democratic alternatives: Essays in honour of John Loxley* (Winnipeg: Arbeiter Ring, 2005), 43–67.

55 Teschke and Lacher, "The changing 'logics' of capitalist competition," 577.

56 T. O'Lincoln, "Australia's imperialist insurance policy," Class and struggle in Australia seminar series, Australia National University (October, 2004), <dspace.anu.edu.au/bitstream/1885/42698/1/Australia_imperialism.pdf>, retrieved July 2008.

57 In the Canadian context, writers like Linda McQuaig and James Laxer typify this problematic position.

58 The U.S. also supports and relies to an extent on a network of client states outside the core as regional enforcers of its imperialist interests, such as Israel or South Africa. On South Africa as a regional power used by the U.S., see Bond, *Looting Africa*, 112-129.

59 O'Lincoln, "Australia's imperialist insurance policy."

60 O'Lincoln discusses the Australian intervention in East Timor. I discuss Canadian involvement in the coup in Haiti in chapter five. On Canada and Guyana, see D. Black and P. McKenna, "Canada and Structural Adjustment in the South: The Significance of the Guyana Case," *Canadian Journal of Development Studies* (vol. 16, n. 1, 1995), 55–78.

61 Harvey, "In What Ways Is the 'New Imperialism' Really New?"

CHAPTER 2:
Empire at Home

The Canadian state's relationship with indigenous people provides a sharp example of the policy of accumulation by dispossession, and serves as a potent reminder of Canada's imperialist history. Any discussion of Canadian imperialism really must begin at home. Indigenous nations are Canada's very own Third World colonies, created and managed as part of an intensive, ongoing colonial project, and they bear the scars of that history.[1] First Nation communities—an archipelago of Bantustan-like territories carved out of much larger traditional territories that were taken by the imperial power—have rates of poverty, illness and suicide several times higher than the rest of Canada, while they have no meaningful right to self-determination. In many First Nation communities in recent years people have lived under boil water alerts because of E. coli outbreaks and a lack of clean water; tuberculosis has made a comeback; poverty reaches levels found in the Global South; and extended families live in overcrowded substandard houses that would be condemned if they were found anywhere else in the country. These are living conditions which belie the image of a tolerant, pacific and caring Canada. But indigenous communities are also spaces of defiance and hope, as they continue to resist the Canadian colonial project and fight for their political, economic and cultural independence.

Present-day Canada was the first territory that Canadian capital, aggressively supported by the state, had to transform in its own image. Laws protecting private property, the privatization of natural resources and their subordination to profit-driven intensive exploitation, the establishment of international borders to manage human migration and protect nascent Canadian industry from international competition, a market in human labour—none of these things (all necessary conditions for the development of a capitalist economy) appeared ready-made to Canadian corporations. There were hundreds of indigenous nations living across present-day Canada on land rich in resources, that did not wish to participate in the state and big business's plans for them and their land. But it was precisely the natural wealth of indigenous land and the labour of indigenous peoples (and poor immigrants) that provided the necessary basis for Canadian capital to grow and prosper in the first place, and to eventually move abroad to become a globally competitive force. It was on indigenous lands that mines were developed, oil discovered, private farms to feed the growing urban centres established, railways connecting the vast Canadian market laid, roads to transport goods carved out of the landscape and tourist resorts built. The whole foundation of Canadian capitalism rests upon indigenous land and resources. The growth of Canadian capitalism could only be achieved, then, by imperialist means. Canada's existence is premised on the forceful subjugation of indigenous nations and their resources to its interests.

But not only did the domestic imperial project give Canadian business the financial foundation to, over time, move successfully onto the international stage, the process of building an empire at home also served as a lesson for building it abroad. The domestic political economy of Canada has provided valuable life lessons for Canadian corporations and the state: that, among other things, subordinating the colonized to your interests by market mechanisms rather than simply by force is an important longer-term imperial strategy; that bureaucratic-administrative mechanisms with an air of impartiality can advance imperial interests while absorbing the more creative and militant energies of the colonized; that while military force is on its own insufficient for advancing imperial ambitions, the empire should always be willing and prepared to use violence or threaten its use to defend its aims when necessary; and that the ideological discourse that inevitably surrounds imperial aggression—that it is about promoting civilization (sometimes articulated as "economic sustainability" these days) and helping the savages to help themselves—which is rooted in deeply derived notions of European (and especially British) racial superiority, is a central tool in empire building that justifies the domination and suffering of whole nations of people. These features of the Canadian imperial project are replayed throughout the course of Canadian history—in slightly different forms in different time periods, of course—time and time again, like a nightmare from which the colonized cannot escape.

The colonization of indigenous nations is not simply a matter of historical curiosity, however; it is central to contemporary Canada. The project is not complete; and the most recent phase of global capitalism—neoliberalism—has sped up the process of accumulation by dispossession, in turn placing greater pressure on indigenous nations and their lands, and intensifying a conflict that is woven, unlike any other, so indelibly into the heart of the Canadian fabric.

A History of Dispossession and Exploitation

Dispossession and exploitation of indigenous peoples is a defining historical feature of the relation between pre-Canadian colonial administrations and Canada, on the one hand, and First Nations on the other, and so it is useful to frame current colonial developments with a brief discussion of their historical context. The strategy of dispossession got fully underway in the early to mid-nineteenth century as the capitalist economy emerged. There were previous transformations in indigenous communities as a result of the fur trade and early European contact and settlement. New technologies were employed in traditional activities, traditional subsistence was balanced with new trading relations with fur trading posts, which included the introduction of wage labour for a small layer of indigenous people, harvesting was intensified in order to feed a growing population living near the posts, and conflict between indigenous nations in some cases increased as they vied for trading relations with Europeans and increasingly scarce natural resources. And missionaries—often different sects competing with one another—certainly sought to convert indigenous peoples and win their souls to Christ. But the wholesale eradication of indigenous economies and cultural practices did not become a generalized and to some degree urgent policy until capitalist relations developed. Until the mid-nineteenth century indigenous peoples in many parts of the country, including in the north and areas in British Columbia, the prairies, northern and southwestern Ontario and northern Québec still retained some measure of control over their natural resources. While indigenous military strength framed any considerations for appropriating their lands, traditional forms of indigenous social organization, knowledge of the land, and hunting and trapping skills were necessary ingredients for the success of the European powers during the fur trade. It was with the decline of the fur trade and the emergence of industrial capitalism that indigenous rights, land tenure and culture became a systematic target of the colonial governments and the Canadian state.[2]

Thievery, Treaty Making and Treaty Breaking

One of the most common strategies of dispossession was the naked theft of indigenous land, made possible by the military power and violence of colonial governments and the Canadian state. Much of present-day Canada, including almost all of British Columbia, large parts north of 60, and northern Ontario and Québec, were in fact taken without any treaty signed, against the will of, and without any compensation to, the original inhabitants of these lands. Much like the enclosures in England from the sixteenth to the eighteenth centuries where peasants were forcibly removed from common land for the sake of newly emerging capitalist interests, indigenous land throughout much of Canada was forcibly enclosed and alienated from its indigenous inhabitants through the nineteenth and twentieth centuries. The land was in turn transformed into the private property of early capitalists and British settlers.[3]

Another strategy of dispossession was the treaty process itself. Canada entered into the treaty process in order to facilitate rapid capitalist development in certain parts of the country and, in some cases, as a result of indigenous resistance to land expropriation. Canada never sought a fair or equitable negotiation of lands and rights with indigenous people. Wherever Canada was able, it exploited its military strength and the economic vulnerabilities of its negotiating partners as much as possible to limit their rights and their treaty lands. The core position Canada took into the various treaty negotiations was extinguishment of what today is referred to as aboriginal title: that is, Canada would only conclude a treaty if its indigenous negotiating partners conceded to it their collective stewardship of their traditional lands and resources, and any rights they may claim by virtue of their being First Nations with a historical tie to the territory. Reserves negotiated in the treaty process have covered only a fraction of traditional lands, which was an intentional strategy to make it extremely difficult for indigenous communities to sustain economic independence and avoid capitalist market relations (a point discussed further below), while insuring capital's access to natural resources.[4] Despite the niggardly approach Canada took in the treaty-making process, it still systematically ignored much of its treaty obligations to First Nations. Treaty lands have regularly been flooded by hydro mega-projects, carved up by highways, shrunk by real estate developments, stolen by the military for bases, implemented with smaller boundaries than those agreed upon by First Nations, and destroyed by industrial sewage and run-off from mills and mines. Infrastructure development on treaty land or in very close proximity to it has wrought ecological devastation for many communities and destroyed resources they relied on to maintain their economies and cultures. Canadian negotiators also allegedly inserted clauses restricting rights and access to resources (game and fish, for example) that indigenous negotiators never agreed to during negotiations. In British Columbia in 1911, furthermore, the Province reserved to itself the right to recover reserve lands it decided were not being used by indigenous communities. Over 30,000 acres of reserve land were subsequently taken by British Columbia on this pretext.[5] As Michael Coyle observes, "[i]n this way the traditional economies of First Nations were sterilized."[6]

Even where treaties were in place, Canada still maintained its right to expropriate indigenous land. After Confederation in 1867, the forced alienation of reserve lands was in fact explicitly prohibited by government statute. Land would have to be voluntarily surrendered by First Nations. However, from its beginning, the Canadian state reserved the right to expropriate indigenous land for "public purposes," such as railway, road and other infrastructure construction. Canadian law allowed for the superintendent-general of Indian Affairs to lease lands, supposedly for the benefit of indigenous people who were engaged in "occupations that precluded them from cultivating the reserve lands to which they were entitled."[86] This is an important power for Indian Affairs, given how (as I discuss below) it sought to push indigenous peoples into wage labour. Early twentieth-century additions to the right to expropriation included leases for surface rights related to mining and the right to dispossess indigenous peoples of reserves that had cities of a minimum of 8,000 residents grow up next to them. It is important to stress here, when considering this provision, that no consent was required from indigenous individuals or their communities. And while communities were supposed to be financially compensated for the forced alienation and sale of their lands, Indian Affairs systematically refused to do so.[8]

Exploiting Vulnerabilities: Creating an Indigenous Labour Market
Creating a working class out of indigenous peoples also figured prominently in the state's colonial plans. Establishing the conditions whereby indigenous people have no alternative but to turn to the labour market in order to make a living—to sell their labour to someone else for a wage—has always been an aim of the Canadian state. In many parts of the country—from British Columbia to the northern prairies to northern Ontario to the Maritimes— newly emerging capitalist industries, especially, but not only, in resource sectors, relied heavily on indigenous labour, as colonial settlement was limited. In British Columbia, for example, until late in the nineteenth century indigenous peoples were the demographic majority.[9] George Walkem, premier of British Columbia, observed in 1875 that indigenous labour is "invaluable in the settled portions of the province."[10]

Given the labour conditions and wages of capitalist industry at the time, and the life away from one's community it entailed for indigenous workers, such a labour market would not create itself. Producing an indigenous working class required limiting the opportunities offered to indigenous peoples by their traditional economies, leaving them little choice but to accept market relations as a new (and alien) governing force in their lives. This is one of the main reasons why Indian Affairs opted in its treaty negotiation policy in the nineteenth and twentieth centuries for thousands of small isolated reserves rather than fewer very large ones, which it did actually consider as a possibility for a time (the other reason was the dangers of united indigenous resistance and a near uprising in interior British Columbia in 1877). Smaller reserves were intended to make it extremely difficult to live off of traditional economic practices. Reserve locations, as Peter Usher argues, often had little to do with the traditional territories of indigenous communities, and had more to do with the demands of the emerging capitalist economy. Reserves were viewed, in other words, as a reserve labour pool for the benefit of capital, as well as a way of keeping indigenous peoples off of coveted resources.[11]

Not surprisingly, then, we find, as Frank Tough remarks in his study of late nineteenth-century northern Manitoba, that for many indigenous peoples, "as the treaty process had dispossessed [them] of their resources, they really were left with no option but to sell their labour."[12] The policy of labour market integration was a central part of the 1966 Hawthorn Report, which argued that indigenous people should be assimilated into the labour market and traditional pursuits should be de-emphasized. Welfare policy was also used to exploit the economic vulnerability of indigenous communities in order to force their reluctant members into market relations. Indian Affairs officials claimed economic dependency was an almost inherent predisposition of indigenous people that needed to be broken, and so welfare was denied to able-bodied First Nations or punitively designed to encourage people to enter the labour force instead. As a result, in certain parts of the country—particularly British Columbia, the northern prairies and the Maritimes—wage work did in fact become an important source of income for indigenous people.[13]

Training in Misery and Suffering: Moral Reform of the Colonized

Moral training and the imposition of "British" values were also actively pursued in the effort to establish indigenous subservience to Canadian authority and the needs of capitalist accumulation. Certainly the banning of spiritual and cultural practices like the potlatch and the sundance were bound up with the general desire on behalf of Canadian authorities to do away with traditions that were central to indigeneity and which were not conducive to market relations in the indigenous community. Moral training in the context of colonial relations has always been a very racist practice. The uncivilized "Indian" was seen to require the intervention of Europeans who know what is best for them, who can assist them in integrating into Canadian society. As one colonial official in British Columbia remarked, indigenous people are "most filthy in their habits and extremely debauched and sensual, syphilitic complaints of the very worst kind being prevalent among them ... The Indians must disappear before the march of civilization."[14] Here we witness the fabrication of the savage as what Himani Bannerji describes as people of the body; the physicality and hyper-sexuality of the irrational primitive looms large in Canadian colonial discourse, with the fear that it could infect Canada's white bourgeois moral order.[15]

While not strictly reducible to the newly emerging capitalist economy (for some missionaries the path to salvation for the savage was the main concern), moral reform was nevertheless shaped by it. By using indigenous peoples to demarcate the boundaries of "uncivilized," moral reform agents and state officials were able to demarcate "civilized": moral resolution, self-discipline, industry, Canadianness—these were defined against a specific kind of indigenous identity. But it is also clear that the uncivilized were such because they needed to learn discipline, self-responsibility and a good work ethic. According to Indian Affairs officials and other agents of moral reform, including some missionaries, a key way to accomplish this was employment in capitalist industry (individual, as opposed to collective, farming was also seen in this manner). In turn, the unwillingness of indigenous people to fully integrate themselves into the labour market was a sign of their moral weakness. That indigenous labour would be performed for non-indigenous employers who happened to need indigenous people with a good work ethic and discipline never compromised the civilizing argument in the eyes of the civilized. Moral reform and market relations dovetail nicely with one another.[16]

Moral training was also a very gendered practice. That many indigenous cultures did not share the same gender dynamics as Canada's was a sign to Canadians of their uncivilized nature. And if women played an integral role in certain traditional practices in some communities, whether as political leaders, engaging in farming, or participating in trapping or the hunt, then gender reform could also prove to be a means to undermine indigenous culture. Wives of missionaries, moral reformers and governmental officials, for instance, "sought to destroy the fabric of First Nations life"[17] through the reproduction of Canadian gender norms through domestic training and teaching indigenous women proper housekeeping and food preparation skills.[18]

One of the harshest examples of the strategy for moral reform was the forceful removal of indigenous children from their families and their subsequent placement in residential schools where they were isolated from their communities and its traditions, language and customs. Residential schools were viewed by state officials and the church as an antidote to the political, economic, cultural and spiritual resilience of indigenous peoples. If other reform efforts did not take, then the answer was to completely obliterate young children's connections to indigenous culture by kidnapping generations of them and reprogramming them: without knowledge of their spiritual traditions, hunting and trapping skills, language and other cultural practices, indigenous youth would have little choice but to integrate into Canadian society. Imposing the capitalist work ethic on defiant savages, the schools became bastions of physical and sexual abuse, forced labour and death from disease.[19]

Canadian Apartheid

The legislative backdrop to Canada's relations with indigenous peoples was the Indian Act. The Indian Act was part of a series of racist laws, including South African Apartheid, designed in the nineteenth and twentieth centuries by the British colonial settler states to manage colonization.[20] The Act and its various colonial measures were imposed on indigenous communities without their consent or consultation, and in some regions, such as Ontario and Québec, long after treaties, in which First Nations never conceded their political sovereignty, were signed. The Canadian state established, through the Indian Act and successive federal ministries subsumed under various economic ministries like "Mines and Resources" or "Northern Development," a nexus of administrative and legal measures that constitute "a totalitarian 'cradle-to-grave' set of rules, regulations and directives to manage Native lives."[21]

Framed by a white supremacist conceit that legitimizes the state's Constitution of indigenous people as uncivilized and therefore in need of guardianship by white people, the Act and the practices surrounding it have been central to the state's strategy to undermine indigenous self-determination and self-sufficiency. Under the Act, Canada arrogated to itself total political authority over reserve communities, and imposed the band council governing system in place of traditional decision-making structures (only a small percentage of reserve residents vote in band council elections). To this day the Minister of Indian Affairs still has the authority to overturn band council decisions. The Act also defined "Indian" (based on the amount of "Indian blood" someone has), in the process determining who had the right to live on a reserve and participate in programs established for First Nations. In effect, the creation of the "status Indian" restricted access to treaty and other rights to reduce the financial burden of indigenous rights on the treasury and force those without status to integrate into mainstream Canadian culture. "Indians" living on reserves throughout the country and off reserves in Manitoba, British Columbia and the Northwest Territories (where there had been recent unrest) were also declared ineligible to vote (since they were not "civilized" enough for this responsibility) in federal elections in 1885, while most provinces passed legislation prohibiting "Indians" from voting in the late 1800s and early 1900s. Men could give up their status in return for the right to vote. Federally, indigenous people did not achieve suffrage until 1960. Québec was the last province to grant indigenous people the vote, in 1969. Under the Act, indigenous women automatically lost their "Indian status" if their husbands decided to give up their own for the right to vote, or if they married non-indigenous men.[22]

Meanwhile, the Indian Act also established special Indian Agents who were to enforce the Act's regulations. As representatives of the state, Indian Agents in the late nineteenth century and for much of the twentieth century were endowed with the highest political and legal authority on reserves. They had the powers of police and justice of the peace, being able to charge and sentence individuals who disobeyed the Act and its regulations (for consuming alcohol, for example), were able to overturn decisions of the band councils and administered the reserve community's funds, including welfare. They were also charged with being the eyes and ears of Indian Affairs, providing surveillance on reserve communities. This involved using the pass law (which was introduced after the 1885 war and existed in law until 1951) to inhibit indigenous movement off reservations. Since growing numbers of indigenous people from the late nineteenth century onwards were engaged in at least part-time wage labour off reserve in many parts of the country, it is obvious that an aim of the pass law, and the Indian Agents enforcing them, was to keep community members from pursuing traditional forms of subsistence off of state-designated reserve land, even if the reserve land was unsuited to support an entire community, as it often was by state design. And when federal gaming and fishing legislation prohibited reserve residents from participating in traditional hunting and fishing practices on reserve, Indian Agents had a role in enforcing these laws as well. Indian Agents would also patrol the reserve, looking for individuals on relief who might be spending money on alcohol or other immoral pursuits.[23]

It was also under the Indian Act that gift-giving festivals such as the potlatch were outlawed from 1880 to 1951. These festivals promoted, on the one hand, economic redistribution, which constituted a barrier to the more competitive capitalist ethic and to dependence on market relations, and, on the other, traditional indigenous leadership structures.[24]

Resistance

Canada's history, however, is not one simply of colonial domination. It is also a history of struggle and resistance. The continued existence of indigenous nations in Canada is a testament to their struggle to survive in the face of centuries of imperialism. In the last two decades, as I will discuss later in the chapter, indigenous resistance has grown more consistently militant. But the revolts at Oka, Gustafsen Lake, Burnt Church, Six Nations and others are really the most recent in a long tradition of militant indigenous resistance that mark Canadian history and which have to a significant degree shaped the nature of the colonial relationship between the imperialist nation and those opposed to it.

As I noted earlier in the chapter, one of the pre-Canadian colonial governments' and the Canadian state's motivations for pursuing treaties was indigenous resistance to land expropriation; the colonial governments could not simply take the land as it wished. The so-called Robinson treaties of 1850, for instance, which cover parts of northern Ontario along Lake Superior, are the direct result of the militant defiance of a couple of Ojibwa communities in the face of a rush for copper in their territories. Communities shut down mining operations and were allegedly prepared to mobilize 1,000–2,000 people against the encroachment, forcing the government to the bargaining table. In British Columbia in 1877, the threat of war from a Secwempec and Okanagan federation forced colonial administrators to concede to some of their demands for larger reserves with better access to traditional harvesting grounds. Despite very difficult conditions on most reserves, indigenous peoples resisted full absorption into the labour market, often hunting, trapping and fishing illegally, while some of those who did work in capitalist industry got involved in union and strike activity. Residential school history is also replete with acts of defiance, some explicit (running away, talking back, refusing to work), others less so (talking behind teachers' backs, fouling the food of teachers and other authorities). This resistance was typically met with unmitigated viciousness.[25]

Indeed, violence often had to be employed by pre-Canadian colonial authorities and Canada in order to control indigenous defiance. Indigenous communities along the coast of British Columbia in the nineteenth century were only subordinated to colonial authority in the face of British and Canadian gunboat diplomacy, the destruction of villages and public hangings of individuals accused of resisting encroachments onto their lands. The expansion of the capitalist state west of Ontario, central to the establishment of a pan-Canadian capitalist market and an agricultural industry to feed the growing industrial centres of southern Ontario, met fierce indigenous opposition, led by the Métis. The opposition broke out into a war in 1885 (the so-called Riel Rebellion) that Canada, despite some losses, eventually won. In addition to those indigenous people killed in the war, nine were murdered on the scaffold and forty-four were imprisoned. In the Mohawk communities of Awkwesasne and Six Nations at the Grand River, the band council colonial governance structure was imposed only after violent interventions by the RCMP. To this day the councils do not have the support of large sections of those communities (and many more communities besides).[26]

Despite this violence, however, Canada has not defeated indigenous people or crushed their emancipatory spirit; the dialectic of resistance and domination, central as it is to Canadian history, persists. First Nations continue to struggle for dignity, equality and self-determination, while Canada seeks to intensify its colonial project.

Canada and Indigenous Peoples in the Neoliberal Age

The development of neoliberalism in Canada has led to a renewed intensification of accumulation by dispossession directed against indigenous people. Neoliberalism, as discussed in the first chapter, involves the restructuring of labour markets and the search for new spaces for the accumulation of wealth. Within Canada, indigenous land and labour figures centrally within the state's and corporations' neoliberal project: the success of neoliberalism is in large measure contingent on the increased penetration of indigenous land and the commodification of their labour power. While accumulation by dispossession has been a key historical moment in the development of Canada, because of their resistance to the Canadian state project, large sections of the indigenous population have nevertheless not been fully integrated into market relations. Considerable portions of their land, much of it resource-rich, have not been subject to capitalist development. The frontier of capitalist expansion still has significantly further to go in Canada.

In a context in which, on the one hand, corporate Canada is aggressively pursuing a cheaper and more flexible labour force as part of its agenda of neoliberal restructuring, and, on the other, the non-indigenous Canadian-born population growth rates remain low while indigenous peoples' are comparatively high, indigenous labour has become highly prized. This is particularly the case, furthermore, in the resource industries where investments are typically located in rural areas in close proximity to reserve communities. As Deb Simmons argues, dispossessed and/or desperate indigenous people, subject to a systematic discrimination expressive of the deeply rooted racist character of Canada, offer a potentially significant pool of cheap labour. Indeed, the proletarianization (the transformation into individuals who make their living by selling their labour for a wage) of indigenous people, and the latter's resistance to this process, is a key concern of the state's policy toward them. Laliberte and Satzewich, in their study of the agro-industry in Alberta, note that "[t]he proletarianization of Native people was (and is) a well known objective of the Indian Affairs Branch of the federal government." Reservations were organized, and are still viewed by government, they maintain, as a pool of cheap reserve labour.[27]

This focus on the labour potential of indigenous people appears to have sharpened since the emergence of neoliberalism. Labour force issues relating to indigenous people, including their consistently lower participation rates than non-indigenous Canadians (which can be ten percent or more lower than the rest of the population for reserve communities), has become a very consistent theme in Indian Affairs studies since the 1980s. Indian Affairs' studies commonly note the significant growth rates of the indigenous population, which are much higher than that of the non-indigenous population. But not only is their growth rate significantly higher, more importantly, their working-age population (typically measured at 15 yrs of age and older) is growing at a much faster pace than that of the non-indigenous working-age population. As one study stresses, "The Aboriginal workforce will grow at twice the rate of the total Canadian labour force in the next ten years."[28] In northern Ontario, the northern prairies and north of 60—areas of interest for natural resource companies and where the state is actively promoting resource development—indigenous people already constitute a large part of the population: eighty-five percent in Nunavut, fifty-one percent in the Northwest Territories and twenty-three percent in the Yukon.[29]

Promoting the market integration of First Nations is a preoccupation in Canada, matched only by the state's promotion of resource development in indigenous communities. Although the state's efforts here are presented to indigenous people and the public more generally with a charitable veneer—"economic development," "sustainability" and "self-government" are typical buzzwords in government literature—and in the interests of the colonized first and foremost, the reality remains that "economic development" of indigenous communities is premised on the negation of their self-determination. The Canadian state's and bour-geoisie's efforts to create a world after its own image in indigenous communities requires, after all, the exploitation and degradation of natural resources essential to the subsistence of community members and the social, cultural and economic sustainability of their nation, and the mobilization of their labour away from tra-ditional community practices toward the capitalist market. And these development projects are finite, with companies leaving communities after they have stripped the land bare and indelibly altered the local ecosystem. Such investments—the profits over which indigenous people have no control—cannot offer mean-ingful long-term economic development for First Nation com-munities as they are presently constituted. Not surprisingly, then, and to the chagrin of the state and capital, many members of the indigenous population continue to resist their full absorption into capitalist relations. State reports often reflect on the difficulties of getting indigenous people to sell their labour for a wage or will-ingly permit the penetration of their communities by resource companies. Indeed, to the extent indigenous people, especially on reserves, participate in the wage economy, it is often to support traditional subsistence activities. Indigenous people in an Ojibwa community, for instance, express a common disdain for the for-mal economy when they assert, according to Peters and Rosen-berg, that it contradicts their values, and that they do "not consid-er the exchange for money a satisfactory arrangement because it meant that workers were not partners in joint-labour exchanges, but 'slaves'."[30] The continued resistance by indigenous people to market relations and capitalist development on their land are inti-mately bound up with one another, as the loss of land to develop-ment invariably threatens traditional subsistence practices which can serve as a buffer to the waged economy, and express their on-going struggle for self-determination—a struggle which marks the limits of capitalist expansion in Canada. In response, the Canadi-an state is engaged in a sustained effort to dispossess indigenous people of their land, ranging from legal manipulations to outright violence, as the pressures of capitalist expansion over the last two decades have intensified, indeed militarized, the colonial conflict between Canada and indigenous nations.[31]

Mining and Oil and Gas Industries:
The Search for Land and Labour

Before considering some of the Canadian state's current tactics of dispossession, it is worth looking a little more closely at the mining and oil and gas industries, which provide a clear example of the tensions between capitalist development and indigenous self-determination.

Mining is a very important sector of the Canadian economy. Over the last decade, mining companies, actively promoted by the state, have been expanding their activities into regions of the country—north of 60, northern and interior British Columbia, northern prairies, northern Ontario and Québec—where capitalist development has hitherto been limited. At the global level, Canada is now the top destination for exploration capital, with the Northwest Territories, British Columbia, Ontario, Québec and Nunavut attracting the largest share of international investment over the last couple of years. Canada has the largest concentration of mining companies in the world, with interests in over 3700 properties. (It is worth noting, though, that unlike in any other major destination for mining investment, domestic companies have the largest stake in Canada's mining industry.)[32]

While Canada is rich in numerous mineral resources, much of the exploration frenzy is currently driven by the search for diamonds, which were first discovered in the Northwest Territories in the early 1990s. Exploration investment in the Northwest Territories, where the first major deposit was discovered, increased by 122 percent between 2003 and 2004 alone, as more diamond finds were made. But the search for diamonds has expanded beyond the Northwest Territories, with considerable sums of money invested in dozens of exploration projects in a few provinces. By 2009 Canada had four diamond mines in operation (three in the Northwest Territories and one in Ontario) with advanced development projects in the Northwest Territories, Québec and Saskatchewan. Canada is now one of the largest diamond-producing nations in the world.[33]

As mining expands geographically in Canada, indigenous labour and land has become central to the success of the industry. The Mining Association of Canada notes that "[m]ost mining activity occurs in northern and remote areas of the country, the principal areas of Aboriginal populations."[34] Natural Resources Canada reports, meanwhile, that approximately 1,200 indigenous communities are located within 200 kilometres of an active mine, and this will only increase as exploration intensifies. The location of the majority of its operations is significant, because it brings the mining industry squarely into conflict with indigenous land rights. First Nation communities claim (either through treaty or as unceded territory) much of the land mining companies seek to exploit, and either want control over proposed projects or oppose them outright given concerns about ecological damage to traditional territories and economies. The industry has a long established and well-earned reputation for damaging the environment surrounding mines through the toxic chemicals integral to its activities, the common practice of dumping tailings in local water supplies and the generally destabilizing effect industrial development has on the natural habitat. In Dene territory in Saskatchewan, to provide one example of mining's destructive nature, more than 1.7 million tons of radioactive waste and tailings were dumped in and around Great Bear Lake during the 1940s and 1950s. All food sources were contaminated, while cancer rates rose steadily in the local communities. A similar history stalks communities in the Northwest Territories, near where companies are searching feverishly for diamond deposits: Dene workers at a uranium mine in Port Radium in the twentieth century suffered shockingly high cancer rates; the community became known as the "village of widows."[35]

Yet the state and politicians are actively promoting mining development in regions of the country in which indigenous people constitute a large part of the population or have significant land claims. This is the case in northern Ontario, British Columbia and north of 60. It is worth noting here that north of 60, which is a site of increasing mineral exploration but has the largest proportional indigenous demographic makeup in the country, the federal government has full legislative authority over local finances and land use because the territories do not have provincial status. If these regions of proportionally large indigenous populations had provincial status, then indigenous people there would in effect exercise significant control over the land and its use and over any natural resources development that was allowed to take place (as a province would). But there is no sign of any of the three territories north of 60 getting provincial status. As a result, any royalties made from the mines go straight into the pockets of Canada, not local communities.[36]

The location of mines is also very significant in a context in which, as industry and government studies indicate, mining is facing a labour shortage.[37] Indigenous labour, in turn, is explicitly identified as central to the expansion of the industry. "Workforce diversity," as one industry-wide study expresses it, is a necessity for mining.[38] But not only will the mining industry and indigenous communities benefit when indigenous youth "acquire the skills and experience they need to meet the demands of the marketplace," Indian Affairs exclaims in an unabashed mobilization of nationalist sentiment, "the entire country … benefits."[39] It is perhaps true that the mining industry's stated desire for indigenous labour is sometimes used as public relations, drawing attention in its glossy brochures to the benefits their investments will bring communities in terms of steady wages; but the need for indigenous labour is stressed enough by the industry, and often in documents that are not necessarily for indigenous consumption, that it is likely real need being expressed rather than simply public relations. The Prospectors' and Developer's Association of Canada's memorandum of understanding with the Assembly of First Nations (AFN) calls for greater industry-First Nation cooperation around resource development and integration of indigenous peoples into the labour market.[40]

Indigenous communities, however, remain unsold on the benefits of mineral development and wage exploitation in mines. Opposition to mining remains strong. And so, not surprisingly, their resistance to the industry has become a focus of concern. The high value placed on a traditional "lifestyle"—as some industry commentators describe it, as it if it is just a fad indigenous people have been slow to get over—which, one study laments with some degree of bewilderment, leads communities to resist wage work in spite of high unemployment on reserves, is now considered a challenge to the industry. Integrating indigenous people into the labour market in rural areas is a real concern. But equally pressing for the industry is the persistent struggle in many communities against mining investment and the subsequent lack of an "effi-

cient regulatory regime"—due to indigenous resistance to mining development—facilitating companies' activities. Indigenous
assertion of title and land rights slows the mine development
process considerably, eating into profits and creating a climate
of insecurity that is potentially scaring away investors. As the vice
chairman of Toronto-based Barrick Gold, the world's biggest gold
producer, complains, "the painfully slow resolution of Aboriginal
land claims" is one major inefficiency facing industry growth in
Canada today (the other being an internationally uncompetitive
tax regime); and "mining is much too important to Canada to be
undermined by issues like these."[41]

The mining industry and the state have responded with a public relations effort aimed at selling mining and wage labour to indigenous peoples. Public relations has become very important for
the industry, given its less than stellar reputation when it comes to
its treatment of the environment and workers. Thus mining now
supposedly offers sustainability, a strong economic base and cultural respect to rural indigenous communities. The industry and
the state also, as part of their public relations campaign, like to
promote their consultations with First Nation communities, and
the environmental impact studies they conduct, which supposedly make indigenous concerns and rights central to new developments. In reality, however, impact agreements and consultations
are really another strategy—with a little more sugar-coating—to
ensure dispossession. More often than not consultation is limited and little to no benefit to the First Nation community is realized. Here is one first-hand reflection on mining from Chief John
French of the Takla nation, Tse Keh Nay, of British Columbia:

> To us, today's mining boom looks a lot like the old fur trade and gold
> rush. Strangers come into our territory without permission, take our
> resources, spoil our land, and then walk away with the profits, leav-
> ing us with the mess ... Much glowing talk is made of paying workers
> $94,500 per year and of the $7 billion in investments provincially, yet
> far too little of that is realized in our communities. Instead, our com-
> munities remain in abject poverty, living in overcrowded, mould-rid-
> den homes on tiny reserves. All the while, government and industry
> continue to suck our lands and resources out from under us.[42]

Dispossession, the expansion of capitalist relations and corporate profits are the true goals, regardless of the PR pitch.

Conflict with indigenous peoples is also a common feature of the activities of the oil and natural gas industries, which share similar sentiments to those expressed by the mining industry. Oil and gas deposits and pipelines used to transport the resources, located in rural and northern areas, often are on or close to indigenous communities. They also require transformation of the surrounding ecosystems in order to be developed. Beyond the drilling for the subsurface deposits and the actual pipelines, the projects, like mines, require roadways to be built, land to be cleared and power lines or even power-generating stations to be constructed—all of which can be disruptive to indigenous communities and their ability to engage in traditional subsistence practices. Not surprisingly, then, indigenous communities commonly seek to win some control over these projects or to stop them outright. A large part of the Alberta territory providing the oil for the current boom is in fact on stolen Cree and Dene land—land never surrendered by First Nations. A major pipeline project, which will provide key infrastructural support to the oil boom in the near future, is planned through Dene land in the Mackenzie Valley. These are just two quick examples, but they demonstrate the tensions at the heart of the most important projects in the Canadian industry, based as they are on the exploitation of indigenous land. These tensions are likely only to increase in the coming years, as the oil and natural gas industries expand rapidly in Canada. Investments continue to flow into the Alberta Tar Sands and other regions such as B.C.—where money on bids for new exploration land outpaced Alberta in 2008—as the Canadian oil industry booms in the context of surging worldwide oil prices amidst uncertainty in the Middle East. Many more developments are being planned by the oil majors. Meanwhile, corresponding to the oil boom, according to industry observers the country's pipeline network must double in size by 2015 to meet the forecast production increases.[43]

Addressing the barriers indigenous people present to oil and gas development is a common theme in industry documents. Land claims impeding investments and court decisions putatively giving indigenous nations the upper hand against industry (which is nowhere near the case), are a source of constant consternation. Industry representatives, like their mining counterparts, are demanding a clearer and more efficient regulatory process, which would involve limits to indigenous communities' ability to delay projects. The Canadian Energy Pipeline Association, for example, demands that "[t]he Government of Canada must communicate to Aboriginal Peoples the importance of de-linking land claims issues from commercial project proposals and demonstrate that Aboriginal issues will be expedited if they do so."[44] In other words, indigenous peoples *may* get faster treatment to their historic claims if they give up one of their main sources of bargaining power: impeding or shaping commercial developments on their land!

The Harper Conservative government has made the development of the North a key part of its agenda. Canada and the oil and gas and mining industries are salivating at the prospect of a resource boom in a region that has remained largely undeveloped (from an industry perspective). But Harper is well aware of the resistance in the region to capitalist development. Speaking at the Artic Games in early 2008, he noted that "[t]here are some here who retain an older, anti-development view of the North. Our government does not share that ... Our government believes in northern economic development now and in the future. The Great White North is as much a part of Canada's identity as the red maple leaf."[45] Resistance to development, in other words, is backward, while its pursuit is the fulfillment of Canadian identity and Canada's own manifest destiny.

While less frequently discussed in oil and gas industry documents than in those of the mining industry, greater indigenous integration in the labour market is raised as a concern. Recent growth in the industry is threatening to outstrip the labour supply in Alberta and the Yukon. An internal migration wave to Alberta from across the country has helped to keep the labour market from becoming too tight (which typically leads to increased wages and better working conditions). But, according to some observers, greater indigenous labour market participation is still needed, especially given that many of the projects are in rural areas close to indigenous communities. The government-supported Petroleum Human Resources Council of Canada cites indigenous people as an important pool of labour that needs to be better integrated into the industry, as labour shortages are expected to persist, if not worsen, in the coming boom years. The industry needs "to attract under-represented groups," such as indigenous people (and immigrant labour and women); but it also must "improve retention" of indigenous workers who are not entirely committed to the capitalist labour market.[46]

As slick as the black gold for which it is drilling, the industry stresses "Respecting Cultural Differences" (the name of one document), and talks about building "enduring and mutually beneficial relationships" with indigenous communities. Sounds nice. But the Lubicon Cree, whose unceded traditional land supplies a great deal of the country's oil wealth, are likely not convinced; nor are those Dene opposing the Mackenzie Valley pipeline. As sugary sweet as the industry's claims about building good relations with indigenous peoples may sound, the stealing of land, attempts to develop land without indigenous consent and the environmental backlash of the developments tell the truth. Even the Canadian Association of Petroleum Producers' own claim about its "Aboriginal Affairs Framework," which it says was developed to support the industry's goal of "timely access to resources ... and secure and efficient access to markets," displays a contradiction at the heart of its business that no PR campaign could gloss over. It is extremely unlikely that indigenous communities, at risk of losing their land, culture and self-determination would agree with oil corporations, driven by the almighty pursuit of profit, about the meaning of "timely," even if they agreed on the "access."[47]

Mining and oil and gas investments regularly (almost as a matter of course) conflict with indigenous interests. They are not alone in creating conflict, however, even if they are on the cutting edge of it. Many industries come into conflict with indigenous communities; one only need take a cursory look at recent conflicts that have made headlines to realize how many industries need to exploit indigenous land (and in some cases labour). Mining, oil and gas, real estate development, tourism, highway construction, fisheries, hydroelectric development, lumber and ranching all have contributed to conflict with indigenous people.

There is, in other words, much at stake for Canadian capitalism with respect to indigenous peoples' struggle for their self-determination. It is an impediment that must be overcome—a barrier to the success of Canadian capitalism. The settlement of disputes, as the Canadian Council of Chief Executives puts it in their pragmatic, calculating fashion, will "help to create a more predictable and stable business environment." [48] Maybe corporations would be happy with settlements that did give indigenous people something socially just, if industry got all it wanted too; but in reality, as industry and most indigenous people wishing to maintain the possibility of self-determination know, it is much more of a zero-sum game than that. Corporations and their industry associations can talk about respect for indigenous culture, about improving the lives of indigenous people and the viability of their communities—but in the end, capitalist exploitation of land and labour and indigenous rights cannot coexist in a mutually beneficial balance. There is, however, little evidence that capitalists and the state would ever strive for that balance: getting them to pay any attention to indigenous rights has had to involve determined resistance by First Nations. Corporations and the state seek first and foremost to expand capitalist relations throughout the country. If the soft measures do not work, they will quite willingly make recourse to fraud, theft and force—like any other advanced capitalist power—to get what they want.

Dispossession By Treaty: The Comprehensive Claims Process
One of the principal means by which the state seeks to dispossess indigenous people of their land is through the formal comprehensive land claims process. Comprehensive claims pertain to indigenous communities that have never signed a treaty. Although forced on Canada and the provinces by indigenous resistance to capitalist development in their territories, the comprehensive claims process has been promoted by Canada and the provinces, in the face of this resistance and the prospect of it growing more militant, as the legitimate legal avenue to settle outstanding territorial and treaty issues. Nevertheless, as befitting a colonial project, the comprehensive claims process has been framed in such a way as to make impossible a fair and timely settlement for indigenous nations. When the framework is established by what are essentially colonial occupying governments and their legal system, without acknowledgement of the historic wrongs done to indigenous people or that the latter never ceded their sovereignty to the Crown, then there can be no pretense to equality between the participants—the colonized and the occupiers. The fact that it can take decades for a comprehensive claim to be resolved, and years

before the first stage of the extremely bureaucratized process is even initiated after a claim has been made by an indigenous nation, expresses, furthermore, the commitment of the Canadian state to a fair settlement. This amounts to decades more for corporations to potentially expropriate and ecologically damage indigenous territory, and for poverty and economic desperation in indigenous communities to increase.

The comprehensive claims process was designed to undermine indigenous sovereignty. Writing on the British Columbia Treaty Commission (BCTC), indigenous writer and activist Taiaiake Alfred describes the comprehensive treaty process as a failure for indigenous nations, and "at its core morally bankrupt" and "illegitimate."[49] It is organized with the purpose of promoting the state's colonial agenda and facilitating the penetration of indigenous territory by resource companies. A large proportion of comprehensive claims are from B.C., since Canada and British Columbia had a policy of not negotiating treaties (with the exception of a few on Vancouver Island from the mid- to late nineteenth century until late in the twentieth century). B.C. took indigenous land claims seriously in the 1990s only after a resurgence of indigenous activism that threatened the stability of, and investor confidence in, the province's resource sector. According to a representative of British Columbia in the Nisga'a negotiations, the Province began pursuing negotiations more seriously because "the fact of the matter is that there were a bunch of wars in the woods going on," which was leading to an "investor chill" that totalled, according to Price Waterhouse, a loss of an estimated $1 billion a year in offshore investment.[50] The aim of the treaty process has been to absorb serious political activity into the safer legal realm and bind indigenous nations into legal manoeuvreing.[51]

The central demand underlying Canada's and the Provinces' negotiating position in the BCTC and the comprehensive land claims process in the rest of the country makes clear Canada's ultimate goal: to solidify the colonial control of indigenous communities and land by denying indigenous nationhood and the illegitimate colonial basis upon which Canada is founded. At the heart of the colonial state's negotiating position is the extinguishment of aboriginal title in return for a relatively small sum of cash— given the wealth that has been made or will be made off of the resources on these lands—and a fraction of traditional indigenous territories. Aboriginal title involves the right to exclusive use and occupation of land, recognized by the Supreme Court as existing in section 35 of the Constitution. Extinguishment therefore involves indigenous nations relinquishing to Canada their political independence and exclusive ownership over and use of their lands. The demand that indigenous nations give up their inherent rights to their land and its resources as indigenous people, and the refusal to engage with indigenous people on a nation-to-nation basis, betrays the profoundly racist premise of the state's negotiating strategy toward them. On what grounds can Canada deny sovereignty to people who have never conceded it, or demand sovereign nations relinquish title to their land as a prerequisite for insuring they have any land or rights recognized by the colonial state? As Alfred forcefully puts it, without treaties between Canada and indigenous people as two equal and sovereign nations, "there cannot be any legitimate occupation of territory by subsequent authorities, only colonial imposition ... Thus there is no legitimate basis for British Columbia's [or Canada's] existence outside of racist arguments rooted in obsolete social doctrines of racial superiority, which allow for a claim of legitimacy and authority based on the inherent right of white peoples to impose their order on non-white peoples."[52]

This is the colonial logic found in the modern comprehensive treaties signed by Canada. There is no serious desire to negotiate a fair or equitable settlement, to right past wrongs or to recognize indigenous sovereignty. In the much criticized (by the political right) Nisga'a agreement in British Columbia, for example, the Nisga'a forfeited their title and got control over only ten percent of their traditional land—small plots which critics suggest will make self-sufficiency extremely difficult, especially given the rate of population growth in Nisga'a communities. British Columbia gets control, then, of almost all of the Nisga'a's traditional territory. Furthermore, the Nisga'a do not even have jurisdictional powers over the rivers and lakes in that ten percent (and have a water allotment under the treaty) or subsurface rights. Under the agreement, furthermore, Nisga'a land is transformed into fee simple title. This means that Nisga'a land is now private property owned by Nisga'a, subject to taxes and governed by the Canadian legal system rather than by aboriginal title. As with property held in fee simple, the Crown has underlying title and can appropriate the land should the owners fail to pay property taxes. Meanwhile, the treaty does not alter existing agriculture and woodlot leases or highway jurisdiction—all of which were established on Nisga'a land before a treaty was signed.[53]

The Nisga'a agreement serves as a model for Canada's comprehensive agreement strategy, evidenced by the fact that all post-Nisga'a negotiations and Agreements in Principle have the same hallmarks. The extinguishment of aboriginal title over most of First Nations' traditional territories, which facilitates corporations' access to their resources with the knowledge that the issue of title will never have to be revisited (the kind of "predictable" and "efficient" access called for in industry documents), is central to these agreements, as is the subsequent transformation of land into fee simple property. They are non-negotiable and no agreement will be signed by Canada unless the indigenous nations concede title. Further, the amount of land being offered, like the Nisga'a agreement, is only a tiny fraction of the First Nations' traditional territories, which will make economic self-sufficiency and self-determination very difficult to achieve, and subsequently increase pressures to accept major economic development projects.[54]

Canada has been the target of criticism by the United Nations' Committee on Economic, Social and Cultural Rights over its insistence on extinguishment as a basis for treaty negotiation. The UN Committee argued that extinguishment is an infringement on the rights of indigenous people to self-determination in international law, and is therefore illegal. In response to criticism from the UN and indigenous peoples, Canada reformed the extinguishment model with its "modified rights" and "non-assertion" language. "Extinguishment" is not used in the Nisga'a agreement, for example. Under the "modified rights" position, aboriginal rights are not nominally "extinguished" but "modified" into rights defined in the treaty; while "non-assertion" entails the indigenous party agreeing to exercise only those rights defined in the treaty and to assert no other aboriginal rights. But, as the UN Committee responded, "the new approaches ... do not differ much from the extinguishment and surrender approach."[55] The modification is in fact tantamount to extinguishment of aboriginal title, as the new modified rights are liberal rights that do not cover rights *as* indigenous peoples or recognize aboriginal title to land indigenous people never ceded to Canada. In the end, aboriginal title is replaced by Crown ownership of the land, while the language of "modified by this agreement" used in the Nisga'a and other settlements, observes Paul Rynard, is an effort by Canada to ensure "that no court will ever rule in favour of the Nisga'a Nation on any basis other than a violation of the specific terms of the treaty—however much future generations might be prepared to reassess the terms of coexistence."[56] This amounts, in effect, to an end run around constitutionally granted aboriginal rights.

In fact, Canada's right to unilaterally extinguish aboriginal title is declared by the Supreme Court's Delgamuukw decision, which was derided by the political right and the resource industry as a major legal coup for indigenous people. Alfred, however, rightly describes the Delgamuukw decision "as a mere refinement of the logic of dispossession that has lain beneath Canadian policy for generations."[57] Here the limits of liberal rights come face to face with the goal of colonial conquest. While Delgamuukw affirms aboriginal title to be a right to the exclusive use and occupation of land protected by section 35 of the Constitution Act of 1982— the part of the decision publicly focused on by the right and the resource industry—it also stresses (in fact, reaffirming past decisions) that that title is not absolute and can be infringed upon. In his majority opinion, Chief Justice Lamar argues that "the development of agriculture, forestry, mining, and hydroelectric power, the general economic development of the interior of British Columbia, protection of the environment or endangered species, the building of infrastructure and the settlement of foreign populations to support those aims, are the kinds of objectives that ... can justify infringement of aboriginal title."[58] As Michael Coyle, who teaches negotiation and mediation at the University of Western Ontario comments, "[o]rdinarily, a law or government action that violates the Constitution will be held to be invalid." [59] But separate rules apply to the colonized and section 35: the violation of indigenous constitutional rights is permitted if the state can prove it has a valid objective in the infringement, the infringement is as limited as possible, there has been consultation with the affected First Nations and compensation is paid. I will come back to what "consultation" means in practice, but compensation is likely little solace for communities affected by mining and hydroelectric projects many of whose members never wanted.

At the same time, though, the Delmaguukw decision also makes it extremely difficult for indigenous nations to prove their aboriginal title to traditional land in the first place. According to the Supreme Court, indigenous nations must provide proof of exclusive occupancy prior to British sovereignty on the land and continuity of occupancy from then until now if present occupation is used as evidence. And for indigenous practices—such as hunting or fishing for either subsistence or trade—to be recognized and protected as aboriginal rights, previous Supreme Court decisions have asserted that First Nations must prove these practices have a cultural continuity with their pre-contact past. In other words, aboriginal rights do not stem from the fact that the indigenous community was a self-governing and sovereign nation prior to contact with Europeans, but from a cultural distinctiveness—an aboriginality—that existed prior to the arrival of Europeans. If a tradition arose from European influence then it is not considered an aboriginal right. Recognizing the difficulty First Nations may have in meeting these requirements, Indian Affairs officials are incorporating this fact into their negotiating strategy in their effort to undermine indigenous land claims by opposing title claims at every turn.[60]

Canada also employs a number of pressure tactics to force the indigenous hand at the bargaining table and ensure it achieves the best possible settlement it can get. This includes the classic divide-and-conquer strategy, isolating small communities from their respective nations and targeting them for negotiations. This tactic was employed in British Columbia against the Lheidli T'enneh, Tsawwassen and Maa-nulth.[61] Canada also exploits the poverty in indigenous communities to force treaties that favour the colonial power. With their legal, research, staff and other fees, negotiations can be quite costly for First Nations with very limited budgets. Indian Affairs, in turn, has a loan fund that most indigenous negotiating partners rely on. The terms and conditions of the fund, however, weaken the indigenous bargaining position and make it impossible to walk away from the negotiations without facing significant financial penalties. The loans are time sensitive, putting a premium on settling the agreement rather than holding out for better terms, while they (and the interest) are typically repaid out of the financial settlement that comes with the agreement. Thus if negotiations stall, indigenous people face serious debt owed to Canada without any means of covering it. The possibility of military or paramilitary force against those communities brazen enough to assert their rights beyond the bargaining table also remains a significant pressure tactic, which I will come back to.[62]

Extinguishment is a powerful arsenal in Canada's imperial strategy; former Assembly of First Nations leader Matthew Coon Come remarks that it "is brutal conquest attempted with a fountain pen." Given that many of the collective rights of indigenous people are linked to their lands and resources, the severing of that relationship to the land via extinguishment undermines their ability to realize their rights while allowing corporations access to their resources.[63]

Dispossession by Slow Bureaucratic Grind: The Specific Claims Process

The specific claims process is another bureaucratic tool that facilitates the dispossession of indigenous peoples. Specific claims arise from Canada's and the provinces' failure to fulfill existing treaty obligations or from the inappropriate administration of indigenous land and other assets under the Indian Act. The specific claims process, run out of Indian Affairs, has been so bureaucratic, corrupt and incompetent that even a Senate committee studying the process could find no other conclusion but to condemn it. The Senate report is even titled *Negotiation or Confrontation: It is Canada's Choice*—recognizing that the process has leading to a growth of militancy among indigenous peoples tired of waiting for justice from Indian Affairs. The process is so bureaucratic that it can take up to twenty years from the time a claim is first filed before it is settled. And as I noted earlier, Canada and the provinces have regularly—as a matter of course—abrogated treaties. As a result, from 1970–2006 1,337 specific claims have been submitted. But only 275 have been resolved. These claims could collectively represent a multi-billion dollar liability for Canada. Phil Fontaine, Chief of the Assembly of First Nations, estimates that it could take

130 years to resolve all those backlogged claims. This problem has been compounded by government cutbacks to commission staff. The result for indigenous communities bound up in this process is potentially twenty or more years of treaties going unfulfilled—of land being taken or ecologically damaged, or of monies owed by Canada not being paid.[64]

And what chance do indigenous nations have of getting their land back after it has been appropriated by Canada and developed? After resorts, highways, railways, housing developments and, in some cases, cities have been built on it? What chance would the Six Nations of Grand River, who stopped a real estate development near Caledonia through direct action, have of getting back Kitchener-Waterloo, which was built on their unceded land, for instance; or the Stony Point community at Ipperwash of reclaiming all the treaty land on the shores of Lake Huron on which cottages were subsequently built? This situation is more than a mere echo of Israel's facts-on-the-ground argument it uses against the Palestinians: the parameters of negotiations narrow with the facts of settler colonization on the ground. Once major developments are undertaken, the colonizing state argues, you cannot really go back. This amounts to an *ex post facto* defence of stealing the land: you may have some claim to the land, but we have since appropriated and invested millions of dollars into it and settled colonists on it, so you cannot have it back. The fact of colonial practice becomes the defence for colonial practice.

Bureaucratic lethargy is not the only problem with the process, however. As the Senate report notes, "everything is done on Canada's terms and the government is both defendant and judge."[65] Yet even when a settlement is offered, there is often a catch. One witness testifying before the Senate committee complained:

> when we had an opportunity to negotiate a settlement on one of our Douglas Reserve claims in Chilliwack, one of the pieces of land they offered us was a swamp ... They offered us a swamp that they wanted to turn into a bird sanctuary. It would have remained a bird sanctuary, but we would have owned it ... One of the other pieces of land they offered us was a rocket range that DND [Department of National Defence] did not need anymore, but it would have cost millions to cleanup because unexploded bombs and munitions remain in those areas.[66]

The net result of the specific claims process is mounting frustrations on the indigenous side, and public warnings that direct action may be the best way of advancing their cause. One witness from British Columbia testifying before the Senate committee angrily remarked, "[M]ake no mistake about it, unless real reform occurs soon, it is only a matter of time before incidents like Oka, Ipperwash and Caledonia occur in communities across British Columbia. Time is running out. Our patience is wearing thin."[67]

In the summer of 2007, the Conservative government, amidst growing unrest in First Nation communities and threats of blockades over unsettled claims, was prompted into introducing modest reforms into the process. However, the Conservatives' reforms still fall short on a couple of key issues. The proposal establishes an independent appeals tribunal comprised of Superior Court judges to decide on claims when negotiations fail and to hear appeals on claims rejected by Indian Affairs. While the AFN can make suggestions on which judges it would like to see on the tribunal, the decision nevertheless remains with Canada, and the judges are still representatives of the colonial state. Meanwhile, the Conservatives are limiting appeals to those worth $150 million or less and have earmarked only $250 million per year for total settlement expenses. The $150 million may cover many claims, but for those First Nations rightfully seeking more, it is an arbitrary and thus unfair cut off; and the overall budget cut off will limit the number of settlements possible in a year, making the process slower than it needs to be.[68]

The Duty to Consult

Some observers have claimed that indigenous peoples have been dealt a victory by the Supreme Court with its demand that Canada has a duty to consult with First Nations before development projects are undertaken on or near their land. The duty to consult has been developed in a number of Supreme Court decisions, including Sparrow, Delgamuukw, Haida-Takhu River and Mikisew Cree. The duty arises from the principle of the "honour of the Crown" with respect to its relationship to indigenous communities, as stipulated by the Supreme Court. According to the Court, this means that the state, in historically recognizing some form of aboriginal rights (to hunt or fish on traditional territories, for instance) from the Royal Proclamation through to section 35 of the Constitution, has a responsibility to accommodate indigenous interests in cases where things like development projects (establishing a mine, for instance) could negatively impact indigenous rights, either by proceeding on territory that indigenous communities assert a right to but which right has not yet been formally proven or recognized by Canada, or by proceeding on territory in close proximity to treaty land.[69]

Given the existence of aboriginal rights, in other words, the state cannot simply ignore indigenous concerns relating to development projects on or near their lands; it must accommodate these concerns, which the Court suggests can be done by consulting with the First Nation communities in question. Canada, the Supreme Court argues, must commit to "a meaningful process of consultation in good faith."[70] The extent of consultation will be determined on a case-by-case basis, but for projects that could potentially involve significant impact on indigenous lands, consultation could entail submissions by indigenous parties for consideration by the state and corporations or participation in the decision-making process.

To the extent it limits the ability of Canada to run roughshod over them, the duty to consult appears to be an important step forward for indigenous rights. There are some important limits to the duty that should give us pause for concern, however. To start, what is meant by "good faith"? This is not made clear by the Supreme Court, and that is a major gap. After all, consider the way in which Canada approaches the comprehensive and specific claims processes. From an indigenous perspective, that approach would come nowhere near "good faith," as the whole strategy of the state here is to undermine indigenous interests. Without any clear stipulation of what "good faith" is, should we expect anything more from Canada than what we see in other areas of its colonialist relationship with First Nations, where the interests of capitalist accumulation are front and centre?

The Supreme Court also makes clear certain limits it explicitly puts on the duty to consult. According to the Haida decision, in cases where the expected infringement of indigenous rights is minor, the duty is simply to discuss important decisions to be taken regarding indigenous lands. That is less like consultation, and more like informing indigenous peoples about what is already planned. In cases where title still has to be formally proven to the state, according to the Haida decision, "there is no duty to agree; rather, the commitment is to a meaningful process of consultation. As for Aboriginal claimants, they must not frustrate the Crown's reasonable and good faith attempts, nor should they take unreasonable positions to thwart government from making decisions or acting in cases where, despite meaningful consultation, agreement is not reached."[71] So Canada can undertake consultations that, as noted above, may not meaningfully exhibit real "good faith," and if agreement is not reached by the indigenous party, then ... too bad, and do not interfere further. Put more sharply, the Court asserts in the Haida decision, "[t]his process does not give Aboriginal groups a veto over what can be done with land pending final proof of a claim."[72]

Thus if the indigenous community does not want the development project on its traditional lands, but has yet to prove its title to the territory in question, or wants to stop a project that is not on its land but which will impact it nonetheless, it really has no power to do so; the only real power it has through the legal channel here is to consult about it. If the consultations do not yield what the colonized want, then (again) ... too bad. The whole premise of the duty to consult, in other words, is the historic colonial relationship between Canada and indigenous nations, and no real justice can be derived from it. In essence, it allows indigenous people some nominal input in corporate and state development plans rather than recognizing their right, as nations that have not conceded their sovereignty, to be self-determining in their territory—all the while absorbing their political energy and resources into another bureaucratic process.

The limits of the duty to consult were made very clear to the Kitchenuhmaykoosib Inninuwug First Nation (KI) in a May 1, 2007, Ontario Superior Court of Justice ruling. KI has been opposing the Platinex mining company's plans to explore on its traditional lands near Big Trout Lake, 500 kilometres north of Thunder Bay. KI surrendered the lands in a 1929 treaty, but retained its rights to hunt, fish and trap on the land, subject to the Crown's development of it. In an earlier decision, the Ontario Superior Court of Justice ruled that the KI's aboriginal right to the territory in question could be irreparably harmed by Platinex's plans if it proceeded without consultation. A nine-month injunction against development was subsequently issued. When the nine months were up, and KI still had not reached an agreement with the Crown over the use of the land, KI sought to extend the injunction. This time, however, the judge refused, stating that the consultation was a "reasonable and responsible beginning of accommodating KI's interest and, at this point in time, is sufficient to discharge the Crown's duty to consult."[73] It is hard to understand how these nine months of consultation, which produced no agreement, could have changed the judge's earlier view that Platinex's plans could irreparably harm KI's rights. What is clear, however, is that Dalton McGuinty's provincial Liberal government opposed consultation from the beginning, and argued that the Ontario Mining Act, which allows for corporations to conduct exploration without consulting First Nations, trumps section 35 rights. This is the government the KI had nine months to negotiate with.[74]

The Supreme Court also stipulates that the duty to consult is the legal responsibility of the state, though it may delegate procedural aspects to "third parties," i.e., corporations. This is what is done with environmental impact assessments, which according to the Court constitutes reasonable consultation. Increasingly, Canada is delegating the consultation responsibility to corporations via these assessment processes. But they are hardly fair and equitable, and typically do not represent meaningful consultation. Teillet observes that the "environmental assessment is simply another mechanism by which government dispossesses Aboriginal peoples from their lands and resources."[75] Input by indigenous groups and scientific experts on their behalf in the review process is severely limited, indigenous communities have nowhere near the funds to shape the assessment that multinational corporations do and rights obtained by corporations in the agreements are fully exploited while those of indigenous communities commonly go unfulfilled.[76]

In the assessment hearings surrounding BHP Billington's massive Ekati diamond mine project in the Northwest Territories, for instance, funding for interveners was a mere $245,000 (in contrast, the Pearson International Airport expansion review panel was given over $1 million for interveners), scientific experts intervening on behalf of the indigenous participants were in some cases given only a few minutes to testify and the company's extremely technical environmental assessment was given to indigenous groups only in English and at a time when many people were out of their communities for harvesting activities.[77]

Furthermore, how seriously can the duty to consult be taken when we consider policy for staking mining claims across the country? Most provinces have a version of the free entry system, which grants mining companies the right of entry and access on all Crown lands, the right to locate and register a claim without consulting the Crown, and the right to acquire a mineral lease with no discretion on the part of the Crown. There is no room for prior consultation under such a policy, which gives carte blanche to companies to invade indigenous land. Corporations can stake indigenous territory without even being registered with the state. As part of its big push to develop large parts of its territory, British Columbia even introduced internet claim staking as part of its 2005 Mining Plan, which allows companies to stake online. The mining plan actually designated over eighty-five percent of the province's land open to exploration, even though approximately ninety-seven percent of it is unceded indigenous territory.[78] In Ontario, mining is actually exempt from the province's environmental assessment policy. In a declaration order that allows for the exemptions, the Province states that "the Crown and the public will be interfered with and damaged by the undue time and expense required to prepare environmental assessments for undertakings that are expected to have insignificant effects on the environment."[79] This is particularly troubling since the federal government often forgoes its own assessments assuming that provinces will be doing so.

Justice in the Legal Realm?

It is clear that however much people may talk up the significance of section 35 and the formal protection supposedly granted indigenous peoples in the Constitution, and regardless of the volume of court proceedings pursued under it and their supposedly pro-indigenous decisions, it is not defending indigenous rights. As aboriginal rights lawyer Jean Teillet argues, "With the hindsight of 25 years, we can ... see that this purpose is not being readily achieved by s. 35 ... Indeed, it seems obvious now that this objective cannot be achieved by court rulings."[80] In practice, formal rights continue to be circumscribed or ignored. As a matter of course, the state has interpreted its responsibilities outlined by s. 35 and court decisions, such as they are, as narrowly as possible.

Thus the bourgeois legal realm provides a solid option for the state in its pursuit of expansion into indigenous territory. While the legal arena is typically presented by Canadian politicians, businesses, lawyers, the media and even some indigenous leaders as a neutral ground where the rights and responsibilities of the parties entering it can be weighed in a fair way by learned and impartial officials, at the end of the day it is an institutional feature of a colonial state, arbitrating laws written by administrators and representatives of a colonial state, and ultimately presiding over and sanctifying an occupation of nations most of whom never ceded their sovereignty to Canada. How much trust can be put in a legal system whose laws pertaining to indigenous nations are rooted in the historical context of colonialism and are designed to maintain the dominance of Canada, and which, even when they circumscribe state and corporate practices, are regularly circumvented by the state and corporations?

The legal system simply was not designed to defend indigenous rights. The law and court decisions have historically always been shaped by the need to reconcile indigenous existence in Canada with the capitalist accumulation of wealth. Indeed, racist and discriminatory treatment has been a barrier to gaining redress in the courts for much of the twentieth century. Until late in the twentieth century, indigenous people had only limited access to records relating to their treaties and land transactions. The state claimed that indigenous people were incapable of handling the responsibility of keeping and using the records pertaining to treaties and land surrenders. Requests for these records, usually when indigenous people were attempting to press treaty claims through legal channels, were regularly denied. Indigenous people were also by law unable to hire lawyers to assist them in gaining redress through the court system from 1927 (when the government amended the Indian Act in a context of increasing pressure surrounding land claims) until the 1950s.[81]

That indigenous peoples can now access the court system does not meaningfully change this status quo, rooted in Canadian history. Even when seemingly progressive positions are taken by the courts or set out in legislation, a closer look reveals their nuances that insure corporate investment can nevertheless continue: thus the duty to consult at best gives indigenous people some input into development projects that will proceed whether they want them to or not, aboriginal title is really simply a burden on underlying Crown title that must be proved on a case-by-case basis, and the state's ability to extinguish constitutional aboriginal rights is enshrined in Supreme Court decisions.[82]

Assimilation:
Liberalism and the Destruction of Indigenous Culture

Canada also continues to pursue its assimilationist policy against First Nations. The assimilationist strategy has deep historical roots. For more than a century the state has sought to destroy the economic and cultural fabric of First Nations and integrate indigenous people into the labour market. But none of the various schemes employed historically to achieve this—residential schools, resisting fair treaty settlement, job training programs, etc.—have been fully successful. The proportion of indigenous peoples living off-reserve has grown over the last fifty years to over fifty percent, but there are still a lot of people on reserves, while many indigenous persons in urban centres have strong ties to their First Nation community. The assimilation project is very far from complete.

Besides the assimilationist potential of whittling away indigenous land through the claims processes or destruction of traditional territories by economic development, Canada is also pursuing assimilation directly in a number of specific public policy initiatives. This includes the channelling of billions of dollars in federal funds into job-training programs to train indigenous peoples for, and encourage their participation in, the labour market. But perhaps the most important has been the effort to undermine the Indian Act. I noted above the racist character of the Act, but that is not the reason that Indian Affairs and successive federal govern ments of both the Liberal and Conservative variety have sought to undermine it. The Indian Act also recognizes certain collective aboriginal rights that Canada would like to eradicate in order to assimilate indigenous peoples into the individualist and capitalist Canadian order. The White Paper written for the Pierre Trudeau Liberal government (with Jean Chrétien as Indian Affairs minister) in 1970 was an attempt to assimilate First Nations and do away with the Indian Act. The plan, which was stopped by fierce indigenous opposition, was to eradicate collective aboriginal rights and to treat indigenous people, in turn, as regular citizens whose individual rights would be guaranteed, like other Canadians, under federal and provincial law. It was argued that poverty and discrimination toward First Nations was rooted in their particular status not as individual Canadians but as aboriginal peoples. Collective rights as First Nations were a barrier to the realization of equality that could only be achieved through liberal principles.

In 2002, the Liberal government (under Prime Minister Jean Chrétien's leadership) proposed the First Nations Governance Act (FNGA), which was another attempt to replace collective aboriginal rights with liberal individualist ones. It also ultimately failed amidst strong indigenous opposition. Like the Trudeau government's White Paper before it, the FNGA was written with very minimal indigenous input. It sought to essentially transform reserve communities into municipalities, where indigenous people would have individual rights rather than collective rights and be able to hold and sell private property. Becoming a municipality is obviously a far cry from being self-determining, and if anything increases indigenous governments' dependence on and responsibility toward the federal government. The FNGA also did not address outstanding land issues on which First Nations have been demanding action.[83]

The Stephen Harper Conservative government has moved in the same direction. Whatever criticisms Liberals may make of the Conservative position toward indigenous peoples and the Indian Act, it is right in line with their policies, even if the Conservative approach is more piecemeal. By the time Jim Prentice was one-and-a-half years into his tenure as Tory Indian Affairs minister in 2007, he had set in motion several significant reforms to the Indian Act and the reserve system without directly calling for its replacement, although that is clearly what is happening. One of the reforms is the push for individual property ownership on reserves. In the 2007 federal budget, the Conservatives allocated

$300 million for the establishment of the First Nations Market Housing Fund, which will allow indigenous people to purchase or build on-reserve housing. The Conservative Party's policy on indigenous peoples states that one of its goals is to "[s]upport the development of individual property ownership on reserves."[84] Prentice himself has suggested the reason for substandard and overcrowded housing on reserves is the lack of private property, which is "the whole basis of wealth creation in our society."[85] But who would be most likely to buy private property from indigenous lands: impoverished indigenous people, or non-indigenous developers? The Tories have also sought to include the Indian Act under the Canadian Human Rights Act, which indigenous critics argue is an assault on the collective nature of indigenous rights, replacing them with individual rights recognized under Canadian law. Prentice even publicly mused about moving whole communities off of reserves and into urban centres as a way of addressing poverty and inadequate housing, education and healthcare in First Nation communities.[86]

As Colin Scott argues, the "old orthodoxy" of assimilationist policy "is well entrenched among federal and provincial politicians" today.[87] I would add that is obviously well entrenched among Indian Affairs officials and a significant section of the general public too. The explicitly racist language of the past may not be employed by contemporary politicians and Indian Affairs officials, but the preconceived notions behind their policies are the same. How else can one defend the refusal to negotiate with indigenous people on a nation-to-nation basis even when the latter never conceded their sovereignty to Canada, or justify the insistence on assimilation when indigenous peoples clearly do not desire such an outcome? In other words, on what grounds other than racism can the attempted conquering of indigenous peoples be made acceptable? Or can indigenous culture be treated as inherently inferior to its mainstream Canadian counterpart and the cause of much of what ails indigenous people? Simply allowing for self-determination, addressing land claims fairly, and proper financial compensation for all that has been taken from First Nations (such as the corporate profits that have been made off their resources) could go a long way to addressing poverty in their communities.

We can see the influence of scholars such as University of Calgary political scientist Tom Flanagan in the views of Indian Affairs officials and Conservative (and Liberal) politicians. Flanagan was a founder of the Reform Party and has been a Conservative Party adviser. He is a strong advocate of assimilation, including the introduction of private property in indigenous communities and the end of aboriginal rights and status. In his book *First Nations? Second Thoughts* he calls indigenous people uncivilized. He laments the loss of the concept of uncivilized to (according to him) cultural relativism, and advocates for its return to public discourse. According to Flanagan, "European civilization was several thousand years more advanced than the aboriginal cultures of North America, both in technology and social organization ... European colonization was inevitable and, if we accept the philosophical analyses of John Locke and Emer de Vattel, justifiable." Of course, he does not explain why the original European colonists in North America could not survive without the assistance of uncivilized indigenous peoples, or that the latter had developed very successful economic, trading and political systems which enabled them to flourish in the many different ecologies of the continent. It is worth noting that John Locke was an intellectual in the employ of English agrarian capitalist and colonial administrator the First Earl of Shaftesbury, and developed his ideas on what constitutes "civilized" in order to justify land expropriation in England and the Americas. Flanagan also assumes that any society without hierarchical leadership and private property, or whose communities have small populations, is uncivilized (too bad for people living in small rural towns). The colonial power he defends is conveniently the de facto measure of civilization.[88]

Anti-indigenous racism also bursts into the wide open during confrontations surrounding indigenous mobilizations. One of the most recent manifestations of this very ugly side of mainstream Canadian culture was broadcast nationwide at the Six Nations reclamation near Caledonia, where local residents engaged in violence against indigenous activists and spewed racist rhetoric while carrying Canadian flags and singing the national anthem. For those on the left who see nationalism as a progressive organizing force, the scenes from Caledonia should be a harsh wake-up call.

Resistance and Confrontation Redux

The last twenty years have been witness to a renewal of indigenous militancy, as direct conflict between indigenous nations and state authorities has increased in response to the pressures of geographical expansion, growing poverty and the refusal of the state to meaningfully address First Nation concerns. The Canadian state's ability to impose unjust settlements on indigenous nations and continue to parcel away their land is dependent, as we saw earlier in the chapter, on the balance of forces between them. The increasing use by indigenous communities of roadblocks, occupations and armed stand-offs like those at Oka, Gustafsen Lake and Burnt Church, and the spread of the militant warrior movement, has limited the state's colonial ambition in some important instances.[89]

Probably the most commonly cited flashpoint was the 1990 Oka revolt, with its images of camouflaged and masked Mohawk warriors standing off against the Canadian military. Lasting several months and broadcast daily on national television, Oka brought the conflict over capitalist development (in this case nine holes of golf at a country club) and indigenous rights onto the national stage in a way it had not been for some time. At Oka, despite the military and police action, and violence meted out against warriors and community members reclaiming their traditional lands, the golf course was never extended. While there is still no final settlement at Caledonia, the Grand River Six Nations community has successfully stopped Henco Industries from building a new subdivision on their lands. Although Dudley George was killed by an Ontario Provincial Police (OPP) bullet, Ipperwash Provincial Park and the army camp, both of which were built on stolen Ojibway Stoney Point land, have not reopened. In southern Manitoba, the Roseau River First Nation won seventy-five acres of new reserve after threatening a railway blockade in the summer of 2007 because of the slow pace of their specific claims negotiations. The concession from Conservative Indian Affairs Minister Jim Prentice came in the context of growing threats of direct action by indigonous activists, and the potential that some participants in that summer's national aboriginal day of action organized by the Assembly of First Nations, such as Roseau River, would push the boundaries established by the AFN for its tightly controlled protest.[90] These are but a few examples of direct action (or the threat of direct action) success against Canadian colonialism. The successes of direct action, combined with the one-sided character of the colonial court system and the slothful negotiating pace of the federal and provincial governments, has raised the profile of "confrontational" tactics. And why would we expect anything different? As activist and community researcher Deb Simmons argues, "[t]he pressures for the alienation of Aboriginal lands emerge as the common element in widely contrasting conditions of struggle" that indigenous people are engaging in today.[91] We should not be at all surprised to see an increasing recourse to railway blockades, roadblocks and land reclamations across the country as First Nations assert their rights. Indigenous activists are hard to ignore when crucial economic infrastructure like a railway is shut down. The warnings for patience from the conservative leadership of the Assembly of First Nations and the threats from politicians, such as those from Conservative Indian Affairs Minister Jim Prentice (who in the summer of 2007 raised the prospect of financial penalties and police action against communities that engage in direct action) increasingly fall on deaf ears when land is being stolen from indigenous people.[92] Indeed, so heated did the tensions between indigenous activists and government become in the summer of 2007 that, while making threats against militant activists, Prentice announced a plan to address the land claims backlog and even to revamp the claims commission by giving it some independence from Indian Affairs (in addition to granting new land to Roseau River). But the backlog at the land claims commission is so extensive it will require massive amounts of money before any meaningful progress is made. There is no indication that any change will be made to Canada's comprehensive claims negotiating strategy with its demand for extinguishment and the forfeiture of most of a community's traditional lands. Thus the proposals may give the superficial appearance that Canada is working to improve its relations with indigenous nations, but the changes do not fundamentally alter Indian Affairs' position or rectify in any significant way the profoundly colonial bias in the claims processes. Most importantly, no tinkering with Indian Affairs or the claims processes, and no Supreme Court decision, can change the basics of capitalist economics: there will be constant pressure by corporations and the state to expand into First Nations' territory. Consequently, indigenous anger will not dissipate, and direct actions will likely continue.[93]

This is the price of imperialism. These conflagrations, where indigenous peoples must physically assert their opposition to Canadian colonialism, forcefully display the colonial tension that is more than a mere hangover of the original European settlement of present-day Canada; it is a historically rooted and ongoing conflict over the future of the country and its resources. Canada is, for the moment, willing to endure this conflict, whatever the costs. This is the dialectical interplay—the shifting balance of forces between the colonizer and the colonized—of empire building. Even in the face of indigenous defiance, the state is not yet ready to seriously reconsider its policies. The state still considers militarization and the deployment of increasing levels of violence as a potential option for dealing with insurgent First Nation activists. The Sûreté du Québec (SQ) after the Oka Revolt, and the RCMP after the Gustafsen Lake stand-off both increased their militarization considerably in preparation for future confrontations, and aggressive policing more generally has become an important part of state policy toward indigenous direct action.[94]

Dispossession and Mega Development:
The Fight Over the Future of Indigenous Land
There are many important struggles against dispossession in Canada today: Six Nations near Caledonia, Tyendenega Mohawks near Belleville, Secwempec at Sunpeaks, Salish at Bear Island and Grassy Narrows near Kenora, to name just a few. These are struggles, involving direct action (blockades, reclamations and occupations of government offices) and police repression, which will help to define the future of Canada and its domestic empire. I want to highlight a few other examples that involve megadevelopment plans. These are projects that the state and large sections of Canadian capital are heavily invested in, because they will lay a much-needed infrastructural foundation for capitalist expansion in Canada. They will be conducted on a scale that requires significant long-term investment from corporations, and offer these corporations the potential for hefty long-term returns. The massive scale on which these projects are undertaken will impact

whole regions of Canada, including large indigenous territories. These cases are a clear illustration of the irreconcilable conflict at the heart of the contemporary Canadian project: the expansion of Canadian capitalism necessitates access to indigenous land and involves corporate practices that strike at the very heart of indigenous cultures, economies and societies. If these projects proceed, indigenous communities standing in their way will be irreversibly transformed, if not destroyed.[95]

Mackenzie Valley Pipeline

Heralded by proponents as "the next Alberta," the Mackenzie Valley in the Northwest Territories is the site of the largest infrastructure development project—the Mackenzie Valley pipeline—ever planned in Canada. Viewed as an incredibly important project by Canada, Alberta and the oil and gas industry, the proposed pipeline will stretch 1,350 kilometres from Inuvik near the Arctic Ocean south through several Dene communities to the Alberta Tar Sands, with other smaller feeder lines built along the length of the main line. It will carry gas from three fields owned by Imperial Oil, Conoco Canada and Exxon Mobil, and Shell to support oil extraction in Alberta. Alberta's Tar Sands account for twenty-six percent of Canada's current oil production, but could grow to seventy percent by 2025. In order to fully exploit Alberta's oil wealth, however, greater infrastructural development is needed, and the Mackenzie Valley pipeline is seen by the oil industry and Canada as the solution. The initial costs for the project were estimated at $7 billion, but by the end of 2007 they had risen to $16.2 billion.[96]

Initial plans for a pipeline were actually made in the early 1970s. However, they met strong opposition from indigenous communities in the region, most of whom had no land claims agreement with Canada and had not been consulted about the project. Canada was in turn forced to establish a public inquiry, headed by Judge Thomas Berger, into the impact the pipeline would have on the surrounding environment and the local Dene communities. At the time, indigenous militancy was on the rise in Canada, inspired by Third World anti-colonial movements. The Indian Brotherhood of the Northwest Territories passed a declaration of Dene Nationhood, stating their right to self-determination and a just land settlement, and their opposition to the pipeline had widespread support among other indigenous nations in Canada as well as non-indigenous supporters. This context helped to shape Berger's conclusion that a moratorium on development should be called until land claims in the region could be settled. The push for a pipeline has picked up steam again in the last decade, though, driven by the increase in world oil prices and Canada's renewed imperial offensive against First Nations, involving the expansion of the domestic frontiers of Canadian capitalism. It has also been partly facilitated by the signing of comprehensive treaties with a number of Dene communities along the pipeline route (the Inuvialuit, Gwich'in and Sahtu Dene), and the potential agreement between these communities, Canada and the oil companies that would give the communities ownership over a portion of the pipeline.[97]

While support exists for the project in some of these communities, opposition remains strong in others. This is the case particularly in the Deh Cho First Nation community in the southern Northwest Territories, which covers approximately forty percent of the pipeline route. Unlike the three other indigenous communities along the pipeline route where support for the project is strongest, the Deh Cho have not completed a land claim agreement. A treaty was signed between the Deh Cho and Canada in 1921, but the Deh Cho argue that they never extinguished their aboriginal rights or control over their traditional lands. Canada claims the Deh Cho extinguished their rights. The Deh Cho's fear is that the pipeline will be like any other development project in Canadian history: it will bring great riches to corporations and the state, while devastating indigenous communities. Some indigenous skeptics point to the diamond mines in the region, from which they argue their communities have little to show, as reason to be cynical about another major resource development project. The pipeline, however, would have a much more far-reaching impact on the region than the diamond mines. If built, such a massive project will leave its indelible mark in the Mackenzie Valley. Whole towns, some ten times the size of existing communities, will be created to support the building project; sand, gravel and water supplies will be exploited for the building of roads and support of the new towns; permanent above-ground infrastructure, such as compressor stations (to recompress the gas and keep it flowing south) will be established, including on watersheds; and it is likely that oil and gas exploration will increase along the pipeline route. Given some of the estimates for gas reserves within proximity of the pipeline, it is possible the pipeline could operate for at least fifty years. That is fifty years of further development and of resource exploration.[98]

Indigenous opponents are also concerned over their lack of control of resource royalties. It is important to recall that because of the territorial status of the Northwest Territories the land is owned by Canada, which also collects all royalty resources from non-renewable resource extraction. This means that the people of the Northwest Territories, the majority of whom are indigenous, have no control over their resources and the profits that are made from them. They can only hope that Ottawa agrees to reinvest those profits back into their communities—but that is far from guaranteed; it is unlikely, especially if one looks at the example of diamond mining in the territory, that the majority of the revenues Canada makes off of the pipeline will find its way back into the indigenous communities. The Government of the Northwest Territories (GNWT) is trying to negotiate a devolution of power from the federal government around the pipeline, particularly with respect to the collection of royalties. So far they have not had success. Even if they were to be granted some royalty rights from Ottawa, the actual value of resource royalties in the territory are not publicly disclosed. This real lack of transparency makes it difficult for the GNWT to negotiate devolution (which it is pinning its hopes on in order to raise the indebted territory's revenues) or for indigenous communities to negotiate pipeline agreements with Canada and the oil companies. How can they possibly negotiate a fair agreement if they do not have all the information necessary to negotiate one?[99]

The current royalty regime employed by Canada in the Northwest Territories is also cause for concern. Royalty rates, covered under the Canadian Petroleum Resources Act, are based on the "net profit" based royalty regime. Under this regime, expenses, including exploration expenses anywhere in the Northwest Territories, are subtracted from royalties or revenues, and while companies are recouping their initial investment, royalty rates remain extremely low, starting at one percent of gross revenue and gradually rising to a maximum rate of five percent. After the initial investment has been recouped the royalty rate is the greater of five percent of gross revenue or thirty percent net revenue. In Alberta and British Columbia, by contrast, royalties are collected using the ad valorem regime, in which a percentage of the gross value of production is collected (in Alberta, it was thirty percent in 2004). Profits from most mine and petroleum operations in the Northwest Territories remain confidential, but observers estimate that the existing Norman Wells oil field has provided a very high rate of return, lining the already well-lined pockets of the overlords at Imperial Oil (the field's owner) even further. The field is estimated to have made a 75.7 percent average return on investment from 1998 to 2004. Resource companies in the Northwest Territories, in other words, are not faring badly. From 1998 to 2004, however, Canada collected nearly $120 million in royalties from this field under the current royalty regime, but if it had been using the regime and rates applied in Alberta, it would have collected over $660 million. Thus not only are royalties in the Northwest Territories controlled by Ottawa, but also their income is well below that of other provinces where indigenous people do not comprise such a large part of the population.[100]

Despite these incredibly high profit rates, furthermore, the oil companies have actually been trying to lower the royalty rates, and in the summer of 2007 threatened to pull out of the project altogether due to rising costs, though the Conservative government was quick to assuage oil company concerns by suggesting it was willing to reduce royalty fees. The Deh Cho, meanwhile, are demanding in their land claim settlement negotiations powers for oil and gas taxation, which also led Imperial Oil to threaten to pull out of the project in 2005, before the most recent threat. The federal Liberal government of the day, like the Conservatives two years later, displayed its unyielding flexibility to the already rich oil lobby by promising the oil companies that no new taxes would be imposed on the pipeline.[101]

While the pipeline will affect hunting and trapping practices that have provided food and cultural sustainability for indigenous people in the region, critics of the pipeline argue that it provides only a short-term development strategy. Indeed, even oil industry executives admit the short-term nature of any development resulting from the pipeline. Most of the jobs that will result will be short term, related to the construction phase. And even if the pipeline is in use for fifty years, and bringing in fair royalty revenues to the local communities (that is a big "if"), the nature of the development involved means that at the end of the pipeline's lifetime there will be little left for region's population by way of spin-off. The Northwest Territories under these conditions will almost certainly remain a "dependent resource colony of the Department of Indian Affairs and multinational corporate capital."[102] Worse still, other remote areas that have undertaken significant and rapid resource development projects have experienced strong inflationary pressures. The costs rise in the immediate term, but when the inflationary pressure dissipates as the boom subsides, costly debt incurred from local community investments at the time of the boom (inflated by boom prices) will remain. Such are the risks of boom-and-bust economics.

According to the Deh Cho, the proposed framework for reviewing the project lacks clarity and does not ensure meaningful public participation from First Nations. The GNWT is cash-strapped and unable to adequately fund indigenous input, and Indian Affairs has offered little to help the communities prepare. This is especially unfair given the vast scale of the project, and the resources the oil industry can put into the assessment process. Imperial Oil's Environmental Impact Statement is more than 1,000 pages long. Without meaningful First Nations' input, the assessment will be considerably off-balance, tilting toward corporate interests. The problem with the assessment process is not just in the preparation, however, it is in the follow-up as well. Without proper funding, how can indigenous communities ensure that any environmental measures proposed will be followed? According to indigenous opponents of the pipeline, some of Justice Berger's original recommendations around protecting a sustainable renewable resource economy have not been adequately followed by Canada, as local renewable resource authorities do not have the resources to evaluate the impacts of the pipeline.[103]

The support that does exist among indigenous people is coloured by trepidation and some degree of desperation. The project is seen as a great opportunity to bring wealth and economic self-sufficiency into poor communities, while there is a recognition that although gas supplies are finite, the potential damage to their traditional economies and cultures is long term. Their support rests on the hope that a full and honest environmental assessment will be provided with indigenous input, a transparent and effective regulatory process will be put in place and a fair share of profits from the project will flow into local communities. But this is a risky gamble for communities, given the potential impact the project will have on them, the lack of clarity on expected corporate profits, the weak royalty regime in place, Canada's control over the Northwest Territories and the one-sided way in which the review process has been conducted thus far. As the chair of the Sahtu Renewable Resources Board concedes, "[t]here are regulatory agencies ... but the kind of atmosphere we had in the Berger days needs to surface a little more."[104]

As we have seen, historically it took serious political organization, and a willingness to engage in direct action, to win concessions from Canada and corporations. Given the enormous profits at stake for corporations and Canada in the Mackenzie Valley, it is likely that the situation there will be no different for First Nations.

Northern Ontario Development

A major battle is being waged between a number of indigenous communities in northern Ontario, on the one hand, and Ontario, Canada and resource corporations, on the other, over the latter's plans to develop northern Ontario. The region north of the 51st parallel has hitherto not been subject to extensive development, though it is rich in subsurface mineral deposits and timber. The region's boreal forest is one of only three of the world's original forests with large areas still intact. It is north of the so-called cut line which lies roughly at the 51st parallel and marked the limit of commercial logging until recently, when Ontario decided to expand the frontiers of capitalist development in the province. Part of the push for development in the area is also driven by diamond mining giants like De Beers and Kennecott, which are spurred on by lucrative finds in the Northwest Territories and James Bay, where the Victor mine is due to open soon and will impact an area four times the size of Toronto. If the Province and corporations get their way, northern Ontario will be forever changed, as it faces the biggest wave of development in its history. In the region lies the

potential for vast profits, but they can only be realized if corporations and the state can defeat the indigenous opposition.[105]
Ontario claims that this time around development will be done
differently. However, indigenous activists claim that thus far there
is little different about the approach. Indigenous rights are being
trampled on as corporations, supported by the Province, rush to lay
claim to the region's immense wealth in natural resources. First Nations point out that fish stock and the migratory patterns of game
have already been altered by some of the initial development.[106]

The recent fight between the Kitchenuymaykoosib Inninuwug
(KI) Cree First Nation and junior mining company Platinex has
thrown into relief the struggle over the future of northern Ontario.
In 1929, KI signed the adhesion of James Bay Treaty 9. As part of the
adhesion, KI received a reserve of 8,800 hectares located near Big
Trout Lake, approximately 500 kilometres north of Thunder Bay.
KI claims, however, that the calculation of the area of its reserve
was improper, and in May 2000 filed a specific claim for 51,000
more hectares of its traditional land for its reserve. Platinex owns
mining leases to KI traditional land, however. Given the slow pace
of the specific claims, KI's land could be pillaged long before a decision is made in the case. Platinex and KI first began discussions
in 1999 about development in the area. When KI decided that discussions were not compliant with the consultation protocol the
community developed, it ended the discussions and notified Platinex that any previous agreements were null and void.[107]

Members of the KI community and other local First Nations
are very wary of corporate-led development on their lands. All but
two KI voting-age residents have signed a petition opposing development. A moratorium on development in the region north of
the 51st parallel has actually been declared by KI and nine other
communities. While the Province allows free entry onto traditional indigenous land, KI Deputy Grand Chief Alvin Fiddler declared,
when the moratorium was announced: "The moratorium is a wake
up call for all those operating under the illusion that there is a 'free
entry' to our traditional lands." The Chief of KI at the time, Donnie
Morris, asserted: "We have said it before and we will say it again.
No exploration means no exploration. Which part of NO does not
the Ontario government understand?"[108] Thus when Platinex tried
to begin exploration for platinum in February, 2007, with Ontario's

approval, it was stopped by KI residents who blocked the company's access road. Platinex was refused entry, and its workers left a week after arriving.

Not deterred by this initial setback, and buoyed by Ontario's support for development and its mining act that allows for free entry staking almost wherever corporations please, Platinex responded in April 2006 by seeking an injunction against the blockade and damages of $10 billion in the Ontario Superior Court. Platinex's case has wide resonance for the resource industry in general, and mining in particular, and has drawn a lot of attention from corporations and industry observers. In response to KI's moratorium and demand for proper consultation, industry analyst Kerry Smith argues dramatically that "[a]ny effort to change the current system would be the death of the exploration business in Canada."[109] Platinex's damage claim is the largest ever made against a First Nation in Canada, and KI leaders estimated it would take them 200 years to pay. KI, however, did not back down. It responded by suing Platinex for $10 million and demanding an injunction against exploration. As one community member walking to the Ontario legislature in Toronto in 2006 to raise awareness of KI's battle said, "[W]e want our children and grandchildren to continue to use the lands and resources to pursue their usual vocation of hunting, trapping, and fishing."[110] This is a battle for the future of KI, and indeed of other northern Ontario First Nations.

KI has also responded with a constitutional challenge, arguing that Ontario's mining act violates its aboriginal rights to be properly consulted before development can take place on their traditional lands. That case is still pending. However, as noted earlier in the chapter, while the Superior Court judge initially issued an injunction against Platinex, halting development for nine months and ordering the Crown to consult with KI, he subsequently reversed that decision on May 1, 2007, declaring that adequate consultation had been given despite no agreement being reached between KI and the province. When KI activists continued to blockade Platinex's operations, they were found in contempt of court and sentenced in March, 2008, to six months in jail.[111]

The battle of northern Ontario is not over yet. Under public pressure, the court eventually released the KI political prisoners from jail. Late in 2009 Platinex agreed to drop its lawsuit against

KI and to sell its exploration claims in the community's territory for $5 million from the provincial government. While this marks a victory for KI, northern Ontario (and in particular the James Bay Lowlands, described by the mining industry as the "ring of fire") will undoubtedly be a site of future conflicts. Exploration claims in the James Bay Lowlands more than doubled to 8,200 from 2007–2009. First Nations north of 51 will continue to assert their right to control development on their territories, and have warned that they will continue to fight the capitalist invasion of their lands.[112]

Manitoba Hydroelectric Development
In the 1970s Manitoba Hydro (a Crown corporation), the Province of Manitoba and Canada planned a massive hydroelectric project in the northern part of the province on the territory of several Cree communities. It involved the diversion of the Churchill River through a control dam into the Nelson River via South Indian Lake, altering the level of South Indian Lake and the flow of the Nelson significantly. Another dam was built at the south end of the Nelson, turning Lake Winnipeg into a massive water reservoir whose natural flows are managed by Manitoba Hydro through the Jenpeg control structure and generating station in order to meet electricity demand patterns in southern Manitoba, Ontario and the United States. The Nelson was converted into a "power corridor" and Lake Winnipeg a massive "storage battery," to support a development scheme that irreversibly transformed 30 million acres of northern boreal forest and rivers. Manitoba Hydro, Manitoba and Canada initially intended to proceed with this project without the consent of the local indigenous communities, parties to Treaty 5, despite the obvious impact development of such magnitude would have on them. It was the resistance of these communities (York Factory, Nelson House, Tataskweyak (formerly Split Lake), Norway House and Pimicikamak (formerly Cross Lake) that forced the corporation and two levels of the state to negotiate the Northern Flood Agreement (NFA) treaty in 1977.[113]

Although no environmental impact study was conducted before the development began, Manitoba Hydro made assurances that the effects on the environment would be minimal. It was wrong. The Nelson River, an important source of fresh water, food and travel for indigenous people, is being killed. Water is contaminated with silt, fish stocks have declined substantially, riverbanks are eroded, travel along the river is unsafe because of the rapidly fluctuating levels that no longer follow a logic with which indigenous inhabitants are familiar, islands are being washed away, logs from dead trees block shoreline access and burial sites have been destroyed by flooding. Meanwhile, flooding has also affected the sources of food for, and migratory patterns of, caribou. The basis of the Cree economy and culture, in other words, is being destroyed by Manitoba Hydro. After thirty years of development, according to one Pimicikamak leader, the number of freshwater lakes in the region declined from thirty to twelve.[114]

Manitoba Hydro, Manitoba and Canada made significant financial commitments to their First Nation partners in the NFA to address the damaging impact of the development. In return for flooding traditional indigenous land, they committed to providing financial support for infrastructural development in communities, land to replace that which is destroyed by flooding, money to replace traplines damaged in the flooding, and money for "the eradication of mass poverty and unemployment."[115] However, they never followed through with these commitments. The negotiations were rushed, and clearly the First Nations were negotiating under duress, as construction for the project had already begun and thus there simply was not time to establish clearer wording and precise definitions of terms in the agreement. Despite earning $20 billion over thirty years from the developments, Manitoba Hydro, Manitoba and Canada used the vagueness in the wording of the agreement to avoid their obligations or to impose a very narrow interpretation on them. According to the Royal Commission on Aboriginal People, "Canada, Manitoba and Hydro did not intend, and have never intended, to cooperate energetically in measures designed and determined to be effective in confronting the adverse impacts of the project. They have instead used every legal device to limit their individual liabilities under the agreement."[116] In response to Cree frustrations with the failure to implement the NFA, Manitoba Hydro, Manitoba and Canada decided to instead negotiate so-called implementation agreements. The implementation agreements, however, are cash buyouts that extinguish all aboriginal land claims and any future claims for compensation, and represent a major step backward from the original

NFA. But after facing environmental catastrophe, threats to their cultural survival, impoverishment and social dislocation because of the hydro megaproject and the stalling on the NFA's implementation, four of the five First Nations signed the implementation agreements. Pimicikamak, politically isolated but defiant, continues to fight for the NFA's proper implementation.[117]

South Indian Lake, another indigenous community which was not a party to the NFA, was ravaged by the flooding from the project. It was not a signatory of the NSA because, despite being a separate community, it was considered by Canada to be a subcommunity of Nelson House and so was not given separate band status. Part of the community was relocated before the development was completed. New houses for the community's relocation were built in southern Manitoba, and according to residents, when the houses were transported up north, the insulation settled in the walls leaving large gaps beneath the roof where heat escapes. Residents still live in these houses. For those who remained in the original community, life was no better. An independent community that engaged successfully in their traditional economy was transformed into an impoverished and dependent one by Manitoba Hydro's ruin of South Indian Lake. Bank erosion, wetland destruction and the degradation of the fisheries among other things undermined the viability of the South Indian Lake economy, and government transfer payments increased exponentially through the 1970s, 80s and 90s, such that now only a fraction of the community's income is generated from non-government sources.[118]

The next phase of hydroelectric development in northern Manitoba is the Wuskwatim dam project. Like its predecessor, it promises to wreak further ecological devastation on already suffering indigenous communities. To head off opposition and divide indigenous communities, Manitoba Hydro signed a Summary of Understandings (SOU) with Nelson House in October 2003. The signing of this agreement is the cause of controversy in the community, because while some members support the SOU many are wary of the agreement and Manitoba Hydro's intentions. The band council that signed the agreement was elected in a very contentious election, which the band's own Election Appeals Committee suggested repeating. The band council's legitimacy has been called into question by many community residents over the election and other tactics it used to build support for the SOU in the community, such as paying residents to attend environmental hearings on the project to publicly demonstrate community support.[119]

Under the SOU, Manitoba Hydro makes a loan to Nelson House so that the latter can buy one-third equity in the Wuskwatim project. Nelson House, in other words, will become minority owners in the project and assume joint financial risk with Manitoba Hydro. As Native Studies professor Peter Kulchyski observes, "[T]hey are not being compensated for developments taking place on their lands, nor are they being made into nation-to-nation partners in economic development. Rather, they are being tossed a bone."[120] Nelson House participation in meetings planning the project is not even mandatory, as corporations involved in the project only need a simple majority to reach quorum at meetings. In short, the SOU which is to govern Nelson House's relations with Manitoba Hydro in place of the NFA treaty (which the community's band council has given up on) is a business deal. It is not a treaty that guarantees constitutionally protected aboriginal rights or financial compensation based on aboriginal title. Indeed, its language on involving Nelson House's participation in the project and on environmental protection and other commitments to the indigenous party is extremely weak and conditional. The weakness surrounding environmental protections is perhaps not that surprising, however, since Nelson House now has an objective interest (as a minority owner using borrowed money) in the success of the project. If the project is financially unsuccessful, not only will Nelson House's lands and traditional economy be destroyed, but it will be in debt to Manitoba Hydro. Minnesota-based political scientist Steven Hoffman, who has researched the impact hydro development has had on Manitoba's northern Cree communities, argues that the SOU "represents not the end of colonialism but its zenith."[121] Aboriginal rights are forsaken for a business relationship and the hope of financial reward based on the project's potential financial success somewhere in the future. It is little wonder that many in the community are opposed to this deal. This is a very dangerous precedent for the way in which indigenous communities address development projects on their land.[122]

The danger is made worse by the real prospect that the Wuskwatim project is only the tip of the iceberg of future hydro developments in Manitoba. If it proceeds, further dams, generating stations and transmission lines may follow, as Manitoba Hydro and the Province seek to build on this victory and look to capitalize on the insatiable demand for energy from business and consumers in the northern U.S. and Ontario. Certainly the Cross Lake community, the lone holdout still fighting for the implementation of the NFA to protect their lands from hydro development, thinks so. Their campaign for the NFA's implementation has become all the more pressing in light of Manitoba Hydro's future plans. Despite the devastation of the development initiated in the 1970s, Cross Lake angrily complains,

> Manitoba Hydro, the Province and Canada continue to push for more hydro power development ... [the] Wuskwatim dam might be completed, Conawapa and Gull/Keeyask dams might get approved, and a massive transmission line connecting the northern generating stations and dams to southern Ontario might be initiated. This could be enough to turn the entire Nelson River system into an industrial sewer, and destroy what remains of our homeland, and our hope.[123]

The SOU could serve as an effective model to tie the hands of indigenous communities while circumventing their aboriginal rights, facilitating Manitoba Hydro's expansion plans. Manitoba Hydro is actually pursuing negotiations with four communities—Tataskweyak (with which it has an agreement in principle), War Lake, York Factory and Fox Lake—that will be impacted by the Keeyask dam project, in order to establish an equity partnership similar to its SOU with Nelson House. Facing opposition in Tataskweyak, Manitoba Hydro paid the band council, which supports the project and signed an agreement in principle with the Crown corporation in 2000, $14 million between 2003 and 2005 for expenses ostensibly related to informing and preparing the community for the dam. This was spent before any community vote on the agreement in principle was taken. Recognizing the danger in equity partnership business agreements, and not seduced by Manitoba Hydro, Cross Lake has instead opted to continuing fighting, engaging in direct actions, such as occupying Manitoba Hydro's Jenpeg generating station, and threatening road blockades.[124]

Manitoba defends the new hydro development scheme as a green, and therefore socially and environmentally responsible, alternative to other forms of energy, such as coal. But for Cree communities directly affected by hydro development, such projects are anything but green. The Pimicikamak community, having first-hand knowledge of the devastation Manitoba Hydro's developments have wrought, calls out Manitoba's deceit:

> The Hydro Project is fueled by a great lie—that industrial-scale hydro is clean, green and renewable. There is nothing clean and renewable about eroding shorelines and waters choked with massive amounts of dead trees. There is nothing clean and renewable about dead fish and animals, floating belly up in the re-engineered waterways. The Hydro Project is fueled by a great theft—indigenous peoples in the north pay the price for cheap power that feeds the south.[125]

The Wuskwatim dam and other Manitoba Hydro schemes may bring cheaper energy to southern Manitobans, Ontarians and Americans in the northern U.S., but it comes at the cost of the ecological destruction of indigenous communities.

A Domestic Imperial Training Ground
Those of us living in Canada need not look very far to witness Canadian empire building first-hand. It surrounds us. Capitalist growth in Canada can only come at the expense of indigenous nations. The struggles in northern Manitoba, northern Ontario and the Mackenzie Valley, among so many others, are a reminder of this: Canada must continuously push deeper into, and politically, economically and culturally subordinate, its very own Third World colonies. The Canadian empire begins—geographically and historically—in these colonies within Canada's own borders, and proceeds outward from there.

In the domestic imperial battleground Canada has faced the challenges of subordinating nations to its political and economic whim; it has developed a confidence in its right to unduly influence sovereign nations, undermine their cultures and drain them of their wealth. A practised imperial hand, Canada has learned to be flexible and rely on a variety of strategies—from the legal realm, to establishing market dependency, to employing force, to proclaiming its humane intentions—to achieve its ends.

But the wealth and resources within Canadian borders are not enough. In the hyper-competitive and ultimately unstable world of neoliberal global capitalism, where the corporation that loses stride in the face of an unforgiving race to control the marketplace can crash and burn before it has a chance to catch up again, Canadian capital must search out new territories to accumulate wealth, grow their business and maintain an internationally competitive position. The fact that indigenous nations do not lie prostrate in the face of the capitalist invasion of their territories, threatening corporate profits and stability, adds further incentive for Canadian capital to expand its interests abroad. Thus Canadian capital's penetration of the Third World within Canada is today matched by its penetration of the Third World abroad. It is to the latter part of the Canadian imperial project that we now turn.

1   Indigenous writer and activist George Manuel, referred to indigenous peoples as the Fourth World. I am simply drawing a parallel here for heuristic purposes between the establishment of colonies in the Third World during the age of classical imperialism discussed in chapter one and Canada's historical and ongoing relationship with indigenous nations within its borders. I am not trying to challenge Manuel's efforts to distinguish a Fourth World on the basis of indigeneity and the absence of a nation-state.

2   V. Satzewich and T. Wotherspoon, *First Nations: Race, Class and Gender Relations* (Scarborough: Nelson, 1993); F. Tough, *As Their Natural Resources Fail: Native Peoples and the Economic History of Northern Manitoba, 1870-1930* (Vancouver: University of British Columbia Press, 1996); J. Teillet, "The Role of the Natural Resources Regulatory Regime in Aboriginal Rights Disputes in Ontario," prepared for the Ipperwash Inquiry. <www.ipperwash.ca>, retrieved February 2007; R. Knight, *Indians at Work: An Informal History of Native Labour in British Columbia 1858-1930* (Vancouver: New Star Books, 1996), 3-9.

3   C. Harris, *Making Native Space: Colonialism, Resistance, and Reserves in British Columbia* (Vancouver: University of British Columbia Press, 2002), 266-267; Knight, *Indians at Work*, 77-82; D. Johnston, *The Taking of Indian Lands in Canada: Consent or Coercion?* (Saskatoon: University of Saskatchewan Native Law Centre, 1989).

4   C. Harris, *Making Native Space*, 265; S. Campbell, "'White Gold' versus Aboriginal Rights: A Longlac Ojibwa Claim Against Damages Caused by the 1937 Diversion of the Kenogami River into Lake Superior," in B. Hodgins, U. Lischke and D. McNab, eds., *Blockades and Resistance: Studies in Actions of Peace and the Temagami Blockades of 1988-89* (Waterloo: Wilfred Laurier Press, 2003), 128-130; Knight, Indians At Work, 109ff.;

P. Elias, *The Dakota of the Canadian Northwest: Lessons for Survival* (Winnipeg: University of Manitoba Press, 1988), 222ff.

5   P. Usher, "Environment, race and nation reconsidered: reflections on Aboriginal land claims in Canada," Canadian Geographer (vol. 44, n. 4, 2003), 368–372; M Coyle, "Addressing Aboriginal Land and Treaty Rights in Ontario: An Analysis of Past Policies and Future Options," paper prepared for the Ipperwash Inquiry. <www.ipperwash.ca<, retrieved February 2007; R. Telford, "Aboriginal Resistance in the Mid-Nineteenth Century: The Anishinabe, Their Allies, and the Closing of the Mining Operations at Mica Bay and Michipicoten Island," in B. Hodgins et al., *Blockades and Resistance*, 80-82; Knight, *Indians at Work*, 108.

6   Coyle, "Addressing Aboriginal Land and Treaty Rights in Ontario," 11, quote p. 15.

7   Indian Act, quoted in Johnston, *The Taking of Indian Lands in Canada*, 74.

8   D. Johnston, *The Taking of Indian Lands in Canada*, 24, 93.

9   Harris, *Making Native Space*, 283 ff; Knight, *Indians At Work*; F. Tough, *As Their Natural Resources Fail*, 200ff; D. Simmons, "After Chiapas: Aboriginal Land and Resistance in the New North America," *Canadian Journal of Native Studies* (vol. 19, n. 1, 1999), 119-149.

10   Walkem quoted in Harris, *Making Native Space*, 284

11   Harris, *Making Native Space*, 283ff; R. Laliberte and V. Satzewich, "Native migrant labour in the southern Alberta sugar-beet industry: coercion and paternalism in the recruitment of labour," *The Canadian Review of Sociology and Anthropology* (vol. 36, n. 1, 1999), 65-70; Usher, "Environment, race and nation reconsidered," 368.

12   Tough, *As Their Natural Resources Fail*, 228.

13   Tough, *As Their Natural Resources Fail*, 223ff; Knight, *Indians at Work*; S. High, "Native Wage Labour and Independent Commodity Production During the 'Era of Irrelevance'," *Labour/Le Travail* (vol. 37, Spring, 1996), 243-264; P. Elias, *The Dakota of the Canadian Northwest: Lessons for Survival* (Winnipeg: University of Manitoba Press, 1988), 222ff; E. Peters, "Developing Federal Policy for First Nations People in Urban Areas: 1945-1975," *Canadian Journal of Native Studies* (vol. 21, n. 1), 61ff; R. DiFrancesco, "A diamond in the rough?: an examination of the issues surrounding the development of the Northwest Territories," *Canadian Geographer* (vol. 44., n. 2, 2000), 114–134; J. Saku, "Modern Land Claim Agreements and Northern Canadian Aboriginal Communities," World Development (vol. 30, n. 1), 143; H. Sewell, *'Enough to Keep Them Alive': Indian Welfare in Canada, 1873-1965* (Toronto: University of Toronto, 2004), 325–330; Laliberte and Satzewich, "Native migrant labour in the southern Alberta sugar-beet industry," 65–85; Brownlie, *A Fatherly Eye*, 101ff.

14 Quoted in Knight, *Indians at Work*, 84–85.

15 H. Bannerji, "Gender, Race, Class and Socialism," *New Socialist* (February-March, 1998), 13.

16 Satzewich and Wotherspoon, *First Nations*, 36ff; Adams, *Prison of Grass*, 132–149; N. Dyck, *What is the Indian 'Problem': Tutelage and Resistance in Canadian Indian Administration* (St. John's: The Institute of Social and Economic Research, Memorial University, 1991), 25-30; Harris, *Making Native Space*, 283ff; Johnston, *The Taking of Indian Lands in Canada*, 80; Sewell, *'Enough to Keep Them Alive'*, 327–328. On the connection between moral reform and wage labour and the moral reform of non-British immigrants in Canada, see my *Cops, Crime and Capitalism: The Law-and-Order Agenda in Canada* (Halifax: Fernwood, 2006). On the making of the English Working Class and moral reform, see E.P. Thompson's *The Making of the English Working Class* (London: Penguin, 1991) and *Whigs and Hunters: The Origins of the Black Act* (New York: Pantheon, 1975).

17 Satzewich and Wotherspoon, *First Nations*, 82.

18 Laliberte and Satzewich, "Native migrant labour in the southern Alberta sugar-beet industry," 66–67.

19 J. Milloy, *A National Crime: The Canadian Government and the Residential School System, 1879–1986* (Winnipeg: University of Manitoba, 1999); B. Schissel and T. Wotherspoon, *The Legacy of School for Aboriginal People: Education, Oppression, and Emancipation* (Toronto: Oxford University Press, 2003), 40-45; A. Grant, *No End of Grief: Indian Residential Schools in Canada* (Winnipeg: Pemmican Publications, 1996), 117–118.

20 On these laws and their relations, see A. Hall, *The American Empire and the Fourth World* (Monteral and Kingston: McGll-Queen's University Press, 2003), 498-500.

21 D. Stasiulis and R. Jhappan, "The Fractious Politics of a Settler Society: Canada," in D. Stasiulis and N. Yuval-Davis, eds., *Unsettling Settler Societies: articulations of gender, race, ethnicity and class* (London: Sage, 1995), 114.

22 On the Indian Act, see A. Hall, *The American Empire and the Fourth World. The Bowl With One Spoon*. Part one (Montreal: McGill Queen's University Press, 2003), 498-499; Satzewich and Wotherspoon, *First Nations*, 36; Brownlie, *A Fatherly Eye*, 81; W. Moss and E. Gardner O'Toole, "Aboriginal People: History of Discriminatory Laws." Background Paper (Ottawa: Library of Parliament, 1991), 3-10, 20-21. The band council system was first established in legislation in 1869, but made its way into the first Indian Act seven years later.

23 Satzewich and Wotherspoon, *First Nations*, 36; Brownlie, *A Fatherly Eye*, 109; Knight, *Indians at Work*, 115

24   Stasiulis and Jhappan, "The Fractious Politics of a Settler Society," 115.

25   Telford, "Aboriginal Resistance in the Mid-Nineteenth Century," 71-84; Harris, *Making Native Space*, 120-121, 286ff; Knight, *Indians at Work*, 17; Grant, *No End of Grief*, 136, 229-231.

26   C. Harris, *Making Native Space*, 120; Knight, *Indians at Work*, 77-84; Adams, *Prison of Grass*, 46-120; H. Adams, *Tortured People: The Politics of Colonization* (Penticton: Theytus Books, 1999), 83-96; G. York and L. Pindeera, *People of the Pines: The Warriors and the Legacy of Oka* (Toronto: Little, Brown & Co., 1991), 159–165.

27   D. Foot, R. Loreto and T. McCormack, *Demographic Trends in Canada, 1996-2006: Implications for the Private Sectors* (Ottawa: Industry Canada, 1998), 11; Simmons, "After Chiapas," 136-137; Laliberte and V. Satzewich, "Native migrant labour in the southern Alberta sugar-beet industry," 2.

28   Ministry of Indian Affairs and Northern Development, Economic Development in Ontario's First Nations Communities, www.ainc-inac.gc.ca, retrieved April, 2005.

29   <atlast.nrcan.gc.ca/site/english/maps/peopleandsociety/populatin/ aboriginalpopulatin/abo_2001/pm_abpopcd_01>, retrieved February 2007. E. Peters and M. Rosenberg, "Labour Force Attachment and Regional Development for Native Peoples: Theoretical and Methodological Issues," *Canadian Journal of Regional Science* (vol. 28, n. 1, 1995), 77; Ministry of Indian Affairs and Northern Development, *Aboriginal Labour Force Characteristics from the 1996 Census* (Ottawa: Statistics Canada, 2001). See also from the Ministry of Indian Affairs and Northern Development, *Québec First Nations: Our Economy, Our Future* (2001), *Implications of First Nations Demography* (1997) and *Gathering Strength: Canada's Aboriginal Action Plan* (1997), all from <www.ainc-inac.g.ca>, retrieved April 2005.

30   Quoted in Peters and Rosenberg, "Labour Force Attachment and Regional Development for Native Peoples," 92.

31   W. Russell, "'The People Had Discovered Their Own Approach to Life'," 132–137; Simmons, "After Chiapas;" High, "Native Wage Labour and Independent Commodity Production During the 'Era of Irrelevance." Furthermore, studies on the earnings of indigenous workers shows that, on average, they earn considerably less than their non-indigenous counterparts, which is perhaps another disincentive to labour market integration, as some may feel that the experience will be yet another discriminatory one. Maxim, White, Beavon and Whitehead, "Dispersion and Polarization of Income Among Aboriginal and Non-Aboriginal Canadians, *Review of Sociology and Anthropology* (vol. 38, n. 4, 2001), 469.

32   A. Lemeiux, 'Canada's Global Mining Presence,' *Canadian Mineral Yearbook, 2004*, (Ottawa: Natural Resources Canada, 2004).

33 Canadian Intergovernmental Working Group on the Mineral Industry, "Overview of Trends in Canadian Mineral Exploration," (Ottawa: Minerals and Metals Sector, Natural Resources Canada), vii; Natural Resources Canada, "Canada: A Diamond Producing Nation," (date unknown). <www.ncrcan-rncan.gc.ca./mms/diam/index_e.htm>, retrieved June 2009; Malatest & Associates Ltd., *A Situational Analysis of the Minerals and Metals Industry.* Report prepared for the Minerals and Metals Industry Sector Study Steering Committee (2004), 5-6, 20; Economist, "Diamonds: Changing Facets," *Economist* (February 24, 2007), 41.

34 Mining Association of Canada, "Aboriginal Economic Development and the Canadian Mining Association," Presentation to the Standing Committee on Aboriginal Affairs and Northern Development (June 10, 1998), 5. <www.mining.ca/english/publications/native.html>, retrieved April 2005.

35 M. Dhillon and A. Libert Amico, "Canadian Mining in Mexico: Made in Canada Violence," <www.miningwatch.ca/index.php?/horseshoe/cdn_mining_mexico> (April 20, 2007), retrieved June 2007. On the "village of widows," R. MacGregor, "Mining spoiled the water, now the animals are all awry," *Globe and Mail* (July 5, 2006), A7.

36 Natural Resources Canada, *Mines and Minerals Sector: Sector Priorities for 2006-2006* (Ottawa: Ministry of Public Works and Government Services, 2004), 2; British Columbia, "B.C. Mining Plan," (Victoria: Government of British Columbia); DiFrancesco, "A diamond in the rough?," 125. Provincial and federal levels of the state each also have extensive incentive regimes, typically involving tax rebates and financial write-offs, to encourage mineral exploration. These are worth hundreds of millions of dollars a year. See Canadian Intergovernmental Working Group on the Mineral Industry, "Overview of Trends in Canadian Mineral Exploration." See also Conservative Indian Affairs Minister Jim Prentice's speech to a Parliamentary committee on Aboriginal Affairs and Northern Development, in which he highlights the importance of mining development in the north.

37 Natural Resources Canada, *Mines and Minerals Sector,* 2; Mining Association of Canada, "Aboriginal Economic Development and the Canadian Mining Industry,"2-4.

38 Malatest & Associates Ltd., *A Situational Analysis of the Minerals and Metals Industry,* 41.

39 Ministry of Indian Affairs and Northern Development, *Québec First Nations,* 1.

40 V. Galt, "Mining signs on with native communities," *Globe and Mail* (March 5, 2008), B7.

41 Mining Association of Canada, Annual Report. Human Resources Committee (2005) <www.mining.ca>, retrieved April 2005; Mining Association of Canada, "Aboriginal Economic Development and the Canadian Mining Industry," 4; Malatest & Associates Ltd., *A Situational Analysis of the Minerals and Metals Sector,* 43J. Quote from Barrick Gold Vice President is Carrington, "Canadian Mining at the Millennium: Challenges to Future Growth." Address to the Autumn Gold Seminar (September 28, 2000), <www.mining.ca/www/Resource_Centre/Speeches.php>, retrieved November 2006.

42 J. French, *TheTyee.ca,* (May 29, 2007).

43 Canadian Energy Pipeline Association, "Industry Viewpoints." <www.cepa.com>, retrieved April 2007; J. Goddard, *Last Stand of the Lubicon Cree* (Vancouver: Douglas &McIntyre Ltd., 1991); N. Scott, "Nexen joins B.C. gas rush, pumps up find," *Globe and Mail* (April 24, 2008), B1. I will discuss the conflict on the Mackenzie Valley pipeline in more detail at the end of the chapter.

44 Quote from Canadian Energy Pipeline Association, "Industry Viewpoints;" <www.capp.ca/default.asp?V_DOC_ID=669>; Canadian Association of Petroleum Producers, *Industry Practices: Developing Working Relationships With Aboriginal Communities,* <www.capp.ca/raw.asp?x=1&dt=100984>, retrieved April 2007.

45 Quoted in J. Cotter, "Harper, on trip to the North, pledges development," *Globe and Mail* (March 11, 2008), A4.

46 Quote from Petroleum Human Resources Council of Canada, *The Decade Ahead.* <www.petrohrs.ca>, retrieved May, 2007; Canadian Association of Petroleum Producers, *Policy Direction for Alberta's Oil and Gas Industry,* <www.capp.ca/raw.asp?x=1&dt=NTV&dn=80955>, retrieved April 2007.

47 Quote from the Canadian Association of Petroleum Producers, *CAPP Aboriginal Affairs Framework* (January, 2004), <www.capp.ca/default.asp?x=1&V_DOC_ID=956&dn=67726&dt=htm>, retrieved April, 2007; Canadian Association of Petroleum Producers, "Respecting Cultural Differences;" Canadian Energy Pipeline Association, "Industry Viewpoints. Aboriginal Relations."

48 Canadian Council of Chief Executives, Human and Community Development: Aboriginal Peoples. <www.ceocouncil.ca/en/human/aboriginal.php>, retrieved April 2007.

49 T. Alfred, "Deconstructing the British Columbia Treaty Process," 1. <www.taiaiake.com>, retrieved April, 2005.

50 B.C. official quoted in C. Blackburn, "Searching for Guarantees in the Midst of Uncertainty: Negotiating Aboriginal Rights and Title in British Columbia," *American Anthropologist* (vol. 107, n. 4, 2005), 589.

51   See also P. Rynard, "'Welcome In, But Check Your Rights at the Door': The James Bay and Nisga'a Agreements in Canada," *Canadian Journal of Political Science* (vol. 33, n. 2, 2000), 215; and Simmons, "After Oka."

52   Alfred, "Deconstructing the British Columbia Treaty Process," 5

53   Rynard, "'Welcome In, But Check Your Rights at the Door'," 223; A. Manuel, "New Relationship or 'Final Solution'—An Analysis of the Certainty Provisions of the Final Agreements Initialed Under the BC Treaty Process," *First Nations Strategic Bulletin* (vol. 4, n. 12, 2006), 2 and "Canada and B.C. Land Claims Policy: Nothing 'New' About the 'New Relationship'," *First Nations Strategic Bulletin* (vol. 4, n. 7 & 8, 2006), 10.

54   A. Manuel, "New Relationship or 'Final Solution'," 1–3; Indigenous Network on Economics and Trade, "Report on Canada's Self-Government and Land Rights Policies to UN Special Rapporteur on Indigenous Peoples," *First Nations Strategic Bulletin* (vol. 4, n. 10), 1;

55   Quoted in Indigenous Network on Economics and Trade, "Report on Canada's Self-Government and Land Rights Policies," 7.

56   Rynard, "'Welcome In, But Check Your Rights at the Door'," 219.

57   Alfred, "Deconstructing the British Columbia Treaty Process," 13.

58   Justice Lamar quoted in Alfred, "Deconstructing the British Columbia Treaty Process," 13.

59   Coyle, "Addressing Aboriginal Land and Treaty Rights in Ontario," 24.

60   G. Dacks, "British Columbia After the Delgamuukw Decision: Land Claims and Other Processes," *Canadian Public Policy* (vol. 28, n. 2, 2002) 244; M. Murphy, "Culture and the Courts: A New Direction in Canadian Jurisprudence on Aboriginal Rights?" *Canadian Journal of Political Science* (vol. 34, n. 1, 2001), 122.

61   In 2007, the Maa-nulth and Tsawwassen ratified an agreement with the B.C. Treaty Commission, while the Lheidli T'enneh rejected theirs. The Tsawwasen and Maa-nulth agreements have been criticized by dissident members who argue a lot was given up for little in return. There were also accusations that the B.C. Treaty Commission spent millions on the Tsawwasen in order to win a favourable outcome, including flying people in from the U.S. and Ontario for the vote. B. Williams, Letter to Prime Minister Harper and Premier Gordon Campbell (July 9, 2007).

62   Indigenous Network on Economics and Trade, "Report on Canada's Self-Government and Land Rights Policies," 9-12; "New Relationship or 'Final Solution'," 1; Rynard, "'Welcome In, But Check Your Rights at the Door'," 217.

63   Matthew Coon Come quoted in Rynard, "'Welcome In, But Check Your Rights at the Door'," 233.

64   Senate, *Negotiation or Confrontation: It is Canada's Choice. Final Report of the Standing Senate Committee on Aboriginal Peoples' Special Study on the Federal Specific Claims Process* (Ottawa: Senate, 2007).

65   Senate, *Negotiation or Confrontation*, iv.

66   Quoted in Senate, *Negotiation or Confrontation*, 12.

67   Quoted in Senate, *Negotiation or Confrontation*, 33.

68   Indian Affairs, "Specific Claims Tribunal Act," <www.ainc-inac.gc.ca/ps/clm/fct3-eng.asp>, retrieved June, 2008; R. Pangowish, "Analysis of Canada's Specific Claims Action Plan," (unpublished, June 15, 2007).

69   Supreme Court of Canada, Haida Nation v. British Columbia, 3 S.C.R. 511, 2004 SCC 73; D. Natcher, "Land use research and the duty to consult: a misrepresentation of the aboriginal landscape," *Land Use Policy* (n. 18, 2001), 113-122.

70   Supreme Court of Canada, Haida Nation v. British Columbia, (Minister of Forests), 2004 SCC 73, [2004] 3 S.C.R. 511.

71   Supreme Court of Canada, Haida Nation v. British Columbia, par. 42.

72   Supreme Court of Canada, Haida Nation v. British Columbia, par. 48.

73   Quoted in J. Melnitzer, "Miner's costly lesson: Consult with First Nations," *Financial Post* (May 16, 2007). <www.canada.com/nationalpost/story.html?id=eeaf2165-e2ce-44aa-94Cfedcbd9be8B10>, retrieved May 2007.

74   Mining Watch, "Ontario Attacks Aboriginal and Treaty Rights in Kitchenuhmaykoosib Inninuwug (KI) Litigation," <www.miningwatch.ca/index.php?/Ontario/NAN_KI_outraged>, retrieved June 2007.

75   Teillet quote from, "The Role of the Natural Resources Regulatory Regime in Aboriginal Rights Disputes in Ontario," 44.

76   Natcher, "Land use research and the duty to consult," 115.

77   Mining Watch, "Mining in Remote Areas: Issues and Impacts," (2001), <www.miningwatch.ca>, retrieved April 2005.

78   Canadian Intergovernmental Working Group on the Mineral Industry, "Overview of Trends in Canadian Mineral Exploration, 109/110; Mining Watch, "Mining's Privileged Access to Land Under Challenge Across the Country," (2007) <www.miningwatch.ca>, retrieved Apri, 2007. On the B.C. mining plan, Mining Watch, "Assault on First Nation Lands in British Columbia," (2005) <www.miningwatch.ca>, retrieved April 2005; Dhillon and A. Libert Amico, "Canadian Mining in Mexico: Made in Canada Violence."

79   Quoted in Mining Watch, "Outrageous! Most mines in Ontario occupe meaningful environmental accoosiiieiii," <www.miningwatch.ca/index.phpf/newsletter_23/Declaration_Order>, retrieved June 2007.

80   Teillet, "The Role of the Natural Resources Regulatory Regime in Aboriginal Rights Disputes in Ontario," 38.

81 Coyle, "Addressing Aboriginal Land and Treaty Rights in Ontario," 18.

82 P. Kulchyski, *Unjust Relations: Aboriginal Rights in Canadian Courts* (Toronto: Oxford University Press, 1994) 1-10.

83 F. Cassidy, "The First Nations Governance Act: A Legacy of Loss," *Policy Options* (vol. 24, n. 4, 2003), 46-50. On the various jobs training programs, see Indian Affairs and Northern Development, "Aboriginal Human Resources Development Strategy," (Ottawa: Indian Affairs and Northern Development, 2003); J. Prentice, Notes for an Address to the House of Commons Standing Committee on Aboriginal Affairs and Northern Development on the Main Estimates of the Department of Indian Affairs and Northern Development (May 29, 2007); and A. Pacienza, "Students in North get work training," Toronto Star (July 10, 2006), A4.

84 Quoted in R. Diabo, "Conservatives Take Over Liberal's Assault on First Nation Rights: AFN's Partisan Politics Proven Futile," *First Nations Strategic Bulletin* (vol. 5, n. 2 & 3, 2007), 2.

85 Quoted in J. Warick, "Ownership remains the issue for First Nations housing," *Regina Leader Post* (September 23, 2006).

86 Prentice, Notes for Address; B. Curry, "Prentice working to make Indian Act obsolete," *Globe and Mail* (December 15, 2006), A6; A. Dobrota, "Mineral-rights fears raised," *Globe and Mail* (November 11, 2006), A8.

87 C. Scott, "Conflicting Discourses of Property, Governance and Development in the Indigenous North," in Blaser, Feit and McRae, eds., *In the Way of Development*, 302.

88 T. Flanagan, *First Nations? Second Thoughts* (Montreal: McGill-Queen's University Press, 2000), 6. He explores "civilization" in chapter three.

89 See T. Alfred and L. Lowe, "Warrior Societies in Contemporary Indigenous Communities," <www.ipperwashinquiry.ca>, retrieved April 2005, for an excellent and insightful study of Warrior Societies.

90 B. Curry, "Ottawa gives land to band threatening to block rails," *Globe and Mail* (June 21, 2007), A1.

91 Simmons, "After Chiapas," 122.

92 B. Curry, "Prepare for long summer of protest, chief warns," *Globe and Mail* (May 15, 2007) p. A1, 8.

93 On the summer of 2007 blockade threats and Prentice's response, B Curry, "Ottawa to address land-claims backlog," *Globe and Mail* (May 16, 2007) A15; B. Laghi and B. Curry, "Ottawa set to empower land-claims panel," *Globe and Mail* (May 17, 2007) A1, 4.

94 *Toronto Star*, "RCMP wants armoured column of its own," *Toronto Star* (July 10, 1997), A12; Waganese, "SQ Rambos On," *Windspeaker* (vol. 8, n. 22, 1991), 4. The shooting death of Dudley George—an unarmed protester from the Stony Point Band occupying unceded land in Southwestern Ontario confiscated by the government during the Second World

War—in the fall of 1995 by the Ontario Provincial Police's (OPP) Tactical Response Unit is a tragic example of this increased level of state violence.

95   There are other examples of megadevelopment projects that are very important to Canadian capital and the state, and which represent a serious threat to indigenous people and their territories, but which I cannot cover here, such as the Vancouver Olympics, British Columbia's mining plan or dam building in the Northwest Territories.

96   Canadian Arctic Resources Committee, "Royalties—A Question of Fairness," <www.carc.org/2005/Royalty%20Release%20D1.pdf>, retrieved June 2007; D. Ebner and S. McCarthy, "Prentice lays down Mackenzie gauntlet," Globe and Mail (June 8, 2007), B1.

97   K. Caine, M.J. Salomons and D. Simmons, "Partnerships for Social Change in the Canadian North: Revisiting the Insider-Outsider Dialectic," Development and Change (vol. 38, n. 3, 2007), 456.

98   Canadian Arctic Resources Committee, Northern Perspectives (vol. 29, n. 1& 2, 2004), 1–4, 13-17; R. MacGregor, "Pipeline rift runs deeper than blood," Globe and Mail (July 3, 2006), A7.

99   Canadian Arctic Resources Committee, "Royalties—A Question of Fairness;"

100   Canadian Arctic Resources Committee, "Royalties—A Question of Fairness;" P. Cizek, "Plundering the North for Hyper-Profits: Non-Renewable Resource Extraction and Royalties in the Northwest Territories 1998–2004," (Canadian Arctic Resources Committee, 2005), 10-11, <www.carc.org/other_publications.php>, retrieved June 2007.

101   Cizek, "Plundering the North for Hyper-Profits;" R. MacGregor, "'This is the next Alberta,'" Globe and Mail (July 1, 2006), A6; Ebner and McCarthy, "Prentice lays down Mackenzie gauntlet," B1.

102   Canadian Arctic Resources Committee, "Royalties—A Question of Fairness;" Canadian Arctic Resources Committee, Northern Perspectives, 5.

103   Canadian Arctic Resources Committee, Northern Perspectives, 2-4, 17.

104   Sahtu Renewable Resources Board member quoted in Canadian Arctic Resources Committee, Northern Perspectives, 12.

105   Mining Watch, "First Nations Declare a Moratorium on Mining Exploration and Forestry in the Far North: No Means No," <www.miningwatch.ca/index.php?/268/Ont_moratorium>, retrieved June 2007.

106   P. Gorrie, "Ontario's last, great wilderness," Toronto Star (August 5, 2006), F1.

107   S. Kerwin, "Analysis of Platinex Inc. v. Kitchenuhmaykoosib Inninuwug First Nation Case," Borden Ladner Gervais LLP Aboriginal Legal Issues e-newsletter (August 16, 2006).

108   Morris and Fiddler both quoted in Mining Watch, "First Nations Declare a Moratorium on Mining Exploration and Forestry in the Far North;" P. Gorrie, "Mining scars run deep," Toronto Star (June 20, 2006), A6.

109   Quoted in Gorrie, "Mining scars run deep," A6.

110 Quoted in MiningWatch, "Northern Ontario First Nation Facing $10 Billion Lawsuit for Blockading Platinex Mining Exploration," <www.miningwatch. ca/index.php?/262/Platinex_blockade>, retrieved June 2007.

111 B. Curry, "Native leaders sentenced to jail in mining protest," *Globe and Mail* (March 18, 2008), A8.

112 K. Howlett, "Mining company surrenders claim to native land in $5-million settlement, opening Ontario's far north," *Globe and Mail* (December 15, 2009), A10.

113 P. Kulchyski, "Manitoba Hydro: How to Build a Legacy of Hatred," *Canadian Dimension* (May/June, 2004), <canadiandimension.com/ articles/2004/05/01/142>, retrieved June 2007; S. Hoffman, "Engineering Poverty: Colonialism and Hydroelectric Development in Northern Manitoba," unpublished draft presented at *Old Relationships or New Partnerships: Hydro Development on Aboriginal Lands in Québec and Manitoba* (University of Winnipeg, February 23, 2004), 5-6.

114 Kulchyski, "Manitoba Hydro," 2-3; Kulchyski, "È-nakàskàkowaàk (A Step Back), 2; Tehaliwaskenhas, "Manitoba Hydro is a Villain—Devastating the Lives of Crees," *Turtle Island Native Network* (June 24, 2003), <www. turtleisland.org>, retrieved June 2007.

115 NFA quoted in Kulchyski, "Manitoba Hydro," 1.

116 Quoted in Hoffman, "Engineering Poverty," 12.

117 Kulchyski, "È-nakàskàkowaàk (A Step Back)," 4.

118 Kulchyski, "Manitoba Hydro," 2; Hoffman, "Engineering Poverty," 9-10;

119 Kulchyski, "Manitoba Hydro," 4–5. As a result of the band council's efforts, and a process that was established to support the dam from the beginning, the Manitoba Clean Environment Commission suggested that the environmental impact of further development would not be significant. See its *Report on Public Hearings: Wuskwatim Generation and Transmission Projects* (Winnipeg: Manitoba Clean Environment Commission, September, 2004).

120 Kulchyski, "Manitoba Hydro," 4;

121 Hoffman quoted in Kulchyski, "Manitoba Hydro, 4.

122 Kulchyski, "È-nakàskàkowaàk (A Step Back)," 5-8.

123 Pimicikamak Okimawin (Cross Lake), "Notice of Indigenous Power," (May 22, 2007), www.manitobawildlands.org/pdfs/PimicikamakPowerNotice. pdf, retrieved June, 2007.

124 CBC News, "Critics Question Manitoba Hydro payments to band," CBC News (April 7, 2005), <www.cbc.ca/canada/story/2005/04/07manitoba-hydro-050407.html>, retrieved June 2007; CBC News, "Band Occupies Manitoba hydro station," CBC News (April 16, 2007), <www.cbc.ca/canada/ manitoba/story/2007/04/16/jenpeg-protest.html>, retrieved June 2007.

125 Pimicikamak Okimawin (Cross Lake), "Notice of Indigenous Power."

CHAPTER 3:
Creating a World
After Its Own Image

An imperial agenda of extending the control of the state and capital within Canadian borders has its correlate in their ever- growing desire to expand their influence and interests abroad, particularly in the Global South. Just as they see the intensification of their domestic imperial project—at the heart of which is the appropriation of indigenous land—as a solution to the problems of capitalist profitability and the increase of global competitive pressures following the collapse of the postwar order, so too do they see a solution to these problems in the Third World's abundant natural resources, cheap labour and growing markets. Not fully sated by the domestic feast, and facing increasing resistance at home, the state and multinational corporations look aggressively abroad to fill their growing imperial hunger for wealth accumulation.

Although separated spatially from the domestic agenda, the international imperial agenda is not an entirely different project; it is a continuation of the former, both geographically and historically. They are both expressions of predatory capitalist expansion and the insatiable thirst for the accumulation of wealth underlying it. Geographically, to the extent Canadian capital cannot completely meet its needs within Canada, it looks internationally to complement its domestic imperial drive. While the specific strategies and tactics used in pursuit of the end goals may, not surprisingly, vary from the domestic to the international arena, those end goals are the same. The Canadian imperial drive, whether at home or abroad, involves aggressive state policies leading to the greater economic penetration of, and influence over, new spaces for wealth accumulation. But the domestic version of this political and economic expansionist agenda is also as old as Canadian capitalism itself, as we saw in the preceding chapter. Contemporary Canadian imperialism, including practices beyond Canadian borders, thus has a long historical legacy. The geographic continuity of Canadian imperialism is also a historical continuity. Imperialism is therefore a central feature of the ongoing development of the Canadian state and capital since their inception. What will be discussed in the following pages—what can rightly be described as Canada's invasion of the South—should be considered in this broader historical context.

The expansion of Canadian capital into the Third World is not an entirely new phenomenon, to be sure. Canadian business has had such interests abroad going back to the late nineteenth and early twentieth centuries. It is important to not lose sight of this aspect of Canadian history, and to not assume that Canada has been simply a benign presence on the world stage for most of its existence. Canadian capital has always had international ambitions supported by the state, even if they have been accelerated and generalized significantly under neoliberalism. Canadian banks such as the Royal and Scotia, for example, built themselves up in part through their activities in Latin America and the Caribbean, where they diligently followed around typically American-backed dictatorships to provide financial services to foreign investors and local elites—and turn a handsome profit all the while.[1] Parts of Latin America, such as British Honduras (now Belize) and El Salvador, were also a site of controversial Canadian mining and energy influence in the early twentieth century. Mining corporations, such as the International Nickel Company's (Inco) in Indonesia and Guatemala, also benefited from brutal dictatorships in the 1960s and 70s.[2]

This pattern of extending economic influence and destructive business investment (for local communities and their environment, at least) into the South has, nevertheless, taken on a heightened significance in the era of neoliberal globalization. Under the pressure of the global profitability crisis of the 1970s and early

1980s, and intensified international competition, the Canadian state and capital are increasingly seizing opportunities to open up foreign markets, gain control over their resources and exploit their labour, while in turn consciously undermining the competitiveness of Third World producers. As a result, Canadian corporations are gaining an unprecedented foothold, and conducting a growing amount of their business in the Third World, going well beyond anything they had accomplished prior to the 1990s.

The Necessity to Expand Abroad

Business leaders and politicians stress that, in order for Canadian companies to grow and remain internationally competitive, they have to expand their interests beyond the limited domestic market and gain access to foreign markets. This is, they argue, one of the key challenges for Canadian business today (and by extension the state). While a domestic market, protected to one degree or another from foreign competition, provides a foundation upon which industrial capitalist economies can mature, it also represents a limit to be overcome. Canadian business and political leaders are no less sensitive to this reality than their counterparts in the rest of the advanced capitalist world. In fact, given the limited size of Canada's domestic market, they are in some cases perhaps more sensitive.

Business Leaders' Perspective

International expansion has had a prominent place on the radar of Canadian capitalists, for example, since the unravelling of the post-Second-World-War-economic boom. As Stephen McBride notes, by the early 1980s larger Canadian capitalists had already begun pushing for the replacement of protectionist policies with the liberalization of both Canadian and international markets, evidenced in their strong opposition to the Foreign Investment Review Agency (which placed limits on foreign investment in Canada) and in their equally strong support for free trade and investment agreements.[3]

Thomas D'Aquino and David Stewart-Patterson, former president and vice-president, respectively, of the Canadian Council of Chief Executives (CCCE), note that "Canada's leading players are all engaged actively in expansion abroad for the simple reason that Canada does not have enough room for them to achieve global scale."[4] In order to build a "world-class" company, Dominic D'Alessandro of Manulife Financial argues, Canadian business cannot rely on the domestic market alone. "We cannot ever have enough market in Canada to make us a player in the world league. Out of necessity, we have to expand abroad." Thus, according to James Stanford, former chairman of Petro-Canada, "Canadian corporations must be equally aggressive [as corporations from other rich nations] in demanding access opportunities around the world."[5] Michael Sabia, former president and CEO of Bell Canada Enterprises and now CEO at Caisse de dépôt et placement du Québec, adds that today's medium-sized corporations "could be the multinationals of the future and public policy has to show a commitment to helping these firms grow and thrive in the global marketplace."[6]

For business leaders expanding abroad is very much about expanding into the Global South. The Canadian state and capital have been eyeing Southeast and East Asia—despite how slow they may have been to get off the mark there relative to other advanced capitalist competitors—as the growth in these regions and the liberalization taking place there will continue to lead to investment opportunities, especially in natural resources and infrastructural development for the telecommunications and transportation sectors. A recent survey of investment intentions found that more Canadian companies than ever were "planning new or expanded investment in Asia over the next few years to build or maintain their stake in the booming markets of the region," and over half of respondents are planning to increase their investments in the region "substantially over the long period."[7]

Latin America, though, is the region that Canadian capital has been eyeing the most closely. It thinks it has a strong opportunity to be a key political and economic player in the region.[8] A study in the mid-1990s by the Conference Board of Canada (a business research organization) on hemispheric opportunities for Canada cited "several forces pulling Canadian companies toward Latin America."[9] These include the economic liberalization that swept most of the region beginning in the 1980s as a result of International Monetary Fund-imposed structural adjustment policies; the need for infrastructural development (involving opening up the banking, telecommunications and energy sectors); and the abundance of natural resources contained there. Richard Waugh, president and CEO of Scotiabank, argues that "throughout our history, Canada by necessity has had to look to international markets to generate wealth," and that for more than a century Scotiabank "has always seen international markets as tremendous growth opportunities." The foreign markets Waugh is referring to, and in which Scotiabank has historically most heavily invested, are in Latin America and the Caribbean. Today, he proudly proclaims (ignoring its historic ties to military dictatorships and ruling elites at the expense of the region's poor), "Scotiabank stands as the leading bank in the Caribbean and Central America ... at least twice the size of any other bank in the region."[10]

The mining industry is also clear about its goals for investment access in South, particularly Latin America. The Canadian mining industry and state, which has supported the former's expansion into the South, are completely in sync with the framework for economic growth articulated by the World Bank. The World Bank has laid out its sharply neoliberal program for the mining industry in Latin America. It has called attention to the problem of indigenous people interfering with mine development, and stressed the need for greater flexibility in labour markets and the importance of liberalizing investment rules by extending corporations' legal rights and guaranteeing them easier access to mineral deposits.[11] Canada's mining industry has been no less ardent in its call for greater protection of corporate rights in foreign markets. Industry organizations have denounced what they view as unfair barriers to accessing the region, including environmental laws or other regulations benefiting "special interests."[12] They have also been strong advocates for limiting royalty rates charged to foreign investors in poor countries, and have pushed for an FTAA (Free Trade Area of the Americas) or other investment treaties that will establish a uniform "process for hemispheric investment," protecting the rights of Canadian companies.[13]

The State's Response

The Canadian state has also since the 1980s stressed the importance of Canadian capital expanding abroad; it has moved to increase its efforts to provide capital with the necessary economic and political climate to facilitate the latter's penetration of foreign economies. This was an important focus of the MacDonald Commission on the State of the Economic Union, which reported in 1985. Charged with recommending a strategy to the government for addressing the country's profitability woes and generally stagnant economy, the commission called domestically for neoliberal restructuring. But it also identified "the developing countries [as] our future." "The potentially vast markets of the less-developed countries," the commission asserted, "while still relatively untapped by Canadian exporters, are becoming increasingly important. Thus, while our present relationship with the Third World may still be dominated by humanitarian considerations, the foundations are now being laid for a mutually beneficial commercial relationship in the future." While the "humanitarian" nature of Canada's relationship with the South is overstated, and the "mutually beneficial commercial relationship" simply misleading (as I note below), the thrust of the statement—that Canada must become more oriented to Third World markets—is nevertheless clear. The commission added that the state must build a more open global economic system for Canadian corporations to operate in, and it was in fact around this time that the state began negotiating the Uruguay Round of the General Agreement on Tariffs and Trade (GATT—precursor to the World Trade Organization), in which the promotion of economic liberalization among poorer countries figured prominently.[14]

The state's preoccupation with expanding Canadian economic interests abroad has become stronger since the MacDonald Commission issued its report. Many are the policy reports stressing opportunities for investment in the South or in a particular developing region. Latin America and the Caribbean is one region that state policy-makers have paid very close attention to, including in market access reports and trade and investment agreement initiatives. This is the result of the region's geographic proximity to Canada, the already considerable scale in which Canadian companies are penetrating various economies there and the clear push by Canadian capitalists, noted above, to increase their presence there still further.

Latin America and the Caribbean are not the only region state officials are watching closely, though. The Standing Committee on Foreign Affairs and International Trade's (SCFAIT) 2005 *Emerging Markets Strategy for Canada*, for example, identifies the importance of exploiting the growing opportunities in Global South economies in general, especially through increasing direct investment, and urges more trade and investment deals to encourage Canadian firms to expand abroad.[15] The SCFAIT's *Reinvigorating Economic Relations Between Canada and Asia-Pacific* observes that "the rapid economic growth in many Asian countries is expected to create considerable opportunities for foreign companies, particularly on the investment side."[16] These opportunities will be particularly strong in infrastructure development, including in the transportation, telecommunications and electricity generation sectors, which are necessary to facilitate this growth, and where Canadian companies are particularly strong (Canada was the fifth largest global foreign investor in infrastructure in 2007), though the report also warns that Canadian firms are falling behind their competitors in exploiting the region's investment opportunities.[17] The Caucasus and Central Asia is another region state officials identify as a potential investment opportunity for Canadian capital. James Wright, Director General of the Department of Foreign Affairs and International Trade, argues that:

> Central Asia and the Caucasus might well represent the last frontier of the wild east. In the modern version of the great game we are seeing a struggle for control of the vast riches—oil and gas, gold, uranium, and other valuable minerals ... Canada has always maintained an interest in Central Asia and the Caucasus, but our engagement has been constrained by the distance, remoteness and the realities of human resource limitations. Over time, this is changing.[18]

In fact, when Wright made his observations (2001) Canada was a significant investor in several of the countries of the region, despite—or because of—the authoritarian nature of many of the governments there. The Canadian state's interest in the economic potential of the region has in fact increased since Canada became an active participant in the occupation of Afghanistan, which I discuss in more detail in chapter six.

Becoming more oriented to the Global South means actively securing access to these markets and protecting Canadian investments in them. Business leaders commonly cite the lack of adequate investment rules in the Global South as a reason for not investing more in the region. This includes supposedly arbitrary regulations (including environmental ones) against foreign corporations, poor protections against technology piracy, unclear rules on state expropriation of foreign investments, limits on repatriation of profits, discriminatory taxes and unreasonably high royalties. As Richard Waugh, president and CEO of Scotiabank notes, while Canadian companies must look abroad to expand their fiefdoms, they must do so "in an uncertain global trade environment."[19] The SCFAIT and state policy-makers also commonly note that while investment opportunities into the South are significant, so are the risks due to what they perceive to be weak regulatory and legal regimes for Canadian investment.[20]

The "Commerce" section of the 2005 *International Policy Statement* highlights the importance to the health of the Canadian economy of Canadian firms spreading abroad and securing access to resources and infrastructure through direct investment. This aspiration for access to the resources, services and people of the South requires, though, a predictable and transparent set of economic rules to facilitate Canadian investment in foreign economies. This can be achieved by "investment rules," which "offer a greater measure of security for Canadian investors and ensure that national policies will not be unduly changed or applied in a discriminatory manner."[21] A central task of Canadian foreign policy, then, is to establish the kind of conditions that will strengthen the international influence and competitiveness of Canadian corporations.

According to business executives, state policy-makers and their supporters in the academy, greater security for Canada's international investors needs to be backed up by enhanced state support at home through greater financial support and more state-corporation partnerships. This, it is argued, will encourage greater research and development and investment in new technologies, and as a result improve Canadian capital's productivity rates and therefore international competitiveness. A good recent example of the push for this kind of corporate-public partnership can be found in the Expert Panel on Commercialization, which issued its two-volume report in 2006. The panel was comprised of business leaders, civil servants and a university president, and argues that Canada's international economic strength, which includes the building of more leading multinational corporations, must be promoted through stronger relationships between government, corporations and universities, increased public financial commitments for corporate research and development and an improved regulatory environment for corporations at home and abroad.[22] Not surprisingly, and despite its advocacy of public funds to build up Canadian companies, nowhere in the report is consideration given to the negative impacts Canada's leading corporations have abroad, especially in the Global South.

Structural Adjustment and Aid Policy
One of the principal ways Canada establishes the conditions necessary to facilitate its imperialist ambition in the Third World has been through its participation in international organizations like the International Monetary Fund (IMF) and World Bank. Canada has, in fact, played an important role in these institutions, and certainly was not forced to support their aggressive imposition of structural adjustment on poor countries. The Canadian state began supporting structural adjustment measures, such as drastic cuts to public spending, aggressive market liberalization and privatization of public services, at the Bretton Woods institutions by the mid-1980s. By the late 80s structural adjustment was strongly endorsed and advocated by the Canadian International Development Agency (CIDA) and the departments of Finance and External (now Foreign) Affairs as part of an effort to facilitate the expansion of Canadian economic interests in the wake of the profitability squeeze of the 1970s and 80s.[23]

Structural adjustment policies have had a well-documented devastating impact on the Third World since they were first imposed in the 1980s, and Canada has met with sharp criticism (both at home and in poor countries) since it began supporting them. In Guyana, Canada was the main target of demonstrations in the late 1980s when it chaired a pioneering Donor Support Group to clear the country's debts with the international financial institutions. Donor Support Groups were established to organize bilateral support from rich nations to help debtor countries pay back the debts owed to the IMF and WB; in turn debtor countries such as Guyana were subjected to onerous conditions in the form of heavy doses of structural adjustment. Black and McKenna report that Canada was seen by other creditor countries as an opportune choice to lead the restructuring of Guyana's economy, as Canadian officials had been active in the World Bank Consultative Group for the Caribbean (and so had a good feel for the economic and political conditions prevailing in the region) and because Canada was perceived to have, relative to other rich nations, a friendlier international image, which would not be the last time Canadian officials attempted to use this image for self-interested economic or political ends.[24]

But Canadian policy-makers were not easily deterred by critics, and remained steadfast in their determination to continue imposing this shock neoliberal therapy in spite of the mounting poverty and social dislocation it wrought. Defiantly answering critics, Marcel Massé, president of CIDA when it first adopted structural adjustment as one of its guiding principles, referred to it as "simply a series of good economic policies that must be applied in all countries." Although the standard of living of the recipients of structural adjustment measures "is one that we should not find acceptable," he acknowledged, it will nevertheless eventually improve people's lives by establishing macroeconomic stability.[25] Likewise a report authored by the Standing Committee on External Affairs and International Trade (SCEAIT) in 1990, incorporating the views of both business leaders and state policy-makers from various departments, defended structural adjustment policies, arguing that "debtor countries must adjust by adopting sound economic policies and ... a significant degree of market liberalization is often appropriate and necessary ... There is no getting around the responsibility for reform which developing countries must themselves shoulder if recovery is to be achieved."[26]

Both Massé's and the SCEAIT's defence of structural adjustment is framed as assistance for the Third World, of course—a tough love approach to economic management that really has the best interest of the poor at heart. Yet, as discussed earlier, poverty continues to worsen for many people in the South more than twenty years since the policies were first prescribed. Despite this, the Canadian push for these harsh restructuring measures has not abated. If ending poverty was indeed the goal of structural adjustment, Canadian policy-makers and other proponents would be due for some serious critical self-reflection. But still they forge zealously ahead. The market liberalization demanded by structural adjustment has contributed—along with other strategies I discuss below—to Canadian companies' ability to penetrate Third

World markets and has thus facilitated Canadian capital's undeniable expansion into the South. Some might suggest that Canadian foreign economic policy since the late 1980s is largely a matter of bad policy decisions shaped by specific institutional actors—such as Massé—without whom Canada might pursue more progressive policy. However, policy is driven by a deeper logic of the need for capitalist expansion.[27]

Structural adjustment is one important part of a broader neoliberal aid agenda that is centred on transforming the values and expectations of Third World communities. Just as the state has sought to impose a capitalist market-based "ethics" and expectations on indigenous people domestically—through residential schools, the Indian Act and so on—it seeks to do so abroad. Telling people the only way they can receive aid is to massively cut back public spending and accept a deeper penetration of market imperatives in their lives, for instance, is in part an attempt to radically alter their expectations of a life not yet fully dominated by the cold, hard "rationality" of the "invisible hand" of capitalism. It is a hard education for people losing their lands and forced to migrate to ever-growing slums on the outskirts of cities, or for people who can no longer access desperately needed public services, but that is the social and economic re-engineering at work in Canadian aid policy. CIDA even funds the integration of this free-market ethic into education systems. For example, it committed $1.5 million from 2004 to 2010 toward a program at the Universidad Nacional de Honduras to assist in the development and implementation of the country's structural adjustment process.[28]

The term "structural adjustment" is seldom used anymore by state officials, because of the continued unrest it has caused throughout the Global South (such as the so-called IMF riots) and the sharp public criticism it continues to face in advanced capitalist countries. Instead, Canada talks about "poverty reduction," and refers to "Poverty Reduction Growth Facility" (PRGF), the term that is replaced "structural adjustment" in IMF and World Bank-speak. But the PRGF programs, and the IMF, World Bank and Canadian attitudes toward the Third World have not changed in any meaningful sense. In its *Report on Operations Under the Bretton Woods Related Agreements Act*, for instance, Canada reiterates its support for structural adjustment, if through more guarded language. It emphasizes "macroeconomic stability" as the tool for poverty reduction, and notes that "much remains to be done to restore fiscal discipline in emerging markets ... a number of structural rigidities" still need to be addressed.[29] Poor countries, in other words, need to cut back spending and liberalize their economies in order to allow capital from the North (including Canada) access. Canadian corporate intervention, not local government intervention, is seen as the way out of poverty for the Third World.

Canada also boasts of its central role in the IMF's and World Bank's adoption of the Poverty Reduction Strategy Papers. They promote the local ownership of the PRGF process, whereby recipient countries are encouraged to develop their own restructuring agendas—supposedly in consultation with civil society groups—which they then provide to and negotiate with creditor nations before loans are released. CIDA refers to this as a program-based approach to aid delivery that is based on creating an ongoing dialogue between donors and recipients. However, even a study published by the IMF on the Strategy Papers argues that they have had no meaningful impact on the adjustment process, and states that the "actual achievements ... far fall short of potential" and "avoid addressing key strategic choices involving 'controversial' structural reforms."[30] The involvement of civil society groups in the process has also been found to be negligible, though in any case their participation in developing a restructuring agenda that will make them poorer and more insecure can hardly be seen as a progressive step forward. Canada's promotion of the Poverty Reduction Strategy Papers, then, is nothing more than an attempt to provide a new gloss to an old and much criticized policy of structural adjustment.

As a guiding philosophy at CIDA, this deep neoliberal restructuring frames Canada's aid policy and its approach to international development. CIDA's programming begins from the uncritical assumption that life in Third World countries will only improve if they allow the free market to flourish without government interference, open themselves up to corporations from the North and establish strong measures to protect private property rights; there can be no other way out of poverty. Tying Canadian aid programs to such things as "locally owned poverty reduction" strategies and "the development of transparent, stable, and effective regulatory and legal structures governing private sector activity," and aligning policy to multilateral institutions such as the IMF and World Bank—these are the themes that litter CIDA policy papers and promotional materials.[31] The agency has consciously used its aid policy as further leverage against governments resistant to IMF and World Bank conditionalities, demanding restructuring in order to get Canadian support. In its 2002 policy statement, *Canada Making a Difference in the World*, CIDA suggests that a "more balanced approach" to poverty reduction is important, but nevertheless stresses that "economic growth is a fundamental prerequisite for reducing poverty in the Third World," and this growth will not occur unless countries open themselves up to economies of the North and pursue the necessary economic restructuring.[32] This sentiment is also echoed in the "Development" section of Canada's *International Policy Statement*, which was produced through CIDA and released in the spring of 2005. Here CIDA blames poverty on economic stagnation and offers the aggressive expansion of free market principles as the solution. All this emphasis on neoliberal restructuring actually comes, it must be stressed, despite CIDA's own acknowledgement—in specific reference to the Americas—that "trade liberalization and opening up to the global economy ... have contributed to growing inequality."[33]

Canadian politicians, public officials and the corporate media may sing the praises of Canadian aid policy, portraying Canada as an exceptionally generous, caring and selfless country. But this portrayal simply does not match the reality. Aid policy has first and foremost always been a political and economic strategy to pursue Canadian self-interest, as Cranford Pratt has shown. The expansion of Canadian international aid in the postwar period was the result of pressures from social movements in Canada for the state to support social welfare abroad as well as at home, but it was in the end also shaped by Canada's geopolitical Cold War aim of containing the Soviet Union. Since the Cold War ended and social movements in Canada opposed to neoliberalism were weakened, however, Canada's international aid program has become much more explicitly oriented to commercial goals.[34] Canadian aid is now another tool to structurally adjust developing nations, promote strong free markets and break down the barriers these countries may have created to limit Canadian (and other foreign) corporations' activities in their markets. According to Brian Tomlinson, "[t]he goal of ending poverty ... usually runs a poor third to Canadian investment and commercial interests."[35] That comment is from a longtime critic of Canadian aid policy; here is a CIDA official's remarks on his agency's Eastern European and Central Asian work: "The first thing to say about our program is that poverty is not our main focus ... transition is our key mandate, specifically the transition to a market economy."[36] As I discuss in more detail in the chapter on security policy, CIDA has also been funding political organizations in foreign countries that oppose governments with which Canada does not have friendly relations.

CIDA may use nice sounding catchphrases like "economic sustainability"—and who would be opposed to this?—but, as David Morrison has pointed out, these kinds of terms are used precisely because they are ambiguous and provide cover for what CIDA is really doing. They do not negate CIDA's overall sharp neoliberal orientation toward the world's poor.[37] Even the infrastructure projects CIDA supports—including energy, transportation and communication systems—are viewed by aid officials in large part as necessary steps to facilitate Canadian capital's expansion into these countries, as capitalist accumulation requires a certain infrastructural foundation on which to proceed.[38] This is reinforced by Canada's decision to focus much of its bilateral aid on countries with the greatest prospects for development, and away from the most impoverished nations. Canadian aid is by and large a subsidy for corporate investment, a cynical strategy of capitalist accumulation imposed on some of the most destitute and vulnerable people in the world.

Canadian aid policy in Africa offers a good example of this strategy. CIDA's "enhanced" aid partnerships (where it placed special focus on specific countries) announced in 2002 and again in 2005 focused on African countries with which Canadian companies have been developing investment relations (typically in mining) or which are rich in natural resources. CIDA declared that it will focus on countries with "good governance" potential, and noted this entails a strong pro-foreign investor climate.[39] In 2009, CIDA replaced these partnerships with its new "Countries of Focus" program, in which 80 percent of bilateral aid will be concentrated on twenty countries. Seven countries are in Africa, but this new program reflects the Harper Conservatives' increased attention to the

Americas, with six countries (one being the Caribbean Regional Program) included from the region. Canada has concluded a trade agreement with two of those countries (Colombia and Peru), is actively pursuing agreements with two others (Honduras and the Caribbean), and has supported coups in two of them (Haiti and Honduras, which I discuss in chapter six).

And what about the Canadian state's actual spending on Official Development Assistance (ODA)? Even if we put aside the self-interested nature of Canadian aid policy for a moment, how well does Canada put its money where its mouth is, to help the world's destitute? The reality is, Canada spends a miserly amount on its ODA. ODA was cut drastically beginning in the late 1980s and 1990s and has not recovered. From the federal government budget years 1989–90 to 1993–94 (the budget years start in the spring), for example, the ODA budget was cut by $1.8 billion, comprising a much larger percentage of total government cutbacks during this period than it made up of actual government costs. Between 1988–89 and 1997–98, the years of the heaviest cuts, ODA decreased by thirty-three percent in real terms, compared to twenty-two percent for defence and five percent for all other programs combined. And while more than seventy percent of the world's poor live in rural areas and depend on agriculture for their livelihood, in the first half of the 1990s CIDA's budget for agriculture, food and nutrition dropped by forty-nine percent in Africa and by eighty-seven percent for the poorest countries in general. Canada's cuts to its ODA were in fact proportionally the highest among donor nations in this period.[40]

More recently, the federal government has refused to meet the United Nations Millennium Development Goals' call for rich countries to increase aid spending to a meagre 0.7 percent of Gross National Income (GNI) by 2015. Instead, in 2006–07 Canada's ODA/GNI ratio was 0.28 percent. That is barely up from a post-cutback low of 0.24 percent in 2003–04—due largely to a rise in one-time contributions in budget year 2004-05—but is still well below its peak in 1986–87 of 0.5 percent, and well below the Organization for Economic Cooperation and Development's Development Assistance Committee's (DAC—a group comprised of the richest donor nations) unimpressive average of 0.47 percent. Canada now ranks fourteenth out of twenty-two DAC members for ODA spending as a ratio of its GNI, and will not come close to reaching the Millennium Development Goals by 2015 at its current rate of spending.[41]

Canada spends more on agricultural subsidies—assisting its own producers against foreign competitors, including from the Third World, and undermining any claim that it supports free trade (a point I return to below)—than it does on international aid (Canada spent $4.2 billion on ODA in 2006–07). Canada's military budget also dwarfs its ODA, with the latter comprising less than a third of the amount spent on the former. The total investment income (including direct, portfolio and "other") earned by Canadian capital in the South is nearly six times what Canada offers in aid. Thus far more wealth is being drawn from poor countries by Canada than is being spent there on aid, while, as I discuss in the next chapter, the investments Canadian corporations undertake are making the lives of people in the Third World worse, not better. Further, we need to recall that, according to Action Aid, on average less than half of the stated ODA budgets of donor countries actually make it to the poor recipients, the rest being spent on bureaucracy, tied aid projects and write-offs. Even if Action Aid's estimation of the amount of wasted aid is high for Canada (and CIDA's annual statistical report does not actually state how much of ODA actually makes it to poor recipients), we are still likely left with ODA being even less than the already low amount announced by CIDA.[42]

Canada likes to trumpet its leading role in supporting African development and Third World debt forgiveness. But when it comes to Africa or debt forgiveness it has little to be proud of. For instance, Canada has been a big supporter of the New Economic Partnership for Africa's Development (NEPAD), which was initiated under external pressure by a number of key African leaders, who then took their proposal to G8 leaders in 2001. Canadian politicians played a central role in developing the African Action Plan—the G8's response to NEPAD. According to CIDA, NEPAD is "a visionary plan to lift Africa out of poverty and into the global mainstream of sustainable growth and development."[43]

So, what is so visionary about NEPAD? Here is how a supportive former British diplomat describes it:

The NEPAD proposals differ from previous African approaches to reviving the continent. Up to now, Africans have tried to put the blame for their troubles onto others: on the legacy of colonialism, on the inequity of the international system, or on the inadequacies of aid flows and international development institutions. This time, [South African President] Mbeki, [Nigerian President] Obasanjo, [Senegalese President] Wade, and their colleagues have accepted that Africans are themselves to blame for their problems and that they must take responsibility for their own recovery.[44]

Truly visionary—from an imperialist perspective. Here is a program in which African leaders are seeking out assistance from the rich nations for a continent whose plight is nothing short of tragic, by devising a program that is premised on ignoring the very reason why the situation is so desperate—the centuries of colonial aggression committed against it. Canada supports a program in which the proposed solution to extreme poverty, as Patrick Bond stresses, is market liberalization and the protection of private property rights for corporations from the North.[45] NEPAD also calls for a rigorous peer review process. Instead of maintaining a more united front in the face of imperial demands from the North as the Organization of African Unity has done in the past, different countries are to instead be graded on their commitment to neoliberal reforms, and their aid will be based on how well they perform on these tests.

But while Canada accepted the new NEPAD approach to development in Africa, it did not endorse its call for significant increase in aid levels. Like its aid contributions to the Global South more generally, Canada's aid contributions to Africa, including debt forgiveness, will do little to help most countries out of their spiral of poverty and dependence on the North. According to the 2005 report of the United Nations Millennium Project, the Millennium Development Goal of cutting world poverty in half by 2015, which rich nations adopted as a target in 2000, will not come close to being reached; and in Africa this goal will not be reached on current development assistance trends until ... 2150.[46] There was a great deal of self-congratulation and back-patting regarding Africa and debt forgiveness by G8 leaders—and their rock 'n' roll cheerleaders Bono and Bob Geldof—at their Glengeagles Summit in 2005. But the aid pledged at Gleneagles—for an extra US$50 billion a year—still comes nowhere near helping poor countries, particularly those in Africa, to pay off debts or tackle rapidly growing impoverishment. Canada in fact made no new significant offer for development assistance of its own, and continues to support the attachment of harsh conditionalities, in the form of structural adjustment measures, to this aid. Despite Canada's and other G8 countries' pronouncements about helping the poor, more wealth will continue to flow out of the Global South to the North in the form of interest payments on loans, than will return in development assistance.[47]

Canada has also been an active participant in the Heavily Indebted Poor Country (HIPC) Initiative. The HIPC Initiative was created by the IMF in 1996 as a debt rescheduling strategy. The idea was for multilateral donor agencies such as the IMF and regional development banks to write off the debts that some of the world's most indebted countries (many of whom are African) owed them.[48] But, in keeping with their neoliberal zeal, and to be sure poor countries do not think that they are going to get off easy, the IMF, supported again by Canada, attaches harsh conditions to the write-offs. In order to be eligible for the write off, the heavily indebted countries must endure six years of structural adjustment to prove their worthiness. Yet for most of the poor countries participating in the initiative, the debts being written off are only a small portion of their total international debt and do not cover most of the debt owed to private financial institutions. It is also debt that they'd actually stopped servicing in any case; in other words, creditor nations are only writing off debts they know will never be paid back.[49] At the end of 2005, furthermore, Canada quietly supported an IMF plan to delay a debt relief package for six countries for whom some G7 members initially discussed granting non-conditional relief to. IMF leaders, backed by Canada, did not like the G7 plan, and exercised their influence to not only delay relief but also to impose new austerity measures on the six countries as a precondition for any future relief.[50]

Canada also has its own bilateral HIPC initiative, established in March 1999. Canada boasts about its bilateral debt relief stance compared to the bilateral initiatives of other rich donor nations (under the Paris Club terms), since it offers a moratorium on debt payments from countries to which it grants HIPC status. Its stated policy is to completely eliminate publicly owed debt after countries have completed the process. That, of course, is not saying much, if the starting point is the policies of other rich donor nations rather than what is socially just for the poorest, most destitute people in the world, or what rich nations really could afford to do. Indeed, Canada's program requires countries to dutifully exhibit respect for austerity measures to be eligible for relief, which "demonstrates the ability to use resources effectively for poverty reduction."[51] Thus far only thirteen eligible countries have been part of Canada's HIPC initiative, and a total of $965 million has been forgiven, a minuscule portion of Canadian GDP.[52] Canada clearly has the ability to provide relief more rapidly (rather than impose austerity measures) or to expand the somewhat arbitrary list of countries who make the HIPC grade if it wished. Canada also calculates the write-offs as part of its ODA, despite a write-off obviously not being the same thing as financial aid. Moreover, Canada continues to refuse to address the issue of odious debt—that debt which was accrued by corrupt dictators who typically spent the money on themselves, their wealthy friends and their militaries for repressive ends rather than on the well-being of their citizens. Thus the poor are being made to pay for the financial mess left them by dictators, who I might add were often supported by rich nations, including Canada.

Of course, there is also no acknowledgement from Canadian officials in all of this that the problems that they are putatively addressing with their development assistance for Africa (and indeed international aid in general)—poverty, deteriorating health, malnutrition, lack of potable water, failed public education systems, among others—are the result of—or at the very least exacerbated by—the conditions of structural adjustment Canada enforces on poor countries in the first place. To the extent that poor nations have become dependent on Canadian aid, it is a dependence imposed on them by Canadian policies.

Investment Agreements

International investment agreements that prohibit economic policies other than neoliberal market liberalization provide another important opportunity for Canadian capital to penetrate the Global South. Not surprisingly, Canada has been actively pursuing a number of investment relationships in the Global South, both multilateral and bilateral, since the early 1990s. Free trade agreements, the WTO investment treaty and Foreign Investment Protection Agreements are the main ways Canada secures access to Third World markets via international agreements.

Free Trade Agreements

As of summer 2010, Canada had enacted seven trade agreements and concluded (though not officially enacted) deals with Jordan and Panama. Its enacted trade agreements are the North American Free Trade Agreement (NAFTA) (with the U.S. and Mexico), the Canada-European Free Trade Association Agreement (involving Iceland, Liechtenstein, Norway and Switzerland) and the bilateral agreements with Israel, Chile, Costa Rica, Peru and Colombia (the Colombian agreement has not yet been enacted in Colombia). The free trade agreements, as I noted in the first chapter, are about much more than free trade. They are also about establishing strong corporate investment rights in foreign economies by demanding the liberalization of various domestic industries, such as mining and natural resources, financial services, telecommunications and agriculture. An economist at Export Development Canada (EDC), a government agency responsible for financing Canadian investment abroad, offers this reflection on trade agreements: "In my view, trade agreements are as much about investments as they are about trade. As a result, the opportunities for international business development are not necessarily limited to existing trading patterns."[53]

NAFTA, which came into effect January 1, 1994, is an important development in international trade and investment treaties. One of the most controversial parts of NAFTA is chapter eleven on investment. Chapter eleven is the cutting edge of investment agreements, enshrining corporate rights. Canada seeks to replicate it in other trade and investment negotiations. It prohibits or limits a series of measures governments have traditionally used to protect local industry against dominant foreign competition, such as rules on domestic content use, technology transfer requirements, partnering with local companies and obligations to invest a certain percentage of earnings in local banks. Meanwhile, it also incorporates the principles of national treatment, which obligates a signatory of the agreement to treat the investors of another signatory country no less favourably than its own investors, and most favoured nation treatment, which requires that a signatory treat investors of another signatory country no less favourably than it treats investors of third countries. On top of this, of course, is its pièce de résistance, the investor-state dispute resolution mechanism, which allows corporations, despite not being a party to the agreement, to sue governments they feel have not met their obligations under chapter eleven, for profits that have been lost or are expected to be lost. Chapter eleven is intended to encourage foreign investment by providing that secure, predictable and transparent legal regime multinational corporations have been demanding. While enshrining corporate rights, NAFTA contains no meaningfully enforceable provisions for labour and indigenous rights or environmental protection. Versions of chapter eleven have been replicated in subsequent free trade deals, though Canada made a few concessions to Costa Rica, such as a clause stipulating a higher than desired earnings deposit rate in Costa Rican banks for the first several years of the agreement. These free trade agreements also do not include enforceable protections for labour rights and the environment, though Canada and Costa Rica added a side agreement to their trade deal that essentially frowns upon reducing labour standards as a means to attract investment.

Latin America and the Caribbean is the region where Canadian foreign direct investment (or Canadian Direct Investment [CDI]) is the most advanced. Tied to this economic interest are a number of trade deals Canada is pursuing. The largest of these is the proposed Free Trade Area of the Americas (FTAA), which would stretch from Canada through Central America and the Caribbean to South America. It would represent a market of more than 800 million consumers with a combined gross national income of US$12 trillion. The U.S. certainly compromises the majority of this potential consumer market, but Latin America also has abundant natural resources and economies that have been liberalizing over the last two decades and which are in need of infrastructural improvements to sustain future economic growth, such as in telecommunications, energy production and financial services. Canada wants to reap the benefits of the changes in this market by securing access to it.[54] Canada has been the most vociferous proponent of the FTAA. The U.S. Congress cooled on free trade in the latter half of the 1990s, making it harder for successive American presidents to successfully pursue the FTAA. Canada took the lead negotiating role in the early stages, chaired the Summit Implementation Review Group, hosted a trade ministerial meeting and several other Summit of the Americas (of which the FTAA is a part) meetings. In this leadership role, Canada has tried to exploit its image as a benign international force to push the agreement through. "We do not have the baggage," one trade negotiator notes when assessing the prospect for FTAA negotiations led by Canada.[55]

A key part of the FTAA deal for Canada is its proposed investment clause. The investment clause is modelled on NAFTA's chapter eleven, and thus includes strong protections for foreign investors, such as national treatment, most favoured nation treatment and an investor-state dispute settlement mechanism. And like NAFTA, while enshrining corporate rights it includes no enforceable protections for labour, indigenous people or the environment. Canada's intention is clear; it "seeks to negotiate investment obligations that will serve Canadian interests by providing for stability, transparency, predictability, non-discrimination and protection for our companies and individuals that invest abroad."[56] In pushing for a strong investment clause, Canada defends its position by inverting the North-South relationship, stressing that it is fighting discrimination by poor countries. It is simply asking for, in other words, equal treatment. Thus for the FTAA, "[u]ltimately, the principal objective is to achieve non-discriminatory treatment of Canadian investment and business operating throughout Latin America."[57]

Due largely to the opposition from a number of South American countries, the FTAA process has stalled. As a result, Canada has sought out a number of other deals. The SCFAIT stresses the importance of signing more investment deals in the region, and recommends that "the Government of Canada aggressively pursue bilateral trade and investment agreements with Latin American and Caribbean countries as well as country groupings."[58] The Southern Cone Common Market (Mercosur) is viewed by many political and business leaders and state policy-makers as the most important country grouping in the region. Established in 1991, it is now comprised of Brazil, Argentina, Uruguay and Paraguay. It is the largest economic market in Latin America and the Caribbean, and is the fifth largest economy in the world. Currently it is a major destination for CDI, and as the region becomes more integrated, including the establishment of a common external tariff, Canada is seeking to ensure its investment access is not compromised. To this end Canada signed a Trade and Investment Cooperation Agreement with Mercosur in 1998, laying the groundwork, it hopes, for improved economic access. Another country grouping Canada has been watching with interest is the Andean Community, which business and political leaders note is "generously endowed with natural resources."[59] It includes Colombia, Peru, Ecuador and Bolivia, and has been a free trade zone since 1993 and adopted a common external tariff in 1995. Canada's economic relationship with the region has grown steadily through the 1990s, although the election of left-leaning governments in Venezuela, Bolivia and, to a lesser extent, Ecuador, has significantly reduced the likelihood of an agreement for the foreseeable future.[60] In 2001, Canada also initiated trade and investment deal discussions with the Caribbean Community, which has a fourteen-country common market, and the Central American four: El Salvador, Guatemala, Honduras and Nicaragua.[61]

The most alarming trade deal in the region, however, is the one with Colombia. Under the Harper Tories, Canada has been actively pursuing a tighter political and economic relationship with the Andean country. I discuss human rights abuses in Colombia tied to Canadian investment in some detail in the following chapter, and the security dimension to this rapprochement in chapter five. Colombia has the worst human rights record in the Western hemisphere, and leads the world by a wide margin in trade union assassinations. Trade unionists, along with indigenous activists, small farmers and peasants, are regularly assassinated, disappeared, tortured and threatened for either trying to defend workers' rights or challenging foreign corporations' access to their land and its resources. While these human rights abuses have been carried out by state security forces, the majority are accounted for by paramilitaries who are nominally independent of the government, but whose ties to the government have been well documented.[62]

Nevertheless, Canada forged ahead with its trade deal. Modelled on previous agreements, it will lock in the rights of Canadian capital in the resource-rich nation. And how will Canada address concerns that such a deal will only worsen the human rights situation? The Tories point to the Labour Cooperation side agreement that accompanies the FTA. The side agreement calls on the two countries to respect basic core labour standards (right to unionize, no child labour, no forced labour, etc.). But there are a number of serious limits to this side agreement that should give us pause. For one thing, there is no standing body established beyond those that might already exist in the respective countries to oversee the side agreement's day-to-day implementation or to which workers can complain when their rights have been violated. In other words, Colombians will have to complain to bodies within the Colombian government. But the Colombian government's record on human rights sharply diminishes the efficacy of the side agreement. There is a provision for either of the partner countries to request a ministerial "consultation" with each other if they feel obligations under the side agreement are not being met (Part Three of the agreement). If unsatisfied with the response, the country that initiated the consultation can then call for the formation of a review panel to report on the claim that obligations are not being followed. But we have to ask: if Canada signs a trade agreement with Colombia after purposefully downplaying the depth of latter's human rights problems, why would it complain about these problems after the agreement comes into force? Further, given the violence and intimidation that is regularly visited upon unionists in Colombia, what is the likelihood of them coming forward to tell their stories, or doing so safely?[63]

The punishment for failing to live up to obligations—mere fines—is also reason for serious reservations about the ability of the trade agreement to deter human rights violations. Imposing fines amounts to a de *facto* decriminalization of violence and intimidation. Moreover, it is not clear in the side agreement that the Colombian government will be held responsible for the actions of paramilitaries, who account for a significant amount of the violence against union activists. They act with the tacit or explicit consent of the military but retain a nominal independence from the government.

Another major flaw of the Labour Cooperation side agreement is that it does not cover indigenous peoples. The Centre for Indigenous Cooperation (CECOIN) reports that not only did the number of violations against indigenous communities increase in the first four years of the Uribe government, but those acts attributable to government security forces increased as well. From 1998 to 2002 there were 298 recorded cases of human rights violations against indigenous peoples committed by government forces. From 2002 to 2006, the years of Uribe's first term, there were 672—a significant increase. State-sponsored assassinations of indigenous activists also increased from twenty-six between 1998–2002 to sixty-two between 2002 and 2006.[64] A little over a month before the signing of the trade deal in Lima, a mass protest of indigenous groups in Cauca, demanding the government fulfill previously made promises around land, education and health, was met with a massive show of force by state security forces. The security forces attacked the protest, injuring more than fifty indigenous activists and killing one. That was the eleventh indigenous person killed in Colombia in the three weeks leading up to and including the protests in Cauca.[65] The military push into indigenous communities in Cauca has increased under Uribe, as the region has untapped (by foreign companies, that is) natural resources. How, then, can Canada talk meaningfully about addressing human rights concerns when the trade agreement ignores one of the most violated groups in Colombia?

Receiving Royal Assent in June 2009 (but waiting for enactment in Colombia), it will likely come into effect well before even the Americans finalize their own deal with Colombia—given the American Congress's efforts to stall the ratification—making Canada a trailblazer of sorts with respect to economic relations with the troubled Andean country.

In June 2009, implementation legislation was passed for Canada's new trade agreement with Peru, which is very similar to the Colombian agreement (including a Labour Cooperation side agreement). This came two weeks after Peruvian President Alan García, sent in a 600-strong police and military force—including armoured personnel carriers and helicopter gunships—to crush a blockade of a major highway by 5,000 indigenous activists. The indigenous activists were protesting García's free trade policies, which include the privatization of large swaths of their land for foreign mining and oil and gas companies. Canada is one of the largest investors in Peru in general and the largest in mining. The military and police assault led to the deaths of at least fifty protest-ers and the disappearance of many—possibly hundreds—more, according to indigenous organizations. Nine police officers were also killed during the assault when indigenous people fought back in self-defence against the massive government show of brutal force. The massacre elicited no response from Canada.[66]

Canada has also been seeking to improve its access to the Asia-Pacific region, though this relationship is far less advanced than the one with Latin America. Canada has been negotiating bilateral trade and investment deals with South Korea and Singapore, and has also supported establishing a regional deal through the Asia-Pacific Economic Cooperation group (APEC).

World Trade Organization

The WTO is another important avenue by which Canada is at-tempting to pry open Third World economies. Besides the various trade-related agreements Canada has signed or been pursuing with the WTO, it has also prioritized the investment agreement currently under negotiation. The agreement is modelled in part on the failed Multilateral Agreement on Investment (MAI), which was the broadest proposed agreement of its kind at the time, and which Canada supported until its death in the fall of 1998. The MAI was negotiated through the Organization for Economic Co-operation and Development (OECD).[67] Many of the OECD coun-tries wanted negotiations for such an investment agreement to be conducted through the OECD because they would not have to make concessions to Global South countries (who are not in the OECD) and subsequently water down the deal. Canada op-posed this position, arguing that not as many investment barriers remained between OECD nations, and that the significant barri-ers were in fact in Third World countries. Thus an international agreement should focus on bringing them down. Canada pushed hard to get non-OECD countries involved in the negotiations. The Canadian position from the beginning of the MAI negotiations in 1995 with respect to the content of the agreement was also one of the more aggressive ones, calling as it did for a replication of the controversial and much-criticized chapter eleven of NAFTA.[68]

Canada is carrying a similar position into the WTO negotia-tions, and is experiencing resistance from many poorer countries who are reluctant to open up their economies to foreign corporations. They fear that their domestic industry (which is not as technologically advanced or competitive as Northern corporations) will be destroyed; public services will be bought off by rich Northern corporations; and natural resources will be plundered with little benefit for the local economy.[69] Some of the improvements Canadian business leaders are demanding to the current working agreement, taken up by Canadian negotiators, involve strengthening the dispute settlement mechanism; protection for intellectual property rights; limits on royalties and state expropriations; and broadening the definition of investment beyond simply direct investment.[70] In short, the state wants Canadian investors to be able to enter Third World countries with few conditions imposed on them. As Canada has pushed for these improvements, it has defended its aggressive positions in part by trying to reconceptualize North-South inequalities, as it does in the case of the FTAA. Despite what appears to be the clearly weaker position of Third World economies vis-à-vis their rich counterparts of the North, Canadian negotiators argue that any attempt to limit liberalization by poorer countries is an unfair and market-distorting practice, suggesting that poor countries' efforts to defend their economies from foreign takeover is the pressing form of inequality between North and South to be addressed. As one policy report puts it, "Canada's objective is to *level the international playing field* in terms of market access," and new WTO rules "must apply equally to all WTO members."[71]

However, Canada has been forced by Third World resistance to reluctantly acknowledge its privilege as a wealthy country of the North. This is expressed in its conceding to certain poor countries' negotiating demands—nominally at least. The demands are for "special and differential treatment." This includes an extended period to fully liberalize their economies in order to improve their competitiveness before foreign companies gain fuller access to their markets, and technical assistance and capacity building support from rich nations, since most Third World countries simply do not have the resources to negotiate an equitable agreement (if such an agreement is even possible) or to ensure WTO (or other) agreements are even implemented and followed properly by their rich country competitors.[72] In response to criticism about its aggressive liberalization positions, Canada has publicly declared its openness to extended liberalization periods for poor countries and promises to assist Third World countries by putting money toward improving their ability to negotiate equitable agreements and to enforce them once enacted.

But behind the rhetoric Canada still negotiates for quick liberalization. Policy documents such as the "Mandate for WTO Negotiations" declares that its negotiators should take a hardline position on poor country demands for "special and differential treatment."[73] Meanwhile, the money it spends on technological assistance is meagre and does little to address the uneven playing field in this regard. As of 2003, Canada had allotted only $35 million of technical assistance support to the WTO and its trade and investment related policy issues, and most of this was earmarked for Central and Eastern Europe.[74] In fact, in the same breath Canada mentions supporting "flexibility" for liberalization and "capacity building," it asserts its desire to ensure poor countries do not get any competitive advantage at its expense: "the balance between substantive obligations for the liberalization and protection of investments on the one hand, and development provisions on the other, must be struck in such a way as to ensure that flexibility does not translate into discrimination."[75] Such a comment is quite remarkable given the significant disparity between a rich advanced capitalist nation such as Canada and poorer nations of the South. At the end of the day, "securing transparent, stable and predictable conditions for long-term cross-border investment" is Canada's first and foremost priority.[76] And rich nations play the dominant role in the WTO—Alain Rugman and Alain Verbeke observe that, notwithstanding efforts to challenge the North, "Developing countries ... have never been important leaders in shaping its policies."[77]

Foreign Investment Protection Agreements
Foreign Investment Protection Agreements (FIPAs) are another way in which the state tries to guarantee corporate access to Third World markets. This has been a useful strategy for Canada since multilateral deals by their very nature are more difficult to successfully negotiate given all the varied interests involved. With FIPAs, on the other hand, Canada targets specific countries for

bilateral negotiations. Since 1994, Canada has signed or concluded twenty-one FIPAs, all with Global South countries.[78] While all
regions of the South are represented in the post-1994 FIPAs, just
under half (ten) are with Latin American and Caribbean countries.
Canada is currently negotiating FIPAs with another seven Third
World nations.

All these deals are modelled on the NAFTA chapter eleven
clause and its unambiguous agenda of enshrining corporate investment rights in international agreements. This includes national treatment, most favoured nation status and severe limits
on expropriation or acts perceived as expropriation. FIPAs also
include NAFTA's investor-state dispute resolution mechanism.
Canada's negotiating practice is to ensure that by signing the
agreements countries are understood to be satisfying the require-
ment of written consent for investor complaints against them to
be taken to the International Centre for the Settlement of Investment Disputes, which is the arbitration body that hears the disputes. Thus FIPAs place significant obligations on foreign governments with respect to how they treat Canadian corporations and
encourage Canadian economic expansion in the South. According to the Department of Foreign Affairs and International Trade,
FIPAs "help to open international markets and make them more
secure for Canadian investors." But not just any markets:

> Emerging economies and those in transition are increasingly im-
> portant destinations for investments made by Canadian investors.
> By specifying the rights and obligations of the signatories respecting
> treatment of foreign investment, a FIPA encourages a predictable in-
> vestment framework and contributes to engendering a stable busi-
> ness environment.[79]

SCFAIT reports argue that FIPAs will be a key way for Canadian
companies to improve their investment access in the Americas
and Asia-Pacific, and suggest signing these agreements should be
a greater priority of Canada.[80]

Like other trade and investment deals, FIPAs have no meaningful protections for labour, indigenous or environmental rights.
Responding to public criticism, the Department of Foreign Affairs
and International Trade did review the NAFTA chapter eleven
clause model it uses for FIPAs (and trade deals) in 2002. But the

changes made were superficial. A government cabinet memo on FIPAs from the fall of 2002 leaked to the Halifax Initiative, a Canadian NGO, essentially reasserts that the agreements' primary role is to provide security and predictability for Canadian corporations in the Third World, where "the rule of law is not firmly established." The memo called, for example, for greater public transparency around the investor-state dispute settlement mechanism, but does not alter it in any fundamental way—corporations are still to be granted significant rights under FIPAs, including the right to sue governments. The memo also calls for Canada to include additional rights for Canadian corporations in the exploratory phase of their investment as part of the new negotiating position. This would protect Canadian investors, particularly natural resource companies that engage heavily in pre-investment exploration, from supposedly discriminatory action long before a mine or oil project is ever developed, limiting even further the ability of local governments to influence Canadian corporations' activities.[81]

Canada now also incorporates an environmental assessment into its FIPA negotiations, but the assessment is only for the impact of a potential investment deal in Canada! Yet investment from most countries of the South is negligible compared to investment from Canadian companies into those countries. A government report on Canada's FIPA with Peru declares that, despite the significant mining and hydroelectric investment by Canadians in Peru, which will increase following the FIPA and which will likely have a discernible environmental implications, considerations of these implications are outside the scope of its environmental impact assessment.[82]

It is also worth considering here that Canadian corporations are more active users of the investor-state dispute settlement mechanism than the corporations of Canada's treaty partners, expressing their interest in aggressively gaining ground in foreign markets. Canada has been the defendant in seven active or previous arbitrations under the NAFTA tribunal, all initiated by American corporations, while Canadian companies have initiated twelve arbitrations against American state governments. This includes a claim by Methanex—a producer of methanol, a key ingredient in the gasoline additive MTBE, which has been linked to health problems—against California, which the company eventually lost; and

Glamis Gold's (now Goldcorp) arbitration over alleged interference of a proposed mining project in Imperial County, California. FIPA arbitrations aren't always publicly disclosed, so they are a lot harder to trace than NAFTA disputes. Foreign Affairs and International Trade Canada, for instance, does not keep a record of them. I have found that Canadian companies have initiated at least four arbitrations under FIPA agreements in the last few years, and are considering two others. These include Scotiabank's arbitration against Argentina's forced conversion of U.S. dollar-denominated bank deposits and loans into devalued pesos following its 2001 financial collapse (as a means of halting the crash and stopping the financial capital flight from the country) and Vanessa Ventures' arbitrations against Costa Rica (over the country's 2002 law banning open pit mining) and Venezuela.[83]

Canadian Multilateralism: Progressive Desire for International Cooperation or Strategic Self-Interest?

Before proceeding further, a few comments on the issue of multilateral versus bilateral political and economic relationships are in order. There is an assumption amongst observers that Canada supports multilateral frameworks because of a progressive foreign policy tradition promoting international political and economic cooperation. These assumptions, however, are quite simplistic and miss much of the motivation underlying decisions to engage in multilateral or bilateral frameworks. It is true that many Canadian policy-makers and business leaders stress the need for operating within multilateral frameworks, such as that which is provided by the World Trade Organization (WTO), agreements such as the proposed Free Trade Area of the Americas (FTAA), or political institutions like the United Nations. But they do so for much more self-interested reasons than most observers give them credit—a cold hard calculus of Canadian business interest rather than some progressive internationalist inspiration.

Multilateral economic frameworks, for one thing, obviously cast a much wider net than do bilateral deals, therefore granting Canadian corporations access to the markets of multiple countries under the rubric of one agreement. It is a more efficient form of negotiation. Multilateral political spaces likewise offer a similar incentive, and if a country wants to shape international policy in some area, bilateral venues are obviously limited in what they can accomplish. But Canadian business and political leaders are also cognizant of Canada's smaller stature relative to other major political and economic powers, and in particular to the United States. They may seek to exploit the opportunities provided them by American imperialism, such as following America's lead in promoting structural adjustment policies in the IMF and World Bank or investing in countries after American intervention leads to the opening of their economies (as in Chile after the 1973 military coup or more recently in Iraq). And while they may side with the Americans in some (though not all) international debates, they also know that Canadian corporate interests are not simply reducible to American corporate interests. Americans are also competitors, vying for the same markets and resources as Canadian capitalists. And, furthermore, as a superpower the United States may ignore, and sometimes trample on, Canadian corporate and political interests. Multilateralism, in this respect, is pragmatic—it can be a check on the unbridled power of Washington, a cautious approach to defending the interests of a more junior imperialist nation. Canada's role in multilateral treaties or organizations should be viewed in this light. Multilateral forums can provide an opportunity for Canadian interests to be heard, or for Canadian goals to be advanced, without always being subjugated by the largest powers. Of course, in order to be successful in such bodies, Canada also needs the support of other smaller advanced capitalist countries that also have interests that do not always coincide with those of the superpower.

But multilateral negotiations can be a difficult road to navigate; the slow pace of negotiations at the WTO (consider here the problems of the Doha round and the difficulty in putting an investment treaty together) and the stalling of the FTAA are a testament to this. In response, Canada continues to try to gain an economic foothold in the Global South by bilateral means, often as a form of insurance in the event that multilateral agreements like the FTAA or the WTO investment deal do not succeed. Bilateral deals are also useful insofar as rich countries like Canada typically argue for the inclusion of at least minimum international standards in negotiations, that is, that the deal being negotiated should not involve standards less than those already established in existing trade and investment treaties. So if, for instance, Canada can get a strong investment deal with one country—giving its corporations strong protection to access that country's markets and re-sources—it will then use that as its minimum standard for future negotiations, whether bilateral or multilateral. This is a safeguard of sorts against the tendency for deals to be watered down in mul-tilateral forums. Further, bilateral deals, the SCFAIT observes, can "provide an advantage for Canada over its competitors in those markets who may not enjoy the same level of access."[84]

Export Development Canada, CIDA
INC and Rewriting Mining Codes

Apart from participation in the IMF and World Bank, and the pur-suit of investment deals, there are a couple of other important ways state agencies facilitate Canadian capital's expansion into the Glob-al South. One is through the financing of corporate investment.

Most of this financing is provided by Export Development Canada (EDC), an arm's-length state agency that offers credit in-surance for Canadian companies investing abroad and loans to their customers. While EDC does not exclusively fund Canadian investments in the Third World, it has nevertheless grown signifi-cantly as markets in the South have been liberalized and Canadian companies began expanding into the region. From 1993 to 1999, for example, EDC's business volume more than tripled to over $40 billion, and it now provides services to over 5,000 Canadian companies. Reporting on its role in Third World investments, the Halifax Initiative writes, "EDC is an important financier of large infrastructure and resource extractive projects, which by nature are more likely than others to have adverse impacts on the poor, labour, human rights and the environment."[85]

Until 2005, EDC did not publicly disclose the projects it was financing, nor did it screen for the projects' environmental and human rights impacts. EDC has in fact been exempted by Parlia-ment from the Access to Information Act. Under public pressure, though, EDC revised its policies: it now takes into account the en-vironmental assessments of potential investments located outside the G7, and discloses those assessments along with the name of the project thirty days prior to its final decision on whether or not it will provide support. It still does not consider the human rights impact on communities where the investments are taking place, however. In the two years following EDC's change to its disclosure policy in 2005, it confirmed financing for nine projects, seven of which were in the natural resources sector (three in both mining and oil and gas, and one in dam building), including Equinox Minerals' Lumwana copper project in Zambia. Four projects under review by EDC were all in the natural resources sector (three mining and one oil and gas). These are Gold Reserve's Brisas gold and copper project in Venezuela, Tiberon Minerals' Nui Phao mine in Vietnam, Falconbridge's Koniambo ferronickel mine in New Caledonia and Qatar Petroleum's Qatar4 Gas Project in Qatar.[86]

Another source of public financial support for Canadian investments in the Third World was the CIDA Industrial Cooperation program (CIDA INC). In 2009 the government renamed CIDA INC the Investment Cooperation Program and placed it under FAIT (Foreign Affairs and International Trade), though it will perform largely the same function. CIDA INC provided financing for Canadian companies to conduct feasibility studies before investing in the South, as well as financing for these companies' customers. Yet the link between the money it spent, on the one hand, and development or the improvement of the well being of people in poor countries, on the other, was quite tenuous. Looking at a selection of seventeen Third World countries in which CIDA INC supported Canadian investment projects for the years 1995 to 2005, we find that over $105 million was spent. Most of it was spent on projects the main beneficiary of which is likely Canadian corporations. Much of CIDA INC's financing went to manufacturing (such as steel, tools and equipment, pulp and paper mills, auto parts), construction, natural resources production, hydroelectric projects, telecommunications and building highways. While people living in the areas where the money was spent may benefit from things like improved roadways, the reality is that the intended primary benefactors are the corporations that will turn a profit from them and other companies who will be more inclined to invest thanks in part to the infrastructure upgrade CIDA INC was supporting. While such things as supplying potable water purification systems contribute to the health and well being of people in poor countries, these are only a very small proportion of what CIDA INC spent its money on. Supporting natural resources development, as I discuss below, does not improve the lives of the poor—rather it typically worsens people's lives. Nor is it easy to conceive of how financing the manufacture of armoured vehicles in Colombia—which CIDA INC did in the 1990s—which has one of the worst human rights records in the world, can help that country's poor.[87]

CIDA has also supported Canadian investment by funding the neoliberal-inspired rewriting of mining codes in Third World countries. Mining reform has been an important feature of the tidal wave of liberalization that has swept across Latin America over the last two decades, and a series of countries, many where Canadian mining companies are heavily invested, have written unambiguously pro-foreign multinational legislation, including Chile, Argentina, Bolivia, Peru and Colombia. The result has been a field day for Canadian mining corporations.

CIDA had a direct role in rewriting two of these countries' mining codes. In 2002, CIDA made a $9.6 million investment in Peru under the Mineral Resources Reform Project. The project was putatively aimed at providing technical assistance and technological support to Peru's Ministry of Energy and Mines to improve its administration of the country's mining and energy sector. But improving its administration involved making its mining laws more conducive to protecting the rights of Canadian corporations. CIDA also spent $11 million from 1997 to 2002 in Colombia, according to an agency official, to help the country "strengthen its institutional capacity in both the Ministry of Mines and Energy and the Ministry of the Environment and the regulatory agencies these agencies worked with."[88] Like improving administration in Peru, strengthening "institutional capacity" in Colombia is a euphemism for neoliberal reform. A central component of CIDA's project was the establishment of Colombia's new and quite controversial mining code. This code allows international capital to freely enter indigenous territories containing mineral deposits, weakens environmental regulations considerably, limits labour rights and significantly reduces the royalty rate foreign mining corporations must pay the Colombian government, from fifteen to four percent. The code demands that small independent miners (typically poor individuals) will lose their mines if they fail to sign a contract with the government within three years. Many miners, however, have not had a chance to sign a government contract, having been forced to leave by paramilitary threats. It also complements Plan

Colombia, which "guarantees private sector control over natural resources, even if this means the forcible removal of the existing population from certain areas of the countryside."[89] These actions are of course defended as contributing to "development" and "poverty reduction," but they are really aimed at facilitating Canadian mining presence. CIDA spending aimed at neoliberalization of foreign economies has goals beyond mining, though. It also funded the liberalization of Colombia's telecommunication sector, a process involving the murder of dozens of trade unionists opposing the project (which I will discuss in the next chapter).[90] On top of the $9.6 million it spent on mining reform in Peru, CIDA spent another $6 million between 2003 and 2009 on public sector reform (aimed at "improving efficiency") and $8.7 million from 2003 to 2008 on developing new institutional and regulatory frameworks in the hydrocarbons sector (promoting "international private sector investment"). In Honduras, as I noted earlier in the chapter, CIDA committed $1.5 million from 2004 to 2010 toward a program at the Universidad Nacional de Honduras to assist in the development and implementation of the country's Poverty Reduction Strategy process, which is the current form by which structural adjustment programs are designed.[91] CIDA's recent work in Haiti (which I will discuss in more detail in chapter five) rates a mention here too. Canadian aid to the most impoverished country in the hemisphere over the last several years has been used, as Engler and Fenton demonstrate, to help prop up a dictatorship that overthrew a democratically elected left-leaning government.[92]

In the international race to gain ground in the Global South, public funds, like those provided through EDC, CIDA INC and CIDA can be an important factor in the success of Canadian capitalists. Canada's pockets may not be as deep as those of the United States or some of the European powers, but its commitment in this regard is not weaker. We might also rethink the role of Canadian aid in Global South countries and simplistic calls for increasing funding for CIDA or the international aid budget. Canadian aid supports Canadian capitalist interests, and thus without a fundamental reworking of aid policy, increased spending will not help the world's poor—indeed, it will likely increase the pain Canada is already causing the Global South.

Human Rights and Foreign Policy: The Corporate Calculus
The other significant way the state supports Canadian capitalists in the Global South is its shameful refusal to enforce human rights standards. According to one energy industry executive, "[i]t's not for Canadians to preach on human rights."[93] During the debate in the fall of 2009 surrounding a private member's bill that would give the state some limited powers to investigate complaints of human rights abuses against Canadian companies, mining industry lawyer Michel Bourassa claimed the "vast majority" of allegations are "unfounded" and that NGOs that raise them do so to "create sort of a story for funding."[94]

The Canadian state has failed to impose any meaningful kind of human rights standards on the actions of Canadian companies—many of whom received public financial support from EDC, CIDA INC and the Canadian Pension Plan for their foreign investments. This is despite growing public pressure to do so following the increased human rights violations in Third World countries associated with Canadian corporate activities. A 2005 report by the SCFAIT calls on Canada to, among other things, hold corporations accountable for human rights violations with which they are associated and to establish a code of conduct, based on principles of corporate social responsibility, for Canadian corporations abroad. The state claims in its response to the Standing Committee's report that ensuring Canadian corporations abide by international human rights law is the responsibility of host states and not Canada, even if those corporations are chartered in Canada and receive Canadian funding to invest abroad. It adds, furthermore, that it does not presently have the legal authority to prosecute Canadian corporations for transgressions made beyond Canada's borders—and it makes no mention of pursuing legislation allowing it to do so. The state also claims there is no internationally accepted norm for socially responsible corporate behaviour, although the literature on social responsibility has become extensive over the last two decades. Nor does it propose any steps to establish such accountability measures. In fact, it stresses the importance of ensuring that any future international agreement on the human rights implications of corporate practices be voluntary, otherwise most countries and their corporations would not participate.[95]

Rather than take any meaningful steps toward the development of a human rights policy to govern the practices of Canadian capitalists abroad, the state instead established a roundtable process (with "stakeholders") in 2006 to discuss the concerns raised in the Standing Committee report. Many critics condemned this process as simply a stalling tactic, noting that it was yet another roundtable process in a long line of roundtable processes that have made no difference to government policy or corporate actions. Indeed, after the stakeholder process completed its work, the state responded, two years later, with its corporate responsibility plan that fails to include an ombudsperson, a proper complaints procedure or a sanctions regime to address corporate malfeasance—all recommendations coming out of the stakeholder process. Canada has created a corporate social responsibility counsellor, but the position is toothless, requiring consent from companies before being able to look into allegations of abuse. The state does add, for good measure, that it in fact supports human rights in poor countries by promoting development, and it does this by supporting World Bank and IMF "macroeconomic stability" measures, i.e., structural adjustment.[96]

The Canadian government has also refused to sign the United Nations' Draft Declaration on the Rights of Indigenous Peoples, which called for the "informed consent" of indigenous people before a development project can be initiated on their land. Under the Liberals, Canada called for revisions to water down the Declaration, which critics claimed set the process back several years. The Tories have simply refused to sign it. An official with the African Indigenous Caucus attending the meetings where the declaration was being negotiated in 2007 accused Canada of promising aid money to African representatives in return for their support in opposing the deal. Canada's failure to support this declaration is an important victory for Canadian natural resources companies operating both at home and abroad, since most of their current and future projects are on inhabited land, and removing the people who stand in the way of their investments is a principal aim of Canadian imperialism.[97]

CIDA has also historically been reluctant to establish human rights measures for its aid program or to tie aid to human rights improvements. This included the CIDA INC program.[98] CIDA

INC had consistently financed investments in countries engaged in human rights violations or in the midst of civil war, including, among others, Indonesia, Nigeria, Afghanistan, Colombia, the Philippines and Sudan. Meanwhile, EDC does not have anything to be proud of in this regard. Despite recent changes to its disclosure policy, it takes into consideration the human rights implications of a project only to the extent they could impact on the profits of the investor.

In the eyes of the Canadian state and capital, investment and profit considerations trump human rights. Here again, Canada really is not any different from other imperialist countries. A key goal of its foreign policy is making the Third World a good place for Canadians to do business, and anything that could interfere with this, including concern for human rights, is perceived as a threat to Canadian interests. In the bluntly honest words of one Canadian business leader, responding to demands that Canada should address human rights abuses in the South: "punitive bilateral action ... In the case of trade, it may hurt Canada more than it will change the behaviour of offending governments."[99] That is the sentiment underlying the Stephen Harper Tories' position on China: despite Harper's public criticism of China's human rights record, his International Trade minister and officials in the Department of Foreign Affairs and International Trade have sought to restore stronger economic relations with it.[100] This is the cold calculus informing Canada's human rights policy: if it undermines corporate opportunities for profit, or gives our international competitors an edge over us, then the best option—the business option—is to disregard it.[101]

Canadian Investment Abroad
Canada's foreign policy has helped to make the Global South an increasingly attractive place to do business. And, as Canada has liberalized markets, structurally adjusted economies and strengthened corporate rights in the Third World, Canadian investment has increased in the region at a considerable pace. Canadian investment in the Global South may not be as extensive as that of the United States or some of the other European and G7 economic powers, but Canadian corporations have not had the head start their competitors have had (given the Europeans

and Americans began empire building in the nineteenth and early twentieth centuries). Canadian investment has nonetheless, by some indicators, been growing at a faster pace than that of the Americans or Europeans.

Canada's place as a major foreign investor, and Canadian capital's penetration of the Global South since the early 1990s, is undeniable. Canadian Direct Investment (CDI) has increased sharply since the early 1990s, and Canada has actually been a net exporter of direct investment since 1997. By 2007, the cumulative stock of CDI had reached $514.5 billion. Measured in investment flows (i.e., foreign investments made in that given year) Canada ranked eighth in the world in 2007 of the top foreign direct investor countries—and has consistently ranked in the top ten in the last several years—with direct investments reaching 150 different countries on all continents, including thirty countries with at least $1 billion in CDI stock (i.e., cumulative direct investment, as opposed to flows).[102] Amongst G8 nations, Canada has the fourth highest ratio of outward direct investment stock to GDP (that is, controlling for the respective size of countries' economies), as seen in chart 3.1.[103]

CHART 3.1: G8 OUTWARD FDI STOCK
AS A PERCENTAGE OF GDP, 1980-2007

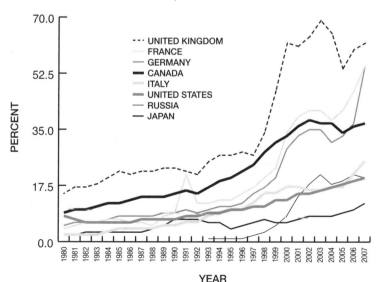

As a sign of the increased importance of foreign investment to Canadian capital, outward investment relative to the economy in 2007 is just over four times the rate in 1980.

Similar to the FDI trend of many other advanced capitalist countries, furthermore, CDI is increasingly going to countries of the Global South. In the early 1950s, this region received approximately ten percent of total CDI stock; increasing sharply in the 1990s, it received just under a quarter by 1998 and by 2007 received over twenty-seven percent. The increase in CDI to the Global South corresponds to the decrease of CDI, as a proportion of the total, to other advanced capitalist countries, as chart 3.2 shows. While the U.S. is still the biggest destination for CDI, for instance, its share of total CDI has declined considerably since the early 1980s. From 1990 to 2006–2007, the share of CDI assets in the U.S. fell from sixty percent to the forty-three-to-forty-four percent range, even though Canadian assets in the U.S., in absolute terms, tripled.[104]

CHART 3.2: CDI STOCK BY REGION AS A
PERCENTAGE OF GLOBAL TOTAL, 1990-2007

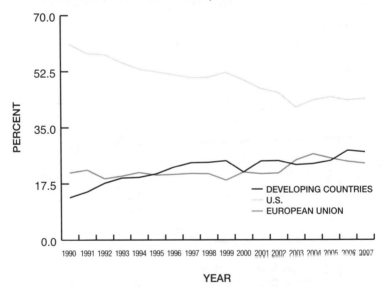

Meanwhile, the ten largest increases in destinations of CDI flows from 1987 to 2007 have all been Global South countries: China (with an increase of nearly 30,000 percent), Peru (19,533),

Chile (12,391), Cayman Islands (7,398), Barbados (7,206), Bahamas (6,766), Colombia (5,585), Costa Rica (2,833), Mexico (2303) and Argentina (1,558).[105]

Canada's growing investment orientation toward Global South countries is also clearly demonstrated in chart 3.3. Here, we see the steady increase, from 1990 to 2005, of CDI stock to Global South countries in relation to the size of the Canadian economy (measured in Gross Domestic Product). In other words, CDI to Global South countries over this period increased at a greater rate than the Canadian economy. This measure also allows us to more accurately compare Canada's investment orientation to the Global South to that of other G7 countries (comparable data for Russia is not available), by accounting for the overall size of their respective economies when considering their foreign investment trends. With the exception of the U.K., Canada's orientation over this period is considerably higher than that of other G7 nations.[106]

CHART 3.3: G7 FDI STOCK TO THE GLOBAL
SOUTH AS A PERCENTAGE OF GDP, 1990-2005

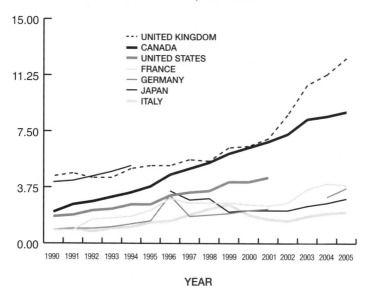

YEAR

Latin America and the Caribbean are the biggest destination for CDI in the South, and as we see in chart 3.4 it has accounted for over seventy percent of total CDI to Global South economies since 1996 and over eighty percent in 2007 (with the Caribbean in particular comprising an average of just under fifty percent over that time period). It is also the only region that experienced considerable growth as a proportion of total growth since 1990. Asia-Pacific's share of the total CDI growth to the South consistently declined over this period, although CDI to this region did increase in absolute terms from $4.1 billion in 1990 to $19.3 billion in 2007. The growth in Latin America and the Caribbean's share of total CDI to the South likely has a lot to do with the significant liberalization trend in the region in the 1980s and 1990s—especially in the financial services and natural resources sectors—and the limited but not completely insignificant history of Canadian investment there in the twentieth century, while the importance of the region for Canadian economic expansion and its relative geographic proximity helps to foster Canada's ambitions for greater political and economic influence there. As you'll note in the chart, Latin America's percentage of the total decreases after 2000 until 2007. But this is the result of the growth of investment in the Caribbean, not a decline in investment to Latin America.[107]

CHART 3.4: CDI BY REGION AS A PERCENTAGE OF TOTAL TO THE GLOBAL SOUTH, 1990-2007

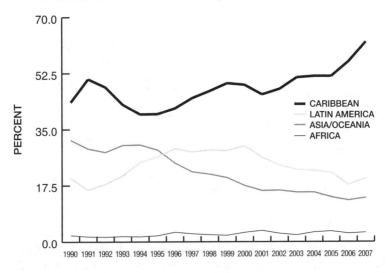

Not surprisingly, then, nine of the ten fastest growing CDI destinations from 1987 to 2007 noted above are in this region, and as we see in chart 3.5, eight of the top ten Global South country recipients of CDI stock in 2007 were in Latin America and the Caribbean (four in the Caribbean and four in Latin America).[108]

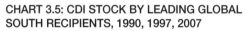

CHART 3.5: CDI STOCK BY LEADING GLOBAL SOUTH RECIPIENTS, 1990, 1997, 2007

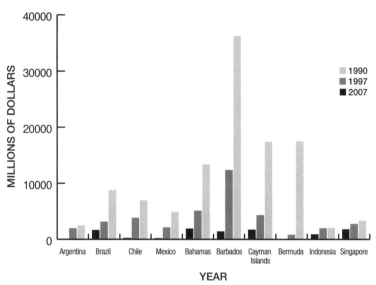

Canadian Direct Investment stock into the Americas, including into non-NAFTA countries, has increased significantly since the early 1990s, making Canada one of the largest foreign investors in the region. By 2006, Canada had actually become the third largest investor in the region. From 1996 to 2006, for instance, Canada was the largest investor in Ecuador, second in Honduras, third in Chile and the Dominican Republic, and fifth in Mexico, El Salvador and Costa Rica. In 2007, Canada was the fourth largest investor in Peru. As I will discuss in a moment, Canadian investment into the Western hemisphere is driven by the finance and insurance and energy and mining sectors. Canadian companies have not penetrated markets as effectively in the Asia-Pacific region as they have in Latin America and the Caribbean, but they do have an important presence in some countries. In Indonesia, Canada was the fifth largest foreign investor in 2005 and tenth in 2006. In Malaysia, Canada was the sixth largest foreign investor in 2006 and tenth in 2007. In the Philippines, Canada was the seventh largest foreign investor in 2006 and eleventh in 2007.[109]

Canadian capital's presence is certainly also being felt in the former Soviet republics of Central Asia. In Kazakhstan, Canada was the fifth largest foreign investor in 2008, with US$945 million invested, most of it in mining. In Kyrgyzstan, Canada was the sixth largest investor in 2007, with US$500 million in assets, again much of it in mining. In Tajikistan, meanwhile, Canada ranked lower as the tenth largest foreign investor in 2007, with US$1.4 million invested.[110]

The importance of the Global South for Canadian corporations can also be seen in its role as an increasingly important source for profits. As chart 3.6 indicates, income from direct investment in the Third World as a proportion of total investment income earned abroad has risen significantly, from just under twenty-five percent for the years 1973–79 to over forty-five percent for 2000–07. Income from the South has actually increased at a much greater pace than has direct investment to the region as a proportion of total direct foreign direct investment, which, as noted above, stood at just over twenty-seven percent in 2007. Direct investment income from the South rose from $1.1 billion in 1990 to $17.9 billion in 2007.[111]

CHART 3.6: GLOBAL SOUTH DIRECT INVESTMENT INCOME
AS A PERCENTAGE OF TOTAL FOREIGN INVESTMENT INCOME

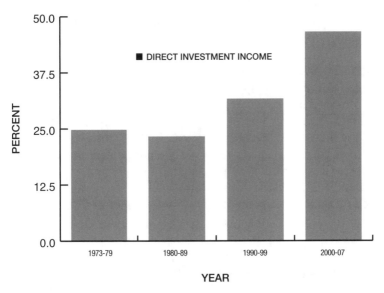

YEAR

Investment income more generally (including direct and port-folio) from the South has increased steadily over the last few de-cades, rising by 535 percent from 1980 to 2007. As a percentage of Canadian-based corporate profits, it peaked in the 1990s at a decade average of 16.6 percent, dropping down to an average of 10.6 percent from 2000–07. The decline in the 2000s, however, was simply the result of a significant surge in domestic earnings. Inter-estingly, foreign profit's peak as a percentage of domestic profits occurs during recessionary periods, as the former decline much less dramatically than the latter.[112]

This CDI, and the handsome profits earned from it, is becom-ing increasingly concentrated among the largest of Canadian cor-porations. Some analysts, in the face of the rise of CDI, may sug-gest that large foreign-controlled domestic corporations account for a large share of it, and that therefore this trend speaks more to the international expansion and influence of non-Canadian com-panies abroad rather than Canadian ones. But non-Canadian resi-dents' share of CDI has been on a long-term decline since the late 1960s, dropping precipitously from thirty-seven percent in 1969 to eighteen percent by the early 1990s. William Carroll finds that "by year end 1996 nearly all large corporations with extensive transnational reach were controlled by Canadian capitalists."[113] Large Canadian-controlled corporations are increasingly accounting for most of the outward investment from Canada. Foreign affiliates of Canadian-based corporations with book values of more than $500 million now represent greater than two-thirds of all CDI.[114]

Canadian investment into the South is led by the "finance and insurance" and the "energy and metallic minerals" sectors (these are the Statistics Canada categories). In 2007, these two sectors together comprised just over seventy-eight percent of CDI stock into the Global South (57.1 percent and 21.1 percent, or $77.6 billion and $28.7 billion, respectively), with "services and retailing" accounting for 11.5 percent and "other" 7.4 percent.[115] However, the growing importance of the South as a destination for Canadian direct investment has also occurred across most sectors. Only one sector—"machinery and transportation equipment"—has declined as a percentage of overall foreign investment since 1990. "Finance and insurance" and "energy and metallic minerals" saw the biggest increases, though the latter's Third World proportion of total foreign investment declined sharply from its high in the late 1990s before rebounding modestly in 2007, likely as a result of increasing popular and governmental challenges to the rights of mining companies in this period.

One of the principal reasons finance and insurance investments in the South have grown so much is Canadian banks' increasing involvement in Offshore Financial Centres (OFC). OFCs are a draw for Canadian (and other foreign) investors looking for places to put their money because of the low or zero taxation rates, limited regulations and the secrecy with which transactions are normally done. From 1990 to 2003, Canadian assets in OFCs grew eightfold, from $11 billion to $88 billion, and by 2003 accounted for a remarkable one-fifth of all CDI—double the proportion of thirteen years earlier. Since 1996, OFCs have been the most popular destination for CDI in the financial sector, and account for two-thirds of CDI assets in the sector. Of the forty-two OFC jurisdictions identified by the IMF, Canadian corporations held assets in twenty-five of them in 2003. The largest growth of CDI into OFCs has been in the Caribbean countries of Barbados,

Bermuda, the Cayman Islands and Bahamas. Other OFC destinations in which Canadians are invested are Singapore, Hong Kong and Malaysia.[116]

While OFCs represent the most liberalized locations for foreign banking investment, banking sector liberalization was undertaken widely across the Global South in the 1980s and 1990s. These reforms allowed for more foreign competition and led to fewer controls on credit, interest rates and international transactions, leading to an increase in speculative inflows, unstable asset bubbles and spectacular meltdowns (I discuss Scotia's involvement in the Argentina meltdown in the next chapter). While banks based in the Global North have traditionally invested in the South to assist their home country corporate customers engage in international trade and investment, since the 1990s these banks have also sought to expand in the South in their own effort to access local markets there that they see "as offering attractive and strategic opportunities to expand," especially in the context of financial sector privatizations. From 1990 to 2003, there was a sharp increase in FDI to the Global South, the majority of which—US$46 billion—targeted Latin America.[117] Over this period, Canadians were the fourth largest financial sector investors in this region, though they were considerably far behind the two largest investor nations, the United States and Spain.[118] Canadian growth in the Americas included Scotiabank's acquisition of thirty-nine branches of a Dominican Republic bank in 2003, adding to its existing twenty-branch network in the country. It also acquired banks in Peru, Costa Rica and Chile in the last few years. Including its Dominican Republic purchase, it spent almost $2 billion in acquisitions in Latin America and the Caribbean between 2003 and 2006. Scotia credited its investments in the region for its record profit earning in the first three quarters of 2006. It has been estimated in fact that Canadian banks earn approximately forty percent of their revenues abroad.[119]

Given their strong balance sheets coming out of the 2007–2009 financial crisis and their strategies for internationalization, the international expansion of Canadian banks is likely to continue for some time. They continue to actively seek opportunities for foreign acquisitions. While the United States is a key target market—with the Bank of Montreal having participated in thirteen takeovers worth $2.1 billion in the Chicago area in the last two decades, TD spending $20 billion on acquisitions since 2005 and the Royal expanding in the Southeastern U.S.[120]—a large proportion of this foreign takeover activity will occur in the South. Although Scotiabank already has a considerable presence in the Americas, as I have noted, it has made its intentions to further increase its acquisitions in the region as well as in Asia clear. Likewise, the Canadian Imperial Bank of Commerce in early 2007 became a majority owner of the FirstCaribbean International Bank. According to CIBC CEO, Gerry McCaughey, this is one step in the plan for expansion: "From a FirstCaribbean viewpoint, we will continue to look at opportunities within the region, and we think growing within the region is of interest."[121] The Royal Bank entered American- and British-occupied Iraq in 2005, as part of an international consortium of thirteen different financial institutions whose aim is to support the emerging investment activities of corporations from the various countries represented in the consortium.[122]

The insurance industry has also been active when it comes to expanding into the South. Some of Canada's biggest and most successful multinational corporations, like Manulife and Sunlife, are based in the insurance industry. And like Canadian banks, they have an eye on the South and its liberalizing markets. Whereas in 1990 foreign branch and subsidiary operations of Canadian insurers accounted for thirty-seven percent of worldwide premiums, by 2005 they accounted for fifty-five percent, or $71.6 billion. Twenty percent of these foreign premiums in 2005, or $14.3 billion, came from Global South countries. Canadian companies also collect significantly more premiums abroad than foreign companies do in Canada. The increase in worldwide assets accounted for by foreign branch and subsidiary operations has also been considerable, rising from thirty-one percent in 1990 to fifty-five percent in 2005.[123]

With a number of major companies, Canada's telecommunications sector is also an important global player despite losses they have suffered in a couple of stock market crises since the late 1990s. Telecommunications has been an important component of increased CDI to a number of Latin American countries, including the Andean Community, where telecommunications CDI is second only to natural resources (oil and gas and mining) and Canadian investors are centrally involved in Colombia. Telecommunications is also a considerable part of CDI in Brazil, Chile and Mexico.[124] But Latin America is not the only region in which Canadian telecommunication companies are seeking business. In late 2006, Nortel Networks won a US$20 million contract to install a 5,000-kilometre optical network across colonial-occupied Iraq. This investment will cover thirty-five cities, and is five times larger than the 1,000-kilometre network the company built between Baghdad and Basra in 2004. Although Iraq had an extensive fibre optics network before 2003, it was largely destroyed in the United States' invasion. Nortel is only too happy to partake in the rebuilding effort, though, turning a handsome profit while ensconcing itself in the country for the long term. According to a company executive, "This is a long-term play for the Iraqi market."[125]

Another Canadian industry deserving of our attention here is arms manufacturing. Although CDI in the arms industry is nowhere near as extensive as it is elsewhere, Canada is nevertheless an important global player in an industry that literally trades in death and destruction. The Canadian industry was the thirteenth largest arms exporter in 2000, tenth in 2001, ninth in 2002, eleventh in 2003, twelfth in 2004 and seventeenth in 2007.[126] From 2002 to 2005, Canada exported $2.1 billion in military goods and technology.[127] These exports range from bullets, to simulation technologies for operating machine guns on attack helicopters, to various technological components for Blackhawk helicopters, to aircraft that with slight modifications are used for combat. Many of these exports, with the government's sanction, go to armies engaged in violent occupations (such as the United States and Israel) and states with a long record of human rights abuses, such as Colombia and Pakistan. Canada's involvement in this deadly industry, and the government's sanctioning of it, often by turning a blind eye, provides a bloody example of that corporate-human rights calculus described above, where the bottom line inevitably wins out. Profit over people is the Canadian corporate mantra in this age of lean and mean global capitalism.

Canada's greatest international presence (and probably most controversial) is in mining, however. As I noted in earlier in the chapter, mining sector reform has been an important part of the overall market liberalization process, especially in Latin America. The Global South, with Latin America front and centre, is now the largest destination for mineral exploration investment. At the same time, Canadian mining industry is the largest in the world. Canadian-based mining companies comprise sixty percent of all mining companies (of a total of 1,138) in the world that spend more than $133,000 on exploration, accounted for over forty percent of all worldwide exploration activity in 2004 and conduct approximately thirty percent of all mining investment worldwide.[128]

Canadian companies also have a much greater international orientation than do other companies, and this orientation has increased rapidly since the early 1990s. For instance, while in 1992 foreign properties accounted for twenty-five percent of all properties held by all Canadian companies worldwide, by 2006 they accounted for more than half. Although Canadian companies are most active in Latin America, as the Canadian industry has moved to gain control of some of the richest mineral deposits in the world, Canadian companies are nevertheless present in all parts of the Global South. Of the top thirty countries in which Canadian mining corporations held properties in 2004, twelve were in Latin America, nine were in Africa and five were in developing Asia-Pacific.[129] By 2004, the larger Canadian companies (defined as those companies that planned to spend at least $4 million on exploration) were expected to spend $305 million on exploration investment in Latin America and the Caribbean, accounting for thirty-five percent of the region's larger company exploration market—the largest by far of all their international competitors. Between 1989 and 2001, seven Canadian companies were among the top twenty mineral exploration investors in the region, and by 2006 the cumulative value of Canadian mining assets was $28.2 billion. In Africa by 2004, the larger Canadian corporations spent more than $100 million on exploration investment, constituting sixteen percent of the total larger company expenditures on the continent. This represented a doubling of the 2003 larger company exploration budgets. Canadian companies of all sizes also had interests in over 600 properties in over thirty-three countries on the continent. In Asia Pacific in 2004, the larger Canadian companies were expected to spend $278 million on exploration, which accounts for one-third of the exploration market in the region and represents a doubling for the total larger Canadian company exploration budgets from 2003. Canadians held interests in

180 properties in Southeast Asia, 160 in East Asia and 180 in the South Pacific.[130]

Canadian Expansion Into the Global South: A Winning Situation For Everyone?

Canadian officials, corporate leaders, politicians and their media allies defend investment deals and Canada's expansion into the South by stressing the contribution these make to international development through direct investment or through poor countries' access to the Canadian market. One of the reasons poor countries will consent to these deals—even if they often do not agree with the laissez-faire terms set by Canadian negotiators—is the need for foreign investment, which they hope will stimulate their economies and provide an opportunity to end the cycle of poverty and debt. This is more an act of desperation, however, then it is of commitment to the unassailable principles of the free market, given the extremely critical state of their economies and the lack of domestic capital to finance development projects. For the free market's record in the South over the last two decades is not exemplary, to say the least.

As I stressed in the first chapter, since investment and spending have been forced open in the 1980s by the advanced capitalist countries, living standards for the average person in the Global South have declined considerably, especially for indigenous peoples and other direct producers—what Mike Davis refers to as the new "passive proletariat"—who have been forced from their land and are migrating to urban slums in record numbers in hopes of eking out an existence on the margins of global capitalism. It takes an extraordinary contortion of all the social and economic indicators to try to prove neoliberal globalization has been anything but a disaster for the majority of people in the Third World, or that there is any meaningful hope for improvement in the near future. The claim that economic security for the poor is just around the corner can only be made so many times before the lie is exposed for all to see.

Studies by the United Nations Conference on Trade and Development (UNCTAD) and the UN Food and Agricultural Organization (FAO) show that poverty has in fact grown fastest in countries that have liberalized the most. Food imports in those Third World countries that have taken considerable strides in liberalizing their agricultural sectors—opening their markets to foreign investment and cutting subsidies, at Canada's and other rich nations' insistence[131]—are rising rapidly, while export levels remain flat as Third World farmers must compete now with more technologically advanced agro-producers from the North who also benefit from agricultural subsidies and import quotas in their home markets. The result is that Third World markets are getting flooded with foreign agricultural products and the domestic diet in the South is becoming increasingly dependent on foreign imports. At the same time, land privatization, which is a fixture of structural adjustment programs and is supported by Canada, is leading to the increased concentration of land in favour of wealthy farmers and multinational corporations, further undermining the livelihood of poor and subsistence farmers.[132]

Natural resources is one of the sectors in which Canada plays a leading role in the South. But mining and oil and gas investment, for example, provide few economic benefits to communities where the development is taking place. As very capital-intensive industries, they do not create a large number of jobs; they also involve significant dislocation of people from their lands and the disruption of traditional economic activities (often through the resulting environmental damage caused by development); and under the NAFTA-style investment clauses and other provisions of the FIPAs and free trade deals, and the mining legislation engineered by Canada in Colombia and Peru, Canadian corporations are obliged to pay very little in royalties and taxes. These investments, in other words, do not contribute in any significant way to domestic growth or sustainability. It should come as no surprise, then, that studies have found that some of the poorest areas in Latin America are those that have been subjected to resource development—much of it done by Canadian corporations. But when countries such as Ecuador seek to place limits on the rights of foreign mining firms, Canada intervenes to actively undermine the effort. In the words of a Corriente Resources representative, the Canadian embassy "worked tirelessly to affect [sic] change in the mining policy—including facilitating high-level meetings between Canadian mining companies and President Rafael Correa."[133]

It should also be noted that the growth of direct investment from poor countries into Canada, relative to CDI into poor countries, is negligible at best. In the government report on Canada's FIPA with Peru, it is actually acknowledged that the deal will have no effect on Peru's investment patterns into Canada. Despite being considered a growing regional power in Latin America, Brazil's investors are also gaining little ground in Canada. Brazilian FDI into Canada grew rather modestly from 1992 to 2002, and by 2003 was only a quarter of CDI into Brazil. At the same time, Canadian investment into the region has risen rapidly. This investment relationship is not unique to the Americas, however. Nearly 100 percent of all inward FDI from the Asia-Pacific region, for example, is accounted for by three investment partners, each of whom is a Global North country: Japan, Hong Kong and Australia. China, in many respects a rising superpower, has shown only limited investment growth into Canada. China's FDI into Canada actually declined in the latter half of the 1990s, and although it has since picked up, Canada's investment into China is still growing more rapidly than China's into Canada.

It cannot really be claimed that foreign investment agreements are about poorer countries gaining access to Canada. Direct investment is still largely a one-way relationship favouring capital from rich countries, with Canadian corporations gaining access to Third World markets, while companies from those markets struggle to make inroads to Canada. As I noted above, furthermore, it is also Canadian corporations—not those of Third World investment partners—making recourse to the investor-state dispute settlement mechanisms in investment agreements to ensure Third World markets are open for business.[134]

Imports from Third World economies have increased, including from Canadian-owned companies with investments in the South. Much of the growth has been in labour-intensive sectors with low wages and poor conditions for workers, like agriculture and clothing. Like other rich nations, though, Canada also still engages in trade-distorting practices such as providing subsidies for its producers and setting import quotas in order to give its corporations a leg up against international competitors. According to the WTO, in Canada "a number of activities remain subject to interventions, notably in agriculture, textiles and clothing, telecommunications, audiovisual, air and maritime transport, and insurance." Canada restricts imports of agri-food and dairy products through a quota system, for instance, where goods are "protected by out-of-quota tariffs that frequently exceed 200%," while "in-quota access is in some instances extremely small."[135] The Asia Pacific Foundation reports that Canada has applied higher duties on more products exported by the Least Developed Countries (LDCs)—the poorest forty-eight countries in the world—than most industrialized countries, including Europe and Japan.[136] And despite Canada's insistence in trade and investment negotiations that poor countries reduce their agricultural sector subsidies, Canada spent an estimated US$6 billion on agricultural subsidies in 2005, and ranked eighth—and ahead of the U.S.—among OECD nations for the percentage that these subsidies made up of farm receipts (at just over twenty percent).[137] David Black finds that, "agricultural subsidies in the rich world [including Canada] for the production of surplus food (which is then pushed onto the world market to the detriment of Africa's hard pressed farmers) exceed Africa's total GDP."[138] Canada's agri subsidies also exceed its ODA budget. At the same time, Canadian producers continue to push for trade protections against foreign competitors they consider to be dumping products onto the Canadian market. By 2002, Canada had undertaken nearly 100 anti-dumping measures at the WTO.[139]

Despite criticism that these policies undermine the Global South's development, Canada has steadfastly refused to meaningfully change its protectionist stance, even for the poorest nations of the world. In 2000, for example, then Trade Minister Pierre Pettigrew announced a market access package for the LDCs that gave duty-free and quota-free treatment to 570 different tariff lines. This was declared with much fanfare by Canadian officials, and was presented as an example of Canada's commitment to international development. What was not publicly mentioned by Pettigrew about this market access package, however, is that the LDCs exported products from only sixty-seven of these 570 tariff lines, and the total value of these products the year the market access package was to take effect was a mere $543,000, or less than 0.2 percent of Least Developed Country exports to Canada. Quotas and tariffs in industries in which LDC's exports tend to be concentrated, such as agri-products, weren't removed.[140]

Canadian negotiators were also some of the most obstinate at the initial collapse of the Doha round of negotiations at the WTO.[141] The Doha negotiations are referred to as the "development" round by rich nations, in an effort to address criticisms their WTO policy stances are driving Third World countries further into poverty. Although Third World countries demonstrated a willingness to compromise and liberalize further in the hopes of improving their access to Northern markets, Canadian negotiators clearly have no intention of budging on the subsidies and quotas Canada provides for its own producers. Canada's persistence, and the Third World's determination to hold its ground, contributed to the eventual breakdown of the negotiations in 2006. Referring to Canada, the Doha negotiations' agriculture committee chair commented in frustration that "Were it not for one developed members' demurral, we could, I feel, at least start going along the operational road to trying to reach certain small steps toward convergence."[142] Canada was still sticking to its hardline protectionist stance in further Doha negotiations in the summer of 2008.[143]

Canada, for good measure, fights the Third World's efforts to gain access to affordable drugs and medicines by invoking the intellectual property rights of pharmaceutical companies. Intellectual property rights, including the WTO's Trade Related Intellectual Property Rights (TRIPS), have been an important and contentious part of international trade and investment negotiations, especially as they related to medicine. Corporations and governments of the North have successfully opposed the trade in generic drugs through stringent patent protections for more expensive brand name drugs, which has the effect of denying people in the Third World access to affordable medicines. Prior to the conclusion of the WTO agreement Canada increased its patent protection for brand name drugs to twenty years. Adding further to health insecurity in the Third World, Canada has also played a central role in trying to block the UN Human Rights Council from recognizing water as a human right and establishing an international watchdog to monitor countries' policies and practices.[144]

The Truth of Canada's Role in the Third World

Like other rich nations, Canada has positioned itself well to exploit the economic vulnerabilities of poor countries in order to pry open and gain influence in their markets. In so far as the economic sustainability of poor countries is tied to the free market and, concomitantly, support from creditor nations, Canada has a good lever to establish a geographic space very conducive to the demands of capitalist accumulation in the age of neoliberal globalization. As a result, the region is becoming increasingly important for Canadian capital, as investment and profits earned in the region continue to grow.

State agencies like CIDA, corporate leaders and their allies in the media will always try to put a positive spin on Canada's role in the South. According to them, it is not a new version of imperialism we are witnessing; it is a contribution to development, helping the world's poor to some day be able to help themselves. But in the light of the impact Canadian policies are having on the world's poor, on the one hand, and on Canadian corporate profits, on the other, such public relations appear as but an echo of the old spin of nineteenth- and early twentieth- century empire building: that the imperial powers were engaged in a civilizing mission. A "white man's burden," as Rudyard Kipling once put it. Indigenous peoples needed European and Canadian generosity to lift them out of their state of savagery. Sometimes, perhaps, the medicine seemed a little harsh, but it was necessary given the backwardness of the colonized. Canada's ruling elite and their media allies are more guarded today about Canada's role. Canada is engaged in "development," not the civilizing of the natives. But the sentiment is the same: structural adjustment, Canadian aid and trade deals—all of which, as I have shown, are framed by Canada's pursuit of wealth and influence in the South and cannot be considered as anything but imperialistic in nature by any honest observer—are portrayed as elevating those incapable of elevating themselves. Another burden for the white person to bear: where would the starving Africans we see on our TV or read about in our morning paper be without Canadian generosity? But behind the discourse lies the miserliness of Canadian aid, the true violence of structural adjustment policies and the devastation of communities across the Third World. Behind the faded image of Canada the saviour is Canada the imperialist, engaged in its own invasion of the Global South.

What I outlined in this chapter is but one way the state works to keep the Global South open for Canadian business, however; it is one end of a continuum of state power, at the other end of which is the recourse to violence and military force. We will focus on the latter exercise of Canadian state power in chapter five. First, however, we take a closer look at the social and environmental costs of the expansion of Canadian capital into the Third World, and the response this is engendering from the region's poor.

1   W. Stewart, *Towers of Gold, Feet of Clay: The Canadian Banks* (Toronto: Shrug, 1982). As Stewart notes, so successful were the Bank of Nova Scotia and the Royal in the Caribbean in the early twentieth century that Canada seriously considered taking over Britain's imperial responsibilities in the Commonwealth Caribbean, taking on its own colonies. Canada's early twentieth-century empire-building ambitions also included British-controlled Central America, where Canadian banks, insurance companies and mining interests were staking claims. But empire building never got off the ground, as by that point British influence was already being replaced by American. The idea was eventually quashed by Prime Minister Robert Borden, who referred to "The difficulty of dealing with the coloured population, who would probably be more restless under Canadian law than under British control and would desire and perhaps insist upon representation in Parliament" (quoted in Stewart, p. 187). On Canada's colonial plans in Central America, P. MacFarlane, *Northern Shadows: Canadians and Central America* (Toronto: Between the Lines, 1989), 17–22.

2   MacFarlane discusses Canadian mining and energy investment in the early twentieth century in Central America. Yves Engler's *The Black Book of Canadian Foreign Policy* (Vancouver: Red Publishing, 2009) provides a good history of Canadian imperial practice, including investment controversies, which renders untenable any claim that Canada has been a model international citizen.

3   S. McBride, *Paradigm Shift: Globalization and the Canadian State* (Halifax: Fernwood, 2001).

4   Thomas D'Aquino and David Stewart-Patterson, *Northern Edge: How Canadians Can Triumph in the Global Economy* (Toronto: Stoddart, 2001), 220.

5   D'Alessandro and Stanford both quoted in D'Aquino and Stewart-Patterson *Northern Edge*, 222 and 228 respectively.

6   Michael Sabbia, "Tackling Canada's Future Prosperity: New Directions for Success." Speech to the Conference Board of Canada (Toronto, April 25, 2006). <www.bce.ca/data/documents/Conference_Board_Speech_en.pdf>, retrieved January 2006.

7   This is from the Asian Investment Intentions Survey. *Investment Executive* (February 14, 2006).

8   N. Strizzi, "Hemispheric Free Trade: Some Important Implications for Canada," *Ivey Business Journal* (vol. 66, n. 2, 2001). Jean Daudelin questions Canada's emphasis on Latin America as an important growth centre and therefore as a region on which to focus its foreign policy energies. The point here, though, is that the Canadian government sees it as a region in which Canada can have a significant influence, and is duly trying to assert its influence there and challenge, as Daudelin notes, Brazil's effort to be the major player through which all outsiders pass in order to make economic and diplomatic inroads. And the Canadian state is obviously not doing this for the greater good of the average Latin American but for the greater good of Canadian capital. See J. Daudelin, "Foreign Policy at the Fringe: Canada and Latin America," *International Journal* (vol. 58 n. 4, 2003).

9   Loizides and Grant, *"NAFTA Extension in the Americas: The Business Case* (Ottawa: Conference Board of Canada, 1994) 2.

10 Richard Waugh, Presentation to the Conference Board of Canada (Toronto, October 13, 2004). <www.scotiabank.com/cda/content/0,1608,CID8209_LIDen,00.html>, retrieved December 2006.

11 World Bank, *Mining Reform and the World Bank: Providing a Policy Framework for Development* (Washington: World Bank, 2003); World Bank, *A Mining Strategy for Latin America and the Caribbean* (Washington: World Bank, 1996).

12 For criticism of environmental laws, Canadian Mining Industry, "Escalating Market Access Concerns and Economic Implications for the Canadian Minerals and Metals Industry." Brief to the 1999 Mines Ministers Conference (Charlottetown: September 13, 1999). <www.mining.ca>, retrieved March 2005. On "special interests," Mining Association of Canada, "Study on the Free Trade Agreement of the Americas (FTAA)." A submission to the House of Commons Standing Committee on Foreign Affairs and International Trade (May 11, 1999). <www.mining.ca>, retrieved March 2005.

13 Mining Association of Canada, "Study on the Free Trade Agreement of the Americas."

14 Canada, *Report of the Royal Commission on the Economic Union and Development Prospects for Canada* v. 1 (Ottawa: Ministry of Supply and Services, 1985), 256. On GATT negotiations, Paterson, 1992.

15 Standing Committee on Foreign Affairs and International Trade, *Elements of An Emerging Market Strategy for Canada.* (Ottawa: SCFAIT, 2005). Committee reports are prepared based upon extensive input provided by Foreign Affairs and International Trade officials, industry leaders and, to a much lesser extent, NGO representatives.

16 Standing Committee on Foreign Affairs and International Trade, *Reinvigorating Economic Relations Between Canada and Asia-Pacific* (Ottawa: SCFAIT, 2003).

17 UNCTAD, *World Investment Report,* 2008, 100, <www.unctad.org/fdi>, retrieved October 2008

18 Quoted in Standing Committee on Foreign Affairs and International Trade, *Advancing Canadian Foreign Policy Objectives in the South Caucasus and Central Asia* (Ottawa: SCFAIT, 2001).

19 Richard Waugh, Presentation to the Conference Board of Canada.

20 Standing Committee on Foreign Affairs and International Trade, *Elements of An Emerging Market Strategy for Canada.* (Ottawa: SCFAIT, 2005). Standing Committee on Foreign Affairs and International Trade, *Advancing Canadian Foreign Policy Objectives in the South Caucasus and Central Asia* (Ottawa: SCFAIT, 2001).

21 Canada, *International Policy Statement: A Role of Pride and Influence in the World.* Commerce section, 1.

22 Expert Panel on Commercialization, Volume One: Final Report of the Expert Panel on Commercialization (Ottawa: Public Works and Government Services of Canada, 2006). <strategis.ic.gc.ca/epic/internet/inepc-gdc.nsf/en/home>, retrieved January 2006.

23 D. Black and P. McKenna, "Canada and Structural Adjustment in the South: The Significance of the Guyana Case," *Canadian Journal of Development Studies* (vol. 16, n. 1, 1995); M. Burdette, "Structural Adjustment and Canadian Aid Policy," in C. Pratt, ed., *Canadian International Development Assistance Policies: An Appraisal* (Montreal-Kingston: McGill-Queen's University Press, 1994), 210-239; C. Pratt, "Humane Internationalism and Canadian Development Assistance Policies," *Canadian International Development Assistance Policies,* 334–370.

24 D. Black and P. McKenna, "Canada and Structural Adjustment in the South: The Significance of the Guyana Case."

25 Massé quoted in Canada, "Minutes of Proceedings and Evidence of the Standing Committee on External Affairs and International Trade" (Second Session of the 34th Parliament, December 7, 1989).

26 Standing Committee on External Affairs and International Trade, *Securing Our Global Future: Canada's Stake in the Unfinished Business of Third World Debt* (Ottawa: Ministry of Supply and Services, 1990), 20–21.

27   This argument can be found in C. Pratt, "Humane Internationalism and Canadian Development Assistance Policies," *Canadian International Development Assistance Policies*, 210-239.

28   Publicly disclosed CIDA programs for specific countries can be found at <les.acdi-cida.gc.ca/project-browser>. Many programs, however, remain undisclosed and require a lengthy and not-guaranteed-to-be-successful Access to Information request.

29   Departments of Foreign Affairs and International Trade and Finance, "Report on Operations Under the Bretton Woods Related Agreements Act (Ottawa: International Trade and Finance Branch, 2004), 10.

30   International Monetary Fund, "Evaluation of the IMF's Role in Poverty Reduction Strategy Papers and Poverty Reduction Growth Facility" (Washington: IMF, 2004) 3,4. See also Canadian Council for International Cooperation and Halifax Initiative, "At the Table or In the Kitchen? CIDA's New Aid Strategies, Developing Country Ownership and Donor Conditionality," <www.halifaxinitiative.org/index.php/Debt_SAP_Reports?AtTheTable>, retrieved October 2006.

31   Quoted in CIDA, *Expanding Opportunities Through Private Sector Development* (Ottawa: Ministry of Public Works and Government Services, 2003), 3, 10. See also, among other things, CIDA, "A Strategy for CIDA in the Americas," <www.acdi-cida.gc.ca>, retrieved June 2006; CIDA, *CIDA's Policy on Poverty Reduction* (Ottawa: Ottawa: Ministry of Public Works and Government Services, 1996). Good background on CIDA's neoliberal orientation and its general role in supporting Canadian economic interests can be found in C. Pratt, "DFAIT's Takeover Bid of CIDA: The Institutional Future of the Canadian Development Agency," *Canadian Foreign Policy* (vol. 5, no. 2, 1998); D. Morrison, *Aid and Ebb Tide: A History of CIDA and Canadian Development Assistance* (Waterloo: Wilfred Laurier Press, 1998); and S. Cox, *Contradictions in Canadian Development Assistance: A Critical Analysis of Canadian Bilateral Aid to Costa Rica, Nicaragua, and Honduras With Reference to Structural Adjustment Conditionality* (M.A. Thesis, York University, 1992).

32   CIDA, *Canada Making a Difference in the World: A Policy Statement on Strengthening Aid and Effectiveness* (Ottawa: CIDA, 2002), 18.

33   CIDA, "A Strategy for CIDA in the Americas," <www.acdi-cida.gc.ca>, retrieved June 2005.

34   See C. Pratt, "Ethical Values and Canadian Foreign Policy: Two Case Studies," *International Journal* (vol. 56, n. 1, 2000/01).

35   B. Tomlinson, "Tracking Changes in Canadian ODA: New Directions for Poverty Reduction? Canadian NGO Reflections," International Journal (vol. 56, n. 1, 2000/2001), 55. B. Tomlinson, "Tracking Changes in Canadian ODA," 55.

36 Quoted in Standing Committee on Foreign Affairs and International Trade, *Advancing Canadian Foreign Policy Objectives in the South Caucasus and Central Asia* (Ottawa: SCFAIT, 2001).

37 Morrison, Aid and Ebb Tide, 319.

38 S. Cox, *Contradictions in Canadian Development Assistance*, 20–21.

39 B. Campbell, "Peace and Security in Africa and the Role of Canadian Mining Interests: New Challenges For Canadian Foreign Policy," *Labour, Capital and Society* (37, 2004), 104–106.

40 D. Black, "From Kananaskis to Gleneagles: Assessing Canadian 'leadership' on Africa," *Behind the Headlines* (vol. 62, n. 3, 2005), 10.

41 See Morrison, *Aid and Ebb Tide* and B. Tomlinson, "Tracking Changes in Canadian ODA." ODA/GNI statistics are from CIDA, *Statistical Report on ODA, Fiscal Year 2006-2007* (Ottawa: CIDA, 2009), 10, <www.acdi-cida.gc.ca>, retrieved July 2008.

42 Data on Third World debt and interest payments to private Canadian institutions is unfortunately not publicly available. Military budget amounts can be found at <www.forces.gc.ca/site/Reports/budget05/back05_e.asp>, retrieved June 2007. Agricultural subsidy amount was drawn from "Agricultural Subsidies," The Economist (July 1, 2006), 88.

43 CIDA, "Canada Fund for Africa: New Vision, New Partnership" (2004), <www.acdi-cida.gc.ca/CIDAWEB/acdicida.nsf/En/REN-218131222-PF5>, retrieved September 2006.

44 N. Bayne, "The New Partnership for Africa's Development and the G8's Africa Action Plan: A Marshall Plan for Africa?," in M. Fratianni, P. Savona and J. Kirton, eds., *Sustaining Global Growth and Development: G7 and IMF Governance* (Aldershot: Ashgate, 2003), 121–122.

45 P. Bond, *Looting Africa: The Economics of Exploitation* (London: Zed Books, 2006), 125ff.

46 D. Black, "From Kanaskis to Glengeagles," 6.

47 J. Dillon, "Reflections on the Gleneagles 2005 G8 Summit," *Kairos: Canadian Ecumenical Justice Initiatives* (July, 2005). <www.kairoscanada.org/e/economic/debt/reflectionsG8summit.asp?id=1>, retrieved Novembe, 2006.

48 Countries qualify for HIPC relief if they qualify under IMF and World Bank arbitrary determinations of whether or not their debt is "sustainable." A country's debt is sustainable if the Net Present Value of the debt is less than twice as large (200 percent) as the country's export earnings, or if annual debt service payments are less than twenty percent of export earnings.

49 For a discussion of this, see Bond, *Looting Africa*, 26. On the Canadian state's participation, see <www.fin.gc.ca/toc/2005/cdre0105-eng.asp>, retrieved January 2007.

50 Social Justice Committee, "Canada's representatives at the IMF agree to suspend G7 debt relief plan for six," <www.s-j-c.net/English/news/ IMFsuspendsdebtplan.html>, retrieved December 2006.

51 Finance Canada, <www.fin.gc.ca/toc/2005/cdre0105-eng.asp>.

52 Finance Canada, "Canada Cancels All Debt Owed By Haiti," <www.fin. gc.ca/n08/09-068-eng.asp>, retrieved July 2009; Finance Canada, <www. fin.gc.ca/toc/2005/cdre0105-eng.asp>.

53 Quoted in L. Pratt, "New business from Canadian-Chilean free trade?" *CA Magazine* (130(2), March, 1997), 11.

54 N. Strizzi, "Hemispheric Free Trade: Some Important Implications for Canada."

55 The trade negotiator is quoted in Purvis, "Canada 2005 Special Report: New Force in the Hemisphere," Time (June 28, 1998), 32; Daudelin, "Foreign Policy at the Fringe."

56 Department of Foreign Affairs, "Investment. Canadian Government Positions and Policies. FTAA." <www.international.gc.ca/tna-nac/other/ invest-en.asp>, retrieved September 2006.

57 Standing Committee on Foreign Affairs and International Trade, *Strengthening Canada's Links With the Americas* (Ottawa: Standing Committee on Foreign Affairs and International trade, 2002), 29.

58 Standing Committee on Foreign Affairs and International Trade, *Strengthening Canada's Economic Links With the Americas.*

59 Standing Committee on Foreign Affairs and International Trade, *Strengthening Canada's Economic Links with the Americas,* 8.

60 Standing Committee on Foreign Affairs and International Trade, *Strengthening Canada's Economic Links with the Americas,* 8.

61 Department of Foreign Affairs, *Opening Doors to the World: Canada's International Market Access Priorities,* 2003 and 2004 editions. <www.dfait-maeci.gc.ca>, retrieved April 2005.

62 Among other sources, see J. Hristov, *Blood and Capital: The Paramilitarization of Colombia* (Ohio University Press, 2009) and F. Hylton, *Evil Hour in Colombia* (London: Verso, 2006).

63 Agreement on Labour Cooperation Between Canada and the Republic of Colombia (2008), <www.hrsdc.gc.ca/en/labour/labour_agreement/ ccalc/index.shtml>, retrieved December 2008.

64 M. Murillo, "Threats Mount Against the Indigenous Social Movement in Colombia," (September 8, 2008), <www.colombiajournal.org/colombia293. htm>, retrieved November 2000.

65 M. Murillo, "Violent History Repeats Itself For Indigenous Communities in Colombia," (October 15, 2008), <www.colombiajournal.org/ colombia296.htm>, retrieved November 2008.

66 Foreign Affairs and International Trade, "Trade Agreement with Peru Opens Doors to Latin America," (June 18, 2009); J. Petras, "Peru: Blood Flows in the Amazon," (June 17, 2009), <www.countercurrents.org/petras170609.htm>, retrieved July 2009; R. Zibechi, "Massacre in the Amazon: The U.S.-Peru Free Trade Agreement Sparks a Battle Over Land and Resources," (June 16, 2009), <upsidedownworld.org/main/content/view/1910/1/>, retrieved July 2009. On Canada's non-response to the repression in Peru, which compares it to Canada's vigorous condemnation of the repression of protests in Iran, see my "Acceptable versus Unacceptable Repression: A Lesson in Canadian Imperial Hypocrisy," (June 30, 2009), <www.counterpunch.org/gordon06302009.html>.

67 The OECD is an organization representing the richest countries in the world.

68 W. Dymond, "The MAI: A Sad and Melancholy Tale," in F. Hamson, M. Rudner and M. Hart, eds., *A Big League Player? Canada Among Nations,* (Toronto: Oxford University Press, 1999), 25–53.

69 While resistance to the North for some political leaders in the Third World is very much about addressing the poverty of their citizens, for many it is more about protecting the interests of local capitalists who simply cannot compete on an even playing field with those from countries such as Canada.

70 SCFAIT, *Elements of an Emerging Market Strategy for Canada. Canada* is seeking a broad asset-based definition of investment, which includes FDI as well as portfolio investment such as shorter term and often-speculative investments like stocks, bonds and mortgages. But as the Department of Foreign Affairs and International Trade acknowledges, "A large majority of members believe that short-term, speculative flows are outside the mandate of the WGTI [Working Group on Trade and Investment]," "Investment. Canadian Government Positions and Other Policies. WTO," <www.international.gc.ca/tna-nac/other/invest-en.asp>, retrieved September 2006.

71 Department of Foreign Affairs and International Trade, *Canada and the Future of the WTO* (Ottawa: Department of Foreign Affairs and International Trade, 1999), 11 (emphasis added).

72 While the discussion here refers to the negotiations for an investment agreement, Global South demands for "special and differential treatment" predate these negotiations.

73 John Dillon, "Free trade deals: what you do not see may be what you get." *Global Economic Justice Report* (Kairos, vol. 2 n. 1).

74 C. Blouin and Ann Weston, "Canada and the WTO Development Agenda," *Canadian Development Report, 2003: From Doha to Cancun: Development and the WTO* (Ottawa: North-South Institute, 2003).

75   Canada's Permanent Mission to the WTO, "Communication from Canada to the WTO working group on the relationship between trade and investment. Development Provisions." July 2, 2002. Paragraph 3. <www.international. gc.ca/tna-nac/documents/w113-e.pdf>, retrieved September 2006.

76   Canada's Permanent Mission to the WTO, "Communication from Canada to the WTO working group on the relationship between trade and investment. Development Provisions." Paragraph 5.

77   Alain Rugman and Alain Verbeke, "The World Trade Organization, Multinational Enterprise, and Civil Society," 84.

78   These countries are India, Jordan, Ukraine, Latvia, South Africa, Romania, Philipines, Trinidad and Tobago, Barbados, Croatia, Chile, Ecuador, Egypt, Venezuela, Panama, Costa Rica, Thailand, Uruguay, El Salvador, Lebanon and Peru. It is in negotiations with Tanzania, Indonesia, Madagascar, Vietnam, Mongolia, China and Kuwait.

79   Department of Foreign Affairs and International Trade, "Investment. Canadian Government Positions and Policies." <www.international. gc.ca/tna-nac/other/invest-en.asp>, retrieved September 2006.

80   These include the previously mentioned *Reinvigorating Economic Relations Between Canada and Asia-Pacific and Strengthening Canada's Economic Links with the Americas.*

81   John Dillon, "Free trade deals: what you do not see may be what you get." See also D. Schneiderman, "Investment Rules and the New Constitutionalism," *Law and Social Inquiry* (vol. 25 n. 3, 2000).

82   Department of Foreign Affairs and International Trade, "Investment. Canadian Government Positions and Policies." See also R. Dattu and J. Boscariol, "Protecting Foreign Investment: What Next?," *Ivey Business Journal* (January/February, 2000).

83   <www.dfait-maeci.gc.ca/tna-nac/dispute-en.asp>, retrieved December 2006. The International Institute for Sustainable Development monitors international investment treaty developments, including arbitrations. <www.iisd.org>.

84   D'Aquino and Stewart-Patterson notably argue for a multilateral system in *Northern Edge*, 266ff, while a number of witnesses at the Standing Committee on Foreign Affairs and International Trade meetings recognized the benefits of bilateral dealings. Canada's pursuit of bilateral economic deals in Latin America is also a way of isolating Brazil, which is seeking to assert itself as the regional power. Not interested in Brazil's ambitions, and not able to get its way with the FTAA and in the Organization of American States (OAS), Canada is trying to circumvent Brazil by making deals with its neighbours.

85 Halifax Initiative, "Canada's Export Development Corporation—Financing Disaster," (Halifax Initiative, 2001). <www.halifaxinitiative.org/index. php/institutions_ECAs/ART3ee78f64b217c>, retrieved October 2006.

86 <www.edc.ca/english/disclosure_9238.htm>, retrieved November 2006.

87 CIDA. Obtained under the Freedom of Information Act, A-2006-00078. The countries I received information on are: Argentina, Bolivia, Chile, Colombia, Paraguay, Ecuador, Peru, Venezuela, Brazil, Guyana, Indonesia, East Timor, Philippines, Afghanistan, Mongolia, Sudan and Nigeria.

88 Quoted in C. Arsenault, "Digging Up Canadian Dirt in Colombia," *Canadian Dimension* (November/December, 2006), 32.

89 J. Hristov, "Indigenous Struggles for Land and Culture in Cauca, Colombia," *Journal of Peasant Studies* (vol. 32, n. 1, 2005) 110; F. Ramírez Cuellar, *The Profits of Extermination* (Monroe, Maine: Common Courage Press, 2005), 38-41; Kuyek, "Legitimating Plunder: Canadian Mining Companies and Corporate Social Responsibility," in L. North, T. Clark and V. Patroni, eds., *Community Rights and Corporate Responsibility: Canadian Mining and Oil Companies in Latin America* (Toronto: Between the Lines, 2006), 209.

90 A. Ismi, "Profiting From Repression: Canadian Investment in and Trade with Colombia," <www.ckln.fm/~asadismi/colombiareport.html>, retrieved July 2006.

91 Some "aid" spending details can be found under country headings at CIDA's "Project Browser," <les.acdi-cida.gc.ca/project-browser>. However, some projects are not publicly disclosed and a long, and sometimes futile, Access to Information request process must be undertaken in order to get this information.

92 Y. Engler and A. Fenton, *Canada in Haiti: Waging War on the Poor Majority* (Halifax: Fernwood, 2005).

93 Quoted in A. Purvis, "Canada 2005 Special Report: New Force in the Hemisphere," *Time* (June 28, 1998).

94 Bourassa quoted in L. Whittington, "Mining companies deny abuses," *Toronto Star* (November 27, 2009), A8.

95 Canada, "Government Response to the Fourteenth Report of the Standing Committee on Foreign Affairs and International Trade—'Mining in Developing Countries—Corporate Social Responsibility," (2005), <cmte. par.gc.ca/cmte/CommitteeList.aspx?Lang=1&PARLSES=381&JNT=08S ELID=e24_&COM=8979>, retrieved November 2006; Halifax Initiative, "Moving Beyond Voluntarism: A Civil Society Analysis of the Government Response to the Standing Committee on Foreign Affairs and International Trade's 14th Report, 'Mining in Developing Countries—Corporate Social Responsibility,' 38th Parliament, 1st Session," <www.halifaxinitiative.org/ updir/Final_Civil_Society_Analysis-Eng.pdf>, retrieved October 2006

96   Mining Watch, "Government Not Serious About Accountability for Extractive Companies," (March 30, 2009), <www.miningwatch.ca/index.php?/corporate_social_res/not_serious_about_csr>, retrieved May 2009; B. Popplewell, "One man's defence of a national reputation," *Toronto Star* (November 22, 2009), A10.

97   Indian and Northern Affairs Canada, "Canada's Position: UN Draft Declaration on the Rights of Indigenous Peoples," (2009), <www.ainc-inac.gc.ca/ap/ia/pubs/ddr/ddr-eng.asp>, retrieved July, 2009; S. Edwards, "Canada set to oppose UN native rights deal," National Post (September 13, 2007), A1; R. SeGuin, "Canada criticized for bid to amend rights deal," *Globe and Mail* (September 26, 2003), A6.

98   Morrison, *Aid and Ebb Tide*.

99   Quoted in Morrison, *Aid and Ebb Tide*, 395.

100 G. York and S. Chase, "Ottawa aims to rebuild frayed ties with China," *Globe and Mail* (January 17, 2007).

101 This cold calculus informing Canada's human rights stance is not necessarily new. At the beginning of the chapter I noted Canadian corporations' historic investment in countries ruled by military dictatorships. Cranford Pratt also discusses Canada's human rights-business calculus with respect to apartheid in South Africa under the Brian Mulroney government in the 1980s. As he shows, Mulroney's orientation toward South Africa was driven by economic opportunism and not by principle. Mulroney's decision to support the anti-apartheid boycott was inspired by a section of the South African ruling class's decision that, given the growing political and economic instability in their country in the 1980s, apartheid was no longer tenable. But when the political and economic situation seemed to calm, and the pro-apartheid section of the South African ruling class regained influence, Mulroney's anti-apartheid position softened. C. Pratt, "Ethical Values in Canadian Foreign Policy." However, as Canadian corporations continue to spread to the Third World at record rates, the conflict between business interests and human rights will only become more pronounced.

102 Statistics Canada, *Canada's International Investment Position*, <www.40.statcan.ca/l01/cst01/econ08.htm, retrieved October, 2008>; UNCTAD, *World Investment Report, 2008*, <www.unctad.org/Templates/Page.asp?intItemID=1485&lang=1>, 76, retrieved September 2009.

103 UNCTAD, World Investment Directory Online, "Key Data," table 23.

104 Department of Foreign Affairs and International Trade, *Sixth Annual Report on Canada's State of Trade* (Ottawa: Minister of Public Works and Government Services, 2005); Industry Canada, *Trade and Investment Monitor* (Ottawa: Minister of Public Works and Government Services, 2003). Data for chart two is drawn from Cansim tables 376-0051

and 376-0053. The former table provides a country-specific breakdown of CDI, while the latter provides aggregated data for regions. Thus total CDI into the Global South is taken from 376-0053. However, the category that most closely corresponds in this table to the Third World is "all other foreign countries," which is non-OECD and -EU countries, and so it is an imperfect account of investment into the South. Table 376-0051 does have specific data for Mexico, which is a member of the OECD, so I added Mexican data to that of 376-0053's "all other foreign countries" to get my Global South totals.

105 Cansim table 376-0051. Latin America and the Caribbean is obviously the most heavily represented region in this grouping. Two other Asia-Pacific countries—Philippines (twelfth) and Malaysia (fourteenth)—make it into the top fifteen fastest-growing destinations of CDI.

106 Data on FDI stock to the Third World is from Source OECD, International Direct Investment Statistics, "Direct Investment By Country," using the "Total World, excluding-OECD" and "Mexico" data sets. Data on GDP is from OECD, "Stat Extracts," <stats.oecd.org/WBOS/index.aspx>, both retrieved October 2008. Data for Italian FDI into Mexico is unavailable for a number of years, though this should not affect the trends depicted in the chart, since Mexico comprised a tiny proportion of Italian FDI to the Third World. Japanese data for 1995 and 1996 is unavailable. German figures for "Total World, excluding OECD" aren't available for 2002 and 2003. And American data for 2002 to 2005 is not available.

107 Data on regional make-up of investment to the Third World is drawn from Cansim tables 376-0051 and 376-0053.

108 The top ten fastest growing destinations from 1987 to 2007 are, in order: China, Peru, Chile, Cayman Islands, Barbados, Bahamas, Colombia, Costa Rica, Mexico and Argentina.

109 For Latin America and the Caribbean data: Economic Commission for Latin America and the Caribbean (ECLAC), *Foreign Investment in Latin America and the Caribbean, 2006* <www.eclac.org/default. asp?idioma=IN, 2007>; ECLAC, Canada's Trade and Investment With Latin America and the Caribbean (Washington: ECLAC, 2003). For Indonesia, "FDI Project Approval," Indonesian Central Bank, <www.bi.go. id/biweb/html/sekiTxt/T3x805.txt>, retrieved October 2008; Malaysia, Central Bank of Malaysia, <www.bnm.gov.my/index.php?ch=109&pg=2 49&mth=8&yr=2008>, retrieved October 2008; Philippines, Central Bank of the Philippines, <www.bsp.gov.ph/statistics/spei_new/tab22.htm>, retrieved October 2008. Data for several countries in Latin America and many countries in Asia-Pacific is quite sparse, so it is difficult to properly situate Canada among other investor nations in them.

110 National Bank of Kazakhstan, "Statistics," (2009), <www.nationalbank. kz>, retrieved July 2009; Natural Resources Canada, *Canadian Mineral Yearbook, 2007* (Ottawa: Natural Resources Canada, 2008); National Bank of the Kyrgyz Republic, "Balance of Payments," (2008), <www.nbkr. kg/balance/Bal_3Q_2008_E.pdf>, retrieved July 2009; National Bank of Tajikistan, "Report On Private Non-guaranteed External Debt and Foreign Investment for the Republic of Tajikistan for 2008," <www.nbt.tj/en/ files/docs/pl_balans/vnesh_dolg_en.pdf>, retrieved July 2009.

111 Cansim table 376-0001. Developing country data here is from the table's "all other countries" category, which excludes OECD and EU nations. Thus my estimate of Global South investment income as a proportion of total foreign investment income is a conservative estimate, as Mexico, which is an OECD member and a major destination for CDI, is not included.

112 Foreign profits are from Cansim 376-0001, "investment income." Domestic profits are from 187-0001, "total all industries, after tax." Developing country earnings are after tax as well. The comparison is imperfect, as the operating profit methodology includes some write downs, such as for inventory, while the foreign investment profits, collected on a Gross Domestic Product (GDP) basis, do not. Canadian-based profits collected on a GDP-basis are not after tax.

113 W. Carroll, *Corporate Power in a Globalizing World*, 74.

114 Industry Canada, *Trade and Investment Monitor* (Ottawa: Minister of Public Works and Government Services, 2003) and Statistics Canada, "Recent Trends in Canadian Direct Investment Abroad: The Rise of Canadian Multinationals, 1969–1992," (Ottawa: Statistics Canada, 1997).

115 Cansim table 376-0053. Data for the Machinery and Transportation Equipment and Wood and Paper sectors is suppressed for confidentiality reasons, so their precise composition of the total cannot be calculated.

116 Statistics Canada, "Canadian Direct Investment in 'Offshore Financial Centres'," (Ottawa: Statistics Canada, 2005).

117 Committee on the Global Financial System, *Foreign Direct Investment in the Financial Sector of Emerging Market Economies* (Washington: Bank of International Settlements, 2004), 6.

118 Committee on the Global Financial System, *Foreign Direct Investment in the Financial Sector of Emerging Market Economies*, 6.

119 Investment Executive, "Scotiabank signs final Dominican Republic agreement," *Investment Executive* (September 19, 2003); Paul Waldie, "Scotiabank in an acquisitive mood," *Globe and Mail* (August 30, 2000), B3; S. Silcoff, "Quietly, Scotia Builds and Empire," *National Post* (August 3, 2007), FP1.

120 T. Perkins and A. Willis, "TD continues to work the U.S. angle," *Globe and Mail* (May 20, 2009) B1, 4.

121 Quoted in A. Willis, "No mergers here, banks look abroad," *Globe and Mail* (January 18, 2007), B3.

122 CMA Management, "Ready for the reconstruction," *CMA Management* (April, 2004).

123 Canadian Life and Health Insurance Association, *Factbook* (Canadian Life and Health Insurance Association, 2006).

124 ECLAC, *Canadian Trade and Investment With Latin America and the Caribbean* (Chile: ECLAC, 2003).

125 C. Maclean, "Nortel's new challenge: Iraq's logistical nightmares," *Globe and Mail* (November 28, 2006), B2.

126 This data is collected by the Stockholm International Peace Research Institute, <www.sipri.org/contents/armstrad/at_gov_ind_data.htm> 1, retrieved October 2008.

127 Foreign Affairs and International Trade, "Report on Exports of Military Goods From Canada, 2002–2005," (Ottawa: Foreign Affairs and International Trade, 2007), www.dfait-maeci.gc.ca/eicb/military/documents/Military_Report2007-en.pdf, retrieved October, 2008.

128 Natural Resources Canada, *Canadian Mineral Yearbook, 2004* (Ottawa: Natural Resources Canada, 2004), 7.3.

129 The remaining four countries are the United States, Australia, Turkey and Sweden.

130 Natural Resources Canada, *Canadian Mineral Yearbook; 2004*; Natural Resources Canada, *Canadian Mineral Yearbook, 2007* (Ottawa: Natural Resources Canada, 2007), 7.1-7.3. The data on number of Canadian companies in the top twenty investors in Latin America from 1989-2001 is from Campodónico and Ortiz, *Caracteristicas de la inversion y del mercado mundial de la mineria principios de la decade 2000*, (Chile: ECLAC, 2002).

131 Canada is a member of the Cairns Group, where it advocates strongly for an end to tariffs and subsidies in the agricultural sector, despite maintaining its own significant trade barriers.

132 J. Madeley, *Hungry for Trade: How the Poor Pay for Free Trade* (Halifax: Fernwood, 2000), 73-74.

133 Kuyek, "Legitimating Plunder," 2006, J. Moore, "Canada throws Ecuador into reverse," The Tyee (July 11, 2008), <News/2008/07/11/CanMining/>, retrieved July, 2008; I. Harris, "Ecuador's Mineral Crossroads: Canada's Commitment?" *Focal Point* (June, 2008), <www.focal.ca/publications/focalpoint/fp0608/?article=article2&lang=e>, retrieved July 2008.

134 Industry Canada, *Trade and Investment Monitor* (Ottawa: Minister of Public Works and Government Services, 2003); Industry Canada, *Trade and Investment Monitor* (Ottawa: Minister of Public Works and Government Services, 2002).

135 WTO Secretariat, Trade Policy Review: Canada. Trade Policy Review Body. <www.wto.org/English/tratop_e/tpr_e/tp_rep_e.htm>, retrieved September 2006.

136 John Wiebe, "Put your tariffs where your mouth is: if Canada truly favours free trade and really wants to help poor countries, why keep them out of our markets?," *Globe and Mail* (April 3, 2002).

137 "Agricultural subsidies," *Economist* (July 1, 2006), 88.

138 D. Black, "From Kananaskis to Gleneagles," 2.

139 WTO Secretariat, Trade Policy Review: Canada.

140 J. Wiebe, "Put your tariffs where your mouth is: if Canada truly favours free trade and really wants to help poor countries, why keep them out of our markets?" and C. Blouin and Ann Weston, "Canada and the WTO Development Agenda."

141 The Doha round was launched in November 2001.

142 Quoted in *Globe and Mail*, "Canada, the bad boy of WTO talks?" (June 23, 2006), A21.

143 J. Simpson, "The ugly Canadian at the global trade talks," *Globe and Mail* (July 29, 2008), A11.

144 S. McBride, *Paradigm Shift*, 117, L. Diebel, "Canada foils UN water plan," *Toronto Star* (April 12, 2008), A1.

CHAPTER 4:
Violence and Eco-Disaster: Canadian Corporations in the Third World

As **Canadian multinational corporations** expand their interests into the Global South, they are leaving a legacy of human tragedy and ecological disaster. Canadian corporations are no different from their counterparts from other core capitalist nations: when they push their way into Third World countries, usually against the wishes of local communities, they do so for one reason and one reason only—profit. Indigenous and labour rights and ecological responsibility are seen as barriers to Canada's corporate interests; indeed, corporations' expansion into the South is motivated in part by the hope that such issues will not interfere with their business plans. To the extent that Canadian corporations ever pay heed to human rights or community demands, it is because fierce, determined and well-organized community resistance has forced them to; it is never done out of altruism.

This chapter offers a survey of case studies of abuses against people and their environment by Canadian capital from a number of different economic sectors, which often has the financial and political support of the Canadian state. The survey is not intended to be an exhaustive documentation of all acts of Canadian corporate malfeasance abroad. That would require a book of its own. The aim instead is to give readers a sense of the widespread nature of this corporate plunder, and to demonstrate that it is not limited to a few isolated incidents that could be explained away as exceptions to the rule of an otherwise humane and environmentally sensitive Canadian capitalism. Abuses of human rights and eco-devastation are in fact a normal part of doing business for Canadian capital, a reality that makes a mockery of the idea that corporations can be socially responsible and should therefore be allowed to self-monitor their international practices. Considering the stories of abuse and devastation that follow, claims of socially responsible practices, as common now on corporate websites as financial reports, ring hollow.[1]

The case studies are all from the last fifteen years. This is not to suggest that Canadian corporate abuses of human rights or of the environment abroad are a new thing; they are not.[2] The primary focus of this book is the contemporary period of neoliberal globalization, in which state-backed Canadian corporate plundering of the Third World is becoming much more commonplace. Thus I am going to focus on contemporary conflicts arising as Canadian corporations circle the globe in the quest of building their new empires. The case studies should make clear that Canadian foreign investment into the Third World, often financed and supported by the state, is an imperialist endeavour that benefits capital at the expense of the world's poor and their environment.

Many of the struggles against Canadian investments discussed in the pages that follow are ongoing. Readers should look for updates from NGO and independent and (occasionally) mainstream media sources.

Mining
Corona Goldfields and Greystar Resources
Vancouver-based Corona, a subsidiary of Conquistador Mines, and Greystar have both had brief but violent turns in Colombia. Given the legacy of violence associated with foreign investment in Colombia, and the recent history of Canadian investment in a number of different sectors there, it is worth looking first at the context which any Canadian corporation is entering when it invests in the country

Rich in resources such as gold, coal, nickel, copper, iron ore, petroleum, natural gas and hydro power, Colombia is one of the most dangerous places in the world to oppose economic restructuring and corporate investment. Privatization, foreign investment and extreme inequalities are maintained through extraordinary levels of military and paramilitary violence. This terror, primarily directed at trade unionists and indigenous peoples and peasants whose land contains subsurface riches, has increased with neoliberal restructuring and the growing presence of foreign, including Canadian, corporations. While the main guerrilla forces, the Revolutionary Armed Forces of Colombia (FARC) and the National Liberation Army (ELN), have also committed atrocities against social movement actors, state security forces and paramilitaries account for the majority of these incidents (see Table 4.1).

TABLE 4.I. SHARE OF RESPONSIBILITY FOR NON-COMBATANT DEATHS AND FORCED DISAPPEARANCES[3]

	1993	1995	1996	1997	1998	1999	2000
Guerrillas	28%	38%	36%	23.5%	21.3%	19.6%	16.3%
Security Forces	54%	16%	18%	7.4%	2.7%	2.4%	4.6%
Paramilitary	18%	46%	46%	69%	76%	78%	79.2%

While the formal separation of military and paramilitary forces was belied in practice by a spirit of cooperation and coordination in pacifying Colombian social movements, the largest paramilitary forces have actually become integrated into Colombia's state apparatus in the last several years under President Alvaro Uribe.[4]

Colombia stands without close rival in the world today for the number of trade unionists assassinated. Since 1991, more than 2,000 labour activists have been killed. Forty-two percent of human rights violations against unionists take place in the mining-energy sector. Ninety-seven percent of the homicides against unionists have been perpetrated by military and paramilitary actors, with three percent being carried out by guerrillas and other armed actors. [5]

Meanwhile, close to four million people have been forcibly displaced in Colombia, two million of them from mining regions as military and paramilitary forces make way for foreign capital.[6] This displacement is bound up with extraordinary levels of violence in the mining zones. In the municipalities of these zones, between 1995 and 2002 "there have been 828 homicides, 142 forced disappearances, 117 people injured, 71 people tortured, 355 death threats, and 150 arbitrary detentions, every year. In addition there have been 433 massacres, which when added to the homicides gives a total figure of 6,625 homicides during those eight years."[7] Whether or not foreign corporations are working directly with paramilitaries (and sometimes they are), they benefit from this culture of violence, which enables them to pursue exploration and resource development on what were once inhabited lands. Furthermore, the violence is compounded by an abysmal social situation. GDP per capita was US$7,900 in 2005.[8] Yet, sixty-four percent of the population lives below the poverty line, twenty-three percent in absolute poverty. The worst rates are to be found in mining zones. Less than two percent of the population owns roughly fifty-three percent of the land.[9] Eleven million of the country's 43,593,000 citizens do not meet their basic food requirements. Adequate health care, education and employment are exclusive privileges of a small elite. This is the context of Canadian corporate investment in Colombia.

In 1997, Corona expressed interest in a gold mine in the town of Simiti, which is located in the southern region of the Bolivar department in the northern part of the country. Thirty-five thousand poor small-scale miners, who had been working the mine for thirty years, along with the Higuera-Palacios family, claimed ownership of the mine. But around the time Corona expressed interest in the mine, according to Francisco Ramírez Cuellar, president of the Colombian Mineworkers Union (Sintraminercol), paramilitaries began appearing in Simiti and nearby communities asserting their goal of handing the area over to multinational corporations. In March 1997, paramilitaries killed nineteen people in communities around Simiti. In April, in the town of Rio Viejo, they cut off the head of small-scale miner Juan Camacho, and placed it on top of a long stick facing the mining zone as a warning about where they planned to attack next. In July, the paramilitaries tortured and killed the vice president of the Agromining Association of the South of Bolivar (Asogromisbol), with which the majority of the poor small-scale miners are associated. Through July/ August of that same year, 5,000 people were forced to flee from their communities by paramilitaries. Killings of poor miners in the area continued through 1998 and 1999. It has been estimated that from 1998 to 2000, paramilitaries killed 259 people in the south of Bolivar, burnt down 689 homes and pillaged seven villages. Conquistador eventually abandoned the Simiti project amidst controversy, though it has interests in other regions of the country, such as in Marmato, where it is alleged to have bought properties from small-scale miners without fully compensating them.[10]

Greystar initially began investing in Colombia in the mid- to late 1990s. Under pressure from guerrillas near one of its projects, the company promised to undertake public works in the area for the benefit of people living there. When it failed to follow through, however, Greystar faced protests and was subsequently expelled from the region. Months later, the Colombian military began operations there to help Greystar recover its machinery. According to locals, these operations led to human rights violations.[11]

The context for mining deteriorated temporarily in the late 1990s. In 1998, Greystar executive Norbert Reinhart was held captive by FARC guerrillas for ninety-four days after he exchanged places with an employee from Terramundo Drilling Inc., a Canadian company contracted by Greystar to drill on its Angostura project, who had been kidnapped. Reinhart was released unharmed, reportedly in exchange for US$200,000 in ransom money, but the incident sparked renewed fears among Canadian mining investors and employees.[12] Growing security concerns were compounded by declining prices in gold on the world market, causing ten Canadian companies—Gran Colombia, Chivor, Latin Gold, Venoro, Odin, Bolivar, Randsburg, Continental, Santa Catalina, and Resource Equity—to abandon the country between 1997 and 1998.[13]

However, the new political and economic context in Colombia—with its neoliberal reforms and the increased strength of paramilitaries—is once again attracting Canadian mining capitalists. There were at least eight Canadian companies in Colombia with fourteen different exploration projects as of 2007.[14] According to data in the *Canadian Mineral Yearbook*, published by Natural Resources Canada, by 2004 Canadian companies held "the dominant share of the larger companies' exploration market in ... Colombia."[15] Furthermore, there are clear signs that the participation of Canadian corporations in the mining sector will increase in the coming years. In 2001 alone, Canadian corporations invested $869 million in the mining and petroleum sectors combined.[16] Greystar renewed exploration in 2003 with gusto. The company now "has eight drill rigs working and [its] successful return has made it something of a poster child for Colombian authorities keen to show that the country is safe for investors and ripe for investment." The Canadian company is understood to be "the vanguard of Colombia's gold mining renaissance, as it puts the troubles of the past behind it and works toward a feasibility study for its 10-million-ounce Angostura gold property near Bucaramanga, in Santander department, having so far spent $48-million on the project." [17] Greystar president David Rovig cites Uribe's so-called peasant militia initiative, a paramilitary force designed to aid the military in controlling Colombia's countryside, as a principal reason for Greystar's return to the country. "The peasant troop initiative and other new ideas are really making a big difference ... It is better because the area is supported by military and by the police and it simply was not in the past." [18]

Barrick Gold

Toronto-based Barrick is the largest gold producer in the world, with properties—and opposition movements challenging its practices—on nearly every continent. As testament to the international unpopularity of the company, May 2, 2007, was the International Day of Action against it. One of Barrick's most controversial projects is Pascua Lama. Pascua Lama is a gold, silver and copper open-pit mine site located in the Andean mountains. It straddles the border between Argentina and Chile, in the province of San Juan in Argentina and on the outer edges of the Atacama Desert in Chile. Barrick bought the mine in 1994, after the introduction of a new mining law led to a wave of foreign investment, led by Canadians, into Chile's mining sector. It plans to sink $1.6 billion into the mine's development. [19] Barrick projects "an annual production of 775,000 ounces of gold, silver, and copper over its first 10 years, with a lifespan of 21 years." [20]

From the beginning, Barrick has faced considerable opposition from community and environmental groups. [21] This opposition was sparked by Barrick's initial plans to relocate sizable portions of three large glaciers blocking certain deposits in the area. According to investigative journalist Jenn Ross, "these glaciers span approximately 24 hectares. The plan calls for moving roughly 10 hectares—about 25 acres—of that surface area, which amounts to 800,000 cubic metres of ice." Raúl Montenegro, an Argentine ecologist based at the University of Cordoba, argues that "Barrick is treating the glaciers like 'piles of ice' rather than essential parts of a fragile desert ecosystem. 'You cannot just pick up a glacier, move it, and then tell the rain to fall somewhere else.'[22]

Resistance has been led by the Coordinator for the Defence of the Huasco Valley, a coalition that brings together many local organizations amongst the 70,000 people inhabiting the waterways connecting the glaciers with the Pacific Ocean. Farmers of grapes, peaches, figs, lemons and avocados, among other crops, cultivate their land in the Huasco Valley, underneath the projected mine site. There is little rainfall in the area, so the crops are dependent on run-off water stored in the glaciers.[23]

Local communities are also concerned about water pollution, a common fear of those living near mining developments. Barrick will use 7,200 kilograms of cyanide daily, and plans to divert rivers in Argentina for cyanide solution production, which is necessary for the extraction of gold. Vice-president for corporate communications at Barrick, Vincent Borg, has also admitted that the company plans to utilize arsenic in its extraction processes. The company assures the Chilean government and community activists that it has taken all necessary precautions to prevent spillage of pollutants into streams and rivers. However, Luis Fara, a farmer and councillor in the adjacent Chilean town of Alto del Carmen, points to the fact that the extreme weather conditions at the high altitude may very well overwhelm the containment systems put in place by Barrick. The U.S. Geological Survey has also recorded three earthquakes in excess of 6.7 in magnitude in the last four years in the area. Aside from potential one-off disasters, the regular functioning of the mine promises to seriously pollute the region. Billions of tons of waste rock are projected to be stored near the Estrecho River: "Waste rock is hazardous due to a process called acid rock drainage, in which sulphuric acid as well as toxins such as mercury, arsenic and cadmium leach out of exposed waste-rock piles." These environmental concerns are intricately intertwined with the livelihood concerns of the farmers in the valley, given that any substantial leakage of cyanide, arsenic or other pollutants would wreak havoc with their means of subsistence. [24]

Protests have included demonstrations of 500 in Vallenar, Chile, on March 21, 2005, over 3,000 in Santiago on June 4, 2005, and urban protests across Chile of over 5,000 on July 10, 2005. Eighteen thousand people signed a petition rejecting the Pascua Lama mining development, and the Citizens' Foundation for the Americas petitioned the United Nations High Commission for Human Rights declaring the project a violation of the indigenous and human rights of the residents of the Huasco Valley. The movement against the Pascua Lama development has been successful in pushing the subject onto the national level of political debate. Chilean President Michelle Bachelet, for example, promised to protect the glaciers as part of her presidential campaign in 2005. In February, 2006, Chilean officials gave a green light to the Pascua Lama project, but, not insignificantly, stipulated that the glaciers must not be relocated. Barrick agreed to this restriction and continued its public relations campaign, promoting the mining development as environmentally friendly and a boon to jobs in a region plagued with high unemployment. However, the Chilean Military Geological Institute, National Agriculture Association, and the Sustainable Chile Programme have all found that the glaciers in the area are already retreating as a result of prospecting and exploration by Barrick. The corporation agreed to pay $60 million to cover any deleterious consequences stemming from mining activities in an apparently somewhat successful bid to quell public discontent. [25]

In a show of support for the project, in his trip to Chile in July 2007, Prime Minister Stephen Harper met with Barrick officials while ignoring meeting requests from Chilean activists concerned about Canadian mining practices. Environmental approvals for the mine were granted in 2007, though the Chilean and Argentine governments continued to discuss how tax revenues on the project would be divvied up into 2009. The anti-Barrick movement was reignited in May 2009 when the company announced it had been given the go-ahead by the Chilean and Argentine governments to begin construction, which it had slated for September 2009. [26]

Barrick's interests in the Ancash region of Peru have also been dogged by fierce opposition and violence. In April 2007, a regional forty-eight-hour strike, including thousands of marchers and road blockades, was called to demand the local government cancel contracts with Barrick and another company, Anatima. Police moved in aggressively to break up the demonstrations, detaining thirty protesters and killing nineteen-year-old Marvin Gonzalez Castillo, shooting him twice. Another protester died of a heart attack after being tear-gassed. But this is not the first incident of violence directed at people demonstrating against Barrick in Peru. In May 2006, community members in Huallapampa gathered to request a pay raise from Barrick. When Barrick refused, demonstrators blocked road access to the company's mines with stones and tree trunks. Barrick called the police, who moved aggressively against the blockades. In the ensuing clashes, two protesters were killed.[27]

Barrick set the stage for violent confrontations in La Rioja Argentina in early 2006, when it announced plans for a gold mining project on Mt. Famatina. Famatina is a 5,800-metre snow-capped mountain that supplies water to a region dependent on its wine, olive, walnut, fruit and vegetable, and livestock agricultural industries. Barrick, however, had the support of local governor Ángel Maza, who had been an advocate of neoliberal reforms in the mining sector and faced corruption allegations over his close relations with the Canadian gold producer.[28]

Maza had worked with former president Carlos Menem to privately rewrite Argentina's mining code, which offered foreign companies significant tax breaks, legal protections and environmental impunity. As soon as Barrick began moving into the region, women in the town of Famatina, concerned about the potential destruction of their agriculture and having experienced previous mining projects that contaminated a nearby river with acid drainage, began organizing the Neighbours of Famatina for Life to oppose the company's plans. The opposition spread rapidly, with neighbourhood councils springing up in the villages surrounding Mt. Famatina. As one activist commented sharply,

> Now they come and tell us about 'sustainable and responsible mining' but we know it does not exist. Instead of tunnels, now they blow up entire mountains with dynamite, grind up the rocks, extract gold with cyanide and acids, using tremendous amounts of water. They take the gold and the rest is called 'tailings.' The tailings and overburden are the remains of our destroyed mountain, which will continue to drain acids and heavy metals for thousands of years and contaminate everything, after leaving us without any water. What is sustainable about this?[29]

As opposition grew, some activists were attacked by police and "anonymous thugs" as they toured the region spreading information about the danger of the mining project. Undaunted, the anti-

Barrick organizing continued to grow in force. Facing a ground-swell of opposition to both Barrick and Maza, the local legislature passed legislation on March 11 to suspend Maza and bring him to trial for corruption over charges of backroom dealing with Barrick. Emboldened by the turning tide against Maza and Barrick, but not fully trusting the political process of politicians whose support, many activists felt, was fair-weather, the opposition decided to blockade the mining camp at Peñas Negras. As a result of these developments, Barrick announced the dismantling of its mining camp and the end of its exploration in the Famatina range.[30]

In 2006, Barrick acquired Vancouver-based Placer Dome Inc., and inherited another legacy of eco-devastation to complement its own. In 2005, Placer Dome had a lawsuit launched against it by the government of the Philippine province of Marinduque for over $100 million. The lawsuit relates to the company's Marcopper mine project, which received US$1.36 million from Export Development Canada (EDC), and seeks money for the cleanup and rehabilitation of polluted lands and water systems, compensation for lost livelihoods and damages for health problems caused by the mine. According to one angry Marinduque official, "after reaping the wealth of our province for decades, Placer Dome left us with nothing but lost lives, environmental destruction and the bill for the cleanup of all the toxic waste that threatens the future of our children and grandchildren."[31] Placer Dome ran the mine from 1969 to 1996, when it closed down. Until 1986, its partner was dictator Ferdinand Marcos (who was deposed that year). Despite protests from area residents, from 1975 to 1991 the company oversaw the dumping of more than 200 million tons of mine tailings into Calancan Bay, severely damaging the food security of twelve fishing villages in the surrounding area. The tailings also leached metals into the bay and are the likely cause of lead contamination found in children from nearby villages. Placer Dome was also responsible for a tailings spill in the Boac River. Three to four million tons of metal-enriched and acid-generated tailings leaked into the river when a badly sealed drainage tunnel at the base of an empty mine pit in a mountain range being used as a storage place burst.[32]

Barrick also acquired the Bulyanulu mine in Tanzania in 1999 when it took over Canadian company Sutton Resources. This project has received $173 million from EDC. The Bulyanulu mine's existence is based on violence and intimidation. In 1996, Sutton subsidiary Kahama Mining Corporation, together with Tanzanian government authorities, forcibly displaced hundreds of thousands of artisanal miners, peasant farmers, small traders and their families from the region surrounding the mine. The removal followed two years of protest against the mine project by the local residents. Residents report that fifty artisanal miners were killed after they were buried alive in mineshafts when Tanzanian authorities and company officials backfilled the shafts. According to the Lawyers' Environmental Action Team (LEAT), an organization defending the Bulyanulu residents killed and displaced in 1996, "The investment stands as a monument to the plunder of the natural resources of poor countries such as Tanzania by the multinational corporations of the rich industrial countries of the North; and the impoverishment and further marginalization of the mostly rural communities in mineral rich areas of Tanzania and elsewhere."[33]

As a result of its efforts, LEAT has been targeted by Tanzanian authorities. Two LEAT members and the chairman of the Tanzanian Labour Party were charged with sedition for their political activities around the Bulyanulu mine in late 2001. One of those persons, Tundu Antiphas Lissu, was out of the country when the charges were laid. Upon his return home in 2002, he was detained by Tanzanian police and held for over twenty-four hours in an underground jail known as "the Hole." LEAT members are prohibited from travelling and speaking about the struggles around the mine. Once again Barrick investment (following up on the groundwork laid by previous owners) proceeds by plunder.[34]

The Bulyanulu mine grabbed the attention of media and critics of Canadian mining companies in November 2007, when Prime Minister Stephen Harper visited Tanzania. Harper's visit to the country involved a meeting with Barrick officials, who are clearly concerned about the growing push in Tanzania for increased royalty rates on its investments in the country. The gold giant is growing fatter off of a liberalized mining market, while Tanzanians continue to suffer from extremely high rates of poverty. As an expression of the tension around Barrick, Harper's visit coincided with a month-long strike of 1,000 workers at Bulyanulu, in which Barrick sought to replace the workers, declaring the strike illegal.[35]

Barrick, either on its own or through its predecessor Placer Dome, has also been linked to human and environmental catastrophes in the Congo and Papua New Guinea. It is important to note that Barrick has also courted controversy in its Canadian investments. In 1995, it bought the Golden Patricia Mine from Lac Minerals. The mine is located in northern Ontario on the traditional territories of several First Nations. Those nations, organized into the Windigo First Nations Tribal Council, signed an agreement in 1988 with Lac Minerals regarding environmental protection and other benefits to be received from the project. But when the ore was depleted in 1997, the Tribal Council found that neither Lac Minerals nor Barrick had fulfilled their end of the agreement around environmental sustainability. Areas of the mine where tailings and waste rock were stored will be toxic forever, and the First Nations were unable to come to any agreement with Barrick about compensation following the closure.[36]

Ascendant Copper and Corriente Resources

Both these Vancouver-based companies have been involved in human rights controversies in Ecuador. Ascendant pursued a project in the Intag region in northwestern Ecuador. Residents in the area around the Junín copper strip mine, and the local Cotacachi government, are overwhelmingly opposed to the project and have carried out direct actions, including road blockades, to express their opposition. The mine would be within the buffer zone of the Cotacachi-Cayapas Ecological Reserve (designated as a "biodiversity hot spot" by the UN), and the communities in the region depend on small-scale farming, coffee production and eco-tourism for their survival, all of which they argue would be threatened if Ascendant were to move ahead with its project. The property was originally owned by Mitsubishi, but that company backed off because of the strong local opposition, and after an environmental assessment it conducted found that the project would cause significant deforestation, local climate change resulting in desertification, contamination of rivers by toxic chemicals and harm to a number of endangered mammal and bird species.[37]

Despite the environmental dangers of the project, and the widespread community opposition, Ascendant continued to aggressively move forward with the project in the late 1990s and early 2000s as international copper prices rose. Ascendant actually claimed it had the support of a local community group called the Corporation for the Development of the Communities of García Moreno (CODEGAM). But CODEGAM's pro-mining agenda was soundly defeated in regional elections in 2004 by anti-mining forces. The company has since admitted it helped to establish CO-DEGAM, and funded it to promote the Junín project and weaken the authority of the Cotacachi government and those who oppose the mine.[38]

Ascendant has also been linked to paramilitaries that have attacked anti-mine protests. Activists say the paramilitaries are funded by Ascendant and linked to CODEGAM. According to the Quito-based Ecumenical Human Rights Commission (CEDHU), Ascendant sent at least 120 armed paramilitaries to storm anti-mining communities that had been blockading the company's access to the Junín mine. The mayor of Cotacachi, a town near the mine, reported that protesters were shot at and pelted with stones. The confrontation escalated when prisoners were taken on both sides. Ascendant CEO Gary Davis denies the pro-mining group members were paramilitaries, and says they were instead agricultural consultants. Davis acknowledges that Ascendant does have security guards protecting company property, but insists their role is strictly defensive. Anti-mining activists counter that these forces have not been strictly defensive, and confiscated a large arsenal of weaponry from the paramilitaries, which they turned over to the government. CEDHU says that thirty-four of the fifty-seven captives taken by the anti-mining demonstrators were former members of the Ecuadorean military, and offered confiscated military ID cards as proof. Anti-Ascendant activists have also reportedly faced death threats and physical intimidation by CODEGAM members while travelling through the region.[39]

One of the persons targeted for his anti-Ascendant work is activist leader and executive director of Intag Ecological Defence and Conservation (DECOIN), Carlos Zorrilla. Zorilla has gained an international profile for his role in building the movement against Ascendant. He visited Canada in 2005 to raise awareness about the struggle against the Junín mine. In 2006, Ascendant allegedly had people infiltrate demonstrations as agent provocateurs. The infiltrators distributed pamphlets supporting the company and tried to delegitimize Zorrilla by claiming he assaulted them at the demonstration and stole $400 cash and a $1200 camera from them. The accusation led to an arrest warrant for Zorrilla, who, in a remarkable article describes being tipped off that police were coming for him and quickly going into hiding in a forest near his house. From his position in hiding, he watched seventeen police officers, some in ski masks, raid his home at six in the morning and threaten his wife and son. According to eyewitnesses, the police travelled in unmarked cars without licence plates, and at least one car belonged to Ascendant Copper. "If they had arrested me," Zorrilla declared in a subsequent visit to Ottawa, "things would have been different. I would not have been standing before you here today. They wanted me dead." The warrant was eventually lifted when supporters, including those outside of Ecuador, pointed out irregularities in the case and called for charges to be dropped.[40]

The conflict between Ascendant and its opponents culminated in September 2007, when the Minister of Mines and Petroleum for the new Ecuadorean government of populist Rafael Correa announced a total prohibition on Ascendant's Junín mine. The government had previously demanded Ascendant cease work, after it rejected the company's environmental assessment for failing to consult local communities and not fully assessing the dangers the project posed to resources and wildlife in the area. The minister stated that the company's activities were illegal because it failed to get authorization from the municipality of Cotacachi before commencing operations, as required under the country's mining law (the company had received permission from a previous government despite opposition from the regional government). Undoubtedly, the fierce local opposition to the project played a part in the decision. The minister raised the violence surrounding the conflict in his announcement and referred to the existence of "parallel armies" operating in the area. The persistent opposition from local communities, including direct action resistance targeting Ascendant property, has led (for now, at least) to a victory against Canadian imperialism in this corner of Ecuador.[41]

Corriente's subsidiary, Ecuacorriente, has also met determined resistance from communities opposed to its Mirador project in the Intag Valley. Local indigenous communities accuse the company of failing to properly consult them, and of consistently understating the impact the development will have on the local ecosystem. Ecuacorriente has nevertheless persisted with its plans. The tensions erupted in a confrontation in December 2006, in which a protest leader, indigenous congressman Salvador Quishipe, claims that he was beaten and nearly suffocated to death at Ecuacorriente's compound, where he was taken after troops dragged him from the demonstration. According to Quishipe, "They bound my hands and feet and ... wrapped my whole head, even my nose and mouth, in packing tape."[42] The CEDHU alleges that other protesters were abused by troops, including a woman who was bound, sexually assaulted and threatened with rape. For his part, Corriente CEO Kenneth Shannon dismisses the allegations, arguing that no company personnel saw any abuses take place at the company compound, and that troops peacefully dispersed an angry mob that shot at them. As a result of the clash, however, Ecuador's energy and mines ministry suspended Ecuacorriente's operations in the area indefinitely. After Ecuador's review of its mining law—a controversial process which saw large segments of the country's indigenous movements criticize Correa for being too soft on large-scale mining—Corriente was permitted to resume operations in 2010.[43]

Anvil Mining

Anvil Mining is a company headquartered in Australia but which was incorporated in the Northwest Territories, trades on the Toronto Stock Exchange, has offices in Montreal and a number of Canadian executives, and whose major shareholder during the time period discussed here was Canadian company Quantum Minerals. It was allegedly involved in a massacre of civilians in Congo's eastern province of Katanga in 2004. But Anvil is only one of several Canadian companies that have been implicated in the Congo's various humanitarian crises. So I want to first take a brief look at the history of foreign intervention in the country and more general Canadian mining involvement.

Very rich in copper, cobalt, diamonds, gold, uranium and manganese, the Congo has been subjected to a long and brutal history of imperialism, coming under Belgian control from 1885 until 1960. Ten million Congolese were killed under Belgian rule, and many more subjected to slavery and torture. U.S. meddling followed the end of Belgian rule, leading to the installation of Colonel Mobutu Sese Seko (who renamed the country Zaire) and nearly four decades of corruption and pilfering the country's resources under his authoritarian command. When Mobutu fell out of favour of the U.S. and other Western powers, they sponsored Rwanda's and Uganda's 1996 invasion (under the pretext of liberating the Congo) and the installation of Laurent Kabila in 1997. But when Kabila's popularity with the imperialists declined only a year later, after expelling Rwandan and Ugandan forces, Rwanda and Uganda invaded again (once again under the pretext of fighting for democracy) and occupied the eastern, resource-rich half. An estimated 2.5 million people have been killed in the war, and another 2.3 million displaced. But while both sides have been implicated in human rights violations, the invaders, according to Human Rights Watch, bear responsibility for most of them.[44]

According to the UN's "Report of the Panel of the Experts on the Illegal Exploitation of Natural Resources and Other Forms of Wealth of the Democratic Republic of the Congo," foreign mining companies have fuelled and profited from the war. The initial draft of the report—which was significantly watered down for its final version after a campaign by the Canadian companies, supported by Canada, cited in it—named several Canadian companies as contributors to the conflict. More than a dozen Canadian companies have invested in the Congo since the initial invasion by Rwanda and Uganda; they are: Kinross, Katanga, Anvil, Barrick, American Mineral Fields, Tenke Mining, Banro Resource, Consolidated Trillion, First Quantum Minerals, International Panorama Resource, Melkior Resources, Samax Gold and Starpoint Goldfields. Even before Laurent Kabila came to power several Canadian companies signed deals with him to exploit the country's mineral deposits. Kabila even sent a representative to Toronto to meet with Canadian mining executives. One observer suggests that the visit may have raised $50 million to support Kabila's final victory over Mobutu. Kabila also reportedly established a circle of Canadian advisers to advance the exploitation of the Congo's resources.[45]

The province of Katanga in southeastern Congo is very rich in mineral wealth, and several Canadian companies, including Anvil, have invested in the region. A report on mining in Katanga by

London-based Global Witness suggests that at least three-quarters of the minerals exported from the region are exported illegally, and that government officials regularly collude with mining companies to enable the latter to avoid regulations and taxes. Miners make two to three dollars a day, commonly work without protective clothing or equipment and many die every year from easily preventable accidents. Wealth flows out of the province and into the hands of foreign mining companies, while people in the region live in penury with little in the way of infrastructure or public services.[46]

Violence in the war-ravaged province is still common, and thus is a part of doing business there. In 2006, three Anvil employees were charged by a Congolese military court with complicity in war crimes committed by government soldiers in 2004. The employees, whose company received a $4 million loan from the Canada Pension Plan for its Dikulushi mine in Katanga, were eventually cleared of complicity by the court in June, 2007. Nevertheless, the court's decision cannot be seen as a genuine vindication of the company's innocence. According to eyewitness reports, in October 2004 the Congolese armed forces violently put down a small uprising in the nearby fishing town of Kilwa. Despite those leading the uprising offering no resistance when the army arrived, as many as 100 unarmed civilians were killed. The soldiers carried out summary killings, arbitrary arrests and torture of suspected rebels and their supporters. Anvil has acknowledged offering logistical support to the army for the operation. Because Kilwa is difficult to access by road, the army used Anvil planes to fly in soldiers from the provincial capital of Lubumbashi. Anvil also provided the army with vehicles to assist in the military assault, to transport people who had been arbitrarily detained and to remove corpses. Anvil claims it had no idea what was planned for the military operation and that the three employees who were charged in the affair were coerced into providing the army with support. The court accepted this defence. At the end of the day, though, Anvil—willingly or not—facilitated this tragedy. Human rights organizations and NGOs monitoring the region have argued that companies that operate in such conflict zones must be aware that their operations can either directly or indirectly result in human rights violations; and, it should be added, it is very unlikely that any multinational corporation would be oblivious to this reality.[47]

The "Kilwa massacre" is not the only incidence of violence surrounding Anvil's operations. Anvil had to temporarily close down its mine in 2006 after protesters burned down a company guesthouse in the town of Kolwezi, killing two people. According to Anvil spokesperson Robert La Vallière, the protesters consisted of illegal peasant miners, but "We do not know what the group is protesting about."[48]

Goldcorp

In 2006, Vancouver-based Goldcorp acquired Glamis Gold Ltd., another Vancouver-based gold mining company, and with it the Marlin mine in Guatemala. The Marlin mine, located in the highlands 130 kilometres northwest of Guatemala City, was a very controversial investment long before it became operational in 2005, with the killing of two people having been linked to the project.

Marlin, which received $63 million from Canada Pension Plan investments, is one of the first major mining developments since the official end of Guatemala's bloody civil war in 1996; and it has been a test case for foreign companies, as the country has been opened up for renewed foreign investment. Much of the bloodshed (over 100,000 people were killed), caused by paramilitary death squads backed by the United States, was directed against indigenous people in the region where Marlin is located, and so the foreign intrusion and the security surrounding it have been cause for considerable concern amongst indigenous people. Indigenous people are also concerned that the mine, which contains as much as 225,000 ounces of gold, will use cyanide to leach out the gold and about 760,000 litres of groundwater per minute, threatening the sustainability of local farming on which they rely. Despite the environmental dangers, indigenous peoples say they were never consulted about the mine. Glamis claimed it organized hundreds of consultation meetings in 2003 and 2004, but indigenous people counter that the meetings were really only promotional sessions that offered no opportunity for meaningful consultation. In June 2005, local farmers organized a referendum on the project, and the mine was rejected by ninety-eight percent of voters. Glamis ignored the results.[49]

Facing an extremely obstinate foreign company, opponents have engaged in direct action against the mine to try and physically stop it from moving ahead. Beginning in December 2004, pro-testers blocked a convoy of mining equipment destined for Marlin for forty-two days. The blockade ended when police attacked it, firing on protesters. One protester, Raul Castro Bocel, was shot and killed and several more were injured. In January 2005, a local bishop led an anti-mine protest of 3,000 people in the provincial capital, and has subsequently faced death threats as a result. Then in March 2005, local resident Alvaro Sanchez was shot dead in the street walking home from a parish church of San Miguel Ixta-huacán by a security guard working for Glamis. That same month, a vehicle belonging to an indigenous leader was torched, and he and two other anti-mine activists received death threats. Clearly, opposing the Marlin mine is dangerous business.[50]

In late 2007 the trial against a group of Mayan farmers known as the Goldcorp 7 began. In January 2007, representatives from com-munities opposed to the Marlin Mine submitted a petition to the company listing their opposition to the project and a number of grievances. Their complaint was dismissed by the company and, according to the community representatives, they were insulted by company officials. On their way home from the company of-fices, the community representatives were attacked by Goldcorp security. Rocks were thrown at them, guns fired and security tried to force one person into a car. The activists managed to defend themselves, but when they reported the incident to police no ac-tion was taken on their behalf. After learning about Goldcorp's re-sponse to the petition, later that same day 600 people from towns that neighbour the Marlin mine began to blockade the roads to the company installations. The National Civil Police's riot squad was called, and was soon joined by upwards of 500 Guatemalan soldiers. Despite the state's aggressive show of force, the block-ades were held for more than ten days, forcing the company to agree to negotiations. But as soon as the blockades were lifted, the company declared it was no longer going to negotiate, and in-stead initiated penal charges against twenty-two local residents. Seven of those people had arrest warrants issued against them. Two community leaders were violently detained by National Civil Police officers—transported in Goldcorp vehicles—at their home in the early morning hours. In a rare positive turn of events that speaks to how outrageous the charges were, however, the judges overseeing the trial eventually acquitted five of the seven and put the other two on probation and levied $500 fines.[51]

Despite Goldcorp's heavy-handed approach to defending its investment, opposition to the project continues. In June 2008, Gregoria Perez, a local Mayan farmer opposed to Marlin, intentionally damaged a powerline Goldcorp ran across her property to feed its mill. When Goldcorp employees went to fix the line they were blocked by anti-Marlin activists. As the fight over the power line, and the mine more generally, continued in July, Canada's Secretary of State (Foreign Affairs and International Trade) Helena Guergis visited Guatemala where she met with representatives of Canadian investors. The press release announcing her visit describes Guatemala as an important partner of Canada in the region.[52]

In June 2009, Goldcorp illegally brought exploration equipment and vehicles onto community and private property of the Mayan Mam population of Sacmuj in the village of Agel after its efforts to purchase land from residents failed. After receiving complaints from local residents, Goldcorp signed an agreement to withdraw its equipment, vehicles and workers on June 12. At the same time, Goldcorp requested and received a police and army presence to, along with private company security, protect its workers. When the company failed to uphold the agreement, exploration equipment and a vehicle were burned. The situation surrounding Goldcorp's presence in Guatemala remains very tense.[53] It is also worth noting that Goldcorp has a number of gold mines in Canada, including one of the world's richest, the Red Lake Complex in northern Ontario. In 1996, Goldcorp forced the Steelworkers (USWA) Local 950 into a bitter strike when the company demanded major contract concessions. Goldcorp used scabs against the union. It turned into the longest strike in Canadian mining history, ending in 2000 when the union, facing a relentless assault by the company, accepted a settlement that called for its own decertification and a small severance payout to its members. Goldcorp broke the union. The mine soon reopened with a new, non-unionized workforce, and a couple of months later a worker was killed while in the crusher facility. Charges were laid by the Ministry of Labour under the province's Occupational Health and Safety Act. Goldcorp ended up paying $281,250 to the Ministry of Labour.[54]

Oil and Gas
Enbridge Inc.

Along with mining, oil and gas is a major draw for foreign investors in Colombia. Its economy is dependent on oil exports. Colombia is the third largest oil producer in the region, and its importance for foreign investors will likely grow should Hugo Chávez continue to limit foreign investment in Venezuela. At the same time, observers, including Colombian officials, acknowledge that the country's vast oil wealth is largely untapped, as Colombia does not have the capital to fully exploit its potential. As part of its broader trend of liberalization, Colombia has opened up its oil and gas industry for foreign companies. This includes a significant reduction in royalties claimed by the government, leading to lofty profits for multinational corporations.[55]

Just as in mining, however, this foreign investment has been surrounded by violence. Oil and gas production in Colombia proceeds through paramilitary and state terror aimed at the dispossession of people living in the way of development projects and the eradication of opposition to corporate expansion. As Grace Livingstone observes in *Inside Colombia*, one of the primary concerns of oil companies operating in Colombia is security. "They have cooperated with military battalions with appalling human rights records and which are known to have collaborated with paramilitary death squads. In Arauca and Casanare, the army had dedicated entire brigades ... to defending oil production. Both of these brigades have been accused of extrajudicial killings."[56]

Livingstone argues that as much as half of the Colombian military's resources are committed to defending oil investments. Colombians living in oil exploration regions have accused foreign companies of providing the incentive, and sometimes the means, for military and paramilitary forces to engage in cleansing operations, clearing oil areas of their human inhabitants. But it is not only local communities who have the misfortune of living near much-coveted oil deposits or along the preferred pipeline routes that are targeted by paramilitary and military squads. From 1993 to 2003, at least 125 activists in Colombia's oil workers' union, often mislabelled as guerrilla sympathizers (as are poor peasants in the way of oil development), have been killed by death squads. In 1998, seventeen other union members were charged with terrorism for unsubstantiated links to guerrilla organizations. The lawyer representing them was also assassinated.[57]

Colombia's largest pipeline is owned by the Oleoducto Central S.A. (OCENSA) pipeline consortium. Calgary-based Enbridge is the biggest foreign investor in OCENSA, owning a quarter of the pipeline, and is its technical operator. Enbridge's involvement began in 1995 as construction commenced, and it operated the pipeline jointly with Calgary-based TransCanada Pipelines (TCPL) until 2000, when the latter sold its shares to Enbridge and Colombia's state oil company, Ecopetrol. Other consortium members include British Petroleum Pipelines, Total Pipeline Colombia and the Strategic Transaction Company. Costing $2.2 billion, the pipeline system spans 800 kilometres and carries 550,000 barrels of oil a day—nearly sixty percent of Colombian oil production—from the Cusiana and Cupiagua oil fields in the central interior of the country to the port of Covensas on the Caribbean coast.[58]

The OCENSA pipeline's construction and security measures surrounding it in the 1990s involved the forced displacement of more than 1,000 peasants living along the route in the department of Antioquia. Two hundred families displaced in this region launched a lawsuit against OCENSA for damages in the late 1990s. Despite disrupting the livelihood of the peasants, OCENSA refuses to properly compensate them. According to Livingstone, "The peasants claim that they have lost their livelihoods as a result of the large-scale disturbance of the land, which contaminated water supplies and eroded the soil on their farms."[59] The peasants now live in poverty without arable land or access to basic services. Given the poverty in the oil-producing regions, it is obvious that royalties do not reach poor Colombians. The families suing OCENSA and their lawyer received death threats for their efforts. The lawyer eventually fled the country and sought asylum in England. The local OCENSA manager was reportedly in contact with the paramilitaries at that time. This displacement, it is important to note, was part of a broader wave of dispossession in the region in the 1990s and early 2000s. Antioquia was governed for a couple of years by future president Uribe, who, as I noted above, has ties to paramilitaries. During his tenure in power in the department, 200,000 peasants were displaced from their lands. The department accounted for eighteen percent of people displaced nationwide, with a considerably higher rate than other regions. The OCENSA pipeline had a role in that.[60]

To secure its investment and ensure local communities or guerrillas did not interfere with the pipeline (the ELN bombed it repeatedly in the mid-1990s), OCENSA contracted Defence Systems Colombia in the mid-1990s. According to a report by Amnesty International, in 1997 "OCENSA/DSC ... purchased military equipment for the Colombian army's 14th Brigade which has an atrocious record of human rights violations." When OCENSA/DSC bought the equipment, soldiers in the Brigade "were under investigation for complicity in a massacre of 15 unarmed civilians in the town of Segovia in April 1996 and for links with paramilitary organizations responsible for widespread human rights violations, including killings, 'disappearances' and torture against the civilian population in the area of the Brigade's jurisdiction." The report adds, "What is disturbing is that OCENSA/DSC's security strategy reportedly relies heavily on paid informants whose purpose is to covertly gather 'intelligence information' on the activities of the local population in the communities through which the pipeline passes and to identify possible 'subversives' within those communities. What is even more disturbing is that this intelligence information is then reportedly passed by OCENSA to the Colombian military, who together with their paramilitary allies, have frequently targeted those considered subversive for extrajudicial execution and 'disappearance.'"[61]

According to another report published in 1999 by organizations monitoring the human rights situation in Colombia, OCENSA and the Colombian Defence Ministry entered into a secret agreement whereby the latter's counter-insurgency brigades would protect the pipeline. Counter-insurgency measures included a curfew in the town of Zaragoza from six o'clock p.m. to six o'clock a.m. for all people living along the length of the pipeline, a security border of 100 metres on either side of the pipeline, with no economic activity allowed within 200 metres of the pipeline, and general intimidation of local communities. Under public pressure, OCENSA reportedly stopped using Defence Systems Colombia in 1999.[62]

Canadian companies are well represented in Colombia's oil bonanza. Other Canadian companies operating in the country include Calgary-based Nexen Inc., Talisman (which I discuss later in relation to the Sudan), Solana Resources, Petrolifera Petroleum Ltd., Pacific-Stratus Energy and Petrobank Energy and Resources. Petrobank was part of a wave of foreign investors entering the Putumayo region following the influx of paramilitaries there seeking to secure the area for foreign investors in the 1990s.[63]

EnCana

Until its departure in 2006, Calgary-based EnCana was the largest foreign investor in Ecuador's oil industry. It boasted several rich exploration and producing properties, and was the largest investor in the US$1.1 billion Oleoducto de Crudos Pesados (OCP) pipeline running through the Amazonian jungle. EnCana's operations were always controversial, and there was fierce indigenous opposition surrounding the OCP Amazonian pipeline project.[64]

Formed out of a merger of the Alberta Energy Company Ltd. and PanCanadian Energy Corporation in 2002, EnCana is the largest North American independent oil and gas company. Its Ecuadorean holdings, including the OCP pipeline, were key parts of the company's international interests. EnCana planned on shipping 80,000 barrels a day through the 500-kilometre-long pipeline, which runs from the Amazon basin through the Andes to the Pacific coast, where the oil is then exported primarily to North American markets.[65]

Community concerns with EnCana investments were many. The threats posed to the Amazonian ecosystem by the OCP pipeline was a central worry. Environmentalists point out that "the Amazon is a globally significant, yet fragile, ecosystem, with large tracts of intact rainforest that indigenous groups depend upon for their physical and cultural survival."[66] Ecuador claims an extraordinary diversity of plant and animal species, some of which are not found anywhere else in the world and are endangered. This eco-diversity was threatened by EnCana's pipeline and its other holdings, including 550,000 acres of undeveloped land in the Amazon in which the company was planning to drill for oil. The pipeline route impacts several protected and ecologically sensitive areas, including the Mindo Nambillo cloud forest; it also runs through the Andes, a geological zone susceptible to earthquakes. Compounding this danger, the heavy crude oil being transported by the pipeline has to be heated at high pressure to twenty-seven degrees Celsius, which increases the risk of accidents and damage to the ecosystem. And indigenous residents in the oil regions are already too familiar with such dangers: there have been thirty major oil spills in Ecuador's Amazon basin in the last three decades, discharging upwards of 400,000 barrels of oil into the ecosystem. Accidents aside, the basic business of oil exploration, production and pipeline construction and use all require the destruction of large swaths of rainforest for the development to proceed. This is typically done without consulting local communities. Hundreds of poor farmers had land arbitrarily bisected by the OCP pipeline and property expropriated without compensation. They took legal action against the OCP, and EnCana countered that the claims have no basis and the litigants are simply trying to milk the company for cash. For the farmland that remains, though, environmental sustainability would always be put at risk by the oil production, which produces toxic wastes that inevitably make their way into the surrounding ecosystem, making it unusable for local populations.[67]

There is a long history of damage to the health and livelihood of indigenous peoples in Ecuador caused by oil production. The oil-producing areas of Ecuador have the ignominious claim to the highest cancer and malnutrition rates in the country. Despite the company's claims of environmental responsibility, people living near EnCana projects reported soil, water and air contamination, which affected crops and livestock. One farmer accused EnCana of actually dumping contaminated water from its oil platform near her property, polluting the local water supply. EnCana ignored her complaints, and she was forced to pay for her own environmental tests, which confirmed her suspicions. EnCana never took any measures to address her concerns, however. Other farmers made similar complaints about EnCana's flouting any serious efforts at environmental responsibility, but have met with the same obstinate response from the company. Quito-based economist Jose Enrique argues that Ecuador's overdependence on oil exports has made the country vulnerable to world market prices for the commodity. The fall in oil prices in 1997–98 contributed heavily to Ecuador's subsequent economic collapse, the brunt of which was borne, as it always is, by the poor. The pipeline will only increase the country's oil dependence, however. Realizing the maximum return on the investments already made in it will require significantly increased oil production, including the opening of hundreds of new wells. This will inevitably put further pressure on the Amazon's delicate eco-balance, as well as on indigenous communities.[68] EnCana had in its employ an armed security force numbering in the hundreds to protect its investments. It claimed the security was necessary because its investments were close to the Colombian border and thus susceptible to guerrilla attack. In 1999, several employees of Alberta Energy were taken hostage for 100 days, though the Colombian guerrilla organizations deny involvement. Local residents maintain that EnCana's security force had more to do with local opposition to the company than did Colombian guerrillas. EnCana security, they argue, worked with the military against them, seeking to put a chill on dissident activity through a show of military force. Since the late 1990s Ecuador has seen massive, tumultuous protests led by indigenous organizations. In 2002, mass strikes and roadblocks in the Amazonian provinces of Sucumbíos and Orellana targeted the oil industry, among other targets, for creating environmental havoc while impoverishing indigenous peoples and harming their health. A state of emergency was declared. Activists in Tarapoa blocked the road leading to EnCana's oil concessions for several days. Military forces landed on EnCana's airstrip and were driven in EnCana trucks by company drivers to the town where they attacked demonstrators. Four protesters were shot. Community members claim that EnCana called in the military and that its security forces participated in the assault. Meanwhile, the Ecumenical Commission for Human Rights made a formal complaint to EnCana about an incident in which the company's security forces made accusations to the Ecuadorean military that the sons of a farmer who had publicly criticized the company were guerrillas. The accusations precipitated a military assault on the family's home. More generally, claims that EnCana security forces mistreated protesters and threatened community members are fairly widespread.[69]

The security stick wielded by EnCana was complemented by its carrot: the Ñanpaz Foundation, the NGO the company owns in Ecuador. Ñanpaz also received funding from the Canadian International Development Agency (CIDA), tying CIDA yet again to a controversial Canadian corporate investment. Nominally established to assist in community development, the NGO has been criticized by locals as incompetent and unaccountable to the community. There is no meaningful community input into what Ñanpaz does. Community activists argue instead the NGO's real goal was to try to co-opt the opposition with talk of community programming and jobs for a few community leaders, while providing the company and its security forces with another way of monitoring dissidents. As a sign of how rooted in the community the NGO was, it operated out of an impenetrable castle-like fortress in Tarapoa, which was surrounded by a high fence and guarded by EnCana security forces.[70]

Because of the prospect for environmental catastrophe represented by the OCP pipeline, and despite threats and violence directed against protesters, the campaign against OCP grew through the late 1990s and the first decade of the 2000s. Several local groups were joined by national organizations such as the National Indigenous Federation of Ecuador (CONAIE), the organization that has led several massive strikes against corrupt neoliberal governments and the selling off of the country's resources to foreign capital, and contributed to the downfall of three presidents between 1998 and 2005. Opposition to EnCana and the OCP boiled over into several mass direct actions against the project through the 2000s. Between August 2005 and February 2006, EnCana's operations were shut down on two occasions and at least two state of emergencies were declared by the government in regions in which EnCana was operating. The states of emergency included the use of military forces to secure EnCana property and the censuring of journalists working in the areas affected by the protests. In February 2006, for example, the pipeline was damaged by protesters and a pumping station in the Napo region crucial to the pipeline was forcibly closed, shutting down operations for several days and leading the government to declare a state of emergency in the area. The local campaign against EnCana was also successful in building international opposition, with campaigns organized against EnCana and the OCP in North America and Europe. Political instability resulting from the mass popular movements opposed to EnCana and the OCP and demanding a greater share of the economic pie, and the political shift to the left in Latin America, most prominent in Venezuela, eventually led the Ecuadorean government to reverse its free market reforms from the 1990s. By the mid-2000s, the Ecuadorean government was demanding a larger share of oil revenues.[71]

In the face of mass direct action and the political shift of the Ecuadorean government, EnCana eventually fled the country. The "Chávez disease," the derisive term company executive Gwyn Morgan uses to describe the shift to the left in Latin America, was too much for the oil giant to bear any longer. It sold its assets in 2006 to a Chinese energy consortium. EnCana's departure did not end its troubles, however. A major oil-producing property it had shares in, which it sold to the Chinese consortium, was subsequently expropriated by the government, which claimed the property was illegally sold to EnCana by another oil company, Occidental Petroleum. As a result, under the terms of its sale agreement with the Chinese consortium, EnCana had to take the financial losses caused by the expropriation, to a tune of US$232 million. EnCana is considering suing Ecuador over this.[72]

Talisman

In the early 2000s Calgary-based Talisman was the subject of an international sanctions and divestment campaign over its role in the Sudanese civil war and human rights disaster. Formed in 1992 when British Petroleum sold its majority stake in its Canadian subsidiary, Talisman is one of the largest independent oil companies in the world, with operations and interests in sixteen countries, most of them in the Third World. It entered the Sudan in 1998. In the mid-1970s American oil company Chevron entered southern Sudan, a region rich in oil but suffering a long history of war and human rights abuses. Chevron sold its interest to Canadian company Arakis after rebels in the south attacked its facilities. In 1998, Talisman took over Arakis, and acquired a twenty-five percent stake in oil exploration, development and pipeline projects operated by the Greater Nile Petroleum Operating Company (GNPOC). [73]

To describe the human rights situation in southern Sudan as bleak would be an understatement. Despite being home to most of the country's richest oil deposits, the region remains economically neglected and desperately poor. Since Sudan gained independence in 1956, residents of the south—who are of black African and largely Christian background, while the residents of the north were mainly Arabic and Muslim—have long sought autonomy from the central government. The struggle for autonomy has resulted in war between the government of the north and para-militaries backed by the government, on the one hand, and rebel forces in the south, on the other. Human rights observers argue the government and paramilitary forces have engaged in wide-spread human rights abuses, involving scorched earth policies, razing entire villages and murdering and enslaving thousands of civilians. The war is motivated in part, observers maintain, to keep control over the oil deposits in the south.[74]

Paramilitary forces known as the *murahleen*, with ties to the Su-danese government including having been first armed by the lat-ter, participate in raids against villages in the southern part of the country, including oil-producing regions. The raids, human rights observers say, are aimed at depopulating regions in the south of the country where there is strong opposition to the central govern-ment and where oil production is located. Men are typically killed in raids, while women and children are taken as loot with govern-ment permission. They end up enslaved. It is estimated that 15,000 Sudanese women and children have been forced into slavery since the beginning of the current phase of the war in 1983. Meanwhile, 50,000 people, primarily from the south of Sudan, have been killed and upwards of 4.5 million have been displaced.[75]

In the late 1990s human rights observers and people living in Sudan's oil-producing region began criticizing Talisman for fuel-ling the war and supporting human rights abuses committed by the military against civilians. Talisman denied the accusations. Under public pressure to take action against the company, Liberal Foreign Affairs minister Lloyd Axworthy called a fact-finding mis-sion headed by John Harker in 1999 to investigate the Sudanese human rights situation and Talisman's role in it. The report con-cludes that foreign oil investment is fuelling the war and human rights abuses committed by the government and government-backed militias. On the one hand, oil revenues are being used by the government to build its military power (the military budget doubled between 1999 and 2001 alone) in order to crush opposi-tion to the government in the south; and military targets include not just armed rebels but villagers suspected of sympathizing with the rebels. On the other hand, according to the report there is an even more direct link between oil production and the human rights catastrophe. Roads and airstrips built by oil companies, including Talisman, have been used by the military to access their targets more quickly than before their construction. Moreover, the military targets include people whose villages stood in the way of oil production and opponents of oil investment. The report notes that many human rights observers have highlighted the military's role in cleansing oil production areas of their human inhabitants. At the same time, while initially denying links to the Sudanese military, Talisman executives eventually acknowledged to the Harker Commission that the military was using the company's airstrips, and was also providing security for its oil fields. The reason such military security is necessary, according to the report, is that many Sudanese living in the oil-producing regions oppose the foreign investment. They claim oil investment is done without their support, under the auspices of a government they do not recognize and with no benefit to them. They asked the commissioners, "Did the Canadian oil company ask our permission to take our oil, and sell it? Why is Canada, a rich country, taking our oil without our permission, and without any benefit to us?"[76]

Having studied the conflict first-hand and spoken with eye-witnesses, the Commission asserted rather bluntly: "We can only conclude that Sudan is a place of extraordinary suffering and continuing human rights violations ... and the oil operations in which a Canadian company is involved add more suffering." Despite this damning report, Axworthy refused to impose sanctions on the company, claiming, in classic political avoidance strategy, that more study was needed. This put Canada a step behind the U.S. in addressing Sudan's human rights tragedy; it had imposed sanctions against the Talisman oil partnership.[77]

With the Canadian government unwilling to sanction Talisman, activists stepped up an international divestment campaign against the company. They began pressuring investors, such as pension funds, to pull their investments out of Talisman in protest of its role in the Sudanese war and human rights abuses. As knowledge of Talisman's practices spread, the campaign picked up momentum. Eventually, pension fund after pension fund began divesting themselves of the company, including the California Public Employees' Retirement System, the Teachers' Insurance and Annuity Association-College Retirement Equity Fund (a U.S. college teachers' pension fund) and the Texas Teachers Retirement

Fund. In 2000, Talisman's shares dropped twenty-nine percent because of the campaign. Even the New York Stock Exchange (NYSE) threatened to delist the company because of its investments in Sudan. As a result of the divestment campaign's success, Talisman pulled out of Sudan, selling its interests in the country in 2002 to the Indian state oil company.[78]

The Sudanese catastrophe is not something Talisman can wipe off its record so easily. In 2001, the Presbyterian Church of Sudan launched a class action lawsuit against the company for complicity in war crimes when it allowed the Sudanese military to use its airfield to attack civilians living near its properties. The case was initially thrown out by a judge in New York, who argued that the plaintiffs had not gathered sufficient evidence to show that Talisman had knowingly helped the military when the latter used its airfields for the assault on civilians, despite arguments by human rights observers and local civilians that Talisman and other investors knew precisely what the military was doing. The Presbyterian Church has appealed the decision. But in another display of unyielding support for the oil giant (under both Liberal and Tory governments), in the spring of 2007 Canada intervened in the case by trying to get the court to throw it out. It argued that if the case were to proceed, it would "create friction in Canada-U.S. relations," and that it would have "a chilling effect on Canadian firms engaging in Sudan." Two former Liberal politicians, the United, Anglican and Catholic churches, members of the Harker Commission and fourteen law professors intervened in response, asking the court to reject the Canadian government's attempt to quash the case. They argued that while Canada publicly declares its support for human rights on the international stage, it has no measures to enforce human rights obligations on Canadian companies operating abroad, while the United States does. Moreover, there are more than 10,000 refugees from the southern Sudan living in the U.S. who were affected by the war and have legitimate claims against Talisman. The case will likely be an uphill battle for the plaintiffs and survivors of the oil-fuelled war, but their continued determination to win some redress for atrocities committed against them in the name of oil investment marks an indelible stain on Talisman's record and on a state willing to defend the company regardless of its practices.[79]

Meanwhile, Talisman is trying to grow its investments in Colombia in the Magdalena Valley, which has a history of paramilitary activity. As noted already in this chapter, resource exploitation in Colombia is typically a very violent process, backed up the military and paramilitary force. Talisman's investments in Colombia should be seen in this light. Talisman was also the target of a Canadian Labour Congress campaign in the late 1990s to get its members to refuse to transport, use or stock the products of companies investing in Indonesia. The campaign was designed to isolate Indonesia in order to force it to end its bloody occupation of East Timor. In 2008, Talisman also announced investments in two oil fields in Kurdistan in northern Iraq.[80]

The Roots of Oil and Gas Imperialism

It is also important to briefly note that many Canadian oil and gas companies that have developed a strong international presence got their start in Alberta's oil fields. But those Canadian investments, just like in the mining industry, are often made on stolen land where the federal and Albertan governments have refused to agree to a just settlement with indigenous communities in order to ensure capital's maximum access to oil deposits. Most of Alberta's oil riches are situated on unceded indigenous territory, while pipelines transporting natural gas to the oil patch or shipping oil from the oil patch to the market often traverse indigenous land.[81] Here again we can note a connection between imperialism at home and imperialism abroad.

Hydroelectric Power
BFC Construction and Agra-Monenco
BFC Construction (now Toronto-based Aecon) and Agra-Monenco (now U.K.-headquartered Amec) are infrastructure development and engineering companies involved in Colombia's controversial US$1 billion Urrá 1 hydroelectric dam project, which was built by an international consortium in 1996. They received a combined US$18.2 million in financing from Export Development Canada, despite the violence and bloodshed surrounding the dam. BFC procured construction supplies for Urrá's lead contractor, while Agra-Monenco was hired to monitor the project's environmental impact and indigenous concerns in the face of public criticism over the dam's impact on local indigenous communities.[82]

The indigenous communities in question are part of the Embera Katio nation, which is situated along the tributaries of the Upper Sinu River, in Colombia's last rainforest along its Caribbean coast. These communities have historically relied on the Sinu water system for their survival. The rivers provided a central part of their diet and served them as a form of transportation. Because the Sinu River figures prominently in the Urrá 1 project, the Embera Katio nation strenuously opposed the dam's construction. The Urrá dam consists of a massive wall that cuts the Sinu River in half. As a result, fish cannot swim past the wall to spawn upriver, depleting their stocks. Communities that were self-sustaining thus lost an important part of their diet and malnutrition increased. One community member reports having "almost fainted at times for a lack of protein," while the children "cry all the time" and "do not have the strength to fight off illness." At the same time, river currents were stifled by the dam, and in their place pools of stagnant water formed that have drawn mosquitoes and led to the spread of dengue and malaria.[83]

The Embera campaign against the dam has included speaking tours by community leaders to raise international awareness about the project, and a successful court injunction against the project because the consortium did not consult with them about its plans. But as is all too common for social justice campaigners in Colombia, Embera activists have paid a very high price for standing up to the foreign corporations. While Colombia's Ministry of the Environment ignored the court injunction and allowed construction to proceed, paramilitaries followed the court case with a campaign of terror. Several Embera leaders were assassinated. As word spread of the destruction caused by the dam, and of the paramilitary's campaign of terror, the Urrá consortium hired Agra-Monenco to monitor the project and report on environmental and indigenous concerns. However, Embera activists claim that the Canadian company served as little more than a public relations arm of the consortium. It typically sided with Urrá in its disputes with the indigenous communities, refused to meet with Embera leaders and refused to discuss the paramilitary activities.[84]

Even after the Colombian government signed a seven-point settlement with the Embera Katio nation in April 2000, which included a pledge to respect human rights and compensation for damage to their land, harassment from paramilitaries continued. Community activists have been subjected to death threats. In September 2000, paramilitaries invaded Embera communities, and on one occasion disappeared twenty-one people, including children, travelling upstream in canoes. It was only after an international campaign was launched to demand their freedom that the captives were released. Paramilitaries killed at least eight Embera activists in the year that followed the settlement with the government. The Embera also report that six members have been killed by guerrilla forces. Negative impacts of the dam continue, with reports of malaria and dengue epidemics in Embera communities.[85]

One Embera leader assassinated for his activism was Kimy Perní Domicó. In 1999 he travelled to Ottawa in 1999 to testify before Parliament's Standing Committee on Foreign Affairs and International Trade about the impact of the hydroelectric project on his community. He explained that his community was not consulted, nor had it been compensated for the damages done to it by the dam. He stressed his community's need for support in their struggle: "We hope you can help us in this process ... The Embera Katio are at a great disadvantage in comparison to the powerful Urrá Company and its foreign investors, Canadians among them." But he ominously added, "Saying these things to you today puts my life in danger ... Already, four Embera leaders have been killed by paramilitary forces for challenging the negative impacts of the Urrá Megaproject ... Anyone who dares to speak out about Urrá is accused of being involved with the (anti-government) guerrillas, and with that pretext, they have declared both our communities and leaders to be a military target."[86]

His plea for help from the Canadian government fell on deaf ears. He returned to Canada in April 2001, where he spoke at the Peoples' Summit in Québec City, which was organized to counter the Summit of the Americas meeting involving all the leaders of the Western hemisphere (minus Fidel Castro). Less than two months after his trip to Québec, he disappeared in Tierralta, Colombia. His body was never found. As part of a peace process involving Colombia's paramilitaries in 2006 (which has not ended paramilitary activity), a paramilitary leader identified Kimy Pernía Domicó as one of their victims.[87]

Fortis Inc.

St. John's-based Fortis is a large utility company with several gas and electricity operations in Canada and the Americas. Its most controversial project is the $44 million fifty-metre high Chalillo dam on the Macal River in Belize, owned and operated by its wholly owned subsidiary, Belize Electric Company Ltd. (BECOL). Chalillo went into operation in 2005. The plans for the dam drew widespread opposition in the early 2000s both within and outside of Belize because of the ecological ramifications. Fortis actually bought the rights to the project from American company Duke Energy, which backed out of the project because of the opposition and negative publicity it was generating. Fortis is not easily fazed by such criticism, however.[88]

Like the many other Canadian investments I have discussed in this chapter, the Chalillo dam proceeds at great cost to the Belizean environment and to those poor local communities whose livelihood depends on the sustainability of that environment. And given their experience with earlier Fortis projects in their area, such as the Mollejon dam, communities along the Macal River have every reason to be concerned about Fortis's latest venture. Communities that fish and drink from the Macal River report that since Mollejon was built in 1995 water levels have dropped considerably and people have suffered skin irritations after bathing in the water. The new dam, it is feared, will impact water levels and quality further. The dam's reservoir will also flood parts of the Mountain Pine Ridge Forest Reserve, Chiquibul Forest Reserve and Chiquibul National Park. An estimated 10 square kilometres of rainforest in the remote valley area along the Macal will be flooded. This area is home to more than a dozen endangered species, including the scarlet macaw, red parrot, jaguar, black howler monkey and tapir (a relative of the rhinoceros). Chalillo will also flood two Mayan ruins, including ancient pyramids and temples, to the anger of Mayan indigenous people who have signed a petition calling for protection of their cultural heritage.[89]

Critics of the hydroelectric project also point to the sweetheart deal Fortis received from the cash-strapped, energy-poor Belizean government. Fortis's ascent to become Belize's major energy supplier, and on such positive financial and legal terms (for the company), comes on the heels of an industry-wide deregulation of public assets and their fire sale to foreign corporations, as Belize scrambles to cover foreign debt obligations and acquiesces to the Global North's push for free market reforms. Fortis will make a lot of money from the project while being insulated from financial and environmental risks related to the dam's construction and operation. Belize's power purchase agreement with Fortis states, for example, that if anything happens to the Macal River or the people and their property as a result of the dam's operations, the company cannot be held liable. In fact, the government agrees to waive Fortis' obligations under all environmental laws and regulations—except those laws the company agrees to follow. Further, if the project is damaged by a natural catastrophe, even if that catastrophe's impact on the dam could have been averted by better planning, the company can still walk away from the project after getting its insurance payout. At the same time, the power purchase agreement locks Belize—and by extension its poor citizens—into a guaranteed price per kilowatt hour deal until 2036 (with guaranteed annual increases) that raises the price of electricity well above what was being paid previously for electricity imported from Mexico. Fortis actually demanded and received—before the dam began operations—electricity rate increases well above what was initially agreed upon, to cover construction costs that skyrocketed beyond the company's initial estimates when it signed the deal for the dam with the government. This while the company's own reports indicate that the dam is not producing the electricity it promised Belizeans. One commentator describes Fortis's profits from the project as "usurious," with the company earning as high as eight times more per kilowatt hour from the Chalillo dam than it does from its dam in Newfoundland and Labrador.[90]

Half a million dollars of CIDA money has gone toward the project in the form of a positive environmental assessment critics say contains inaccurate and misleading information, and of which no public review has been permitted to examine the assessment work. The CIDA-funded assessment was contracted to the Canadian subsidiary of British-based AMEC. This is the company—the former Agra-Monenco—that was contracted to monitor the Urrá 1 dam in Colombia, as I just discussed, and which was criticized by indigenous people in Colombia for being in the pocket of the Urrá consortium. Remarkably, the environmental assessment said the geology where the dam was built is granite bedrock, which Fortis argued was perfect for the dam. But the earth was subsequently proven by an independent geologist to be a much softer sandstone bedrock instead, which critics suggest is far less secure a foundation for a massive dam. A collapse of the dam could destroy villages and possibly lives downstream. But under its agreement with the Belizean government, Fortis would not be liable for the destruction it causes.[91]

Although opponents have thus far been unable to stop the dam, many Belizeans are opposed to it, just as they are opposed to the free market reforms more generally, and have organized to challenge it. Opponents organized an anti-Fortis march in the capital city of Belmopan in 2002. The government responded by organizing a counter march, to which it bused in demonstrators. But when interviewed on TV, the counter-demonstrators could not say what they were marching for. A legal challenge was also initiated by the Belize Alliance of Conservation Non-Governmental Organizations (Bacongo). It wound its way to the Privy Council in London, which is the former British Colony's highest court of appeal. Despite the testimony of a scientist challenging the veracity of the CIDA-sponsored environmental assessment, the British court rejected Bacongo's case in 2004. Belizeans opposed to the selling off of the country's public assets have also formed a new fledgling political party, We the People, which is beginning to contest national and local elections.[92]

Fortis pushes on, though. Its subsidiary BECOL won approval in May 2007 for the construction of yet another dam on the Macal—a US$52 million generating facility at Vaca. This is the third and final phase of its hydroelectric scheme on the river. BECOL has a fifty-year agreement with BEL for the new project, in which the latter will purchase energy from it starting in 2009.[93]

A new government elected in 2008 appears unwilling to completely acquiesce to the Canadian company and has refused Fortis's efforts to further increase rates. Fortis is currently challenging the decision in court.[94]

SNC Lavalin

Montreal-based SNC Lavalin, formed in 1991 from a merger between Canada's two largest engineering firms, describes itself as one of the world's leading engineering and construction companies. It has projects in close to 100 countries, and specializes in designing and building infrastructure projects, including dams and components for dams.[95]

Two of the dam projects that SNC Lavalin has participated in are the Chamera 1, which began operating in 1994, and the Chamera 2, which was completed in 2004, both are located in the state of Himachal Pradesh in northern India. The dams are located thirty kilometres apart on the Ravi River. The company is part of two international consortiums responsible for the respective dams. Canadian companies have a strong presence in both projects. Besides SNC Lavalin, Acres International and Marine Industries are involved. EDC provided $403 million in financing for Chamera 1 and $175 million for Chamera 2, while CIDA provided $245 million for Chamera 1. SNC Lavalin is responsible for the turnkey construction for the dams. As with Fortis and the Chalillo project in Belize, SNC Lavalin and its international partners were able to exploit India's underdeveloped energy industry: unable to meet its own energy demands, the country liberalized its energy markets in the early 1990s, allowing foreign companies to build, own and finance power generators.[96]

The Chamera dams have not been without serious human and environmental consequences. The first dam, constructed without consultation with local villagers, drowned 46,000 trees and eighteen kilometres of forested valleys. Already suffering from severe deforestation, significant parts of the area are being desertified. This has left them susceptible to soil erosion, landslides and destruction of homes, crops and livestock during monsoon season, as the natural barrier to such climatic disasters provided by the forest is disappearing. Hundreds of people were displaced, and lost their jobs and their land after it was submerged. On top of this, fish stocks in the Ravi river have been depleted, the result, according to local residents, of mud that was extracted for the construction of the project not being disposed of properly. To make matters worse, Chamera 1 has also suffered technical problems that increase its environmental risks—leaks in the sluice gates, seeping in the foundations, malfunctioning generators, floating debris, no early warning system and an unstable rock foundation upon which the dam rests have all been identified as potential hazards. Further, the dam (as well as Chamera 2) is built in an earthquake zone which has the highest level of seismic in India. Such are the dangers that an engineering firm hired by CIDA to monitor the dam ominously reported in 1996: "any further indications of structural unsoundness, slides, increasing seepages into the dam, evidence of seepages downstream from the dam, vortices on the reservoir along the right bank, etc. must be considered as potentially catastrophic requiring the immediate controlled lowering of the reservoir and eventually the shutting down of the power plant."[97]

Chamera 2, located, as noted above, a mere thirty kilometres from its predecessor, only extends the potential for catastrophe—more lands to be submerged, greater desertification and increased possibility of disaster. The government acquired land from, and promised compensation for losses to, 339 families for this project. Promises are one thing, follow-through another, however. So, in 1999 families displaced by Chamera 2 joined with families displaced by Chamera 1 to form the Chamera Oustees Welfare Association (COWA). COWA has demanded from state government adequate compensation for lost lands, jobs, and land and timber distribution rights for the dispossessed. It has engaged in a hunger strike and highway blockades to advance its demands.[98]

SNC Lavalin is also leaving its ignominious mark in Vietnam with its involvement in the Dai Ninh dam, one of many dams being built on the Mekong river system. The twelfth longest river in the world, the Mekong and its tributaries provide food, water, transportation and many other daily essentials to sixty million people in six different countries. But the Mekong and the ecosystem it sustains are threatened by plans for massive development projects, as countries in the region look to develop their industrial economies, which requires much-expanded energy capacities. In the last fifteen years more than 100 large dams have been proposed, and some built, along the Mekong and its tributaries. Forty-five of these projects involve Canadian companies and EDC and CIDA support. SNC Lavalin is one of those companies in the thick of things.[99]

The Dai Ninh project, located on the Da Nhim and Da Queyon rivers, is to supply power to Ho Chi Minh City and the surrounding provinces. Construction began in 2002. CIDA paid SNC Lavalin $300,000 in 1994 to do the project feasibility study on the dam, and another $652,000 in 1996 to design it. Critics argue that the dam will flood an estimated eleven kilometres of agricultural land and 9.6 kilometres of forest, displacing 14,000 people and devastating the livelihoods of tens of thousands more poor Vietnamese who live in the area being flooded.[100]

Despite—or, as is more likely, because of—the potential human displacement and destruction of the surrounding ecosystem, SNC Lavalin's feasibility study has been shrouded in secrecy. Local villagers who will be affected by the dam have not been consulted, nor do they have the right to review the project's plans. Probe International's request to CIDA under the Access to Information Act to see the company's feasibility study was denied. CIDA explained to the NGO that SNC Lavalin objected to the study's disclosure, and that a provision in the Act allows the company to keep the study from coming under public scrutiny to protect its business interests. It is hard to imagine that there would be such effort to keep the study secret were the project ecologically responsible and without dire consequences for the people living in area to be flooded. Even the World Bank, erstwhile booster of large development projects, declined support for the dam, pointing to poor resettlement planning.[101]

SNC Lavalin is also doing its best to keep the world armed: it is one of Canada's biggest arms manufacturers. Among many other things, SNC Lavalin's bullets are put to good use by the American military in its illegal and bloody occupation of Iraq.[102]

Roots of Hydroelectric Imperialism

It is worth noting briefly here that again we have a Canadian industry whose corporate giants have grown to international maturity through domestic imperialism. As I discussed in the previous chapter, Canada's hydroelectric industry's rise to international prominence is based on its destruction of indigenous land in Canada in places like northern Manitoba and northern Québec. This is important to remember when studying international Canadian damning projects.

Telecommunications

Nortel Networks

Before the 2008 global financial crash, Brampton-based Nortel was a leading international telecommunications company. It has investments in over 150 countries, with Colombia being one of its fastest growing markets since it began operations there in the early 1990s. While it has suffered a rough patch in many of its global operations since the early 2000s, including in North America, laying off thousands of workers, Nortel has been a major provider of telecommunications infrastructure in some of Colombia's largest markets, and operates the country's largest cellular market.[103]

Liberalizing reforms undertaken by Colombia in its telecommunications sector since the early 1990s are the most advanced in South America. Colombia has one of the largest telecommunications markets in the region, representing a potentially great investment opportunity for foreign corporations, and like a shark circling its prey, Nortel seized the opportunity to gain control over Colombia's telecommunications assets once the opportunity presented itself. It has been supported by both CIDA and EDC. CIDA spent $4 million in 1995 to promote market liberalization in Colombia's telecommunications sector, with the aim of opening the sector up to Canadian corporations such as Nortel. EDC, meanwhile, has provided over $300 million in financing for Nortel's export and investment projects since 1995, helping the company gain a foothold in the growing Colombian market.[104]

As a result of the neoliberal market reforms imposed on Colombia's telecommunications industry, Nortel has become one of the industry's most powerful players, with juicy contracts for infrastructure development and cellular operations throughout the country. It has used this power to further entrench the privatization agenda. Nortel is largely responsible for the liquidation of Colombia's largest telecommunications company in 2003, the state-owned TELECOM, and the privatization of its successor. In the mid-1990s TELECOM signed contracts with Nortel and several other foreign companies to install 1.6 million fixed telephone lines. But under the contracts, TELECOM assumed all the risks of the investment, committing to pay out the difference between profits it guaranteed its foreign partners and the actual profits earned. TELECOM also agreed to guarantee ridiculously inflated profit levels. It was a sweetheart deal for Nortel: signing a contract with a guaranteed high rate of return, regardless of how well its investment actually does. The deal, and its outcome, led to an investigation stemming from allegations of corruption against three former presidents of the state-run utility, although Nortel's contract survived the scandal. The company was contracted to install 200,000 fixed telephone lines for a guaranteed profit of $143 million by 1999. Of course, this profit level was never achieved for Nortel or any of the other foreign companies, which all promptly, and ultimately successfully, sued the state-run utility for over US$1 billion. Nortel received US$57.6 million from TELECOM and another US$80 million from the Colombian government, the latter payout following Nortel's claim that it was still owed money beyond the payments from TELECOM. TELECOM tried to avoid making full payment, arguing it would face financial ruin if forced to do so. But Nortel and other companies, with the support of the American government, leaned heavily on Colombia to ensure payments were made in full. TELECOM also requested financial aid from the Colombian government to keep it from becoming insolvent, but right-wing leaders, including President Uribe, refused to support the state-run company and ultimately liquidated it as part of their overall privatization agenda, which they had been pursuing since the early 1990s with a healthy dose of encouragement from the IMF. The liquidation provided money to make the payments to Nortel and the other foreign litigants, while getting rid of the state-run utility.[105]

Privatization and Nortel's successful entrance into Colombia's telecommunications market has only been accomplished, as is the case typically in the country, through violence and bloodshed. But this has not deterred Nortel. Privatization efforts since the early 1990s have been strongly opposed by the country's telecommunications workers, organized in the Association of Telecommunications Workers (USTC) and the Central Union of Workers (CUT). Privatization has led to the loss of an estimated tens of thousands of unionized jobs in a country already beset by severe poverty and inequality. The liquidation of TELECOM alone led to the layoff of 8,000 unionized workers. The unions have organized a number of mass strikes involving several hundred thousand workers each, marches through Bogota and workplace occupations. The response of the Colombian state has been predictably harsh. In 1992 thirteen union members were tried on terrorism charges and arbitrarily detained for close to a year for organizing demonstrations against privatization. In 1998, seven union leaders were killed during a strike against (among other issues) a proposal to privatize TELECOM. In 2003, as EDC awarded Nortel more than $300 million in a line of credit for a series of Colombian investments while TELECOM was being liquidated and 10,000 unionized telecommunications workers lost their jobs, over seventy opponents of privatization were killed.[106]

Colombia is not the only violence-plagued country that Nortel has entered. In the fall of 2006, it won a US$20 million contract to set up a 5,000-kilometer fibre-optic network across Iraq. This contract follows on an earlier one to build a 1,000-kilometre network from Baghdad to Basra in the south of the country. The new contract is five times larger and covers thirty-five cities. Nortel describes it as a "nationwide optical backbone." The contract is part of a wave of privatizations that has swept Iraq since the illegal American invasion and occupation. Were it not for the invasion and the destruction of Iraqi infrastructure that entailed (the country had an extensive fibre-optic network before the invasion), Nortel's contract would not have been possible. But imperialism pays for capital of the Global North, and Nortel is now one of the direct beneficiaries of American military might. Nortel is not relying on the U.S. military alone to do business in Iraq, however; it also uses private security companies. Thus Nortel enters the nebulous world of outsourced imperial power, relying for protection on companies with little accountability to either the U.S., Iraqi or Canadian governments, and which have also been implicated in human rights abuses and killings of civilians.[107]

Bell Canada International (BCI)

Montreal-based Bell also plays a leading role in the development of telecommunications infrastructure and cellular markets throughout Latin America.

Its Colombian cellular subsidiary is Comcel S.A., which is one of the country's largest providers. BCI's expansion in Colombia, like Nortel's, has taken place since the 1990s as the country's telecommunications market was being opened up to foreign companies and state companies were being sold off. The company's ascendance has therefore come at the cost of the layoffs of thousands of unionized public sector telecommunications workers. And like any other major multinational that enters Colombia, BCI enters a war zone in which foreign companies and their infrastructure are targets of guerrillas, and where human rights abuses are committed by military and paramilitary forces against workers and opponents of foreign investors. During an escalation of bombings targeting corporate infrastructure in the late summer of 2005, Comcel transmission towers and a Comcel station were the biggest telecommunications targets. President Uribe has put such guerrilla activities on the top of his heavy security agenda, as part of his overall plan to make Colombia as attractive to foreign capital as possible. As I discussed above, this security agenda has involved strengthening the hand of the military and paramilitary forces, increased targeting of civilians and worsening conditions for Colombian workers.[108]

Brazil is another country where BCI has exploited opportunities afforded by externally imposed privatization of public utilities. Brazil offers foreign companies like BCI the biggest potential for telecommunications market expansion in South America. It has a large population and growing economy, and it has undergone extensive privatization, deregulation and opening up to foreign capital since the early 1990s, as a result of IMF structural adjustment conditionalities and the inability of the debt-ridden Brazilian government to adequately finance its state-run telecommunications sector. Privatization in the telecoms market since the mid-1990s has earned the country US$82.1 billion of revenue to help pay down its external debt. Thus BCI has set its sights on the country as a major area for investment and growth, refocusing its energies from Asia to Latin America in general and Brazil in particular; and it has successfully increased its market share in cellular distribution and infrastructural development there since the 1990s, winning lucrative contracts from the Brazilian state. It is a major player in the country's wealthiest state, São Paulo. But here again BCI's growth in Brazil has come at the expense of the loss of an important infrastructural public asset and in spite of opposition from telecommunications unions. Privatization has involved workforce reduction, especially of older unionized workers, a significant increase in lower paid workers at the bottom end of the industry to match an increase in a well paid management layer, and the growth of subcontracting and weaker job security.[109]

Garment Manufacturing

Gildan Activewear

Montreal-based Gildan, one of the world's largest T-shirt and sports-shirt manufacturers, has led the movement of Canadian garment producers into countries with cheap labour and very poor work standards. Following NAFTA, which grants Canadian corporations strong property rights in Mexico, and WTO trade deals, which reduce quotas rich countries imposed on textile and clothing imports from developing nations, Canadian clothing manufacturers have increasingly set up shop in the Global South, where labour costs are kept to a minimum and freedom of association often does not exist. Clothing can now be exported with little penalty back to the Canadian or American markets. Major destinations of Canadian companies are Mexico, Central America and the Caribbean basin. These garment companies historically built up their revenues exploiting cheap, mainly immigrant, labour in Canada; it is on the backs of workers of colour in Canada, often working at home at piece rates that fall well below legal minimum wages, that Canadian clothing capitalists have been able to become internationally competitive. But while immigrant labour in Canada is cheap, it cannot compete with labour in countries like Honduras, El Salvador or Haiti. As an executive with Canadian company Gentle Fit Lingerie notes, labour costs in Mexico are "less ... much, much less" than in Canada.[110]

Until 1997, all of Gildan's textile manufacturing was done domestically. But after battling unions defending their mainly female immigrant workforce, it announced in March 2007 that it was closing its remaining textile factories in Montreal and a cutting operation in New York. The decision is the culmination of a gradual shift over the last decade toward moving all its operations abroad to cheaper locales. Gildan also announced the closure of two Mexican factories: even Mexico is not cheap enough for the company. Instead, it is consolidating its operations in Honduras, Nicaragua, Haiti and the Dominican Republic, where labour is dirt cheap. Chief financial officer Laurence Sellyn comments, "Our strategic plan and industry leadership are based on consolidating our manufacturing in offshore hubs."[111] A representative with the union representing Gildan workers at one of their Montreal plants expressed shock at the decision to shutter the facility, considering the union had made concessions in their latest contract and increased productivity.[112]

One case that put Gildan in the spotlight of human rights and labour activists is the El Progreso factory in Honduras. Beginning in 2001, the Toronto-based Maquila Solidarity Network (MSN) and the Honduran Independent Monitoring Team (EMIH) began investigating complaints that labour rights were being regularly violated at El Progreso, the majority of whose workers are women. The story was eventually picked up by the CBC television program Disclosure, which broadcast a program on labour violations at the factory in January 2002. Investigations found that wages were very low and were barely enough to survive on. In some cases, workers' wages were considerably less than what they were paid when originally hired, despite the company continuously increasing production targets. Because wages are tied to meeting production targets, furthermore, many workers reported skipping the breaks to which they were legally entitled and taking short lunches. Overtime pay was also regularly not provided, contrary to Honduran labour law. When questioned about the poor remuneration, Gildan suggested, matter-of-factly, that without the company such poorly educated workers would not even have a job, and that "we must also be honest in our assessment; these types of jobs (sewing operator) even in Canada or the United States do not earn sufficient wages to meet the basic needs of a family."[113]

Wages were not the only complaint of El Progreso workers. Before being hired, and two months after starting, women were forced to take a pregnancy test, and if tested positive they were let go—though the company would claim the reason was for staffing cuts. Pregnancy tests also contravene Honduran law. Health problems associated with poor air quality were also common amongst workers, including sore throats, asthmatic cough and sinus problems. El Progreso is not an isolated Gildan case, though, as similar violations were also found at a Gildan factory in Mexico.[114]

When Gildan workers at El Progreso began to organize for better working conditions, they met fierce resistance from the company. Before the factory was closed down in 2004, an estimated 100 workers who were involved in efforts to unionize were fired. Though official reasons for the dismissals never mentioned the union—some referred to "personal reasons"—it is surely not a coincidence that many union supporters were fired for "personal" or other reasons.[115] Gildan responded to criticism from MSN, EMIH and Disclosure by initially denying claims of labour violations. Its denials were reinforced by the Canadian government, which gave the company, amidst the growing controversy around El Progreso, a CIDA- and Canadian Manufacturers and Exporters-sponsored "Excellence in Corporate Social and Ethical Responsibility" award, draining the prize of any possible meaning it could have. Gildan also threatened legal action against MSN if it continued to circulate its report on the factory, even going so far as to contact the NGO's funders to inform them of the potential lawsuit. Not deterred, MSN continued with its campaign, and in December 2003, together with the Independent Federation of Honduran Workers (FITH) and the Canadian Labour Congress (CLC), filed a formal complaint regarding the firing of El Progreso union activists with U.S.-based labour monitoring organizations the Fair Labor Association (FLA) and the Worker Rights Consortium (WRC). While Gildan offered to cooperate with the FLA, it refused WRC access to the factory or its records. Based on interviews with current and former workers, both the FLA and WRC investigations documented a systemic pattern of labour rights violations. Although the company responded by offering to come up with a corrective plan, at a meeting with the FLA in July 2004 in which it was supposed to provided details on that plan, Gildan announced unexpectedly that it was instead closing the factory down, throwing 1,800 people out of work. [116]

Gildan denies the closing of El Progreso had anything to do with union organizing or its unwillingness to implement meaningful changes to its labour regime. Critics argue that the increasing pressure to change its labour practices, as well as the possibility of a union, lie at the heart of its decision. Why, for example, would Gildan have begun the process of trying to create a company union, as it did, if it was planning on closing the factory? Gildan claimed that it was a cost issue, that it could get cheaper wages in Nicaragua and Haiti. But why then did it leave its other two Honduran factories open, and in fact announce plans for a new one shortly after closing El Progreso? As Lynda Yanz of MSN asserts, "Gildan is non-union everywhere except in Canada [and it has now closed its Canadian operations], and this decision sends a clear message to its other plants: Don't try to organize or you'll be shut down."[117] Although MSN has stated that Gildan is more open to discussing criticisms of work practices since the El Progreso affair, the company is nevertheless relying entirely on Central American and Caribbean sweatshop labour. Another controversial investment by the company is in Haiti. Gildan exploits extremely cheap sweatshop labour in the impoverished and coup-ridden country. While it was already subcontracting to a Haitian company prior to the latest coup in 2004, it will clearly benefit from the removal of the democratically elected President Jean-Bertrand Aristide. I discuss Canada's involvement in the 2004 coup in more detail in the sixth chapter. For now I will note that while Aristide's presidency, whose main supporters were found amongst the most impoverished of Haitians, may not have involved a radical reorientation away from IMF-imposed structural adjustment, he was nevertheless openly critical of the impact of neoliberalism on poor Haitians and of the long history of racist imperialism that the country has suffered. Among other things, he raised the minimum wage and sought to defend the labour rights of the many sweatshop workers toiling for foreign companies in the country's Export Processing Zone (EPZ).

Aristide's efforts at reforms angered the Canadian, American and French states enough that they helped to organize the coup against him. The interim government that replaced him, prominently featuring individuals linked to past military dictatorships, and backed militarily by a United Nations force including Canadian soldiers, moved to weaken labour rights in the EPZ and lower the minimum wage to its pre-Aristide level of just over a dollar a day. The move has been good for business, as Gildan has expanded its operations since Aristide's overthrow. But the Gildan connection to the coup goes deeper. One of the company's local subcontractors is Andy Apaid, who workers allege never honoured the Aristide minimum wage and fired those who challenged his labour practices. He is also accused of forcing workers to attend anti-Aristide demonstrations, as part of the coup plotters' efforts to make it appear to the international community that there was mass opposition to Aristide, when in fact there was not. Apaid was also the leader of the Group of 184 anti-Aristide opposition, which was comprised of business and media owners. With the support

of Canada and the U.S., it helped destabilize the Aristide government in the buildup to the coup. Earlier, Apaid's family provided
financial support to the 1991–94 military dictatorship that came
to power after the first time Aristide was overthrown. Clearly Gildan has some very unsavoury business connections in Haiti.[118]

Other Canadian companies that have operations in the Mexican maquiladoras, Central America and the Caribbean basin include Nygard International, Phantom Industries, Gentle Fit Lingerie, Vogue Brassieres, Western Glove Works, Ballin, Canatex,
Pimlicio Apparel and Canadelle.[119]

Bata

Toronto-based Bata makes and sells shoes, runs 4,600 retail stores
in over fifty countries and operates forty factories in twenty-six
countries. Its international presence is one of the largest, and old-
est, among Canadian clothing companies. It also has a long history of conflict with its workers in the Third World, as it has pursued
a strategy of exploiting cheap and vulnerable labour to maximize
profits. This history includes its operations in Suharto's Indonesia,
where unions were criminalized, and where the company called in
police to attack picket lines. Bata was also an investor in apartheid
South Africa, where it broke unions, paid its black workers wages
that were half of the poverty line at the time and thirty-five percent less than what it paid workers at a factory in a white district,
and imposed "intolerable" working conditions on its employees,
including forced overtime, suspension of lunch breaks and denial
of sick leave.[120]

A more recent example of Bata's conflict with its workers comes
from Sri Lanka. On June 22, 2004, nearly 600 workers—members
of the Commercial and Industrial Workers Union—began a two-
week occupation of a Bata factory in Ratmalana, an industrial area
on the southern outskirts of Colombo. The occupation was a response to continued outsourcing of work to other factories, and
the firing of the local union president on trumped-up misconduct
charges after he uncovered evidence of company corruption related to the misuse of the workers' pension fund. The workers demanded that Bata withdraw its plan to cut the workforce by another twenty-five percent, and let the fired union president's case go
before a labour tribunal. But when a court ruled the occupiers to

be illegally trespassing on company property, police removed the workers, who continued their protest outside the factory gates. On the fifty-second day of the strike, after complaints from company officials that access to the factory was impeded by the workers, police attacked the picketers with tear gas, water cannons and batons. Fifteen workers were arrested, several were severely injured and hospitalized, and all workers involved in the job action were subsequently fired. Later that night after the strike was violently broken, a Bata warehouse on the southern outskirts of Colombo was torched in what police describe as a several-million-dollar case of anti-Bata sabotage.[121]

Financial Services

I have noted that Canadian banks such as Scotia and Royal (RBC) have a long history of imperialist practice. In this manner, they have come to dominate a sizable chunk of the Latin American and Caribbean banking markets. Many of their unsavoury activities are not as visible as those of other industries such as mining or oil and gas, where people are violently dispossessed of their land and their environments poisoned. But that does not mean the banks should escape our critical attention. For as one Scotiabank executive remarked a generation ago, "We've stopped screwing Canadians. Now we're screwing foreigners."[122] If the executive is exaggerating about Scotia's relations with Canadians, he is not about its relations with foreigners. But the banks' involvement in the exploitation of the people and environments of the Global South can be more difficult to trace than in other industries. Their role might entail financing another company's investment that involves human rights and ecological abuse. By the end of the 1990s Canadian financial companies raised more equity capital for the mining industry than was raised in Australia, the United States and South Africa combined.[123] I will provide a few recent examples of the contribution to imperialism in the South by Canadian banks.

Scotiabank

During the Argentine economic meltdown in 2001–2002, Scotiabank's subsidiary, Scotiabank Quilmes, was the target of angry protests by both its customers and workers, was investigated for fraud, and had its operations suspended when the head office in Toronto refused to inject much-needed capital into the subsidiary, leaving both customers and workers in the cold. Eventually the bank sold off its assets and departed the country.

In the fall of 2001, not long after the planes hit the World Trade Center towers, Argentina went into one of the worst economic meltdowns of the global neoliberal era. Once the darling of neoliberal propagandists, held up as an exemplar of the benefits of the tough economic medicine of IMF-imposed aggressive restructuring and market liberalization (including "pegging" the value of the Argentine peso to the U.S. dollar as a means of controlling inflation and government spending), Argentina's fall from grace was quick and, for its working and middle classes, extremely painful. In order to peg the peso to the dollar, Argentina had to purchase dollars (build up its reserves), and to do that it had to borrow heavily from the IMF and international financiers. However, when the economies of the emerging markets of Russia, East Asia and Brazil sank into a deep recession and their financial markets teetered on the brink of collapse in the late 1990s, following a massive and unsustainable influx of capital from the North earlier in the decade, international lenders began to grow apprehensive about the overheated markets of the South. Their demands for repayment of outstanding loans, fearing suddenly that the states of the emerging markets would not be able to cover them, grew increasingly loud. As the world economy faltered, Argentina's economy slid into a prolonged recession beginning in the late 1990s, and its external debt, a direct result of IMF policy and worsened by the global slowdown, grew steadily. Compounding the problem was that by pegging the peso to the dollar, Argentina essentially handed monetary control of its economy to the U.S. (which controls the supply of dollars), and was therefore unable to lower interest rates—a common move to ease the effects of recession (to make it cheaper to borrow money and continue to invest). The IMF insisted the only solution to the faltering economy was to cut domestic spending even further than it had been in the 1990s—and this during a recession.

By the fall of 2001 the government, whose finances were drying up amidst the economic contraction, could no longer sustain its massive external debt, which reached US$150 billion. A whopping thirty percent of gross domestic product was going to interest payments on that debt. Eventually the government had no choice but to default. As the government defaulted on its foreign debt, and private international financiers refused further loans to the country, the crisis washed across Argentina. Companies across industries were drowned in the flood of capitalist market "correction," and unemployment skyrocketed to over twenty percent. The financial system verged on collapse, as banks lost billions of dollars in unpaid loans held by companies that had gone bankrupt. The government unhitched the peso from the dollar in a bid to regain control over its monetary system. But with international investors fleeing the country, demand for the Argentinean currency fled with them, and its value against the dollar started to plummet. Argentineans rushed to the banks to withdraw their savings fearing they would be lost as the currency's value tumbled and banks appeared near death. In order to stave off a complete financial collapse the government imposed sharp limits on bank withdrawals, infuriating the depositors who watched as their savings vanished in the crisis. Angered by rising unemployment, the loss of savings and the prospect of further cutbacks, working- and middle-class Argentineans took to the streets in massive protests, bringing the country to a standstill.[124]

As mass strikes and demonstrations flared up in January 2002, then-president Eduardo Duhalde sought to ease the pressure on Argentineans by forcibly establishing conversion rates for pesos with U.S. dollar deposits and loans that effectively shifted some of the costs of devaluation onto the banks' shoulders (many Argentineans held a portion of their savings and loans in U.S. dollars). Debts owed to the banks shrank in value significantly, and banks had to absorb the financial loss. But the cash crunch meant the banks were unable to lend and thus make money. Foreign banks were also prohibited by the government from seizing the assets of debtors, such as individuals who could not afford to pay their mortgages. The value of Scotiabank's assets dropped by $1 billion with the devaluation of the peso, while the bank eventually wrote down $707 million in 2002 to cover its losses.[125]

Scotiabank's response to the crisis infuriated Argentineans and their government, who charged that the bank's head office in Toronto (along with several other foreign banks) exacerbated the financial crisis by refusing to put more cash into its struggling subsidiary. This would have ensured that, despite the dramatic run on deposits, Quilmes would remain solvent and depositors, many of whom had lost their jobs and were struggling to survive, would be able to withdraw funds to cover basic expenses. Scotia's head office, however, was insistent that it would not be putting any new money into Argentina "unless there are clear rules in place that give confidence that the systemic economic crisis can be turned around."[126] The bank's strategy was to exploit the financial chaos and the hardship Argentineans were enduring. With the support of the Canadian state and the IMF, Scotiabank sought to force further economic restructuring and liberalization of the banking system. Many observers believe this precipitated the suspension of Scotia's operations by Argentina's central bank in April 2002, when the bank could not meet the reserve levels required by Argentinean law.[127]

In early 2002, two Scotiabank Quilmes executives, along with their counterparts from a number of other foreign banks, were the subject of an investigation by the Argentine government. Their offices were raided by police amidst allegations that they contributed to the financial crisis by illegally moving funds out of the country. If proven, this would have amounted to fraud against the bank's customers. But Scotia had the support of the Canadian government to protect its interests. Prime Minister Jean Chrétien expressed his concern about the treatment of Scotiabank to Argentinean president Eduardo Duhalde at a summit meeting on poverty, where Duhalde was looking for financial relief from rich donor nations. The judge was replaced, and nothing came of the investigation. Later in 2002 Liberal finance minister Paul Martin also pressured his Argentine counterpart at IMF meetings in which Argentina was again negotiating financial relief, urging him to rethink the country's treatment of the Canadian bank.[128]

Short on cash during the crisis, Scotia's response to the situation was an obvious attempt to shift the burden of its financial losses onto its customers and workers. The head of Scotia's Argentine operations was charged with "legal disobedience" in July 2002, after Quilmes refused a court order demanding it release frozen funds for its employees, pensioners with savings held by the bank and employees of companies that held accounts in the bank. The bank was refusing the release, claiming it did not have sufficient cash. Scotiabank also refused 1,800 workers back pay and the US$35 million in severance to which they were entitled. One worker angrily noted that "All they care about is their share-holders in Canada ... they seem to have forgotten they also have 1,800 workers with families to support. They have no heart."[129] But while the bank was stiffing its customers and workers, and despite its claims of impoverishment and its failed requests for aid from the Argentinean government, it was able to cover its losses rather quickly. It wrote down its Argentine losses in 2002 while Argentineans were still in the midst of economic chaos. Given the size of Scotia and the value of its global assets and profits, the write-down really made no dent in the company wallet. The losses were recouped by the end of the year. Bank executive Peter Godsoe noted that the losses associated with Quilmes "will have no material impact" on the health of the bank.[130]

As a result of its actions, Scotia drew the wrath of its customers and workers. Demonstrations were held in which people threw eggs and burned tires outside branches. The bank was forced to install metal shutters and hire guards to protect its properties from the angry protesters. Scotia workers organized a one-day strike in Argentina, blocked traffic in Buenos Aires and demonstrated at the Canadian embassy, asking the Canadian government to intervene and assist them in getting their severance pay. They even came to Canada in 2002 to protest outside Scotia's Toronto headquarters.[131]

Although Scotia sold off its Argentinean operations in late 2002, the story does not quite end there. Despite having easily written down its losses several years before, Scotia initiated a lawsuit in 2005 against the Argentinean government for more than $600 million. Scotia accused the government of discriminatory practices when the latter forced the bank to convert U.S. dollar deposits to pesos and refused it the same financial assistance it offered to domestic banks. Scotia claimed these practices contributed to the collapse of its subsidiary, and insisted that the government must compensate it.[132]

Royal Bank of Canada (RBC)

Although RBC has extensive interests in Latin America and the Caribbean, I want to highlight another investment. There is a commonly accepted view that Canada is not involved in the imperialist occupation of Iraq. The Liberal government of 2003, facing widespread opposition to the war both in Canada and abroad, decided to opt out militarily. Nortel's Iraqi contract, discussed earlier, undermines the assumption that Canada has no involvement in the country. Even if Canada has not engaged in the military occupation, Canadian corporations are looking to profit from the rebuilding and privatization projects that the invasion and occupation have made possible. Their opportunity to win a piece of the lucrative spoils of war and occupation will be facilitated by RBC.[133]

In the fall of 2003, RBC joined a financial consortium of fourteen major international companies, headed by the American bank J.P. Morgan Chase & Co. The consortium was established by the U.S.-run provisional authority to facilitate international investment and trade in the war-torn but geostrategically useful country, once an important economic player in the Middle East. RBC was recruited to act as a conduit to Canadian business—providing letters of credit to allow Iraqis to purchase Canadian goods and services—and stands to earn a handsome reward if it gains a longer-term foothold in Iraq and stability (for business and Western powers) returns to the Middle Eastern nation. But what is good for RBC is good for Canadian capital more generally. Before RBC joined the international financial consortium, Canadian companies did not have good access to business opportunities in Iraq.[134]

This Iraq opportunity could not have come without the U.S. invasion. Prior to 2003, the foreign corporate presence in Iraq was limited, and the state played a large role in the economy. Foreign banks had not operated in the country since it undertook a policy of economic nationalization in the 1950s. But now, with a massive wave of privatization imposed by the American occupation authorities and supported by their Iraqi political puppets, and conservative estimates putting the reconstruction costs—excluding military expenditures—at US$500 million a month for the foreseeable future, foreign companies, including banks, are licking their lips at the opportunities now open to them in Iraq. RBC spokesperson Paul Wilson sees a good opportunity for the Canadian bank hedging bets on Iraq's future, explaining that it "expects an adequate return … given that the forecast is $500 million [monthly] in a year, one would expect that Canadian importers and exporters will be involved in doing trade with Iraq."[135] "Adequate" of course is likely a gross understatement. RBC did not build up its international empire over the last century by seeking out so-so returns. Predators never go in half-hearted. To sweeten RBC's investment even further, this will be a very low-risk venture: the bank's financing support is being guaranteed by the American-controlled Development Fund for Iraq, whose revenue source comes from the country's oil export earnings. In other words, the Iraqi people—severely impoverished, malnourished and insecure as a result of the invasion and occupation—are guaranteeing the financial security of the wealthy Canadian multinational's investment: it is being backed by the exploitation of their natural resources. Export Development Canada (EDC), using Canadian public funds, will also offer RBC risk protection. And so it goes. A Canadian bank exploiting naked imperialism, and in the process helping other Canadian companies get their piece of the Iraqi pie.[136]

Another example of RBC's important role in facilitating the international expansion and growth of Canadian capital involves Toronto-based junior mining company Gabriel Resources. Gabriel is seeking to build itself up into a larger global concern through its Rosia Montana gold mine in Romania. Despite intense opposition to the mine both inside and outside of Romania, RBC arranged an underwriting syndicate that raised $254 million in Canada in 2006 and 2007 for the project. The Canadian Imperial Bank of Commerce and Bank of Montreal also provided Gabriel Resources with financing.

The development would be the largest open cast cyanide-leech gold mine in Europe. It would entail the involuntary resettlement of over 2,000 people from their homes, the destruction of important archaeological sites dating from the Roman and pre-Roman period and the destruction of the historic village of Rosia Montana, including several churches and cemeteries. At full production the mine will use thirteen to fifteen million kilograms of cyanide a year, while the adjacent valley of Corna, despite being inhabited, will be used as a tailings pond facility for an estimated 195 million tons of cyanide-laced heavy metal tailings. Gabriel submitted a request to obtain environmental approval in 2004 based on its environmental impact assessment. The assessment triggered a flurry of responses from various independent experts pointing out the numerous deficiencies and false conclusions it contained, and a number of authors of the assessment requested their names be removed from it, claiming that the published version had no relationship with the report the company submitted.[137] Gabriel's plans gave rise to "Save the Rosia Montana," Romania's largest civil society movement, according to some observers. Dozens of organizations and individuals, ranging from the Romanian Orthodox church to the Romanian Academy (the country's most important scientific body) to fifty of the country's most eminent archaeologists and historians, have declared their opposition to the mine.[138] Rosia Montana reportedly received support from the Canadian government. Raphael Girard, Canadian ambassador to Romania from June 1, 2000, to August 31, 2003, relied on information provided by Gabriel on the environmental impact of, and opposition to, the mine in reports to government officials. Not surprisingly, these downplay the size of the opposition and the latter's concerns. He has since moved on from his position as ambassador and taken up a post with the company's board of directors, no doubt to exploit his connections with the Canadian state to help move the project along. He reported to investors in 2005 that the Canadian government is fully behind the mine and is actively lobbying to get it off the ground.[139]

Despite this support, the opposition has managed to stall the mine, at least temporarily, following a legal victory against the environmental assessment in 2007. Romania's Ministry for the Environment subsequently suspended the impact assessment procedure for an undetermined period. Gabriel, though, asserts its intention to fight the ministry's decision and proceed with its project, but the Romanian Supreme Court put up another roadblock when it cancelled Gabriel's permit. In order to continue with the mine, the company will have to reapply for a new permit.[140]

A Trail of Tragedy and Destruction

It is clear that acts of Canadian corporate malfeasance abroad are not those of a few select rogue companies; nor are they isolated to one or two industries. Canadian capitalist plundering of the Third World—hyper-exploiting labour, stealing and destroying land, and violently attempting to thwart opposition movements—has become widespread in the age of neoliberal globalization. When Canadian companies expand their interests around the globe, they leave a trail of human rights violations and ecological devastation.

Canadian capital is also clearly drawing on and reproducing the sharp racial dynamics of imperialism. It is not an accident, as I have noted in previous chapters, that the super cheap and hyper-exploited labour Canadian capital seeks out around the Third World is primarily that of people of colour. Canada structurally adjusts people into poverty and desperation, and then its capital swoops in to feed off their vulnerabilities. But on what grounds can Canadian business and political leaders claim, with straight faces, that paying sweated labour less than poverty-level wages and imposing extremely poor working conditions on people is justifiable? On what grounds can it proceed with its investments on the basis of murder, as it does in Colombia? People of the Third World have been racialized as expendable and unable to care for themselves. Their poverty, in the eyes of the Canadian state and capital, is both an example of their economic and cultural, and indeed civilizational, backwardness, and an opportunity to drain their wealth from them. Thus the idea of empire—the right and indeed the need (for the colonized's own sake) to dominate people of colour in the South—intersects violently with imperial practice. Canadian capitalists may be getting filthy rich, but it is a necessary lesson for the world's poor.

This racist dynamic has been especially obvious in regard to indigenous people. As with the domestic investments of Canadian capital, investments abroad regularly target indigenous communities. Canadian companies, supported by the state, typically ignore indigenous land claims, push indigenous peoples off their land, and proceed with investments that entail devastating ecological impacts without the consent of indigenous communities. These practices are motivated by a profoundly racist view— which is in fact an extension of domestic attitudes—of indigenous peoples as inferior and incapable of having any rights as a people worth respecting. Indigenous nations are clearly situated by imperialists outside the historically rooted European-derived notions of "civilized," which confers to Canadian capital the right to forcefully dismiss their claims. Organizing their world on different ethical, spiritual and socioeconomic principles from the North, they are objectified through their difference as uncivilized and irrational: at best a helpless people who sometimes need the tough medicine of the rich countries; at worst a backward disruption of the capitalist march of progress. Yet there is nothing progressive about environmental destruction, the exploitation of labour or the denial of a nation its right to self-determination. Thus as we have seen, it is often indigenous peoples leading the struggles against Canadian companies. Indigeneity is not defeated, nor is it the cultural flaw of backward peoples; instead, it is a rich source of hope and collective and spiritual strength, drawn on to challenge Canadian imperialism and maintain an inspiring defiance in the face of the continued assaults on their communities.

The case studies provided in this chapter are by no means exhaustive. Not all industries have been covered. For instance, as I pointed out in the previous chapter, Canada has been one of the world's major weapons exporters for some time, and many of its exports have made it into the hands of dictators (in Pakistan under Musharref or in Indonesia under General Suharto); armies enforcing illegal occupations (Indonesia when it was occupying East Timor or Israel in Palestine); or governments engaging in widespread human rights abuses (Colombia, for example). I also have not discussed the specific impact of Canadian support for structural adjustment policies, or for patent protections for pharmaceutical companies this make it harder for people in poor countries to access cheap and desperately needed medicines. These policies, as many critics have pointed out, have brought devastation on Third World countries, condemning billions of the world's poorest to increased poverty, malnutrition and curable diseases. Canada is complicit in this neoliberal terrorism waged by the rich world (usually through the IMF or WTO) against the South.

Besides its role in the IMF and WTO, the Canadian state consistently provides direct support to Canadian corporations as they wreak havoc on the Third World. EDC or CIDA funding, failing to impose human rights standards on Canadian corporations, and exploiting the economic vulnerabilities of poor countries to ensure Canadian companies are well treated—these are strategies the state uses to defend the interests of Canadian capitalists abroad. This is the real Canada: the aggressive imperialist pursuer of economic self-interest.

Canada's participation in the IMF and WTO, EDC and CIDA funding, and refusal to develop human rights policy for Canadian companies operating abroad, are not the only way the state supports Canadian capital. Canada has also been undertaking a significant overhaul of its security policy, which is tied in important ways to its global capitalist ambitions. It is to this security policy we now turn.

1   J. Kuyek offers a devastating critique of the concept, and how its use often has little more than propaganda value for corporations. Kuyek, "Legitimating Plunder: Canadian Mining Companies and Corporate Social Responsibility," in L. North, T. Clark and V. Patroni, eds., *Community Rights and Corporate Responsibility: Canadian Mining and Oil Companies in Latin America* (Toronto: Between the Lines, 2006). See also P. Simons, "The Adequacy and Effectiveness of Voluntary Self-Regulation Regimes, *Industrial Relations* (vol. 59, n. 4, 2004), 101-141.

2   As noted in the previous chapter, Canadian banks built up their empires in part by exploiting investment opportunities in Latin America and the Caribbean provided by American-backed dictators in the late nineteenth and twentieth centuries, while pulling out of and destabilizing countries ruled by left-wing governments, such as Salvador Allende's Chile. Canadian mining companies have a similar historical legacy of their own, violently exploiting the labour and resources of developing nations in the Americas, Africa and Asia-Pacific. Canada was also an important investor—in a number of industries—in General Suharto's Indonesia (1965-1998), which denied the basic civil and political rights of Indonesians and engaged in a brutal occupation of East Timor in which an estimated one-third of the population was killed. See S. Scharfe, *Complicity: Human Rights and Canadian Foreign Policy: The Case of East Timor* (Montreal: Black Rose Books, 1996); E. Briere and D. Devaney, "East Timor: the slaughter of a tribal nation," *Canadian Dimension* (October, 1990), 31-35.

3   W Avilés, 'Paramilitarism and Colombia's Low Intensity Democracy,' Journal of Latin American Studies 38 (2), 403. Derived from the Colombian Commission of Jurists.

4   F. Hylton, *Evil Hour in Colombia* (London: Verso, 2006), 109ff; G. Livingstone, *Inside Colombia: Drugs, Democracy and War* (London: Pluto Press, 2003), 119.

5   International Confederation of Free Trade Unions (ICFTU), *Annual Survey of Violations of Trade Union Rights*, 2006, <www.icftu.org/displaydocument.asp?Index=991223986&Language=EN>, retrieved January 2007. C Campbell, 'Addicted to Blood Coal,' *Maclean's*, 20 March, 36; F Ramírez Cuellar, *The Profits of Extermination* (Monroe, Maine: Common Courage Press, 2005), 86-87.

6   Hylton, *Evil Hour*, 4; and Ramírez Cuellar, *The Profits of Extermination*, 84-85; J. Hristov, *Blood and Capital: The Paramilitarization of Colombia* (Athens: Ohio University Press, 2009), 2.

7   Ramírez Cuellar, *The Profits of Extermination*, 85.

8   Central Intelligence Agency (CIA), *CIA: World Fact Book* (Washington, D.C.: CIA, 2006), <www.cia.gov/cia/publications/factbook/geos/co.html>, retrieved January, 2007.

9   Ramírez Cuellar, *The Profits of Extermination*, 82-83.

10 Ismi, "Profiting from Repression," 27-28; Ramírez Cuellar, *The Profits of Extermination*, 39-40.

11 Ramírez Cuellar, *The Profits of Extermination*, 39.

12 The Vancouver Sun, 'Colombia not Safe, Foreign Affairs Ministry Says,' *The Vancouver Sun* (May 4, 2002), A2. Forrest Hylton provides a portrait of the 1990s: "If multiple sovereignties and fractured territories had been a notable feature of the political landscape in the 1980s, both the insurgencies and the paramilitaries made qualitative leaps in control over resources, population, territory, and transport routes during the 1990s. This was achieved through greater recourse to terror, especially on the paramilitary side, as counterinsurgency operations were increasingly privatized and subcontracted," Hylton, *Evil Hour*, 80.

13 Ismi, "Profiting from Repression."

14 <www.northernminer.ca>. Retrieved January 2007.

15 Lemeiux, 'Canada's Global Mining Presence', 7.12.

16 C Arsenault, 'Digging up Canadian Dirt in Colombia,' *Canadian Dimension* (November/December 2006), 32-35.

17 Both quotes on Greystar's new presence in Colombia from P. Harris, "Colombia's Troubles Pale Next to Golden Opportunities," *The Globe and Mail* (January 4, 2006), B6.

18 Rovig quoted in W. Stueck, "Miner gives Colombia another chance," *Globe and Mail* (October 14, 2003), B9.

19 K. Patterson, "Struggle at the Top of the Andes," *The Ottawa Citizen*, (October 1, 2006), A6.

20 T. Clark, "Canadian Mining in Neo-liberal Chile," in L. North, T. Clark and V. Patroni, eds., *Community Rights and Corporate Responsibility: Canadian Mining and Oil Companies in Latin America* (Toronto: Between the Lines, 2006), 105.

21 *National Post*, "Barrick Gold Tells Chilean Hearing It is 'Perfectly Feasible' to Move Three Glaciers," *National Post* (April 20, 2005), FP3; *National Post*, "Greens Bid to Block Barrick in Chile, *National Post* (February 10, 2006), FP4; J. Ross, "Moving Heaven, Earth and Glaciers," *Toronto Star* (June 4, 2005), H5; and S. Pratt, "Are Mining Companies Running Over Human Rights in Foreign Lands?" *Edmonton Journal* (October 30, 2005), A18.

22 Quoted in Ross, "Glaciers Under Threat," 16-19.

23 Ross, "Glaciers Under Threat," 16-19.

24 Clark, "Canadian Mining in Neo-liberal Chile," 106; Ross, "Glaciers Under Threat," 16-19; and quote is from Patterson, "Struggle at the Top of the Andes," A6.

25 Clark, "Canadian Mining in Neo-liberal Chile," 108; Ross, "Moving Heaven," H5; Ross, "Glaciers Under Threat," 16-19; Patterson, "Struggle at the Top of the Andes,"A6; R Foot, "Anti-Mine Protesters Greet Harper on Chile Visit," *The Vancouver Sun* (July 19, 2007), C4; D. Estrada, "Activists Try to Block Start of Pascua Lama Mine," *Inter-Press Service* (May 18, 2009).

26 Estrada, "Activists Try to Block Start of Pascua Lama Mine."

27 Corpwatch, B*arrick's Dirty Secrets: Communities Respond to Gold Mining's Impact Worldwide* (2007), 4. <www.corppwatch.org/article. php?id=14466>, retrieved June 2007.

28 D. Modersbach, "Argentina: Famatina Says NO to Barrick Gold," (March 20, 2007), <www.miningwatch.ca/index.php?/Barrick/Famatina_update>, retrieved June 2007.

29 Activist quoted in Modersbach, "Argentina: Famatina Says NO to Barrick Gold."

30 Modersbach, "Argentina: Famatina Says NO to Barrick Gold." The quote is from Modersbach as well.

31 Quoted in Mining Watch, "Philippine Province Sues Canadian Mining Giant Placer Dome," (October 4, 2005), <www.miningwatch.ca/index. php?/Marcopper_Mine/Marinduque_suit>, retrieved June 2007.

32 C. Coumans, "Philippine Province Files Suit Against Placer Dome—Background," (October 4, 2005), <www.miningwatch.ca/index.php?/Marcopper_Mine/Marinduque_suit_backgnd>, retrieved June 2007.

33 Lawyer's Environmental Action Team, *Robbing the Rich to Give to the Poor: Human Rights Abuses and Impoverishment at the MIGA-Backed Bulyanhulu Gold Mine, Tanzania*. Submission to the Extractive Industries Review of the World Bank, Maputo, Mozambique, (January 13-17, 2003), <www.leat.or.tz/activities/buly/eir.submission>, retrieved June 2007.

34 Mining Watch, "Human Rights Advocate Jailed in Tanzania," (January 3, 2003) <www.miningwatch.ca/index.php?/Tanzania_en/Human_Rights_Advocat>, retrieved June 2007. Mining Watch, "Tanzanian Environmental Activists Persecuted for Speaking Out Against World Bank Group Gold Mine," (May 10, 2002). <www.miningwatch.ca/index.php?/Tanzania_en/Tanzanian_Environmen>, retrieved June 2007.

35 A. Freeman, "Controversy over mining overshadows health initiative," *Globe and Mail* (November 27, 2007), A23.

36 Corpwatch, *Barrick's Dirty Secrets*, 17.

37 Mining Watch, "Will Ascendant Copper Be Stopped in its Tracks?" (August 25, 2006), <www.miningwatch.ca/index.php?/Ecuador_en/Ascendant_

injunction>, retrieved July 2007; Mining Watch, "Ecuador" (2007), <www.miningwatch.ca/index.php?/Ecuador_en>, retrieved July 2007; Friends of the Earth, "International Investment Complaint Filed Against Canadian Mining Company," (May 18, 2005), <www.miningwatch.ca/index.php?/oecd_complaint_ascen>, retrieved July 2007.

38   A. T. Males, "Letter from the Mayor of Cotacachi Cantón, Ecuador, to the Toronto Stock Exchange" (March 8, 2005), <www.miningwatch.ca/index.php?/Ecuador_en/Cotacachi_TSX_en>, retrieved July 2007.

39   K. Patterson, "Canadian miner battles Ecuador opposition," *Edmonton Journal* (December 15, 2006), A14; Vancouver Sun, "Vancouver-Based firm in Ecuador says it hired security guards, not paramilitary forces," *Vancouver Sun* (December 8, 2006), F7; Mining Watch, "Ascendant Copper Agrees to Curtail Activities" (March 30, 2007), <www.miningwatch.ca/index.php?/Ecuador_en/Ascendant_signs>, retrieved July 2007.

40   Sister Elsie Monge, "U.S. Citizen Linked to Transnational Mining Company Ascendant Copper Infiltrated Demonstration, Now Presents False Accusations Against Intag Community Leader," (Quito: Ecumenical Commission on Human Rights, October 18, 2006), <www.miningwatch.ca/index.php?/Ecuador_en/CEDHU_en>, retrieved July 2007; K. Patterson, "UN probes claims mining interests framed critic: Ascendant's copper mine plan under fire," Vancouver Sun (December 20, 2006), D10; C. Zorrilla, "Police Raid on My House," (October 27, 2006), <www.zmag.org>, retrieved July 2007; Zorrilla quoted in Mining Watch, "Luck of the Draw: Carlos Zorrilla visits North America" (May 29, 2007), <www.miningwatch.ca/index.php?/Ecuador_en/zorilla_visit>, retrieved July 2007.

41   J. Kneen, "Ecuador: Government Shuts Down Ascendant Copper's Junín Project," Mining Watch Alerts (September 28, 2007); Mining Watch, "Ascendant Copper Ordered to Cease Work," <www.miningwatch.ca/index.php?/Ecuador_en/ACC_EIA_rejected>, retrieved July 2007.

42   Salvador Quishipe is quoted in K. Patterson, "Canadian CEO denies abuses at mine protest," *The Ottawa Citizen* (January 18, 2007), A12.

43   D. Hasselback, *National Post* (March 6, 2007), SR 1; Patterson, "Canadian CEO denies abuses at mine protest," A12; S. Santacruz, "Regulations Lift Mining Ban, Uncertainty Persists," *Ecuador Mining News* (December 9, 2009), <www.ecuadorminingnews.com/news.php?id=124>, retrieved December 2009.

44   A. Ismi, "Congo: The Western Heart of Darkness," *Canadian Centre for Policy Alternatives Monitor* (October, 2001).

45   Ismi, "Congo."

46   E. Mekay, "Minerals Flow Abroad, Misery Remains," *Inter Press News Service* (July 5, 2006), <www.corpwatch.org/article.php?id=13858>, retrieved July 2007.

47 *Calgary Herald,* "Two jailed for life in Congo Massacres," *Calgary Herald* (June 29, 2007), A22; D. Lewis, "Congo wants Anvil staffers tried in war crimes case," *Globe and Mail* (October 17, 2006), B15; Mining Watch, "Anvil Mining and the Kilwa Massacre, D.R. Congo: Canadian Company Implicated?" (June 16, 2005), <www.miningwatch.ca/index.php?/Congo_DR/Anvil_Mining_Kilwa>, retrieved July 2007.

48 W. Stueck, "Fiery protest prompts mine closing," *Globe and Mail* (April 27, 2006), B5.

49 A. Koehl, "Billions, Millions, and the Peasant," (January 18, 2006), <www.miningwatch.ca/index.php?/Glamis_Gold/Koehl_billions>, retrieved July 2007; K. Patterson, "Canadian mine strikes lode of unrest," *Ottawa Citizen* (April 26, 2005), C3.

50 Patterson, "Canadian mine," C3; W. Stueck, "Clashes reported in Guatemala over Glamis mining project," *Globe and Mail* (January 13, 2005), B14.

51 Rights Action, "Trial of 'Goldcorp 7'Begins Monday, November 12," Rights Action Update (November 10, 2007); Intercontinental Cry, "Goldcorp seven verdict is in," (December 17, 2007), <intercontinentalcry.org/goldcorp-7-verdict-is-injustice-in-guatemala/>, retrieved January 2008.

52 A. Hoffman, "Goldcorp bested by Mayan mother," *Globe and Mail* (July 10, 2008), B1; Foreign Affairs and International Trade, "Secretary of State Guergis to Visit Belize and Guatemala," (July 10, 2008), <w01.international.gc.ca/MinPub/Publication.asp?Language= E&publication_id=386372&docnumber=159>, retrieved July 2008.

53 Rights Action, "After Goldcorp illegal tried to take control of more lands, Maya Mam people of San Miguel Ixtahuacan are threatened with more 'criminalizatin'and repression," e-mail alert (June 12, 2009).

54 Mining Watch, "Goldcorp Analysis," (September, 2007), <www.miningwatch.ca/updir/Goldcorp_Analysis_Sept_2007.pdf>, retrieved October 2007.

55 J. Gradon, "It is difficult but manageable, says the nation's oil boss," *Calgary Herald* (March 12, 2000), A11; C. Howes, "The oil imperialists: The Westeren Canadian Sedimentary Basin, source of Alberta's wealth, is drying up. So Exploration companies have a new tool: their passports," *National Post* (November 13, 1999), F8; <www.enbridge.com/about/enbridgeCompanies/international>, retrieved July 2007; S. Pearce, "Tackling Corporate Complicity: Canadian Oil Investment in Colombia," in L. North, T. Clark and V. Patroni, *Community Rights,* 162.

56 G. Livingstone, Inside Colombia: Drugs, Democracy and War (London: Latin American Bureau, 2003), 108.

57 Livingstone, *Inside Colombia,* 117; S. Pearce, "Tackling Corporate Complicity," 160ff.

58 Ismi, "Profiting From Repression," 10; <www.enbridge.com/about/enbridgeCompanies/international>. In the 1990s, TCPL assisted in the

construction of the Thai portion of the Unocal/Total gas pipeline originating from Burma. Unocal was accused of using, with the consent of the Burmese dictatorship, slave labour on the pipeline in Burma.

59 Livingstone, *Inside Colombia*, 112.

60 Hylton, *Evil Hour*, 93; Ismi, "Profiting From Repression," 10; Ismi, "Enbridge Spreads Disaster in Colombia," *Canadian Centre for Policy Alternatives Monitor* (July, 2004).

61 Amnesty International quoted in Ismi, "Profiting From Repression," 10.

62 Ismi, "Profiting From Repression," 11. OCENSA's secret agreement with the Colombian Defense Ministry was reported in the Chicago Colombia Committee's and the Colombia Labour Monitor's *Colombia Bulletin*.

63 G. Leech, "Plan Petroleum in Colombia," *Canadian Dimension* (July-August, 2004), 42-45; S. Polczer, "Colombia courts Calgary for increased oil production: Country 'great place to do business,'" *Calgary Herald* (June 10, 2006), C4.

64 N. Drost and K. Stewart, "EnCana in Ecuador: The Canadian Oil Patch Goes to the Amazon," in *Community Rights*, 113-114, 118.

65 Drost and Stewart, "EnCana in Ecuador," 113-114. In 2008 EnCana announced plans to split into two companies in 2009, one that will focus on natural gas the other petroleum.

66 Drost and Stewart, "EnCana in Ecuador," 117.

67 Drost and Stewart, "EnCana in Ecuador," 117-118; T. Levine and G. Michalenko, "The route of the problem: cloud forest defenders want proposed pipeline moved," *Alternatives Journal* (Summer, 2002) 7.

68 Drost and Stewart, "EnCana in Ecuador," 119-120; Levine and Michalenko, "The route of the problem," 8.

69 Drost and Stewart, "EnCana in Ecuador," 121-122, 128.

70 Drost and Stewart, "EnCana in Ecuador," 122; Levine and Michalenko, "The route of the problem," 8

71 *Globe and Mail*, "EnCana's Ecuador pipeline resumes shipments," *Globe and Mail* (March 2, 2006), B16; Globe and Mail, "Ecuador state of emergency over oil pump hijacking," *Globe and Mail* (February 23, 2006), B16; A. Valencia and C. Andrade Garcia, "EnCana shuts down operations: Company hit by attack on properties," *Calgary Herald* (August 19, 2005), D4.

72 D. Yedlin, "South America choosing perilous path," *Globe and Mail* (May 23, 2006), B2; Calgary Herald, "EnCana leaves Ecuador with $1.4B," *Calgary Herald*, (March 1, 2006), F4; C. Cattaneo, "Ecuador file hits EnCana Q2 earnings," *National Post* (July 26, 2006), FP 7. Gwyn Morgan quoted in C. Cattaneo, "'Don't tar us with one brush,' Colombia says: Country welcomes Western oil firms," *National Post* (June 13, 2006), FP2

73 <www.talisman-energy.com/about_us/history.html?disclaimer=1>, retrieved July 2007.

74　K. Vick, "Sudan: Oil Money is Fueling Civil War," *Washington Post* (June 11, 2001); Harker Commission, *Human Security in Sudan: The Report of a Canadian Assessment Mission*, prepared for the Minister of Foreign Affairs (Ottawa: January 2000), executive summary, <www.reliefweb.int/library/documents/cansudan2.pdf>, retrieved July 2007, 3-4, 8-10.

75　Harker Commission, *Human Security in Sudan*, 3-4, 8-10; R. Re, "A Persisting Evil: The Global Problem of Slavery," *Harvard International Review* (Winter, 2002), 32-35; Vick, "Sudan: Oil Money is Fueling Civil War."

76　C. Varcoe, "Oil Hot Spots: Hunting for oil can be a risky business in some parts of the world—but it is a risk Canadian producers are willing to accept," *Calgary Herald* (February 19, 2000), D1; Harker Commission, *Human Security in Sudan*, 14.

77　Harker Commission, *Human Security in Sudan*, 15; C. Varcoe, "Oil Hot Spots, D1; Canada and the World Backgrounder, "Energy Ethics," *Canada and the World Backgrounder* (March, 2000), 11.

78　J. Bagnall, "Ottawa must halt firms working in genocide zones," *Times-Colonist* (October 11, 2007), A12; M. Bourrie, "Canada: Oil Company Targeted for Ties to Sudanese Military," *Inter Press Service* (February 7, 2000), <www.corpwatch.org/article.php?id=317>, retrieved July 2007.

79　K. Patterson, "Ottawa opposed on Talisman war-crimes case; Eclectic group challenges intervention," *The Gazette* (June 12, 2007), B5; K. Patterson, "Government backs Talisman in U.S. suit; Warns war crimes case could 'create friction,'" *Ottawa Citizen* (May 26, 2007), A4. The suit was filed under the U.S. Alien Tort Claims Act.

80　On Talisman in Colombia, <www.talisman-energy.com/operations/rest_of_world.html>, retrieved July 2007; J. Baxter, "Companies, products linked to Indonesia: Labour organization urges boycott," *Ottawa Citizen* (September 15, 1999), A4; N. Scott, "Talisman strikes deal for Iraq fields," *Globe and Mail* (June 24, 2008), B1.

81　See, for example, T. Gordon, "Colonialism and the Economic Crisis in Canada," (April 18, 2009) <www.zmag.org/znet/viewArticle/21193>, retrieved April 2009. Perhaps the best-known First Nation community resisting oil development in Alberta is the Lubicon Cree. John Goddard provides a useful history of this struggle in *Last Stand of the Lubicon Cree* (Vancouver: Douglas and McIntyre, 1991). See also the Friends of the Lubicon at <tao.ca/~FOL/>.

82　<www.aecon.com/This_Is_ Aecon/>, retrieved July 2007; <www.amec.com/about/about_landing.asp?pageid=7>, retrieved July 2007; P. Knox, "Agency under fire over dam development," *Globe and Mail* (November 16, 1999), A15.

83　Halifax Initiative, Reckless Lending, vol. 2, (2003), <www.halifaxinitiative.org/updir/Reckless_Lending_v11.pdf>, retrieved July 2007, 13; Embera member quoted in CBC News, "Colombian Indians battle dam for survival," (July 5, 1999), <www.cbc.ca/world/story/1999/07/05/colombia990705.html>, retrieved July 2007.

84   Halifax Initiative, *Reckless Lending*, vol. 2, 13-14; CBC News, "Colombian Indians battle dam for survival."

85   Halifax Initiative, *Reckless Lending*, vol. 2, 13-14.

86   Domico quoted in R. Foot, "PM's visit to Colombia raises spectre of slain aboriginal," *Ottawa Citizen* (July 16, 2007), A5.

87   Foot, "PM's visit to Colombia raises spectre of slain aboriginal," A5.

88   P. Kedrosky, "Power rumble in Belize jungle," *National Post* (January 31, 2004), FP11.

89   K. Loverock, "Chalillo chill: Critics slam the dam that a Canadian company wants to build in Belize's Valley of the scarlet macaw," *Alternatives Journal* (Spring, 2002), 27-28; Kedrosky, "Power rumble in Belize jungle," FP11; J. Wells, "Reason to rethink Belize hydro dam," *Toronto Star* (December 10, 2003), E1.

90   Stop Fortis, "Power Purchase Agreement," <www.stopfortis.org/BelizeDamDay3_14_06.html>, retrieved July 2007; Stop Fortis, "Fortis/BEL Raises Rates Yet Again," (January, 2006)," <www.stopfortis.org/Update01_18_06.html>, retrieved July 2007. Quote is from Loverock, "Chalillo chill," 28; M. Cutlack, "When the dollars run out: Belize keeps selling off its assets to foreign companies. Now the country is bleeding itself dry to pay electricity, telephone and water bills," *New Statesman* (March 4, 2002), 34-35.

91   Loverock, "Chalillo chill," 28; Kedrosky, "Power rumble in Belize jungle," FP11; Wells, "Reason to rethink Belize hydro dam," E1; Wells, "Reason to rethink Belize hydro dam," E1.

92   Cutlack, "When the dollars run out," 34-35; Kedrosky, "Power rumble in Belize jungle," FP11.

93   Calgary Herald, "Fortis wins run-of-river project," *Calgary Herald* (May 31, 2007), E4.

94   G. Pitts, "Planting the seeds of empire," *Globe and Mail* (July 7, 2008), B3.

95   <www.snclavalin.com/en/6_0/6_4.aspx>, retrieved July, 2007; D. MacDonald, "Staid but steady: Investors warm to SNC-Laalin's building business," *Montreal Gazette* (August 11, 2001), C1.

96   National Post, "Consortium wins contract for $500M Indian project," *National Post* (June 10, 1999), C2; A. Swift, "India looking for Canadian help to produce power," *Montreal Gazette* (June 20, 1995), C3; Halifax Initiative, *Reckless Lending*, vol. 2, 7.

97   Halifax Initiative, *Reckless Lending*, vol. 2, 7-8.

98   Tribune, "Chamera oustees: 50 more seek compensation," *Tribune* (July 5, 2003), <www.tribuneindia.com/2003/20030705/himachal.htm#3>,

retrieved July 2007; Halifax Initiative, *Reckless Lending,* vol. 2, 8; Tribune News Service, "Chamera Dam oustees meet Governor," *Tribune* (July 20, 2000), <www.tribuneindia.com/2000/20000720/himachal.htm#4>, retrieved July 2007.

99   <www.irn.org/programs/mekong/>, retrieved July 2007; <www.threegorgesprobe.org/probeint/mekong/cdn/index.htm>, retrieved July 2007.

100   <www.irn.org/programs/vietnam/index.php?id=01july.vietnamprojects. html>, retrieved July 2007.

101   <www.irn.org/programs/vietnam/index.php?id=01july.vietnamprojects. html>.

102   D. MacDonald, "Staid but steady," C1.

103   <www.nortel.com/corporate/cm/index.htm>, retrieved Jul, 2007; A. Ismi, "Profiting From Repression," 25.

104   A. Ismi, "Profiting From Repression," 14-15; A. Ismi, "Nortel Implicated in Disastrous Liquidation of Colombia's Telecom," *Canadian Centre for Policy Alternatives Monitor* (October, 2004), <www.ckln.fm/āsadismi/ nortel.html>, retrieved July 2007.

105   Ismi, "Nortel Implicated in Disastrous Liquidation of Colombia's Telecom."; *Toronto Star,* "Nortel to receive $80 million U.S. in compensation from Colombia," *Toronto Star* (March 4, 2004), C4; *National Post,* "Colombian Telecom pays Nortel US$56.7M," *National Post* (August 3, 2002), FP5; L. Acosta, "Colombia probing irregularities in Telecom joint venture contract: Revenue deal with Nortel," *National Post* (January 26, 2002), FP5.

106   Halifax Initiative, "Export Development Canada and Human Rights— Risk or Rights?" (June, 2006), <www.halifaxinitiative.org/updir/Policy-Brief-EDCandHR.pdf>, retrieved October 2006; Ismi, "Nortel Implicated in Disastrous Liquidation of Colombia's Telecom."

107   C. McLean, "Nortel's new challenge: Iraq's logistical nightmares," *Globe and Mail* (November 28, 2006), B2. Nortel quote from Nortel, "National Optical Backbone Network to Deliver Communications Services for Iraqi Residents and Businesses," Press Release (November 20, 2006), <www. nortel.com/go/news_detail.jsp?cat_id=-8055&oid=100210025&locale= en-US>, retrieved July 2007.

108   A. Ismi, "Profiting From Repression," 24; <www.bce.ca/en/investors/ investmentoverview/investingbce/>, retrieved July 2007; J. Guillermo Londoño, "Attacks against electricity towers increase 87.6% during 2005," *El Tiempo* (January 11, 2006)

109   J. Barham, "Bell-led group wins Brazil licence," *National Post* (April 24, 1999), D9; R. Gibbens, "BCI sees huge growth in Latin America: 'Our strategy to refocus ... will pay off handsomely,'" *National Post* (May 3, 2001), C9; S. Guimarães, "Brazil's Telecom Unions Confront the Future: Privatization, Technological Change, and Globalization," *International Labor and Working-Class History* (Fall, 2007), 44, 50-51.

110 Maquila Solidarity Network, *A Needle in a Haystack: Canadian Garment Connections in Mexico and Central America* (Toronto: Maquila Solidarity Network, 2000), <en.maquilasolidarity.org/en/node/459>, retrieved September 2007; Gentle Fit executive quoted in *A Needle in a Haystack*. On Canada's garment industry, see R. Ng, *Homeworking: Home Office or Home Sweatshop? Report on Current Conditions of Homeworkers in Toronto's Garment Industry* (Toronto: OISE, 1999).

111 Sellyn quoted in P. Delean, "Gildan to shut last two local plants," *Montreal Gazette* (March 28, 2007), B1.

112 Maquila Solidarity Network, "Gildan Announces Closures of Canadian, US and Mexican Factories," (March 27, 2007), <en.maquilasolidarity.org/en/gildan/announcesclosures>, retrieved September 2007; M. Logan, "Alleged Union-Buster Expands in South," *Inter Press Service* (February 5, 2004), <www.corpwatch.org/article.php?id=9875>, retrieved September 2007.

113 Maquila Solidarity Network, *A Canadian Success Story, Gildan Activewear: T-shirts, Free Trade and Workers'Rights* (Toronto: Maquila Solidarity Network, 2003), <en.maquilasolidarity.org/sites/maquilasolidarity. org/files/Gildan%20report%20web%20version.pdf>, retrieved September 2007, 20ff. Gildan quote p. 25. On Gildan's Third World growth strategy, see also J. Sanford, "Beat China on Cost: Gildan taps other labour pool—and trade pacts," *Canadian Business Magazine* (November 7-20, 2005), <www.canadianbusiness.com/managing/strategy/article.jsp?content=20060109_155539_4340>, retrieved September 2007.

114 Maquila Solidarity Network, *A Canadian Success Story, Gildan Activewear*, 20ff.

115 Maquila Solidarity Network, *A Canadian Success Story, Gildan Activewear*, 20ff.

116 Maquila Solidarity Network, "Chronology of Gildan Activewear El Progreso Case," <en.maquilasolidarity.org/gildan/chronology>, retrieved September 2007.

117 Campaign For Labor Rights, "Gildan Tries to Cut and Run!" <www.clrlabor. org/alerts/2004/july25-gildan.htm>, retrieved September 2007. Yanz quoted in R. Gibbens, "Gildan closing plant in Honduras," *Montreal Gazette* (July 16, 2004), B5.

118 D. Evans, "Another Canadian connection in Haiti: Clothes to die for," www. sevenoaksmag.com (February 12, 200); A. Fenton, "Gildan Activewear: taking sweatshops to new depths in Haiti," Znet (July 24, 2004), <www.zmag. org/content/showarticle.cfm?ItemID=5927>, retrieved September 2007.

119 Maquila Solidarity Network, *A Needle in a Haystack*.

120 <www.bata.com/about_us/bata_today.php>, retrieved September, 2007; Scharfe, *Complicity: Human Rights and Canadian Foreign Policy*; R. Pratt, *In Good Faith: Canadian Churches Against Apartheid* (Waterloo: Wilfred Laurier University Press, 1997), 114-116.

121 <www.solidaritycenter.org/content.asp?contentid=476>, retrieved September 2007; Asian Human Rights Commission, "Sri Lanka: Brutal force used to disperse unarmed and peaceful workers," (August 19, 2004), <www.ahrchk.net/ua/mainfile.php/2004/772>, retrieved September 2007; A. Warnakulasuriya, "Police say Bata fire sabotage," *Daily News* (August 14, 2004), <www.dailynews.lk/2004/08/14/new03.html>, retrieved September 2007.

122 Quoted in W. Stewart, *Towers of Gold, Feet of Clay: The Canadian Banks* (Toronto: Shrug, 1982), 183.

123 B. Campbell, "Peace and Security in Africa and the Role of Canadian Mining Interests: New Challenges for Canadian Foreign Policy," *Labour, Capital and Society* (n. 37, 2004), 110.

124 S. Healy, "Argentina's Market-enforced Crisis," Znet (February 18, 2002), <www.zmag.org/content/showarticle.cfm?ItemID=1600>, retrieved September 2007.

125 C. Barraclough, "That Sinking Feeling," *Newsweek International* (August 19, 2002, 28; A. Mandel-Campbell, "Scotiabank 'has no heart,' says Argentine staff: Holding one-day strike: Bank says still working with authorities to resolve issues," *National Post* (May 30, 2002), FP4.

126 Scotia official quoted in H. Scoffield, "No cash for Argentina: Scotiabank," *Globe and Mail* (May 1, 2002), B3.

127 Scoffield, "No cash for Argentina," B3.

128 K. Kalawsky, "Police raid Scotiabank Quilmes: Files seized from Argentine bank," *National Post* (March 6, 2002), FP4; D. Bueckert, "Judge replaced in Scotiabank case; Argentina's Duhalde informs Chrétien in Mexico," *Toronto Star* (March 22, 2002), E3; P. Morton, "Canada leans on Argentina: Martin calls for action; officials tell Dodge Scotiabank unit could reopen this week," *National Post* (April 22, 2002), FP1.

129 Scotia worker quoted in A. Mandel-Campbell, "Scotiabank 'has no heart,' says Argentine staff," FP4.

130 National Post, "Argentine Judge charges former Quilmes exec: 'Legal disobedience,'" *National Post* (July 17, 2002), FP8. Godsoe quoted in Calgary Herald, "Bank of Nova Scotia branches closed by regulator," *Calgary Herald* (April 20, 2002), D3.

131 Barraclough, "That Sinking Feeling," 28; A. Mandel-Campbell, "Scotiabank 'has no heart,' says Argentine staff," FP4; D. Plumb and D. Helft, "Scotiabank might be stuck: Quilmes unit could be forced to pay off its Argentine depositors," *Montreal Gazette* (May 10, 2002), C10.

132 S. Stewart, "Scotiabank pressing Argentina for redress," *Globe and Mail* (April 8, 2005), B4.

133 Anthony Fenton points out that while the Canadian military has not formally engaged in action in Iraq, Canadian senior officers have worked

with occupation forces and police officials have trained Iraqi police units. A. Fenton, "Dedication to the war of terror," *New Socialist* (n. 62, 2007), 26-27.

134 J. Demers, "Ready for the reconstruction," *CMA Management* (April, 2004), 53.

135 Paul Wilson quoted in S. Stewart, "RBC eyeing vital trading position with Iraq bank," *Globe and Mail* (September 8, 2003), B1.

136 B. Schmick, "Morgan Chase leads consortium to manage billions in assets," *Globe and Mail* (August 30, 2003), B6. Stewart, "RBC eyeing vital trading position with Iraq Bank," B1.

137 Bank Track, "RBC," <www.banktrack.org/?show=dodgy&id=109>, retrieved July 2008.

138 Mining Watch, "Stop the Canadian Government from Supporting the Rosia Montana Gold Mine," <www.miningwatch.ca/index.php?/Gabriel_ Resources/Rosia_Montana_UA_070905>, retrieved July 2008; M. Potter, "Transylvania tug-of-war; Toronto-based Gabriel Resources wants the pot of gold beneath the Transylvanian hills," *Toronto Star* (April 27, 2008), A8; Bank Track, "RBC."

139 Mining Watch, "Stop the Canadian Government from Supporting the Rosia Montana Gold Mine."

140 Bank Track, "RBC;" *Globe and Mail,* "Romania cancels permit for Gabriel's gold play," *Globe and Mail* (December 10, 2009), B14.

CHAPTER 5:
Making the World Safe for Capital

Any country with imperial ambitions backs up its dreams of global power with some degree of military might. That is a historical truism, as sure as an empire's fall. It is no less true of the imperial project today as it was when Britain was imposing its sunset empire on intransigent populations in the nineteenth century. The reality of empire building is such that the fancies of the powerful cannot be realized without recourse to force, or at least to its ever-present threat. Whether direct colonization or the contemporary market-based form of imperialism, imperial domination always produces resistance from its subjects.

Today, the United States, without a major imperial rival (at least for now) and pursuing its imperial goals largely by market means, has built up the most powerful military in human history.[1] That military is a key feature of the American imperial project. But what about the Canadian military? How are we to understand its role in the world today? Or that of the broader Canadian security apparatus? We often hear that Canada's military is weak and under funded—laughable compared to that of the other advanced capitalist powers—or that Canada's post-Korean War military tradition transcends war for the higher purpose of peacekeeping. These views suggest that the military is incapable of projecting, and/or is unwilling to project, Canadian power at home or abroad. This is not true.

Current developments in Canadian security policy must be placed in the context of the important transformations in Canadian capitalism discussed in chapters two to four of this book. Canadian security policy is not designed or implemented in a political and economic vacuum. It is taking shape amidst the extensive domestic and international expansion of Canadian capital. Policy-makers in Foreign Affairs and the Department of National Defence (DND) are not ignorant of this expansion, nor are they unaware that its sustainability requires a certain kind of political order—a political order amenable to free markets and strong private property rights. Considerations of the security and well-being of the Canadian economy—of Canadian capitalism—are key to both Canada's domestic and foreign public policy. They are never far removed from discussions of the "national interest," which the current security agenda is being designed to defend. Even the "War on Terror," with its nominal stress on fighting Islamic fundamentalism and the threats to freedom and democracy the latter supposedly poses, should be viewed in this context. It is no coincidence that the Global South—its threats to international order, its lack of stability and so on—figures so prominently in the War on Terror and broader thinking on Canadian security policy by military and political leaders, going back to the end of the Cold War. Nor is it a coincidence that some political and military leaders are describing indigenous activism within Canadian borders as a national security threat.

Canadian capital needs force to back up its search for new markets and spaces of accumulation. The second and fourth chapters showed that there is serious resistance to this agenda. Sometimes the resistance directly targets Canadian investments, other times (and in varying forms) it more broadly targets the general conditions of the neoliberal global order—pro-foreign investment climate, strong private property rights, political and economic stability, etc.—that facilitate Canada's aggressive penetration of new markets. Now, Canada can rely to some extent on the United States for security purposes and, equally importantly, on alliances like the North Atlantic Treaty Organization (NATO).[2] It is not a superpower and on its own simply does not have the military clout of the U.S. or NATO.

But to be able to rely on its alliances and to have any influence on them, Canada has to give something back to them. As military and political leaders argue, Canada has to be a contributor and not just a sponge on the security resources of others. Moreover, what if Canadian interests somewhere are threatened independently of those of other capitalist powers? We have seen several examples of this in the previous chapter. Perhaps the best example of such a scenario, though, exists within Canadian borders. Indeed, you cannot understand Canadian security policy without considering First Nations: Canada's military and paramilitary forces were in fact first forged in wars against indigenous people. Just as Canadian capitalist expansion begins at home, so does Canadian security policy. Given both its independent security concerns and its desire to be a more meaningful contributor to its military alliances, the development of a stronger security apparatus (including a more robust and combat-capable Canadian military with a more aggressive domestic and global orientation) has become a priority for the Canadian ruling class. And military power is not the only way in which security is being pursued by Canadian capital and the state. As I discuss below, local police forces, paramilitaries and mercenaries (now called private military companies) are increasingly used to defend Canadian interests. Any discussion of Canadian security policy must therefore take into account the role of non-military agents.

Indigenous Nations: The Security Threat From Within

It is not an overstatement to suggest that over its relatively short history the Canadian state has viewed indigenous struggles as one of the most pressing security challenges it faces, if not the most pressing. Indigenous peoples' continued existence within Canada as nations is a reminder of the fragility of the Canadian state project; every demand for or defence of land, every assertion of political sovereignty, is a threat to that project and a sharp reminder of its irreconcilability with First Nations' aspirations for liberation from colonialism.

Military and paramilitary assaults against indigenous nations have been a formative part of Canada's development. The military and the Royal Canadian Mounted Police (RCMP) (in a previous incarnation the Northwest Mounted Police [NWMP]) cut their teeth fighting First Nations for their land, resources and political and economic sovereignty. The first real test for the fledgling Canadian army was the Northwest War in 1885 (discussed in chapter two). Six thousand soldiers were sent to defeat the Métis-led struggle after the NWMP, Canada's first line of offence against the assertion of Northwest sovereignty, was defeated at Duck Lake. The NWMP/RCMP would be used throughout the nineteenth and twentieth centuries across the country to implement the numbered treaties and impose land expropriation, the Indian Act and the band council structure on recalcitrant communities. In the Mohawk communities of Six Nations and Akwesasne, for example, the RCMP had to deploy paramilitary force to impose band councils when the majority in both communities refused to recognize them. In Akwesasne one Mohawk was killed during the assault in 1899; in Six Nations the RCMP invaded twice to enforce Canadian sovereignty over the community, once in 1924 and again in 1959.[3]

Neoliberalism and Paramilitary Power
As the pressures of capitalist expansion have picked up in the neoliberal era, so too has the recourse to force in an effort to subdue indigenous resistance. Indeed, prior to the Afghanistan war, the largest Canadian military operation since the Korean War was at Oka in the summer of 1990, where 2,500 soldiers, surveillance aircraft and armoured personnel carriers (APCs) were deployed on August 14 after Mohawk Warriors beat back a Sûreté du Québec (SQ) invasion of Kanehsatà:ke territory. The failed SQ assault and the subsequent military buildup was all for a golf course expansion at a country club on sacred Mohawk land. The standoff between the Warriors and the military lasted until September 26, when the Mohawks withdrew from the blockades after having critical supplies cut off by the military but having ultimately stopped the golf course expansion.[4]

The increase of indigenous militancy and the influence of Warrior Societies in some First Nation communities following Oka became a matter of serious concern to Canadian political leaders and the security establishment. They were worried about increasingly bold assertions of political and economic independence by indigenous peoples. According to journalist David Pugliese, in late 1993 and early 1994 senior officials from DND, RCMP and the Canadian Security Intelligence Service (CSIS) developed a military and paramilitary assault strategy on three Mohawk communities. Akwesasne, Kahnawà:ke and Kanehsatà:ke (the latter two having been involved in the Oka revolt) were being targeted because of the powerful role Warrior Societies played in the communities politically (subverting the colonially imposed band councils), economically (through alleged cigarette manufacturing and distribution) and defensively. That Warrior Society members and other indigenous activists had support from large sections of their communities did not matter; their ascendance was a sign of defiance toward the Canadian state that was not to be tolerated. Colonial control would be reimposed by force.[5]

The invasion plan, which was submitted to the then federal Liberal cabinet, called for an assault force of 800 RCMP officers, backed by several thousand soldiers, to take control of the three reserves. The military would also conduct covert intelligence gathering, although the communities had apparently already been subject to electronic eavesdropping by the Communications Security Establishment (an intelligence agency that conducts communications surveillance). The military's highly secretive commando unit, Joint Task Force 2 (JTF2), which was nominally established to fight terrorism, was ordered to prepare for country-wide actions by indigenous people in response to the invasions, including attacks on key infrastructure such as water treatment plants and highways. Other military units around the country were also ordered to prepare to move into volatile areas to quell uprisings the invasions might spark. Pugliese estimates that a quarter of the Canadian military's combat power was put at a high state of readiness.[6]

Hoping to keep its plans a secret, the military engaged in a coverup by referring to the assault buildup as an "exercise" and refresher training for soldiers who had been peacekeeping. Nevertheless, some newspapers reported that something beyond a mere exercise was clearly taking place. One Montreal newspaper reported that the military was planning to support the RCMP for a major assault of some kind, another that soldiers were preparing for counter-smuggling operations, most likely in indigenous communities. With the plans no longer a secret, and with a real potential for widespread bloodshed on both sides, the Liberal government eventually backed down. It would turn to tax breaks on legal cigarettes to target smuggling, but not directly confront the power and influence of the Warriors and other anti-band council activists. However, JTF2 was used to continue surveillance in Mohawk communities, gathering information on cigarette smuggling while familiarizing themselves with the trails and back roads in the targeted areas.[7]

Not long after the plans for the invasion of the Mohawk communities were put aside, a major security offensive against First Nations occurred at Gustafsen Lake in British Columbia. A couple dozen Secwempec activists began a reclamation on June 15, 1995, of a sacred ancestral burial site that had been turned into a rancher's property. It eventually became a thirty-six-day standoff with RCMP paramilitary forces that combined very aggressive intimidation tactics with a high level of incompetence.

When an RCMP emergency response team, dressed in camouflage, tried to infiltrate the reclamation in an intelligence-gathering mission in early August, the indigenous activists fired warning shots over their heads, believing them to be local racist vigilantes. The RCMP responded by surrounding the reclamation with 400 heavily armed emergency response team (ERT) officers, land mines, five helicopters, two surveillance planes and nine APCs borrowed from the military. They also commenced a smear campaign, grossly exaggerating the size of the reclamation and the activists' arms cache. The RCMP also claimed—but could never substantiate—that the indigenous activists had been firing on them after the standoff began. For their part, the indigenous activists claimed RCMP officers tried to provoke them and opened fire on them at random—accusations that were later proven in court.[8]

The confrontation actually erupted into an armed battle on September 11. It was initiated after a pickup truck carrying indigenous people hit an RCMP-placed land mine as it was leaving the reclamation. RCMP ERT officers then drove at the damaged pickup in an APC, prompting the indigenous people to fire at it with their hunting rifles. The ERT officers responded by firing some 2,000 rounds out of the APC's gunports as the Secwempec activists turned and ran back to the encampment. But as the activists desperately ran for cover, another ERT unit across a lake from the APC began firing on them as well—but hit the APC, whose occupants continued firing believing they were under attack from the members of the reclamation. Luckily, none of the indigenous people were killed in the RCMP attack.[9]

On September 17, the First Nation activists withdrew from the reclamation. All told, the RCMP fired an estimated 77,000 rounds of ammunition over the course of its siege. They also requested support from JTF2, which the commando unit publicly declined. However, according to Pugliese, local police officers claimed that in fact the commando unit was present at the siege conducting intelligence gathering, and some reclamation participants insist that it was in fact JTF2 firing on them during the September 11 battle.[10]

Conflicts between indigenous peoples reclaiming stolen land or defending their rights, and state security forces continued through the 1990s and into the present. In 1995, the Ontario Provincial Police's (OPP) Tactics and Rescue Unit (TRU) Team, with an assault force of over forty well-armed officers, attacked in the dead of night unarmed Stoney Point activists reclaiming Ipperwash Provincial Park, killing Dudley George and badly wounding several others in the process (I discuss this incident and its background in chapter two). The attack followed Premier Mike Harris's angry demands that the indigenous people be removed from the park. The use of racist slurs and threats of violence against the indigenous activists by the OPP officers was common before the attack. TRU Team members also celebrated the killing of George by making two different T-shirts and mugs. The mugs have an OPP shoulder flash with an arrow through it, and "Team Ipperwash" written on it. One set of T-shirts had the TRU symbol (a sword) breaking an arrow in half over an anvil.[11]

While the military was not mobilized for this action, the OPP's Tactics and Rescue Unit (TRU) has trained with JTF2 and actually hired an ex-member of the commando unit as an instructor in the 1990s.[12]

In 2000, the RCMP and Department of Fisheries and Oceans (DFO) enforcement officers moved in on the Mi'kmaq community of Burnt Church in order to keep the First Nation from exercising its aboriginal rights to fish, which was affirmed in the Supreme Court's Marshall decision. The state claimed it was enforcing conservation, when in fact the much larger non-indigenous commercial fishery represented more than ninety-five percent of the local industry. The decision to move in was made after Mi'kmaqs, with the support of Warrior activists from around the country, defended themselves against the racist violence of non-indigenous fishers, who shot at indigenous activists, destroyed indigenous traps and hurled racist slurs (some of which was caught on television). The Mi'kmaq and their supporters allegedly trashed three fishing plants in retaliation and set up a blockade on the only access road into the fishery. Eighteen Mi'kmaq were arrested by local police before the RCMP and DFO intervened. DFO targeted indigenous boats on the water by running its own vessels at them. The blockade eventually ended peacefully, but with a cloud hanging over the ability of indigenous peoples to practice their aboriginal rights. The RCMP spent $3.7 million policing the stand-off, while the DFO spent $13.8 million.[13]

Six Nation activists are currently engaged in their reclamation of unceded land near Caledonia, Ontario, (the Douglas Creek Estates) that was going to be turned into a subdivision. The reclamation began in 2006. The OPP raided the reclamation in the early hours of April 20, 2006. They took down barricades and arrested twenty-one people, but the indigenous activists mobilized their forces that same day, pushed the OPP back and re-established their barricades and the reclamation. The barricades across Highway 6 have since come down, but the activists remain and the land has not been developed. In its first two years the OPP spent tens of millions of dollars policing the reclamation, maintaining twenty-four-hour surveillance and rotating more than 2,500 officers through its Caledonia operations.[14]

Coups, Political Prisoners and Plans for Future Military Conflict
In March 2008, the SQ demonstrated that violent intervention by paramilitary force to impose government-friendly leaderships in First Nation communities is not a thing of the past. In what residents of the Algonquin community of Barrière Lake, located 250 kilometres. from Ottawa, describe as a coup d'état, SQ officers forcibly entered their community of 650 to remove a customary leadership, which had not been subject to the Indian Act's band council system and which had the support of the majority of the community. The SQ-enforced coup followed the Department of Indian Affairs' decision to remove the traditional chief and council and replace them with a small and unpopular faction.[15]

Barrière Lake's conflict with Canada goes back to at least the 1960s, when the federal and Québec governments forced the First Nation community off of its traditional lands and onto a 0.2 square kilometre plot near Rapid Lake. With no community centre or high school, only one phone line for the entire community and serious overcrowding in substandard houses (in some cases up to eighteen people live in small dwellings with unfinished basements and leaky roofs), the reserve is badly underserviced by Indian Affairs. To make matters worse, resource development has wreaked havoc on the ecosystem of Barrière Lake's traditional territory. Hydro development has damaged waterways. Logging companies have cut over traplines, destroyed moose habitat (moose have been a staple of the community's diet) and sprayed the area with industrial herbicide.[16]

The community has remained defiant, however. As the presence of logging companies grew significantly in the late 1980s, it began mounting blockades against them. When wood supply to mills was cut off, Canada and Québec decided to come to the negotiating table, and in 1989 signed off on the Trilateral Agreement, which includes an integrated resources management plan to be negotiated between the two levels of government and the First Nation community. But neither Canada nor Québec is genuinely interested in fulfilling the terms of the agreement. Canada was to provide funds for the preparation of independent wildlife and forestry studies. Instead, after signing the agreement it sat on the funds, drawing more protests from Barrière Lake members. Québec, meanwhile, has walked away from negotiations on a number of occasions.[17]

When it was clear Canada and Québec were reluctant to fulfill their responsibilities under the Trilateral Agreement, the First Nation community began to mobilize again. In response, Canada turned to the old colonialist measure of divide-and-conquer in an effort to destabilize Barrière Lake's popular and defiant leadership. In the 1990s Indian Affairs began supporting a small opposition group within the community that was more compliant with Canada's and Québec's interests. Then, in 1994, the SQ charged Barrière Lake leader Chief Jean Maurice Matchewan with assault, based on information from two members of the opposition faction. His bail conditions prohibited him from returning to the community. That was followed by the arrest of band administrator, Michel Thusky, for supposedly detaining two police officers in the band office. He was also forbidden under his bail conditions from returning to the community. The cases were subsequently thrown out, but the government and police did effectively tie up the community's leadership in legal troubles for a year.[18]

In 1995, Québec began making accusations of sexual misconduct on the reserve and financial misconduct by the community leadership. The accusations were again based on information provided by the minority opposition, and were again proven to be false. The opposition faction then set themselves up as a government-in-exile in the town of Maniwaki, 130 kilometres south of the community, with funding from Indian Affairs, and hired the law firm of Thompson Dorfman Sweatman to file a motion with the federal government to have Barrière Lake's traditional council removed from power. It was later discovered that the law firm also represented forestry company Domtar, which has investments in Barrière Lakes territory. The opposition's manoeuvreing culminated with the first attempted coup, when Indian Affairs replaced Barrière Lake's leadership with the minority opposition faction in 1996.[19]

But the residents remained defiant, and blockaded their own reserve to keep the opposition from entering their community. Faced with the resistance, Indian Affairs cut off all government funding to the reserve, which was already suffering from ninety percent unemployment and extremely poor living conditions. But community members refused to give in, and lived for over a year without water, electricity or schooling for their children. They survived entirely by living off their land as best they could given the decades of environmental destruction caused by resource development. And when logging companies tried to move back into areas that had previously been protected, they were met once again by blockades. With mills facing shutdowns as a result, Indian Affairs dropped its effort to replace the community's leadership, and when elections were subsequently held, the opposition was soundly defeated.[20]

Unfortunately, Barrière Lakes confrontation with Canada and Québec did not end there. Both Canada and Québec have walked away from the Trilateral process again, shamelessly claiming that it has taken too long to implement. The First Nation's traditional leadership subsequently initiated a lawsuit against the governments for failing to uphold their end of the Trilateral Agreement. The lawsuit would not be completed, however. When Matchewan was reelected as chief in 2006, Indian Affairs refused to recognize him. Instead, citing the community's budget deficit and supposed leadership uncertainty as reasons, it put Barrière Lake under Third Party Management in which an external consultant unilaterally runs the reserve's affairs. Matchewan was subsequently charged with marijuana- and firearms-related offences. He was replaced by supporter Benjamin Nottoway in 2007. The opposition faction opposed Nottoway's ascendance to power, though, and began actively lobbying Indian Affairs for recognition as the new leadership in the community. Indian Affairs responded by stating that it would only deal with the opposition, and when community members began protesting the latter groups and threatened to banish its leader Casey Ratt, the SQ moved in and installed the opposition into power, arresting several people in the process. While claiming to represent a majority, Ratt has refused to participate in elections. At the same time, he plans to drop the community's lawsuit against Canada.[21]

Around the same time that Barrière Lake's leadership was removed, a series of confrontations between indigenous activists and companies seeking to exploit their unceded land in Ontario led to a number of arrests by police forces. At one point in 2008 twelve indigenous people were sitting in jail in Ontario for their political activism. Six were from Kitchenuhmaykoosib Inninuwug (whose fight against Platinex is discussed in the second chapter), one was from Ardoch Algonquin (who are fighting Frontenac Ventures) and five were from Tyendenaga (who are fighting a gravel quarry on the Culbertson Tract). Although most of those activists were eventually released from jail, the experience is a chilling reminder of the lengths to which the state will go to keep indigenous people under its thumb. The full force of the state's coercive apparatus is brought to bear on those indigenous peoples willing to step outside the parameters Canada has set for its colonial relations with First Nations.

These are a few examples of conflict between indigenous peoples and Canadian security forces. But if there is still any question as to the seriousness with which the state takes indigenous militancy, or the degree to which military power is considered a serious option to crush indigenous aspirations for political and economic self-determination, it should be laid to rest by DND's counter-insurgency manual. The manual discusses strategies to defeat insurgencies against governments, including deadly force, deception and misinformation campaigns. While it discusses insurgencies in the Third World, an early draft produced in September 2005 includes First Nations as examples of insurgents the military has previously faced and may face yet again. It argues that:

> The rise of radical Native American organizations, such as the Mohawk Warrior Society, can be viewed as insurgencies with specific and limited aims. Although they do not seek complete control of the federal government, they do seek particular political concessions in their relationship with national governments and control (either overt or covert) of political affairs at a local/reserve ('First Nation') level, through the threat of, or use of, violence.[22]

DND backpedalled on its inclusion of First Nations in the draft manual when it was made public, and the reference was omitted from subsequent versions. But that does not mean the military's mindset has changed along with its public relations effort. Given its recent history, there is no reason to assume that it does not consider indigenous communities to be security threats.

The spectre of indigenous activists as security threat was raised again in a Senate committee meeting by former general, and now Liberal Senator, Roméo Dallaire in April, 2008. Referring, in the context of plans for the 2008 Assembly of First Nations (AFN)-organized day of action, to the demographic growth of indigenous peoples and the insufficient funding they receive, Dallaire asked: "Isn't there an internal security risk that's raising itself more and more as the youths see themselves more and more disenfranchised and, in fact, that they could actually, if they ever coalesced, bring this country to a standstill?"[23]

With indigenous militancy firmly ensconced in Canadian security thinking, and indigenous activism continuing to grow, the threat of a paramilitary assault on Mohawk communities has been raised once again by the RCMP and the Ministry of Public Safety and Emergency Preparedness. In May of 2008, they released the *Contraband Tobacco Enforcement Strategy*, which calls for "coordinated surge enforcement operations in high-risk locations" between the RCMP and local police forces. While nominally about targeting the "organized crime" behind the manufacture and sale of contraband tobacco, and thus defending the profits of tobacco companies and government taxes made off of the tobacco industry, it is clear the implications of the strategy extend well beyond cigarettes. The strategy identifies three Mohawk communities—Akwesasne, Kahnawà:ke and Six Nations—as the primary sources of illegal tobacco in Canada. These happen to be communities with active Warrior Societies and a long history of direct action to defend their land, and which continue to assert their political and economic sovereignty. Six Nations is also currently engaged in a land reclamation. Any action against the cigarette industries in these communities is thus clearly a political one. The report acknowledges, for instance, that the tobacco industries are "viewed by some as avenues to develop self-sufficiency and autonomy in Aboriginal communities." And if in the process of moving against the contraband industries the First Nation organizations most defiant toward Canada are weakened, then, from the state's perspective, all the better.[24]

Several months after the RCMP's and Ministry of Public Safety and Emergency Preparedness's report was released, it was reported by several Mohawk nation members that CSIS was trying to recruit Mohawk informants in order to gather information on individual activists, political protests, the contraband tobacco industry and community factions. Several individuals were approached for information, and at least one was threatened when he was not forthcoming to the CSIS agents. This spying was likely done with high-level government knowledge, too. According to former service director Reid Morden, such spying activity would require approval at the ministerial level or higher.[25]

If indigenous peoples figure prominently in contemporary security planning, their role as a source of threat and danger has become deeply ingrained in the military consciousness. It is no coincidence, for instance, that, as Sherene Razack points out, Canadian soldiers operating abroad sometimes describe their location as "Indian country."[26] Indigenous people and territory here are conflated in the soldier's mindset with hostile and unfamiliar populations and terrain that need to be subdued. They are a symbolic reference point for the foreign and dangerous even on missions halfway around the world. They also serve as a practical reference point to measure foreign combat experience. Former commander of the Canadian Forces in Afghanistan, Brigadier General Tim Grant, compared the difficulties of policing the Afghanistan-Pakistan border regions, where sympathies to the Taliban are high and governments do not have strong political control over local populations, to the difficulties the military had in Mohawk communities during the Oka revolt. "There is a tribal structure there that's been in place for a long time," he noted, "and for the federal government to come in and try and regulate it, Pakistan has the same challenges that we had during the Oka crisis."[27]

So long as indigenous people refuse to bow down before Canadian imperialism, the state's option of military or paramilitary force remains real. There is a long tradition of violence and coercion against indigenous resistance in Canada, and there is every reason to believe that it will continue, especially as capitalist pressures for First Nation land and resources intensify. Indigenous land, and to some degree indigenous labour, is a crucial piece of the Canadian capitalist puzzle. For Canadian capitalism, and the returns to capital, to grow, indigenous lands must be seized and self-determination stifled, by, as we have seen, any means necessary. Dispossession is at the core of the domestic neoliberal project.

Adding to the prospect for deployment of military power, furthermore, is the ironic fact that an estimated eighty percent of military assets are located on indigenous land or near indigenous communities: the military has a vested interest in containing indigenous rights.[28]

Immigrant Threat to the Nation
Canada's security establishment also likes to raise the threat posed by immigrants of colour. The immigrant-as-security-threat—and as potential sources of moral, political and racial contamination—is as old as Canada itself, and is an expression of white settler Canada's deep-rooted racial character. Non British immigrants (racialized as non- or not-fully white) have been viewed as both a threat to the nation and a source of cheap labour. Canada's "whiteness" has been aggressively mobilized to limit the rights and expectations of non-British immigrants whose labour is

nonetheless desperately needed to fuel Canada's growing capitalist economy. A labour force with limited rights, the logic goes, is a labour force that is vulnerable and therefore cheap and hopefully compliant. But to ensure that compliance, and to protect Canada from the uncivilized customs and habits of racialized immigrants, harsh security measures against them are pursued.[29]

There is a long history of such measures against racialized immigrants, ranging, for example, from the police surveillance, and eventual exclusion of, Chinese workers in the early twentieth century or the deportation of immigrant workers deemed communist in the 1930s. The most recent incarnation of the immigrant-as-security-threat is framed by the War on Terror, which reached a fever pitch following 9/11. The omnipresent perceived threat of terrorists who will exploit our liberties to destroy our freedoms has enabled governments to pass aggressive and broad security laws (such as the Anti-Terrorist Act), which narrowly circumscribe immigrants' rights, and increase the use of already existing laws targeting immigrants (such as security certificates).[30]

The state's pursuit of these measures is not simply about terrorism. In fact, post-9/11 legislation does not represent a break from a previous agenda, but an acceleration of an older one. Governments began implementing restrictions on immigrants and refugees' right to enter the country well before 9/11. It has become increasingly difficult for people born outside Canada to enter the country with the chance of becoming a citizen unless they are financially well established, while increasing numbers of immigrants were finding themselves in detention centres in Toronto and Vancouver. But with its use of broader surveillance measures and more punitive treatment of immigrants of colour, the War on Terror offers good ideological cover ("the terrorists will attack Canada if Canadians do not remain vigilant") for creating a climate of fear and vulnerability among immigrants. Some of the more egregious parts of the Anti-Terrorist Act have been withdrawn by parliament in the last couple of years because of growing public criticism, such as preventive arrests (which allowed police to detain someone seventy-two hours without charge) and investigative hearings (where a suspect can be forced to testify), but the Act remains and the Harper Tories have discussed trying to reinstate these sections. Indeed, without sustained opposition that is willing to challenge this security agenda and the racialized context of fear framing it on a unambiguous anti-racist basis, these policies will define the existence of immigrants within Canada for the foreseeable future.

Canada's Burden:
Bringing Stability and Human Rights to the Global South

As important as these domestic threats are for Canada's ruling elite, Canadian security concerns extend well beyond Canadian borders despite Canada having no clear foreign enemy and not being at meaningful risk of attack. Since the end of the Cold War, and long before the attacks of September 11, 2001, Canada's military leaders and policy-makers have been at pains to point out that the global security situation confronting Canada's more pressing than it was before the Soviet Union fell. It would be easy to write this warning off as the result of the self-preservation instinct of military officials seeking to prove their continued relevancy to their paymasters. But the security threat themes raised repeatedly in the speeches and writings of Defence officials, and their articulations of the transformation war has undergone in the new world order, suggest more is going on here. Indeed, the new doctrine surrounding security threats and military engagement that DND has been developing since the end of the Cold War corresponds very well to the new form of imperialism.

Contemporary Imperialism and Military Power

Ellen Wood's discussion of the role of military power in the new imperialism in *Empire of Capital* is useful for our understanding of Canadian developments. Wood notes that "we are now discovering that the universality of capitalist imperatives has not at all removed the need for military force."[31] Even though direct military colonization of countries is no longer the *modus operandi* of imperialist powers, military force is as relevant to empire building as it has ever been. Imperialism has taken a largely market-based form, as Global South countries are ensnared by international market imperatives in which imperialist countries hold all the power and reap all the benefits. But just like domestic markets, the global market, producing sharp inequalities and discontent, requires state power to enforce its rule. Thus "while market imperatives may reach far beyond the power of any single state, these imperatives themselves must be enforced by extra-eco-nomic power."[32] For this reason, Wood argues, the contemporary imperialist system is dependent on a network of stable, reliable and compliant subordinate states which can facilitate the global expansion of capital from the North.

So the flip side of an imperialism based on the power of global capitalist market forces rather than on direct military-backed colonization is the imperialists' dependence on local states. The necessary stability for an imperial system based on local sovereign states to run smoothly has little chance to be realized, however, given the poverty, insecurities and massive disparities of wealth and power those global market forces produce. The dangers to the imperialist order here are many. Democratic states may allow for the rise of popular forces that have no interest in being compliant to imperialism and seek instead to roll back the gains accorded to the wealthy and powerful by neoliberalism. In some cases, authoritarian governments—such as Iran today—may for a variety of reasons (political, economic and ideological) refuse to offer their unquestioning obedience to the empire. These are the "rogue states" of the new world order, designated as such not because they represent a meaningful direct threat to countries of the North (which they do not) but because they seek to operate outside the global rules established by the superpower and other imperial forces of the rich world. At the same time, extreme poverty and the legacy of colonial meddling—sometimes leading to civil strife articulated along ethnic and/or class lines—may undermine the stability of some states needed for their effective insertion into the imperialist state system, while potentially destabilizing their neighbours. The imperialists refer to these as the "failed states," though, as I will show, the definition of failed is quite arbitrary and suitably elastic depending on the particular interests of countries of the North. The point, in any case, is that imperial powers of the North understand that military force is necessary to maintain the global status quo in an inherently unstable world order.[33]

As David McNally points out, military strategists for the superpower have for some time emphasized the role of the Global South in producing security threats. Their reports, going back to the 1980s, stress that most armed conflicts of the last half century have taken place in the South; the United States military is now more likely to face so-called asymmetric threats—guerrillas, insurgents, "terrorists," organized crime, etc.—rather than a large, modern army; America's enemies will not give up; and, therefore, these security threats in the South will be a permanent feature of global capitalism. These are the strategic observations shaping American military doctrine today, as the superpower prepares itself to be able to rapidly intervene throughout the South and fight many low-intensity battles against asymmetric threats. Just as the capitalist market is global, so therefore must be America's military capabilities; and just as the security threats are a permanent part of globalization, so must be America's war to contain them. This is the burden of the American military. "No longer is imperialism simply about policing an identifiable territory or region," observes McNally, "now it entails securing the entirety of the world market."[34]

While the American ruling class's doctrine of permanent war on the South was being developed well before 9/11, the threat of terrorism provides that doctrine with solid ideological cover. George W. Bush described the War on Terror as "a task that never ends," suggesting there will always be enemies of "freedom" who will threaten the security of America and other countries of the North.[35] "Terrorist" is also a suitably vague, and therefore flexible, label. The terrorist can be found virtually anywhere: thus while much of the focus has been on the Islamic terrorist (who can be found in the Middle East, Africa, South Asia and Southeast Asia), American policy-makers have also discussed the dangers of non-Islamic "terrorists" operating in the Andean region, especially Colombia. This, not coincidentally, is the region that has seen the strongest resurgence of militant left-wing social movements in recent years. 9/11 has also obviously enabled the U.S. to formalize the new doctrine of war with two offensive wars. Both of those wars, furthermore, have demonstrated America's willingness to preemptively attack another country on the extremely fragile grounds that the latter might pose a future threat to the superpower. The right to preemptively attack others is a powerful weapon; one that is a flagrant violation of international law but which is clearly intended as a sharp warning to any foreign country or social movement that might oppose imperialism.[36]

Imperial powers like the U.S. have also increasingly taken to justifying their military interventions on humanitarian grounds.

"War to defend market access," McNally comments, "sounds just a bit too crass, even imperialistic. Consequently, heads of state have taken to invoking human rights, freedom and defence of civilization as the touchstones of military policy."[37] Failed states are not only a threat to the North; they are also a threat to their own citizens. If governments in these countries are unwilling or unable to protect their citizens, then it is the responsibility of those of the North to step in and do so—even if not asked. Military intervention, then, is a benevolent act. But as I noted above, "failed" is a highly politicized designation. Lurking not far in the background of the discourse on humanitarian intervention is the old racist trope that the South is a place of inexplicable savagery and violence—helpless without the support of the civilized nations. Imperialist powers have always cast their invasions of other nations in a positive light.[38]

Canadian Foreign Security Policy

The writings and speeches of Canadian policy-makers and political and military leaders show a broadly similar line of thinking to that in the U.S. An imperialist military orientation to the world is being sketched out by military and political leaders. Since the early 1990s there has been a consistent focus on the Global South in Canadian security policy. In the post-Cold War era, Canada has focused upon the security threat posed by the uncertainty, instability and unpredictability of the Third World. National security must be designed to maintain order against these threats when they arise. There is a longing for the "stability" of the Cold War expressed in security documents. According to the 1994 Defence White Paper, for instance, "Cold War stability has given way to instability and uncertainty—the world is in many ways a more dangerous place than it has been for the past 40 years … If anything, we are in a more unstable and unpredictable international environment [than the] balance of terror that has hung over the world since 1950." The White Paper goes on to argue that the country must "prepare for instability because instability in the world will inevitably affect Canadians and their interests."[39]

In a 1998 speech, Major General C. Couture captures the theme of the loss of international stability and predictability with the end of the Cold War well, observing that, at least during that era, "We knew the enemy's capabilities, their doctrine, their points of attack." "[T]his nice, neat predictable future" during the Cold War allowed military planners the comfort to develop a "specified response to a predicted situation." But that comfort left Canada illprepared for the world to come. Now "the international security environment is increasingly complex, unstable and unpredictable." The threats are no longer modern armies like that of the Soviet Union; they are asymmetric enemies such as urban and rural guerrillas destabilizing their regions of the world. They are also the "failed states" and "the stateless actors who have no interest in diplomacy ... who view Soft Power as only being soft."[40]

This position on international security has continued into the twenty-first century. The defence section of the 2005 International Policy Statement, stresses among other things the threat of instability posed by failed and failing states, terrorism and "regional flashpoints," all of which are located in the Third World.[41] Bill Graham, Liberal Defence Minister from July 2004 to February 2006, contended that "the dangers of the Cold War have been replaced by new and evolving threats." The threats are caused by failed and failing states, global terrorism and the proliferation of weapons of mass destruction. As a result, "today's military operations are more complex, dangerous and demanding" than they were in the past.[42] Tory Defence Minister from February 2006 to August 2007, Gordon O'Connor, also observed "that, since the end of the Cold War, there has not been a direct conventional military threat to Canada," yet "the world remains a very unpredictable and dangerous place." "Canada's defence," he argues, "is ... tied to stability in the rest of the world," thus the military must be prepared to intervene in foreign countries as a matter of containing instability.[43] DND's counter-insurgency manual argued that insurgencies against states, most of which are located in the Global South, are on the increase and threaten the stability of the global order. They are a product, according to the manual, of the end of the Cold War, which "created an unstable security environment that supported the growth of insurgent conflict." The manual is an effort to prepare the military for fighting insurgencies in the Third World.[44]

In short, the idea of the Global South as a dangerous and potentially hostile place, and the most likely location of future military missions, is firmly entrenched in Canadian security thinking.

This sentiment is echoed in the Conservative Governmnet's Canada First Defence Strategy published in May 2010. Since 9/11, the discussion of global instability and threats to Canada has become wrapped up with the War on Terror. "Terrorism" is commonly cited as the most pressing asymmetric security threat facing Canada. But military developments post-9/11, it must be stressed, have only carried forward an already existing security agenda of a indeterminate war for stability with the Global South; they do not represent a fundamental break in policy direction. Since 9/11 the omnipresent spectre of terrorism has been quite successfully exploited by political and military leaders to advance an agenda developed long before the attacks on the World Trade Centre and the Pentagon.[45]

But what exactly is this stability, predictability and certainty Canada wants? One can be excused for being sceptical toward political and military leaders' claims about the threats to stability emerging from the Global South. The veracity of some specific threats to Canada highlighted in DND's security analysis—such as narco-trafficking, the proliferation of weapons of mass destruction, overpopulation, refugee flows, the spread of infectious diseases—are questionable and superficially examined at best. There is no meaningful evidence to suggest that Canada or any other country of the North is seriously endangered by any of these things; nor do DND or Canadian politicians raising concerns about them seek to muster such evidence. References to them appear to be crude attempts to stoke general fears about the omnipresent dangers of the uncivilized South in order to direct security policy in a specific direction.

More commonly mentioned threats, such as terrorism and failed states, do not hold up much better to close scrutiny. Terrorism, as I have already argued, certainly provides a good cover for the international expansion of the military, but there has never been any compelling evidence presented by Canadian security agencies that Canada is at risk of terrorist attack from groups based in the Global South (or in Canada, for that matter). The only Canadians who have experienced attacks from forces in the South are soldiers participating in the occupation of Afghanistan. Like terrorism, the failed state rationale is weighed down heavily with ideological baggage. The direct danger supposedly posed to Canada here is the terrorists who apparently have safe haven in such countries, and who for some unexplained reasons might want to launch an attack on Canadian soil. It would be a mistake, however, to think that the Canadian ruling class has no concern with instability or a lack of predictability or uncertainty in the Third World. The concerns become clearer when we peel off the shallow ideological veneer of terrorism, failed states, weapons of mass destruction, refugee flows and so on and consider what is really at stake in the Third World. The discourses on security and foreign economic policy mirror one another in important ways. Both discourses constantly refer to the lack of stability, certainty and predictability facing Canada in the South. This is not a coincidence: security policy is not being developed in a political and economic vacuum. Consider what motivates the Canadian state's interest in the Third World. As I have argued in the preceding chapters, its principal interest in this region is the successful expansion of Canadian capital and the accumulation of wealth. It only makes sense that this interest—the reason why Canada is engaged in the Third World to begin with—would frame its security concerns, and that concerns raised in the security agenda would therefore echo those raised in foreign economic policy. As it has become heavily invested in the Global South, in other words, Canada's ruling class has developed a strong interest in the region's stability, certainty and predictability. Anything undermining that becomes a security threat.

This stability is pursued by Canada in a number of ways. Recall, for example, the meaning behind CIDA's and Foreign Affairs' promotion of "good governance" in its aid policy: it is equated with state structures that promote neoliberalism and market liberalization. Structural adjustment policies and trade and investment agreements are also ways of encouraging neoliberal stability. Militarism is one more strategy within the overall agenda of remaking the South—one end of the state power continuum for imposing a certain kind of order in the Third World. This agenda and the continuum of policy tactics used to advance it are summed up fairly well in comments by former Tory Defence Minister Peter MacKay on Canada's goals in Afghanistan. In Afghanistan, he states, the Canadian Forces are working "with other departments and agencies [Foreign Affairs and CIDA] ... to establish the good governance and development that are vital to long-term stability."[46]

In some instances policy-makers are explicit about economic interests needing to be defended. *Shaping the Future of the Canadian Forces: A Strategy for 2020*, DND's long-term strategic planning document published in 1999, notes, on the one hand, that "[d]isparities between the developed and developing nations will remain" in the coming decades, but argues, on the other, that one of the important trends that will shape Canadian security thinking is "Canada's need for international trade and the global stability which permits that trade to flourish." The defence of free markets, despite their impact on the South, is thus highlighted as a key feature of the "strategic environment" facing Canada.[47] Likewise, during his tenure as leader of the military, General Maurice Baril argued bluntly that "[o]ur economic future depends on the global stability required to trade freely with other nations. As a major trading nation, we are therefore compelled by interest to protect and promote international peace and security."[48] Economic security has also been an important focus of the Canadian Security Intelligence Service (CSIS), Canada's intelligence agency, since the end of the Cold War. One CSIS report notes that "[i]n today's competitive global economy, highly developed industrialized countries such as Canada face increasingly aggressive competition from developing nations ... One of the most effective and least costly means for countries to make up economic ground is to engage in economic espionage."[49]

Economic concerns are inextricably bound to Canada's security policy. It is hard to conceive of a military policy that has at its core the stability of economic forces that act like a stranglehold on the Third World as anything but imperialist.

A Peacekeeping Nation?

Despite the direction in security policy I have discussed so far in this chapter—and the military interventions I discuss below—the idea that Canada is foremost a peacekeeping nation still has a lot of currency among Canadians. But this is a myth—a well-established one to be sure—that simply does not hold up to scrutiny. Peacekeeping is a marginal, if not irrelevant part of current Canadian foreign policy. Of the 72,784 military personnel on UN peacekeeping missions in 2006, fifty-six, or 0.077 percent, were Canadian. Canada ranked fifty-second—tied with Mali—out of the ninety-seven countries contributing soldiers to UN peacekeeping missions that year. In the 2006–07 budget year, Canada spent $6.2 million on peacekeeping. That same year, it spent at least $1.4 billion waging war in Afghanistan. Combat is the Canadian military's first priority; peacekeeping is an afterthought.[50]

Former Liberal Defence Minister Bill Graham declared in a speech in 2005 that "Traditional 'peacekeeping' … is, for the most part, a remnant of the past."[51] The 2005 defence section of the International Policy Statement says little about peacekeeping, except to note that "most of the Canadian Forces' major operations have borne no resemblance to the traditional peacekeeping model of lightly armed observers supervising a negotiated ceasefire. Missions are now far more complex and dangerous, with our troops frequently deployed to failed and failing states such as Haiti and Afghanistan where there is little if any peace to keep."[52] The International Policy Statement instead focuses on the need to make the military more combat-capable since future missions will involve armed engagement against enemies.

Some observers suggest the promotion of Rick Hillier to Chief of Defence Staff in 2005 was part of the effort by the then Liberal government to transform the military into a combat-capable force. Hillier has been nothing if not blunt in his views of what role the Canadian military should play in international affairs. Following his promotion, Hillier confidently asserted: "We are not the Public Service of Canada. We are not just another department. We are the Canadian Forces and our job is to be able to kill people."[53] Hillier set out immediately to try to build up the military's size and capacities, advocating strongly for increased funding for weapons and initiating an aggressive recruitment campaign. He also created Canada Command to transform the different components of the military into a more integrated expeditionary force better able to confront security challenges at home and abroad. Hillier was also quite clear on where security threats will emerge—where Canadian soldiers will be killing people. In an article published before his ascendancy to leader of the Canadian Forces, Hillier argued that driving the transformation of the military were the post-Cold War era asymmetric threats to global stability. "Those threats will have to be dealt with where they will be most common—amongst populations in developing, or failed, states that need our help."[54]

The Stephen Harper Tory government has continued along this foreign policy path, stressing the need for Canada to be willing and prepared to send the military for combat missions in the supposedly dangerous parts of the world. Instability and threats to Canadian security—"That is the reality and will be the reality of our world for the foreseeable future," declares Harper. "That means we will need a strong, multifaceted military, backed by the political will to deploy." And unless Canada is willing to participate in military actions abroad, he argues, it will fail to earn international respect and will be a marginal global player: "Countries that cannot or will not make real contributions to global security are not regarded as serious players."[55]

So foreign military interventions for which Canadian political and military leaders are planning are not about peacekeeping. The language of peace may still be used now and then—though with increasingly less frequency—but there is little peace involved in the kind of missions Canadian policy-makers have in mind today. Graham's use of "traditional" as an adjective for peacekeeping in the quote provided above, for instance, may suggest there is a more modern kind of peacekeeping still performed, but we should be careful here because the new language around supposed peace missions, such as "peace support" or "peace enforcement," is, as a number of observers have argued, little more than code for missions involving military combat, taking sides with particular parties in a conflict and intervening in countries without being requested by those countries' governments—in other words, missions that have nothing to do with peacekeeping.[56]

"Peace" as an adjective for foreign interventions in security policy discourse (whether for "support" or "enforcement") has as much substance as "humanitarian intervention," a concept which figures very prominently in the security lexicon. Canada's political and military leaders constantly repeat, by rote, the humanitarian character of security policy—even if people have to be killed to make the point, as Hillier stresses. Without war, Canadian leaders insist, there is little chance of humanitarian support; indeed, one of the more popularly espoused military doctrines today collapses humanitarian relief and war into a single coherent mission. Military and political leaders commonly refer to the "three block war" doctrine now, which was originally articulated by American military strategists. It holds that future military engagements will involve combat in one block, patrolling streets and maintaining order in another and providing humanitarian relief in a third— all at the same time and involving the same subject population. There is, in other words, no humanitarianism without war—a convenient conclusion for those who wish to extend their military power into foreign countries.

However much military missions are cast with a humanitarian inflection, there is little substance to such claims, as I discuss in the next chapter with respect to Haiti and Afghanistan. Canada has no meaningful interest in global humanitarian causes—its aid and international trade and investment policies should have revealed that some time ago. And this is clearly reflected in its military interventions. These missions are about fighting enemies and enforcing a specific kind of "peace" on people—one conducive to the North's political and economic interests. The true nature of humanitarian intervention is summed up well by Canadian intellectual and Liberal Michael Ignatieff, who is also one of the most prominent intellectual defenders of the new imperialism. He argued in 2003 that "[t]his new imperialism ... is humanitarian in theory but imperial in practice; it creates 'sub-sovereignty,' in which states possess independence in theory but not in fact." Imperial states, he adds, must seek to maintain order in regions of interest to them.[57]

The Responsibility to Protect Doctrine

One of the most recent and concerted efforts to elaborate, defend and promote the concept of humanitarian intervention is the Responsibility to Protect (R2P) doctrine, which was written in 2001 by the International Commission on Intervention and State Sovereignty (ICISS). Canada was a major force behind its development—Ignatieff was in fact one of its authors—and the adoption of the motion supporting its principles by the United Nations. (International law has not actually been amended at this point to address those principles, however.) Not surprisingly, Responsibility to Protect is presented with a progressive veneer: it promotes military intervention to assist people suffering a supposed humanitarian crisis in failed or failing states where governments in those states are either unable or unwilling to stem the crisis. But beneath the progressive façade is an attempt to radically alter the legal and customary norms regarding the principle of nation-state sovereignty, which should be cause for alarm.

Responsibility to Protect promotes a significant shift in thinking on the principle of nation-state sovereignty, and essentially advocates a rewriting of international law embodied in the UN Charter. Developed after the Second World War, the UN Charter holds the principle of state sovereignty in very high regard, on the grounds that it will limit interstate conflict. The Charter limits one country's right to invade another country unless the first country is under ongoing attack or faces the threat of imminent attack by the second, and the UN Security Council has not had an opportunity to address the situation. But the ICISS argues that the principle of state sovereignty is anachronistic in the post-Cold War era of failed and failing states, and indeed has already been abrogated for humanitarian purposes in the 1990s, such as in the NATO invasion of Kosovo. Responsibility to Protect, as the argument goes, is therefore simply an effort to bring international law up to date with existing practice in order for countries with the capacity to do so (almost always wealthy countries) to be better able to protect the human rights of people in other countries. Thus Canada is a major player in the effort to reshape international law and practice surrounding the principle of sovereignty. The 2005 defence section of the International Policy Statement reflects this, as it drops the need for consent of target countries from its list of criteria for participation in UN missions.[58]

Foreign policy commentator Kim Richard Nossal notes that the rhetoric surrounding Responsibility to Protect and humanitarianism is not matched by reality, pointing out the Canadian state's failure to intervene in Darfur despite the well-documented humanitarian crisis there. But Nossal incorrectly assumes that the disjuncture between rhetoric and reality is because Canada simply wants to present a certain kind of image of itself but has no intention of backing it up when push comes to shove. But Canada, we need to remember, intervened in Haiti and used Responsibility to Protect as justification. The issue is not so much that Canada does not want to back up its high-minded rhetoric; it is that Canada has self-serving reasons for intervening in some places and not others. Sudan does not rate very high on Canada's list of imperialist priorities, whereas Haiti, located in a region in which

Canada has significant and long-standing political and economic interests, does.[59] Humanitarian justifications for military invasions, including Responsibility to Protect, are not only threadbare, but they are also arbitrary. After all, what constitutes a failed state? Why are some states, like Haiti, failed and worthy candidates for intervention, while others, such as Sudan, do not warrant intervention? Responsibility to Protect mentions things like states causing or failing to address ethnic cleansing and mass starvation as examples of "failed," but no reasonable person could claim those things were occurring in Haiti in 2004 when Canada intervened. And, as I discuss in the next chapter, Canada's intervention led to an increase of human rights abuses—some of them committed by the UN force that Canada was a part of, others by right-wing political forces with the tacit consent of the UN force. Moreover, there is no discussion by proponents of Responsibility to Protect of why some countries may have become unstable, if in fact they have. There is no discussion of the role of policies—both direct and indirect—of countries of the Global North in causing instability in the South. In the case of Haiti, Canada and the United States supported opposition groups that mobilized to destabilize the country and weaken the Aristide government.

The failed designation, then, is a deeply political one. Its aim, when attached to doctrines like Responsibility to Protect, is to legitimize imperialist interventions into sovereign nations. States that are seen as threatening to the neoliberal order risk provoking a military response from the powers of the North on the grounds they cannot properly care for themselves. As Venezuelan President Hugo Chávez, critic of neoliberal global capitalism and no stranger to foreign interference from imperial powers, argues with respect to Responsibility to Protect: "[T]his is very suspicious ... Tomorrow or sometime in the future, someone in Washington will say that the Venezuelan people need to be protected from the tyrant Chávez, who is a threat ... They are trying to legalize imperialism within the United Nations."[60] Recall (again) how Canada defines "good governance." The refusal to adopt the neoliberal free market model by definition constitutes bad governance. How great do we suppose the distance is from bad governance to a failing state, if the only possible path to development is adherence to strong free market principles? The refusal to adopt neoliberal doctrine is viewed as irresponsible and a sign that a country is taking a turn for the worse. When the Third World state that opts out of neoliberalism subsequently is faced with the withdrawal of aid money, capital flight or the funding of right-wing opposition groups, causing some degree of instability, however minor, imperialist nations can then seize upon these as justification for intervention.

Sherene Razack argues sharply that the idea of humanitarian intervention draws on the old racist imperialist tropes of the uncivilized character of people in the Third World, thus providing imperialist countries like Canada a useful pretext, cloaked in humanitarian principles, for military intervention in the Third World. The people of the failed or failing states are simply unable to protect themselves from want and suffering. It is up to those of us in the North—it is in fact our responsibility—to intervene and bring order and stability to them. Indeed, so backward and helpless are they that war must be waged against them in order to protect them from the savagery of their own society. As Razack asserts, imperialism is more than just accumulation; it is also about an idea: "the need to and the right to dominate others *for their own good*, others who are expected to be grateful."[61] "Their own good" often means political subordination to Canada and the North, a strong free market and greater integration into the neoliberal global economy. That imperialist policies have never been of any help to their victims does not matter. The racist narratives told in Canada about the Third World by policy-makers and the media, and filtered down into the public's common-sense views of the region, divorce the peoples of the Global South from any meaningful historical context. Suffering or instability are thus viewed "as though they have risen up from the landscape itself and not out of histories in which the West has featured as a colonizing power. No longer anchored in a history," the problems "seem to be properties of certain people and certain regions."[62] The problem is of backward cultures and irrational peoples of colour, who pose a threat to not only themselves but the civilized North. So the cause of most of the problems the South experiences—imperialism—can now be portrayed as the solution. This is the imperialist parlour trick lying behind Canadian doctrines like the Responsibility to Protect.

Rethinking a Canadian Mythology—A Final Note on Peacekeeping
It must be stressed here, though, that even the supposed golden age of Canadian peacekeeping in the postwar period is largely a product of myth-making. It may be that Canadians such as Lester Pearson played important roles in promoting peacekeeping in the UN, but the story is not as simple or optimistic as proponents of peacekeeping mythology suggest. Many on the mainstream left in Canada, such as the New Democratic Party or the Council of Canadians, base their criticisms of Canada's role in Afghanistan on an uncritical notion of Canada as a peacekeeper: Canada should not be waging war in Afghanistan, the argument goes, it should instead get back to its progressive history of peacekeeping, where the military did good in the world, unlike imperialist forces. But Canadian peacekeeping has a questionable history. Given the realities of Canada's peacekeeping record, it cannot be the cornerstone of progressive Canadian foreign policy. Building solidarity with people suffering at the hands of Canadian foreign policy cannot be accomplished with a myth of progressive Canadian peacekeeping as a premise.

For starters, the Canadian military has historically always been more than a peacekeeping force. As I discussed earlier in the chapter, the military's response to indigenous uprisings in the Northwest Territories in 1885 or at Oka in 1990 were certainly not peacekeeping missions. Since the Second World War, the Canadian military has participated in at least five imperialist interventions in foreign countries: Korea (1950–1953), Iraq (1991), Yugoslavia (1999), Haiti (2004) and Afghanistan (since 2002). Canada did not participate in the Vietnam War. But it did sell billions of dollars of war materials to the U.S. at the time, and used its seat on the International Commission of Control and Supervision— the international force established in 1954 to oversee the implementation of the Geneva Accords that ended the First Indochina War—to support the American war effort. Canada sent two naval destroyers to the region near the end of the U.S. war to back up Canadian soldiers serving with it. And while Canada did not officially participate in the 2003 Iraq War, Canadian soldiers and officers on exchange programs have nevertheless been fighting with the American military and taking command positions in the occupying forces.[63]

In the 1970s Canada planned independently of the United States two unilateral military interventions in the Caribbean, one in Grenada in 1974, the other in Jamaica in 1979; and two plans for multilateral invasions of Haiti in the 1980s and 1990s. Although the planned interventions in Grenada and Jamaica did not happen, they demonstrate the willingness of Canadian politicians and military planners to intervene on their own in a foreign country, in a clearly non-peacekeeping role, to protect Canadian investments.

The Jamaican case is worth noting. Through the 1960s and 70s Canada's economic ties with Jamaica grew significantly, particularly in the aluminum industry. This investment was led by Alcan, which had several major projects in the country. In 1972 the left-wing Michael Manley was elected prime minister. As part of Trudeau's efforts to strengthen the economic bonds between the two countries, Canadian aid to Jamaica increased in line with Canadian investment over this period. However, Canada had concerns about the possible influence of Cuba on the far left wing both inside and outside of Manley's People's National Party, fearing Jamaica would be tilted strongly to the left economically and Canadian investments would be threatened by nationalization. So through the 1970s Canada, with the support of Jamaican authorities, quietly participated in espionage against supposed Cuban influence in the country. But Canadian concerns about the Jamaican left increased further after the United States initiated a destabilization campaign against the Manley government (through an economic embargo and political interference) when it introduced restrictions on foreign investment (which did not target Canadian investors). Fearing the possibility that American interference in the country and the weakening of Manley's government might actually lead to a radical shift to the left and embolden supposedly Cuban-backed forces to try to bring down the government and seize foreign assets, Canada planned a military intervention in 1979 to physically protect Canadian investments against seizure by radical forces. The plan called for sending a battalion group from the Royal Canadian regiment, to be accompanied by three destroyer escorts, one helicopter-carrying destroyer and a support ship and its four landing craft.[64]

Actual peacekeeping missions were, furthermore, always framed by Cold War realities and Canada's ties to its allies. As

Alistair Edgar rightly observes, "the popular image of Canada, Canadian foreign policy and Canadian defence policy as 'helpful fixers,' or as selfless boy scouts in an otherwise realist-oriented world, does not mesh with the full range of calculations that actually lay behind those policies."[65] For instance, the 1956 Suez Crisis, in which Britain, France and Israel invaded Egypt after Nasser moved to nationalize the Suez Canal, is generally viewed as a watershed moment in the development of UN peacekeeping, with Lester Pearson playing the major role in promoting the use of peacekeeping forces. But Pearson's motivation was to use the UN forces to help Canada's long-standing allies, Britain and France, save face when they found themselves in a potentially dangerous military situation. Britain and France were pressured by the United States, seeking to consolidate itself as the main imperial hegemon and to assuage Soviet opposition to the invasion, to back off lest the region become destabilized further. In general, the principal goal of peacekeeping was not humanitarian; it was to maintain global stability and prevent the two superpowers from getting directly involved in conflict with one another.[66]

Canadian peacekeeping missions have also not been without controversy. Canada's peacekeeping mission in Somalia in the early 1990s ended in disgrace, when Canadian soldiers shot two Somalis (one fatally) in the back, tortured to death another and took trophy photos of the incident, and were caught spewing racist hatred on video. While the level of brutality of the Somalia mission shocked Canadians, it demonstrated the explosive racial dynamics that frame peacekeeping, where primarily white soldiers from the Global North are tasked with maintaining order among peoples of colour in the Third World. Sherene Razack argues that, as with so-called "humanitarian" missions more generally, peacekeeping is rooted in the historical legacy of racist colonial projects imposed on people in Third World countries. Why peace is absent in a country is seldom discussed, and so abstracted from historical context the locals appear as savages for whom violence is commonplace, while Canadians appear as civilized saviours once again coming to the rescue of those who cannot help themselves. On occasion that savagery overwhelms Canadian soldiers and pushes them to the brink, as supposedly happened in Somalia. While the soldiers' murderous behaviour was not excused in the ensuing public inquiry, the narrative presented it as the product of Somalian savagery rather than a racist imperialism of which peacekeeping is a part.[67]

Lastly, Canada has always been a major arms exporter, contributing to conflict abroad while presenting itself as a peacekeeping nation. The Canadian arms industry, supported by the state, has supplied the war machines of countries with dismal human rights records like the United States, Israel, Indonesia, Turkey, Peru and Colombia to name a few. Canada's arms exporting policy, in other words, has facilitated brutal imperialist occupations and campaigns of terror against subject populations. In the past several years, Canadian exports have grown such that Canada is now consistently in the top ten—reaching as high as fifth in 2003—of the world's military exporters.[68]

When you add together Liberal and Tory leaders' behind-the-scenes support for the U.S.'s ballistic missile defence plan (after the Liberal government publicly declined to support it), Canada's participation in nuclear alliances like NATO and NORAD (with the former maintaining a first strike nuclear policy), Canada's recent refusal to back an international agreement to ban the use of cluster bombs (which have a reputation as being particularly deadly for civilians); and Canada's attempt to dilute a new treaty on extraordinary rendition (i.e., enforced disappearances), it is hard to escape the conclusion that Canada is contributing to the militarization of the world.[69]

Building Up the War Machine

Observers of the Canadian military commonly note that the latter has been so severely neglected by various governments that Canada's ability to project its power abroad and work with allies to keep the world safe from various threats like terrorism and rogue or failed states has been severely weakened. Interestingly, while Canada's military expenditures in the postwar period were (not surprisingly) a fraction of those of the United States, Canada's budgetary increases and decreases until 2001 closely followed those in the U.S. The exception was the Vietnam War period. Military spending for both countries increased sharply in the early 1950s as the Cold War heated up, contracted from the second half of the 50s to the mid-1960s when the U.S.'s spending increased during the Vietnam War until it declined in the 1970s, and picked up again in early 1980s when the Cold War was rekindled, only to decline slowly through the 1990s. The 1990s in fact saw the military budgets of all G7 countries cut back, with concerns raised by military officials and critics of the cuts in these countries about outdated technologies and shrinking troop size. The Canada-U.S. spending patterns also hold when they are measured against Gross Domestic Product (GDP) (i.e., when they are controlled for by the size of the countries' respective economies). So while Canada's spending-to-GDP ratio has been lower than that of the United States since at least the Second World War, both countries' ratios followed a similar pattern until 2001.[70]

Canadian military spending did not follow the U.S.'s in the years following 9/11, as the latter's war machine shifted into high gear for the invasions of Afghanistan and Iraq. It is also true that Canada's spending-to-GDP ratio is lower than that for most NATO countries and other major non-NATO military spenders. However, Canada's spending has been increasing considerably in recent years, and in absolute numbers it is a relatively big spender. The increased military spending really took off in earnest under the Liberal government in the years following 9/11 and has continued under the Conservatives. Increased military spending has strong support from corporate leaders. Canada's military spending is projected to increase by just over $18 billion from 2005 to 2010 alone, and by some accounts by as much as $50 billion over the next two decades, although the global economic crisis of 2008 will likely lead to a scaling back or delaying of some of this spending. This military spending is addition to the $8 billion governments have spent on other security agencies like CSIS, the RCMP and the Canada Border Services Agency for the "War on Terror." In 2007 Canada was the thirteenth biggest military spender in the world (constant [2005] USD), and sixth largest in NATO. So Canadian spending is not insignificant on a global scale. Countries ahead of Canada include the superpower and those vying to compete with it (the U.S., China and Russia); large G7 economies with a history of colonial empires (the U.K., France, Germany and Italy); and those whose militaries have been built up by the Americans to advance the latter's influence in different regions of the world (Japan, South Korea and Saudi Arabia). At the same time, though, from 2000–2007,

Canada had the ninth highest rate of spending increase amongst the world's top spenders, and third highest in NATO.[71]

The increase in military expenditures is clearly aimed at improving Canada's capacity to project its power and influence in the world in order to impose its brand of stability—that is, free markets—on the South. That is what lies behind the renewed buildup of the military. Politicians and military leaders repeatedly stress that, in order to meet its security needs in the post-Cold War era, Canada must develop a military that is lighter and able to address asymmetric threats rather than conventional armies, is easily deployable to the far reaches of the globe, and can be deployed for long periods of time. The new military must also improve its capacity to apply deadly force—if enemies are uninterested in diplomacy, then soft power approaches to addressing international security issues, such as diplomacy and peacekeeping, will have less of a role to play in the future. The implication of this, of course, is that Canada must make heavier investments to improve its war-fighting capacities. The bump in DND's budget in recent years, then, will likely be part of a longer trend of consistently larger DND budgets. As General Baril argues: "Complex and prolonged military operations are to become the norm," so Canada needs a "modern, task-tailored, and globally deployable combat-capable forces that can respond quickly at home and abroad."[72] The central role of the emerging new-look Canadian military has been described by the chief of land forces, Lieutenant General Andrew Leslie, as counter-insurgency—vital experience in which, he notes, the military has gained in Afghanistan—and explicitly not peacekeeping. In keeping with recent trends in Canadian security thinking, he suggests this counter-insurgency will take place in the "failed" states of the Third World.[73]

The Canadian military went from a regular force of around 60,000 in the early 2000s to 66,000 in 2009, with further plans for increase in the next decade (though it is still a way off from the 89,000 it had at the end of the Cold War). The largest chunk of funding, though, is going to new technologies and weapons. Canada is committing several billion dollars over the 2005-2010 period to, among other things, sixty-five new fighter jets, fifteen surface combat ships, mobile gun systems, unmanned aerial drones, armoured vehicles that can withstand improvised explo-

sive devices (IED), transport aircraft (to move troops and equipment efficiently around the world), support ships for refuelling
and resupplying other ships at sea and transporting troops, a new
airforce unit with the capacity to rapidly deploy and set up an
operating airfield anywhere in the world, utility trucks and a half
dozen large icebreaking ships for patrolling the Arctic and defending Canadian claims to the region, and a new military overseas spy
agency known as the Human Intelligence Unit. Again, some of this
spending may be delayed or scaled back in the wake of the global
economic crisis, but the state is still clearly planning on proceeding with much of it. Colonel Michel Drapeau sums up the current
transformation of the Canadian military well: "[W]e're acquiring
the capacity to project forces overseas into difficult areas by buying the equipment that will allow us to go there ... This government [the Conservatives] wants to make sure the Canadian military is now a force to be reckoned with."[74]

DND has also quietly bolstered its Special Forces units as part
of its agenda of targeting asymmetric threats. While Ottawa discloses very little on Canada's special forces, we know that they are
highly trained commandos who can be rapidly deployed for both
reconnaissance and combat purposes. Some military observers
suggest that such forces are crucial to Canada's ability to conduct
independent operations in the future in order to defend Canadian
interests. The Joint Task Force 2 (JTF2), discussed above in the section on First Nations, is the more well-known of these units. It is
currently being expanded from 300 to 600 members by 2011, and
DND committed to building specialized training facilities for it in
2005. Apart from its domestic operations, JTF2 is alleged to have
operated in Afghanistan since at least 9/11 (an ex-member alleges
the unit was there long before 9/11), Haiti while Aristide was removed from power (where it secured the airport for his removal),
Nepal where it trained the army of the authoritarian monarchy to
fight against Maoist guerrillas, and in a number of Latin American
countries, including Colombia and Peru. DND also established
a new special forces unit, the Canadian Special Operations Regiment (CSOR) operating out of Petawawa, with the aim of having
750 elite soldiers by 2011. The CSOR will be a complement to the
JTF2 within the new Canadian Special Operations Forces Command (CANSFOCOM).[75]

On top of its efforts to develop its own forces, DND also has a $16 million a year program to support the development of other countries' militaries. The Military Training Assistance Program (MTAP) provides language, officer and "peace support" operations training to roughly 1,300 military personnel from sixty-three different Global South countries a year. Sixty of those are "Tier One" countries, which means the training is entirely paid for by Canada. According to its directorate, the MTAP serves to "promote Canadian foreign and defence policy interests." It "uses the mechanism of military training assistance to develop and enhance bilateral and defence relationships with countries of strategic interest to Canada," and in the process raises "Canada's independent national profile as a valuable player in the international arena."[76]

It happens that many of the "Tier One" countries are ones with which Canada has, or is hoping to develop, strong economic ties. These include countries with records of human rights abuses, such as the Philippines, Tanzania, Peru, Argentina, Honduras and Ecuador, where social movements have organized against Canadian investment projects. The MTAP is also used to build backing for military engagements Canada supports while laying the groundwork for working with militaries that participate in the program. Eleven of the participating countries have served alongside the Canadian military in the International Security Assistance Force in Afghanistan. It is not a stretch to suggest, though, that the program is actually aimed at facilitating foreign interventions by the Canadian military in the future. MTAP's 2005–2006 Annual Report actually states that "MTAP-trained countries are likely to cooperate with, and offer the Canadian Forces access to their country and their forces, when necessary."[77]

Paramilitary and Private Military Power

The military is not the only way Canadian interests are secured abroad. Local police, paramilitaries and private military companies (or mercenaries, as they used to be called) play an important role in advancing Canadian investments in the Third World. While these forces will not replace traditional militaries, they can be a supplemental resource to militaries in larger conflicts (such as paramilitaries in Colombia's war against the Revolutionary Armed Forces of Colombia [FARC] or private security companies in occupied Iraq). They are also an effective weapon to address localized "instabilities," such as opposition to investment projects. In the case of police and paramilitaries, they have the benefit of being locally available and thus can be quickly deployed, often at no cost to the company. Private military companies offer a more cost-efficient means of addressing disturbances to the local imperial order than a traditional military, since unlike a standing army they are contracted for a specific operation or set of circumstances. They also all have the benefit, especially police and paramilitaries, of creating good public relations distance between the company involved and the human rights abuses that typically take place when investments are being defended.

Canadian companies have made good use of these tools of imperial enforcement. As we saw in the last chapter, police and paramilitaries have been used to great effect by Canadian companies, across industries, in Colombia, Argentina, Ecuador, Guatemala, Sri Lanka, Tanzania and the Congo. And that is the tip of the iceberg. In all of these cases, Canadian investment opportunities have been made available or defended by police and paramilitaries at considerable human cost. People have been killed, beaten and threatened by paramilitaries and police defending Canadian projects.

Private military companies have been contracted by Canadian companies operating abroad, often in conflict zones, to secure investments on numerous occasions that we know of, though companies tend to not readily disclose such things. South African-based Executive Outcomes (EO)—established by a former special operations officer in the apartheid-era South African Defence Forces—was contracted by Calgary-based Ranger Oil in Angola in 1993 to take back an oil depot that was seized by right-wing anti-government militia, União Nacional para Independência Total de Angola (UNITA). Ranger was bleeding money without access to its depot, but the Angolan government was unable to muster the force required to dislodge UNITA. After a short but bloody fight, EO handed Ranger back its depot. EO also worked for Vancouver-based DiamondWorks (now called Energem Minerals) in Angola to protect its Yetwene mine after it was attacked by UNITA soldiers. American security firm Airscan, which was involved in a 1998 cluster-bomb attack—supposedly targeting guerrillas—in Colombia that killed eighteen unarmed civilians, including nine children, provided security in the Sudan for Canadian oil company Arakis.[78]

State agencies also use modern-day mercenaries. CIDA, whose aid work tends to parallel Canadian foreign investment patterns in the resource industry, and which may therefore make enemies of local communities, has contracted American firm ArmorHoldings (which has operated in Colombia) to guard its office in the Congo. The Golan Group, run by former Israeli special operations and intelligence personnel, has provided security to Canadian diplomatic missions in Central America.[79]

There are also a number of Canadian-based private security companies operating abroad. They include Globe Risk, Executive Security Services International and Garda. Globe Risk executive Alan Bell notes the growth potential for private military firms with the international expansion of capital: "The easy places in the world have been maxed out ... Now the real business potential is in places like South America and Central Africa"—regions of instability, he suggests, where firms like his will be in high demand.[80] Globe Risk has worked for resources companies in Latin America and led Canadian mining executives in the hunt for diamonds in Sierra Leone.[81]

The biggest Canadian private security firm is Garda, which has made a fortune in Iraq since the occupation began. It describes itself as the fifth largest security company in the world, having swallowed up sixteen firms in Canada, the U.S. and U.K. since 2005. It has 1,800 personnel providing security to diplomats, aid workers and companies in Iraq and Afghanistan, where profit margins for private armies are extremely high. In essence, Garda is the private face of an occupying military force, freeing up traditional military soldiers to focus on the war against the Iraqi resistance forces. Not surprisingly, it has been targeted by groups opposing the occupation. Despite the growth of the industry and its controversial and murky nature, there is no Canadian law regulating the operations of Canadian-based security firms working abroad.[82]

Interoperability with Allies

It is commonly argued that what drives Canadian security policy today, including the considerable budget increases DND has received in recent years, is interoperability with the United States. Interoperability refers to the push toward enhanced compatibility of, and collaboration between, the Canadian and American militaries in the areas of technology, communications and war doctrine.

There has in fact been a close working relationship between Canadian and American security sectors and defence industries going back to the Cold War. This is perhaps best exemplified by the North American Aerospace Defence Command (NORAD), which was established 1958 to conduct aerospace surveillance over North America. The Canadian and American militaries have also long participated in exchange programs for soldiers and officers, while DND has bought American-developed defence technologies with an eye to maintaining compatibility with the U.S. military. However, there has undoubtedly been strong emphasis on the importance of interoperability with the U.S. in recent years from political, military and business leaders. While the push for increased interoperability began before 9/11, the War on Terror has created the space to push the agenda further.[83]

Examples of more recent cooperation between Canadian and American security apparatuses include: soldier and officer military exchange programs; the Great Lakes-Saint Lawrence Seaway Cross Border Task Force, which targets the illegal trafficking of people and goods across the maritime border; the December, 2001 Smart Border Agreement aimed at collaboration on land borders (including sharing of databases and plans for biometric screening) to facilitate trade while fighting terrorists; increased coordination between the Ministry of Safety and Emergency Preparedness and the Department of Homeland Security; and increased sharing of information between CSIS and the FBI, which is what led to the extraordinary rendition of Maher Arar and possibly several other Canadian men to Syria where they were tortured and abused by Syrian authorities. (Intelligence sharing agreements between the two countries go back decades.) There have also been discussion between Canadian and American authorities following 9/11 about creating a common North American security perimeter, although that project, which is far from a foregone conclusion, is nowhere near being realized.

What we are witnessing, it is worth stressing, is less about a full-on integration of security apparatuses and more about increasing collaboration between them. There is certainly no case to be made at present that Canadian security apparatuses will be cease to be independent entities and become fully integrated with their American counterparts. Further, most though not all of the examples of increased collaboration involve North American security, rather than more advanced interoperability of forces that can project North American power internationally. That is where interoperability is at present most advanced, and not surprisingly since Canada and the U.S. share a very long border. This is not to suggest that interoperability will not go further in the future. It may very well. But while we should be attentive to increased collaboration, especially around domestic North American security concerns but also in military adventures like Afghanistan, it is a mistake to ignore the continued independence of Canadian security policy, including its application abroad. Canada does not do everything the U.S. does or wants it to do (not formally participating in Iraq being a good example), and it has its own specific imperialist interests it needs to defend where it cannot always rely on the superpower.

It is inaccurate to see Canadian collaboration simply as a response to American demands. Unfortunately, the mainstream left in Canada clings to this idea. Linda McQuaig's *Holding the Bully's Coat* is a good example. It is true that the U.S. put greater pressure on Canada after 9/11 to collaboratively enhance continental security and to become a partner in the War on Terror, and some Canadian politicians and business leaders argued that Canada should comply lest its economic ties with the U.S. be weakened. But it is by no means clear that American business leaders—who do a significant amount of their trading and investing in Canada— had any serious interest in letting their economic ties with Canada weaken or would have allowed cross-border slowdowns to interfere with trade for very long. Further, the adoption of increased security measures in North America, and a more aggressive international security position by Canada post-9/11, is not, as I have argued, an about-face by Canadian leaders. Canadian business, military and many political leaders are quite happy with a tougher and more expensive security stance. 9/11 afforded them the opportunity to carry this agenda forward, with the U.S. pushing it for good measure.[84]

Working with the Americans in some areas of imperialist practice does in fact makes sense for the Canadian ruling class, particularly in the area of security where the superpower is much more advanced. While Canada's rulers may dream of a stronger military and more effective security apparatus, Canada obviously does not have the same capacity to project power and enforce global imperialism the way the U.S. does (nor does any other country). At the same time, since Canada shares a common border and a continent with the United States (and Mexico) collaboration on continental security is not that surprising. Thus, as I have stressed throughout this book, working with the U.S. in security as in other policy areas involves a balancing of interests for Canadian imperialists: using opportunities the superpower provides for advancing their interests, while making sure that, as a sub-superpower, their interests are not trampled by the Americans.

The push by Canada's military and political leaders for increased interoperability does not just pertain to the U..S.. There is also considerable stress on interoperability with NATO in the same speeches and documents that discuss relations with the U.S.. This is important, as we get a better understanding of the significance of interoperability if we do not isolate Canada's relations with the U.S. from the broader push toward interoperability with other imperial powers, as writers like McQuaig do. While the U.S., as the superpower, is the unofficial leader of NATO, the alliance includes other smaller imperial powers. It represents a coordinated attempt by the imperialist countries of the West to address common security threats to the regional and international stability of the global order, as led by North American and European capital. When we put Canada's relations with the U.S. in the broader international context of its support for NATO, we can see that the goal of its security policy is not to go against its own self interest to blithely appease the Americans but to participate in those alliances that work to defend the imperialist system of which Canada is a part. The U.S. plays an important role here; so too does NATO (I discuss NATO further in the section on Afghanistan in the next chapter).

Canada simply does not hold the bully's coat. It has imperialist ambitions of its own, and that is what drives its security policy. Pretending otherwise takes the responsibility for Canadian actions out of Canadian hands, where they belong.

Canada's Dirty Hands

Responsibility for Canadian foreign and security policy rests in the hands of the Canadian state and the powerful economic forces in Canadian society pushing for these policies. The increased spending and ideological focus on the Third World is translating into a more aggressive military and diplomatic posture, which is aimed at promoting Canadian interests both as an individual imperial power and as a member of the imperial axis of the North. Direct Canadian support for coups and repression and participation in military occupations and human rights disasters are a common feature of Canadian policy. They are not anomalies.

In the next chapter we will look at some case studies of Canadian security policy in action, as Canada gets its hands dirty in the South.

1   In the first chapter I discuss the connections between market-based and direct colonization forms of imperialism, suggesting that they are part of the same continuum of imperial state power

2   NATO is the security wing of the richest (Western) countries in the world, plus a few others drawn in from Russia's former sphere of influence in Eastern Europe as a way of isolating the former world power.

3   J. Granatstein, *Canada's Army: Waging War and Keeping the Peace* (Toronto: University of Toronto Press, 2002), 28ff; G. York and L. Pindera, *People of the Pines: The Warriors and the Legacy of Oka* (Toronto: Little, Brown and Co., 1992), 160-161.

4   The federal government bought the land from the town of Oka. York and Pindera, *People of the Pines*, offers an excellent account of the Oka Revolt. See also Alanis Obomsawin's National Film Board-produced documentary, *Kanehsatake: 270 Years of Resistance* (1993).

5   D. Pugliese, *Canada's Secret Commandos: The Unauthorized Story of JTF2* (Ottawa: Esprit de Corps Books, 2002), 33-34.

6   Pugliese, *Canada's Secret Commandos*, 35.

7   Pugliese, *Canada's Secret Commandos*, 36.

8   Pugliese, *Canada's Secret Commandos*, 53.

9   Pugliese, *Canada's Secret Commandos*, 53.

10 Pugliese, *Canada's Secret Commandos*, 54.

11 Ontario, *Report of the Ipperwash Inquiry* v. 4 (Toronto: Queen's Printer for Ontario, 2007), 28-30.

12 Pugliese, *Canada's Secret Commandos*, 79.

13 W. De Lint, "Public Order Policing in Canada," background paper prepared for the Ipperwash Inquiry (2004), 15–16; T. Alfred and L. Lowe,

"Warrior Societies in Contemporary Indigenous Communities," background paper prepared for the Ipperwash Inquiry (2204), 24.

14 H. Lindsay, "Gaining Ground: Six Nations Reclamation," *First Nations Strategic Bulletin* (vol. 5, n. 1, 2007), 8-9; M. Nelson, "Fantino will beef up Caledonia's OPP squad," *Hamilton Spectator* (January 10, 2007).

15 M. Lukacs, "Coup d'état in Indian Country," (April 8, 2008), <www.rabble. ca/news_full_story.shtml?x=69793>, retrieved April 2008.

16 C. Angus, "The Algonquins of Barrière Lake: Against All Odds," *First Nations Strategic Bulletin* (vol.4, n. 9), 2-3.

17 Angus, "The Algonquins of Barrière Lake," 3.

18 Angus, "The Algonquins of Barrière Lake," 4.

19 Angus, "The Algonquins of Barrière Lake," 4.

20 Angus, "The Algonquins of Barrière Lake," 5.

21 Angus, "The Algonquins of Barrière Lake," 6; J. Barrera, "B.C. Chiefs enter fray at Barrière Lake," *Ottawa Citizen* (March 25, 2008), <www.canada. com/ottawacitizen/news/story.html>, retrieved May 2008; J. Barrera, "Reserve in turmoil," *Ottawa Citizen* (March 15, 2008), <www.canada.com/ ottawacitizen/news/story.html>, retrieved May 2008; J. Barrera, "Riot police ensure calm at Barrière Lake," *Ottawa Citizen* (March 12, 2008), <www. canada.com/ottawacitizen/news/story.html>, retrieved May 2008.

22 The counter-insurgency manual is quoted in B. Curry, "Forces' terror manual lists natives with Hezbollah," *Globe and Mail* (March 31, 2007), A1.

23 Dallaire is quoted in B. Curry, "Tories warned about stand on natives," *Globe and Mail* (April 9, 2008) A10.

24 RCMP, *Contraband Tobacco Enforcement Strategy, 2008* (Ottawa: Public Safety and Emergency Preparedness, 2008). The first quote is from p. 36, the second p. 31.

25 J. Friesen, "CSIS turning to natives in search of information," *Globe and Mail* (November 29, 2008), A4.

26 S. Razack, *Dark Threats and White Knights: The Somalia Affair, Peacekeeping, and the New Imperialism* (Toronto: University of Toronto, 2004), 17.

27 Grant quoted in Canadian Press, "Less fight in Taliban, says commander," *Canadian Press* (March 30, 2007), <winnipegsun.com/News/ Canada/2007/03/30/3870062-sun.html>, retrieved March 2007.

28 P. Lackenbauer, "Aboriginal Claims and the Canadian Military: The Impact of Domestic Strategy and Operations," Conference of Defence Associations Institute First Annual Graduate Student Symposium (November 13-14, 1999), <www.cda-cdai.ca/symposia/1998/98lackenbauer.htm>, retrieved February 2008.

29 For a brief overview of this history, see my *Cops, Crime and Capitalism: The Law-and-Order Agenda in Canada* (Halifax: Fernwood, 2006), 113-128.

30 See, for example, R. Daniels, P. Macklem and K. Roach, eds., *The Security of Freedom: Essays on Canada's Anti-Terrorism Bill* (Toronto: University of Toronto Press, 2001) ; C. Bell, "Subject to Exception: Security Certificates, National Security and the 'War on Terror,'" *Canadian Journal of Law and Society* (vol. 21 n.1, 2006), 63-83; N. Sharma, "White Nationalism, Illegality and Imperialism: Border Controls as Ideology," in K. Hunt and K. Rygiel, eds., *(En)gendering the War on Terror* (Aldershot: Ashgate, 2006), 121-144.

31 E. M. Wood, *Empire of Capital* (London: Verso, 2003), 153.

32 Wood, *Empire of Capital*, 154.

33 Wood, *Empire*, 155ff.

34 D. McNally quote is from *Another World is Possible: Globalization and Anti-Capitalism* (Winnipeg: Arbeiter, 2006), 237. The U.S. security studies McNally refers to are: Washington's Commission on Integrated Long-Term Strategy (1988), U.S. Strategic Air Command (1990), Secretary of Defense's Bottom Up Review (1993) and the Quadrennial Defense Review (1997). It is also important to note that U.S. military strategists have also discussed since the 1990s their concerns over the emergence of a new inter-imperial rival, usually referring to Russia and China.

35 Bush quoted in McNally, *Another World is Possible*, 238.

36 The right to pre-emptive attack can be found in the post-9/11 United States Security Strategy as well as various speeches by Bush.

37 McNally quote is from *Another World is Possible*, 240.

38 For an excellent critique of peacekeeping in particular and the notion of humanitarian intervention more generally, see S. Razack, *Dark Threats and White Knight*.

39 1994 Defence White Paper quoted in D. Hooey, "The South as a 'Threat'? [Re]Assessing North-South Dimensions of Canadian National Security," *Canadian Journal of Development Studies* (v.19, n. 3, 1998), 469. Hooey also provides a good overview of central role of the South in Canadian security analysis.

40 Couture quote is taken from Major General C. Couture, "Speech to the Canadian Defence Association Institute," (November 14, 1998), <www.forces.gc.ca/site/newsroom/view_news_e.asp?id=444>, retrieved January 2008.

41 Canada, "Canada's International Policy Statement—Defence," (Ottawa: Ministry of Supply and Services, 2005), 5-6.

42 B. Graham, "Speaking Notes for the Honourable Bill Graham, P.C., M.P. Minister of National Defence at the Annual Conference of the McGill Institute for the Study of Canada," (February 18, 2005), <www.forces.gc.ca/site/newsroom/view_news_e.asp?id=1609>, retrieved January 2008.

43 G. O'Connor, "Speaking Notes for the Honourable Gordon J. O'Connor, P.C., M.P. Minister of National Defence at the Conference of Defence

Associations Institute Annual General Meeting," (February 23, 2006), <www.forces.gc.ca/site/newsroom/view_news_e.asp?id=1860>, retrieved January 2008.

44 DND, "Counter-Insurgency Manual," Chapter Two, par. 35.

45 Discussions of terrorism following 9/11 can also be found throughout post-9/11 speech and documents at <www.forces.gc.ca>. On Canada's support for Israel, see Dan Maloy's articles on <www.znet.org>.

46 See M. Neufeld, "Pitfalls of Emancipation and Discourses of Security: Reflections on Canada's 'Security With a Human Face,'" in S. Arnold and J. Marshall Beier, eds., *(Dis)Placing Security: Critical Evaluations of the Boundaries of Security Studies* (Toronto: York University Centre for International Security Studies), 19-34. Neufeld critiques the "human security" agenda of the Liberal government in the 1990s. Although the agenda never really took off, and is no longer part of foreign policy discourse, Neufeld argues that traditional notions of security were never at threat of being supplanted by it. He also discusses the importance of free markets to Canada's international security interests. MacKay quote is from P. MacKay, "Speaking Notes for the Honourable Peter G. MacKay, P.C., M.P. Minister of National Defence, for the Diplomatic Forum," (September 10, 2007), <www.forces.gc.ca/site/newsroom/view_news_e.asp?id=2454>, retrieved January 2008.

47 Department of National Defense, *Shaping the Future of the Canadian Forces: A Strategy for 2020*," (DND: Ottawa, 1999), <www.cds.forces.gc.ca/00native/docs/2020_e.doc>, retrieved January 2008.

48 General Maurice Baril, "About the Canadian Forces—Speech to the Huron College History Club," London, Ontario (October 14, 1999), <www.forces.gc.ca/site/newsroom/view_news_e.asp?id=452>, retrieved January 2008.

49 CSIS, "Economic Security, Backgrounder No. 6," (Revised October, 2006), <www.csis-scrs.gc.ca/en/newsroom/backgrounders/backgrounder06.asp>, retrieved February 2008.

50 S. Staples, "Marching Orders: How Canada abandoned peacekeeping—and why the UN needs us now more than ever," (Ottawa: Council of Canadians, 2006), 1, 9; M. Valpy, "The myth of Canada as global peacekeeper," *Globe and Mail* (February 28, 2007), A8. While Staples is useful for empirical information on Canada's contribution to peacekeeping, I strongly disagree with his uncritical view on it.

51 Graham, "Speaking Notes for the Honourable Bill Graham."

52 Canada, "Canada's International Policy Statement—Defence," 8.

53 Hillier quoted in Chase, "Outspoken general bows out with no regrets," A13.

54 S. Maloney, "Soldiers Not Peacekeepers," *Walrus* (March, 2006), <www.walrusmagazine.ca/articles/2006.03-national-affairs-canadians-kandahar/>, retrieved April 2008; Staples, "Marching Orders," 4. Hillier's

quote on the military's job being to kill people is from S. Chase, "Outspoken general bows out with no regrets," *Globe and Mail* (April 16, 2008), A13. His quote on developing states is from "Army transformation: punching above our weight," *The Army Doctrine and Training Bulletin* (Fall-Winter, 2003), 3.

55   Harper quoted in C. Clark, "Compromise on Afghanistan muffles election drumbeat," *Globe and Mail* (February 22, 2008), A4.

56   Edgar, "Canada's Changing Participation in International Peacekeeping and Peace Enforcement," 110-112; Dorn, "Canadian Peacekeeping," 17.

57   Ignatieff is quoted in A. Bendaña, "Fragile Premises and Failed States: A Perspective from Latin America," in *Fragile States or Failing Development? Canadian Development Report 2008* (Ottawa: North-South Institute), 82. The quote originally appeared in a March 2003 article in the *Naval College War Review*, entitled "The Challenges of American Imperial Power."

58   International Commission on Intervention and State Sovereignty, *The Responsibility to Protect* (Ottawa: International Development Research Centre, 2001), <www.idrc.ca/openebooks/960-7>, retrieved December 2006. On efforts to rewrite international law in the interests of the new imperialism, see M. Mandel, *How America Gets Away With Murder: Illegal Wars, Collateral Damage, and Crimes Against Humanity* (London: Pluto Press, 2004). Mandel also provides a sharp critique of the Kosovo, Afghanistan and Iraq wars. Interestingly, Canada's efforts in challenging the principle of sovereignty, goes at least as far back as the Mulroney government. See also Edgar, "Canada's Changing Participation in International Peacekeeping and Peace Enforcement," 110-112; and Dorn, "Canadian Peacekeeping," 17.

59   K. Nossal, "Ear Candy: Canadian Policy toward humanitarian intervention and atrocity crimes in Darfur," *International Journal* (vol. 60, n. 4), 1017-1032.

60   The Chávez quote is taken from A. Fenton, "'Legalized Imperialism': 'Responsibility to Protect' and the Dubious Case of Haiti," *Briarpatch* (December-January, 2005-06), 18.

61   Razack, *Dark Threats and White Knights*, 10. The emphasis is in the original.

62   Razack, *Dark Threats and White Knights*, 16.

63   J. Elmer and A. Fenton, "Canadian General Takes Senior Command Role in Iraq," *Global Research* (January 25, 2008), <www.globalresearch.ca/index.php?context=va&aid=7897>, retrieved May 2008; Y. Engler, *The Black Book of Canadian Foreign Policy* (Vancouver: Red Publishing, 2009), 128.

64   S. Maloney, "Maple Leaf Over the Caribbean: Gunboat Diplomacy Canadian Style?" in A. Griffiths, P. Haydon and R. Gimblett, eds., *Canadian Gunboat Diplomacy: The Canadian Navy and Foreign Policy* (Halifax:

Centre for Foreign Policy Studies, Dalhousie University, 2000), 147-184. That was not the first time the Canadian navy was sent to defend Canadian investments abroad, however. In January 1932, two Naval destroyers, with two platoons of Canadian soldiers, were dispatched to the Caribbean coast of depression-ridden El Salvador in the wake of a communist-led uprising of workers, peasants and indigenous people against the country's military junta. Montreal-based International Power Co. had a monopoly over electricity generation in the country, and its exorbitant rates had made it a target of anger and resentment amongst El Salvadorans. The Canadian destroyers lined the El Salvador coast with British and American destroyers. While the destroyers did not directly participate in the battle against the uprising, the Canadian, American and British show of naval force, at a time of rapidly declining support for the government, inspired the army's violent crushing of the uprising, which left several thousand dead. P. MacFarlane, *Northern Shadows: Canadians and Central America* (Toronto: Between the Lines, 1989), 44, 49-62.

65   A. Edgar, "Canada's Changing Participation in International Peacekeeping and Peace Enforcement: What, If Anything, Does It Mean?" *Canadian Foreign Policy* (vol. 10, n. 1, 2002), 113.

66   On peacekeeping see also A. Walter Dorn, "Canadian Peacekeeping: Proud Tradition, Strong Future?" *Canadian Foreign Policy* (vol. 12, n. 2, 2005), 8-9; and M. Bouldin, "Keeper of the Peace: Canada and Security Transition Operations," *Defense and Security Analysis* (vol. 19, n. 3, 2003), 267.

67   Razack, *Dark Threats and White Knights*, 11-12.

68   See <www.ploughshares.ca> or <www.coat.ncf.ca>.

69   R. Saunders, "'Missile Defense' Alive and Well in Canada," *Canadian Dimension* (September/October, 2006), 23-24; M. Hurtig, *Rushing to Armageddon: The Shocking Truth About Canada, Missile Defense, and Star Wars* (Toronto: McClelland and Stewart, 2004); B. Robinson, "Canada and nuclear weapons: Canadian policies related to, and connections to, nuclear weapons," (Waterloo: Project Ploughshares, 2002), 3-7; G. Galloway, "Canada yet to back ban on cluster bombs," *Globe and Mail* (February 9, 2007), A5; Human Rights Watch, *World Report, 2006*, <hrw.org/wr2k6/wr2006.pdf>, retrieved April 2008.

70   B. Robinson and P. Ibbot, "Canadian military spending: How does the current level compare to historical levels? ... to allied spending? ... to potential threats?" <www.ploughshares.ca/libraries/WorkIngPapers/wp031.pdf>, retrieved January 2008; Granatstein, *Canada's Army*, 420.

71   Staples, "Marching Orders," 1; S. Chase, "Defence plan to cost $50-billion over 20 years," *Globe and Mail* (May 15, 2008), A9; S. Bell, "Canada is a terrorist haven: CSIS," *National Post* (March 1, 2004), A1. Comparative data comes from the Stockholm International Peace Research Institute, "The

15 major spender countires in 2007" and its military spending database, <www.sipri.org>, retrieved July 2008.

72   The Baril quote is from Baril, "Speaking Notes for General Maurice Baril Chief of Defence Staff at the Canadian Club of Ottawa." The themes discussed here, on what kind of military is necessary, are repeated ad nauseum throughout speeches and policy documents that are available at <www.forces.gc.ca>.

73   J. Montpetit, "Canada's peacemaking role to change," *Toronto Star* (November 15, 2009), A7.

74   DND, "Recruiting and Retention in the Canadian Forces," (May 5, 2009), <www.forces.gc.ca/site/news-nouvelles/view-news-afficher-nouvelles-eng.asp?id=2865>, retrieved May 2009; DND <www.forces.gc.ca/site/Reports/index_e.asp>, retrieved May 2008; Moore, "Long-term defence plan set out," A4; M. Hartley, "Rapid-response air unit seen as policy shift," *Globe and Mail* (July 21, 2007), A3; I. Bailey, "Harper plans Arctic patrol fleet," *Globe and Mail* (July 10, 2007), A1; B. Campion-Smith, "Armed forces welcome spree," *Toronto Star* (June 30, 2006), A6. The Drapeau quote is from the Hartley article.

75   Esprit de Corps, "New regiment created," *Esprit de Corps* (January, 2006), 18; S. Maloney, "Commentary on 'Burn the Witch: A Case for Special Operations Forces,'" *The Army Doctrine and Training Bulletin* (Spring, 2000), 72; O. El Akkad, "Proposed army spy unit raises worry," Globe and Mail (May 27, 2008), A5; and Pugliese, *Canada's Secret Commandos*, 66-73.

76   The quotes are all from Directorate Military Training Assistance Program, *2005-2006 Annual Report*, 2, <www.forces.gc.ca/admpol/downloads/MTAP_AR06_E_v.3.pdf>.

77   Directorate Military Training Assistance Program, *2005-2006 Annual Report*, 3.

78   M. Drohan, *Making a Killing: How and Why Corporations Use Armed Force to Do Business* (Toronto: Random House, 2003), 200-207; C. Spearin, "International Private Security Companies and Canadian Policy: Possibilities and Pitfalls on the Road to Regulation," *Canadian Foreign Policy* (vol. 11, n. 2, 2004), 1-2; D. Pugliese, "Guns for hire: Soldier of Fortune," Vancouver Sun (November 12, 2005), C8; R. Morris, "Colombia must pay bombed villagers: court," *Gazette* (May 27, 2004), A21; A. Effinger and C. Donville, "High stakes in arctic diamond rush," *Gazette* (October 8, 2005), B1. Executive Outcomes was dissolved in 1999, though some of its key personnel are involved in the British company Sandlines International.

79   Spearin, "International Private Security Companies and Canadian Policy," 2.

80   Bell is quoted in J. Ferguson, "Protecting employees in a perilous world," *Globe and Mail* (October 27, 2005), E5.

81 Spearin, "International Private Security Companies and Canadian Policy," 3.

82 Pugliese, "Guns for hire," C8; D. Butler, "How a nice Québec firm found itself in a war zone," *Ottawa Citizen* (June 4, 2007), A1; J. Greenwood, "Danger? All in a day's work at Garda," *National Post* (May 30, 2007), FP3.

83 On interoperability with the United States, including in the weapons manufacturing industry, see A. Edger, "Growth Pains or Growing Strains?" *Canadian Foreign Policy* (vol. 8, n. 2, 2001), 1-22. Governmental documents and speeches citing interoperability with the U.S. as a goal are many. They include, among others, Department of National Defense, *Shaping the Future of the Canadian Forces: A Strategy for 2020;*" Baril, "About the Canadian Forces;" G. Macdonald, "Canada-U.S. Defence Relations, Asymmetric Threats and the U.S. Unified Command Plan;" <www.forces.gc.ca/site/newsroom/view_news_e.asp?=1004>, retrieved January 2008; J. McCallum, "Speaking Notes for the Honourable John McCallum Minister of National Defence At a Joint Press Conference to Announce the Canada-US Joint Planning Group," (December 9, 2002), <www.forces.gc.ca/site/newsroom/view_news_e.asp?id=473>. The Canadian Council of Chief Executives (CCCE) also supports increased interoperability with the U.S. and other allies. See CCCE "Defence and Security." See also G. Albo, "Empire's Ally," *Canadian Dimension* (November/December, 2006), 19-22.

84 L. McQuaig, *Holding the Bully's Coat: Canada and the U.S. Empire* (Toronto: Doubleday, 2007).

CHAPTER 6:
Coups, Invasions and Occupations

In this chapter we take a look at a few case studies of Canadian security policy abroad. It does not represent an exhaustive list by any means. It does, however, offer a look at some key examples of violent and manipulative Canadian efforts to forcibly impose its imperial will on Global South countries. The international projection of Canadian power has been disastrous for those on the receiving end.

Reasserting Itself in the Caribbean:
Canada and the 2004 Coup in Haiti

In February 2004 the popularly supported and democratically elected President of Haiti, Jean-Bertrand Aristide, was overthrown in a coup. The coup was led by the country's business elite and paramilitary forces featuring ex-army officers and death squad members active under earlier dictatorships, who were in turn supported by American, French and Canadian imperialism. An excellent history of the coup is provided by Peter Hallward's *Damming the Flood*, while Yves Engler and Anthony Fenton's *Canada in Haiti* demonstrates Canada's central role in the regime change and human rights atrocities that accompanied it.[1]

As Engler and Fenton argue, from Canada's point of view the coup allowed it (and the other imperialist powers) to rid itself of a political nuisance who was not fully compliant with imperialist interests in the Caribbean and who sought to empower Haiti's poor majority. The coup in turn created better investment conditions for Canadian capital (mining and sweatshop manufacturing in particular). But just as importantly, I would add that the coup is also a significant step in Canada's effort to politically and militarily reassert itself in a region it has long viewed as a strategic priority. Canada, as I have noted, has a long economic and military history in this part of the world. But its economic presence has grown considerably since the early 1990s, and its diplomatic and military intervention in Haiti should be seen in that context: Canada is seeking to reimpose itself as a power in the Caribbean. Canada's participation in the coup and subsequent occupation of Haiti was done against the opposition of the Caribbean Community (Caricom), which refused to recognize the post-coup regime. The intervention also offers Canada useful experience for destabilization campaigns and counter-insurgency operations. At the same time, happily taking a lead role in the coup and post-coup "rebuilding" may give Canada some future clout in the region's affairs with the dominant power there, the U.S.—an imperialist insurance policy in the Caribbean for Canadian interests.[2]

Aristide and the Destabilization Campaign
Aristide, a former priest who helped build a movement of the poor to fight a U.S.-backed dictatorship, was first elected President of Haiti in 1990. He was overthrown seven months later in 1991 by a CIA-backed military coup, but returned to power in 1994 with the military support of the U.S. and Canada. In supporting Aristide in 1994, the imperial powers were responding to the brutal repression, instability and international criticism that followed Aristide's ouster. Support came with the condition that he be more compliant with their interests and step aside when his term was finished. He led Haiti, which was becoming increasingly reliant on American aid, in a somewhat more amicable relationship with imperialism until 1996, when his former Prime Minister René Préval won the presidency. Aristide did, however, disband the country's military in 1995, which had been involved in decades of dictatorship and participated in the 1991 coup against him.

Tensions between the Haitian elite and the imperialist powers, on the one hand, and Aristide and his Lavalas party supporters, on the other, resurfaced when Lavalas won a landslide victory in legislative elections in May 2000, and Aristide entered the presidential campaign to replace Préval and handily won the election in November later that year. For the first time, Lavalas had a president and a legislative majority and so did not have to rely on political support from elite-backed parties to get legislation passed. The U.S., Canada, France and the World Bank all cut off aid to the government after Aristide's election, angry that an independent-minded party had consolidated itself electorally and was bold enough to modestly challenge their neoliberal prescriptions for the Haitian economy while pursuing the "popular political empowerment" of the Haitian poor.[3] The successful practice of defiance by the poorest country in the hemisphere was not a precedent the imperialists were willing to let Aristide and Lavalas set. Given the extremely fragile state of Haiti's finances and its dependence on external donors that were withdrawing financial support, reforms were limited. But they weren't insignificant for the country's poor. Despite Haiti's budget being cut in half, its exchange rate collapsing and its Gross Domestic Product falling from a meagre US$4 billion in 1999 to $2.9 billion in 2003 as a result of the aid cuts, the Lavalas government, among other things, increased the minimum wage; expanded schools (more were opened under Préval and Aristide than in the country's 200 years preceding their administrations) and literacy programs; built new health clinics and hospitals; raised taxes on the rich; removed discriminatory restrictions on the use of Creole, the language of the poor majority, in government while creating thousands of new public sector jobs; and increased subsidies on price-sensitive consumer goods. Aristide also sought to strengthen ties with regional governments with less-than-friendly relations with the imperialist powers: he arranged to have Cuba send 800 much-needed doctors and nurses, and began discussions with Cuba, Venezuela and other Caribbean nations for an alternative to the American- and Canadian-led hemispheric free trade strategy.[4]

The imperialist powers had in fact already decided as early as 2000 (if not earlier), following the legislative and presidential elections, that Lavalas and Aristide were problems that would have to be dealt with firmly. As Hallward observes, for the Haitian elite "[i] t was no longer possible to deny the fact that so long as Aristide was around, Lavalas would remain in power for the foreseeable future."[5] With electoral democracy not working in their favour, "[b]y 2000, Aristide's opponents both in Haiti and abroad realized they needed to develop a new and more active program of destabilization and counter-mobilization."[6] The government's agenda of modest social reform would only serve to heighten opposition. Canadian politicians and officials were centrally involved in the destabilization campaign from the beginning and saw it right through to its successful conclusion. They directly funded many opposition groups with very poor human rights records. But they also participated at least twice in high-level meetings with their counterparts from France and the United States to develop a coordinated strategy to undermine Aristide's government. As early as 2000, then Liberal Foreign Affairs Minister Lloyd Axworthy travelled to Washington for a "Friends of Haiti" meeting. Fenton argues that "These 'friends' of Haiti feared that unless Aristide's Lavalas Party was reined in, the neoliberal vision for that country was in dire jeopardy."[7] Then in 2003 Denis Paradis, who would eventually become the Liberal government's Secretary of State for Latin America and the Caribbean and Minister responsible for La Francophonie, hosted a high-level meeting in Meech Lake with representatives from the United States and France, called the Ottawa Initiative on Haiti. While Canada has not disclosed details on what exactly was discussed at the meeting, Montreal-based newspaper L'Actualité reports that participants discussed—approximately one year before Aristide's ouster—the need to remove Aristide and place Haiti under the control of the United Nations. Following the meeting Denis Paradis publicly invoked the Responsibility to Protect doctrine to justify Canada's interference in the country on the grounds that Haiti, under Aristide, was a failed state requiring intervention. Pierre Pettigrew, who succeeded Axworthy as Minister of Foreign Affairs, also reportedly met with key people involved in the anti-Aristide opposition and armed insurgency not long before the February 2004 coup.[8]

Almost immediately after the legislative elections Canada, the U.S., France and the OAS began to publicly question Lavalas's democratic legitimacy. The voter turnout was around sixty-five percent (comparable to recent elections in Canada and the U.S.) and Lavalas handed the elite-backed parties a resounding defeat. Initially the OAS described the election as free and fair; but after prodding from the U.S., OAS spokesperson Orland Marville decided it was in fact flawed. The imperialist powers (and the OAS acting on their behalf) seized on the methodology employed by the non-partisan Haitian Provisional Electoral Council (CEP) to calculate vote percentages for Senate ballots. This was the same methodology used in the previous election without criticism from external forces. They claimed that it led to the conversion of large pluralities into majorities for some Lavalas senators who should have instead been forced into a second round. Although only eight Lavalas senators, who would likely have won the second round handily, were affected, and despite their stepping down to placate the thoroughly defeated opposition, Canada et al. continued to use this incident to suggest the elections were unfair and to justify withdrawing financial support from the government. The imperialist powers also suggested Aristide's election was tainted by a boycott by opposition parties on the pretense that Lavalas would never allow fair elections. Again, it did not matter that independent monitors on the ground in Haiti described the presidential election as fair, or that an estimated sixty percent of voters turned out. Canada and its allies had their story and they were sticking to it.[9]

The imperialist powers also put their support behind the opposition coalitions that formed after Aristide's election—the Democratic Convergence (CD), which emerged first, and the Group of 184 (G184), which included CD members. The coalitions were comprised of capitalists in control of the country's media and its thriving sweated industries in the export processing zones, right-wing politicians and ex-army officers who had been involved in pre-Aristide dictatorships, and various conservative NGOs. The leading figure in G184 was the owner of Haiti's largest sweatshop chain, and business associate of Montreal-based Gildan Active-wear (discussed in chapter four), Andy Apaid.[10]

Around the time Aristide was elected for the second time, the Canadian state cut its funding to the Haitian government, most of which came through CIDA and Foreign Affairs, and instead shifted its support to, in its words, "civil society." But as Engler and Fenton demonstrate, "'civil society' was in effect equated with opposition to Haiti's elected government. Without exception … organizations ideologically opposed to Lavalas were the sole recipients of Canadian government funding."[11] One such organization is the National Coalition for Haitian Rights-Haiti (NCHR-H), a virulently anti-Aristide organization which was funded by CIDA and was the most widely used source detailing Aristide's supposedly authoritarian character by the international media and governments. It levelled accusations of atrocities at the Aristide government that were proven by independent human rights researchers to have been spurious. NCHR-H has been silent about post-coup political repression, but used a CIDA grant of $100,000 to investigate a genocide committed by the Aristide government that has been thoroughly refuted (Aristide's former Prime Minister, Yvon Neptune, was jailed for supposed involvement in it).[12]

The Canadian state also funded several Canadian-based NGOs with ties to anti-Aristide groups in Haiti. Ottawa-based NGO Rights and Democracy, funded entirely by the federal government, wrote a report on Haiti denouncing the Aristide government and describing G184 as "grassroots."[13] It used information provided by NCHR-H. The Concertation Pour Haiti (CPH), a Québec-based network of NGOs, called Aristide a "tyrant," denounced his government as a "dictatorship" and a "regime of terror" and weeks before the coup called for his removal.[14] After the coup they brought NCHR-H coordinator, Yolène Gilles, who named wanted Lavalas "bandits" on Haitian radio, to Canada for a speaking tour. CPH also brought Danielle Magloire, who works for CIDA-funded anti-Aristide feminist organizations. Quick to denounce supposed human rights abuses by the Aristide government, Magloire's organizations have also remained silent about violence and mass rape by government forces following the coup. Magloire would also serve on the Council of Wise People, set up after the coup to pick the interim leader. A number of Québec unions also received hundreds of thousands of dollars from CIDA for work in the Centre International de Solidarité Ouvrière (CISO). They denounced the detention of union activists in Haiti under Aristide, but have said nothing about the targeting of unionists after the coup. CIDA also had Philippe Vixamar on its payroll from 2001 to at least 2005. Vixamar became the Deputy Minister of Justice under the post-coup government where he oversaw police operations and prisoners (discussed below).[15]

CIDA and Foreign Affairs hid their destabilization policy in Haiti behind their much-hyped cover of "democracy promotion."

William Robinson dissects this agenda in the context of American foreign policy in Latin America and the Caribbean, locating its emergence in the shift under Ronald Reagan in the 1980s from supporting military dictatorships, which had helped contain leftist insurgent movements but were nonetheless unable to establish the requisite stability demanded by international capital, to supporting civil society organizations sympathetic to neoliberal restructuring. Campaigns to support right-wing groups against progressive popular forces, once managed by the CIA, are now led by organizations like the National Endowment for Democracy (which funds groups like the International Republican Institute [which was centrally involved in the anti-Aristide campaign] and the National Democratic Institute for International Affairs). Canadian foreign policy is similar here: the promotion of democracy is done within strictly neoliberal parameters; and as we see in the case of Haiti, is aimed at the systematic undermining of governments that dare try to operate outside those neoliberal parameters. Democracy is on the terms of the Canadian state and capital, not those of the people in Third World countries; electoral institutions, "civil society" organizations and civil and liberal rights are manipulated to promote Canadian interests rather than the popular will of people.[16]

Although they were presented as a mass movement broadly representative of Haitian "civil society" by the imperialist countries, Canadian and American NGOs and the international media, in reality CD, G184 and the opposition more generally had little popular support. CD leaders estimated their first major conference in January 2001 would draw 20,000 people; it could only muster a few hundred. But that did not deter the opposition from its aggressive anti-Aristide and -Lavalas position, buoyed as it was by its American, French and Canadian backing. The opposition's strategy was to denounce the authoritarianism of the government to the compliant international media and force concessions from Aristide without dropping its demand for him to step down as president. Between June 2000 and February 2004 the opposition rejected over twenty offers from the government for new elections and power sharing. Knowing Lavalas would win any election, the opposition and its imperialist backers stuck steadfastly to their script that no deal could be reached so long as the autocrat Aristide remained in power.[17]

As the DC and G184 engaged in their strategy for subverting democracy, ex-army officers and death squad members—some of whom had been convicted for their role in massacres following the first coup against Aristide—formed the Front pour la Libération et la Réconstruction Nationale (FLRN) and began waging an armed campaign against the government and its supporters. Aristide's opponents knew that, while they could successfully demonize him to their imperialist backers and an uncritical international media, he remained profoundly popular among the poor majority. Thus, Hallward notes, "[O]n its own, a non-violent destabilization campaign against FL [Famni Lavalas] had little or no chance of success."[18] Based in neighbouring Dominican Republic, which provided a home to Haitian exiles wanted by the government for human rights violations, the FLRN began its armed incursions into Haiti in July 2001. Its initial targets were rural police stations and Aristide supporters in areas of the north, and a bold assault on the presidential palace on December 17, 2001. While police and Aristide supporters were tortured and killed in these attacks, the casualties remained low as pro-Aristide forces managed to keep the FLRN in check in the early stages of the insurgency.[19]

Even though the DC and G184 initially maintained a safe political distance from the armed insurgency, they refused to condemn the paramilitary violence. Instead, the opposition, along with its American, Canadian and French allies, pinned the blame for the violence squarely on the shoulders of Aristide, going so far as to accuse him of staging the attacks to justify a clampdown on his opponents. One of the worst kept secrets of the destabilization campaign, the ties between the DC and G184 and the FLRN, would eventually be exposed by leaders of the paramilitary group themselves, who would occasionally introduce themselves to the Haitian public as the armed wing of the opposition. One of the founders of the FLRN, Guy Philippe, actually acknowledged publicly after the coup that he had been working with G184.[20]

Despite the violence of the opposition—and contrary to claims that Aristide was an authoritarian who survived on political violence—throughout the period leading up to the coup, Aristide never countenanced armed defence against the insurgents. While his government was made vulnerable by the absence of an army or an armed wing of Lavalas, some of Aristide's supporters, located in the slums of Port-au-Prince and other cities, were organized into armed groups (described simplistically by the imperialists and the international media as criminal gangs); and some of these groups on their own initiative justifiably defended themselves against the paramilitary violence. But Aristide never raised a general call to arms to defend Haitian democracy—perhaps helping to seal his fate. Indeed, as Hallward argues, one of the remarkable things about Aristide's second presidency, threatened almost from the get-go by political violence, is how little violence it deployed against the opposition. For instance, none of the prominent opposition leaders were killed or disappeared—a remarkable accomplishment for a Haitian government. Compare this with the political violence of imperialist-backed regimes in Haiti. On the one hand, under the Duvalier dictatorships (1957–1986) an estimated 50,000 killed; Namphry/Avril regimes (1986-1990) 700-1,000; Cédras (1991–1994) 4,000; and Latortue, who followed Aristide (2004-2006), perhaps 3,000 to 4,000. On the other hand, human rights observers not funded by Canada or the U.S. or relying on those in the pay of Canada or the U.S. estimate that during Aristide's tenure at most thirty killings can be attributed to the Haitian National Police—many of whose members were anti-Lavalas—or political groups with only a loose affiliation to Aristide.[21]

The Coup

By the fall of 2003 FLRN attacks had increased in regularity and grown in intensity throughout the country. As of February 2004, the FLRN began what its leaders described as its final push to overthrow the Aristide government. With the assistance of an armed group that had supported Lavalas, which it won over to the anti-Aristide cause through political manipulation and old-fashioned buying-off, the FLRN was gaining momentum and confidence. It managed to overrun the police station and prison, burn the homes of Lavalas officials in the city of Gonäives, and extend its control through the northern half of Haiti and parts of the south. However, the poorly equipped police and Lavalas supporters managed to contain the insurgency so it could not spread further. While violent and bloodthirsty, on its own the FLRN did not appear capable of deposing Aristide. It was well armed, but small and unable to buy off enough of the pro-Lavalas organizations to break their stronghold in most of the country's major city slums.[22]

Enter the U.S. and Canada. By late February time was of the essence for those forces pursuing the removal of Aristide. With the FLRN contained for the time being in the north and parts of the south, pro-Lavalas forces in Port-au-Prince and other major cities were able to begin preparing defences for a future assault from the insurgents. On top of this, Venezuela and other Haitian allies in the region were growing increasingly anxious about the insurgency, and the imperialist countries were concerned that Lavalas allies might begin pushing for a military intervention to defend the government. To head off possible intervention and strike a blow against the pro-Aristide movement, the imperialist powers had to take action. Thus on February 29, the United States, with assistance from Canada (Canadian special forces helped secure the airport), kidnapped Aristide and flew him out of the country to exile in the Central African Republic.[23]

Canada and the U.S. claim that Aristide left the country willingly after calling the American embassy to request assistance for safe passage to the Central African Republic. This claim simply does not hold up to scrutiny, however. First, all available evidence, including the testimony of Aristide himself and his close friends and political confidants, shows that up until the night he was taken out of the country Aristide had no intention of leaving. Aristide claims American embassy officials called him to tell him they wanted to do a joint press conference, and that they would pick him up and take him. Instead, they took him to the airport and forced him onto a plane without telling him where he was going. Second, as Hallward asks, why would Aristide want to go to the Central African Republic, a dictatorial ally of the French government? If he had any say as to where he'd be exiled, why would not Aristide go to a neighbouring ally? Third, U.S. officials suggest they were caught off guard by Aristide's request, yet later that same day the American military was able to quickly send reinforcements to Haiti, with Canadian soldiers following not far behind. And fourth, if Aristide left Haiti of his own free will, then why was he under virtual house arrest and kept from speaking to the international media for several days upon his arrival in the Central African Republic?[24]

The Post-Coup Repression

According to Fenton, the overthrow of Aristide "was immediately followed by a witch hunt and campaign of repression … against supporters of Aristide and his Lavalas Party."[25] Estimates by independent human rights researchers of the number of Aristide supporters killed in the first few days after the coup vary from 300 to 1,000 people, but even the low-end estimate is an indictment on the imperialist-handpicked government of interim leader Gérard Latortue, a neoliberal economist who spent most of the previous twenty years living in Florida and has family connections to paramilitary leaders. The goal of the terror campaign was to physically crush the Lavalas movement's grassroots support. The Haitian elite and their imperialist backers knew they would eventually have to hold elections if the coup were to have any international legitimacy, and that Lavalas would likely win again. While recruiting some of the more opportunist Lavalas politicians would help to weaken the party, on its own that strategy would be insufficient. Mass repression would still be necessary.[26]

Removing Aristide and presenting it as an abandonment of the country by the president served to disorient the Lavalas movement enough to give the coup supporters and their imperialist allies a quick upper hand on the ground. Lavalas militants were quickly contained in the slums of the major cities, and would be preoccupied over the next two years with surviving. Paramilitaries operated with impunity across large parts of the country for several months after the coup. Pro-Aristide demonstrations would be shot on indiscriminately by the new Haitian National Police (HNP) force, which reportedly integrated ex-soldiers and death squad members into its fold. The new police, using arms purchased from the U.S., which lifted its arms embargo against Haiti after Aristide's removal, would also carry out wave after wave of paramilitary assault in the slums. As I noted above, an estimated 3,000 to 4,000 people, most of whom were Lavalas supporters, would be killed during the Latortue regime. Lavalas leaders as well as grass roots activists were targeted. Several thousand more Lavalas supporters would be jailed. A Port-au-Prince prison, built to hold 500 people, held more than 2,000 in squalid conditions by the spring of 2006. Only eighty-one of those prisoners had been convicted of a crime. This was all done under the watch of CIDA-paid Deputy Minister of Justice, Philippe Vixamar.[27]

The post-coup campaign of repression against Lavalas supporters was made possible by Canadian military power, which was part of a UN Security Council-sponsored mission initiated hours after Aristide's ouster. Five hundred Canadian soldiers supported the Latortue regime between March and August, 2004, a period in which the repression was at its most intense, while, according to Engler and Fenton, reports placed JTF2 members in the country as late as mid-2005. While the HNP was responsible for the brunt of the repression, Canadian (and American, French and Chilean) soldiers participated in the initial assaults on the Lavalas strongholds. Residents in the slums that were subjected to HNP attacks reported that the more heavily armed Canadian and other foreign soldiers were sent in first to soften up their neighbourhoods—including breaking down barricades erected for self-defence and forcing the pro-Lavalas forces onto their heels—for the HNP. August Heleno Ribeiro, the former Brazilian commander of the UN mission in Haiti, told a congressional commission in Brazil that "we are under extreme pressure from the international community to use violence."[28] He identified Canada, the U.S. and France as the biggest proponents for using a heavier hand against Lavalas supporters.[29]

Despite the ferocity of the assaults against Lavalas supporters, Canada would still claim in 2006 in regards to the security situation that "there are still many challenges that must be overcome." To that end, it pushed a declaration through the UN General Assembly calling for greater reinforcement measures by UN soldiers and police officers to promote security in Haiti. This led, according to a Canadian government report, to "[m]ore robust operations" by the UN force and the HNP in late 2006, which "further improved the security situation." At the time, the police component of the UN force was led by a Canadian.[30]

Canada also spent nearly $20 million directly on the HNP from 2004 to 2006 under the Latortue regime under the Interim Co-operation Framework; it also contributed another $10 million to an OAS project on the criminal justice system that included the HNP. The $20 million went to the establishment and training of the HNP—the same HNP involved in massive rights violations. One hundred RCMP officers were sent to Haiti to help train and integrate ex-soldiers into the new police force. The effort to train the HNP to make Haiti "more secure" includes training on patrols, crowd control and intelligence. Canadian police officers also "are actively involved in operational planning and implementation." CIDA also spent $800,000 on the correctional system to ensure, among other things, a "strategic plan" was developed and that personnel were trained in the plan, and that "civil society" was consulted in the "judicial reform process." Not surprisingly, CIDA is silent on the swelling prison population, the squalid conditions prisoners face and the fact that the majority of inmates are being held without having been convicted of anything.[31]

As the Latortue regime was rooting out and exterminating Lavalas supporters with Canadian assistance, it also rolled back Aristide's social policies. Literacy programs were shut down, subsidies for the poor were cut, price controls removed, agrarian reforms to help peasants halted, hospitals closed, the already meagre minimum wage was reduced and the collection of income tax suspended to apparently compensate the elite for property damage incurred during the insurgency. An already harsh existence for the poorest people in the hemisphere was made even more desperate.[32]

The military and police spending is part of a broader Canadian engagement with post-Aristide Haiti, which the state describes as "a priority focus for the Canadian government engagement in the hemisphere."[33] Canada is Haiti's second largest bilateral donor. It spent nearly $200 million from April 1, 2004, to March 31, 2006, and has committed another $520 million from 2006 to 2011. On top of its security engagement, Canada also continues to fund at least ten G184 organizations, spending a total of $10 million on them from April 2004 to March 2006. Canada also spent over this same period approximately $39 million on the Haitian government and the World Bank and the Caribbean Development Bank to keep Haiti in line with its structural adjustment conditionalities. The money went to trapping Haiti even further in debt bondage. Canada paid down some of its arrears to its external donors, while assisting external donors to lend the impoverished country money on condition it agrees to further neoliberal restructuring. CIDA helped the Latortue regime to prepare its Poverty Reduction Strategy Paper—that is, its restructuring proposal for foreign donors (see chapter three on PRSPs). According to CIDA, under its watch the Haitian government "has achieved the zero-deficit objectives of the International Monetary Fund."[34]

While Canadian aid was flooding into the country to roll back social policy, repress the opposition and re-engineer the economy, Canadian ambassador Claude Boucher established a Haiti-Canadian Chamber of Commerce in 2004, followed by Canada's first trade mission since before Aristide's election. Canada also spent $20 million on a new embassy, a main focus of which is to promote Canadian business interests. Latortue welcomed Canadian business travellers at the new embassy. Together with the World Bank, Canada has promoted further sweatshop expansion—that is, "export-led development"—as a requirement for economic growth, in an effort to make Haiti a prime destination for Canadian and American capital in search of wages and working conditions on par with those of China.[35]

Canada's post-Aristide foreign policy toward Haiti is similar to that advocated by the Canadian Foundation for the Americas (FOCAL), a right-wing think tank funded by Foreign Affairs that has political leaders' ears on policy matters relating to the Americas. More critical responses fell on deaf ears. FOCAL has an unyielding pro-free market orientation and offers intellectual support and apologia—however unrigorous its arguments—for a stronger Canadian presence in the hemisphere. The Standing Committee on Foreign Affairs and International Trade actually invited FOCAL to present its views on what Canada's role in Haiti should be after the coup. In its submission FOCAL defends Aristide's ouster, describing him—without documentation—as "incompetent, corrupt and frequently brutal." It recommends that Haiti be put under a trusteeship by the international community, and that the latter, including Canada, commit to a long-term presence of ten years to manage Haitian affairs, or conduct what it calls "state building." Equally important for FOCAL, Haiti represents an important opportunity for expanding Canada's influence in the hemisphere: with the U.S. overcommitted elsewhere and unwilling to take on a leadership role, "[T]his is an opportunity for Canada to assert the leadership, which the Prime Minister is seeking ... and raise Canada's hemispheric profile." Clearly this is what Foreign Affairs officials wanted to hear. FOCAL has also been very outspoken on Canadian foreign policy in the Andes, as I discuss below.[36]

2006 Elections

Another area of Haitian political life in which Canada was heavily involved was the 2006 presidential election. By the summer of 2005, the Latortue regime and its imperial caretakers (including the UN) began preparations for a presidential election, which would be held in February, 2006. Despite pronouncements by Canada to the contrary, efforts were made to make the election as unfair as possible. With Aristide still in exile, Lavalas supporters' preferred candidate was Father Gérard Jean-Juste. But before he could have a chance to challenge pro-coup candidates, he was imprisoned on trumped-up charges in July, 2005. Lavalas supporters eventually, if reluctantly, came together to support former president René Préval.[37]

Under the Préval government, over 10,000 voter registration centres were provided for the 2000 elections. By contrast, under the Latortue regime only 500 were set up, and in areas that were inconvenient for people living in Lavalas strongholds. In Cité Soleil, for instance, there are an estimated 150,000 people of voting age, but only 52,000 voter cards were distributed and only 30,000 votes were ever counted for the 2006 election. In 2000, 12,000 polling stations were set up across the country, but in 2006 a much smaller number were set up in only 800 voting centres, which were again located in areas inconvenient for people living in Lavalas strongholds.[38]

Despite the effort to decrease the pro-Lavalas vote, sixty-five percent of eligible voters turned out to vote on February 7, many spending hours walking to voting stations and waiting in line. On February 9, with twenty-five percent of ballots counted Préval led with sixty-two percent, well ahead of his closest competitors. But only two days later, the CEP declared Préval only had 49.6 percent of the vote, and that a second round would be necessary. Tens of thousands of votes, most cast for Préval, were discovered in a Port-au-Prince garbage dump. Seeing that the fix was in, poor Haitians swarmed into the streets and marched on the CEP's headquarters. Anger was directed not only at the CEP, however, but also at the UN mission, which many protesters accused of conspiring with Latortue against Lavalas. Faced with the outpouring of popular anger, and with international media covering the election, the CEP decided to raise the Préval vote to just over fifty percent—

high enough to avoid a second round of voting but slim enough a margin for opponents to argue that his mandate was weak. Given that Lavalas supporters mobilized around his campaign (if not as their first choice), Préval's victory must be read as a strong rebuke of the coup and the forces behind it. Once again, if given the choice (and under extremely corrupt conditions in 2006) the poor Haitian majority elected a Lavalas president.[39]

Canada spent over $35 million, most of it from CIDA, on elections in Haiti from 2005 to 2006 (this included a municipal vote). The money went to providing "technical and material expertise to support the electoral process, and thus the Provisional Electoral Commission."[40] Canadian money was also directed to the hiring, training and deployment of 3,000 security officers, a counting officer, and oversight from observers and Elections Canada officials. Yet there is absolute silence in government reports on the utterly corrupt nature of the presidential election, the systematic attempt to disenfranchise poor Lavalas supporters and the angry protests required to force the government into accepting Préval's victory. It is clear Canada had no real interest in a genuine democratic election, and was attempting to fund a victory for the pro-coup forces.[41]

While his campaign was backed by Lavalas supporters, Préval has governed very modestly. Being dependent on external donors who are neoliberal zealots has considerably narrowed his room for manoeuvre, as has the fate of the Aristide government. Imperial powers continue to meddle in Haitian affairs. UN assaults in the slums continue, if less frequently than under the Latortue regime. And the country's elite remain emboldened by their success against Aristide, who still has not received the green light to return home from exile. Préval has not sought to challenge this state of affairs in a direct way, and in fact has instead pursued alliances with anti-Aristide factions. As a result, conditions for the poor majority have not improved under Préval beyond the reduction in military assaults in their neighbourhoods. The situation remains tense, as the global increase in food prices in 2008 hit most Haitians very hard, leading to riots and violent clashes with UN and HNP forces, which left several people dead.[42]

Canada, through its aid policy and its work with international financial institutions, which have a stranglehold on the Haitian economy, has had a hand keeping the Préval government in check.

Haiti remains a strategic focus of Canadian foreign and security policy in the Caribbean region under the Harper government, just as it was under the Liberals. Harper visited Haiti in July 2007 and declared that "the security of our entire region will be enhanced by greater stability in Haiti."[43] "Stability" obviously means a strong neoliberal orientation and a weakened Lavalas movement, which Canada continues to work toward. The food riots in 2008, caused by a devastating combination of growing poverty and the global rise in food prices, did nothing to change Canada's policy direction toward Haiti, exposing the Responsibility to Protect doctrine for the sham that it is. Canada has also remained silent about the CEP's—which includes Préval appointments—decision to ban the Famni Lavalas, still far and away the most popular party in the country, from the April 2009 senate run-off elections and February 2010 legislative elections based on the flimsy claim that the mandate submitted by Aristide for the party was not authentic. The April, 2009 elections were boycotted by Lavalas supporters as a result, with the CEP estimating voter turnout to be a mere eleven percent and Lavalas supporters suggesting it was more likely two to three percent.[44]

Canadian leaders are quite rightly scorned by Haitians for the despicable role they have played in the impoverished island. But Haitians risk their lives for speaking out against Canada. Outspoken anti-Latortue activist Lovinsky Pierre-Antoine was disappeared on August 12, 2007, just two weeks after organizing demonstrations against Canada's support for the coup, which were timed to coincide with Stephen Harper's visit to the country. Ten thousand people participated in the rally, and forty people were arrested by UN forces. Foreign Affairs and the Canadian embassy in Haiti have maintained a chilling silence on Pierre-Antoine's disappearance, as indeed they do on the continuing problematic human rights situation in the country. In fact, Canada continues to finance the strengthening of Haiti's security apparatus, announcing in the fall 2009 another $15 million for the 2010–11 budget year for the HNP and prisons.[45]

The Haitian intervention must be concluded a success for Canadian imperialism. It played a lead political, economic and ideological role in undermining a democratically elected government. And its military, including its elite commandos, was central in violently subduing the pro-democracy forces in the impoverished Caribbean country, gaining valuable counter-insurgency experience at the same time. Canadian capital has benefited, while Canada's imperial brand received an important boost in a region that remains a strategic priority. This has been demonstrated most recently following the devastating earthquake that hit Haiti on January 12, 2010, which killed an estimated 230,000 people. Undoubtedly, the sheer extent of devastation, caused in part by a toxic mix of substandard building, overcrowding and inadequate health care, is a product of Haiti's economy being run into the ground by centuries of imperialism. Canada dispatched 2,000 troops to Haiti in an effort to demonstrate the rapid-response capacity of its military. Together with the response of its allies, this was the most militarized aid effort in history, leading some Haitians to eventually protest the large military presence of imperial nations, particularly that of the Americans. Canada also organized the first donors' conference in Montreal two weeks after the earthquake. This gathering of the so-called "Friends of Haiti," however, excluded Cuba and Venezuela, despite both countries' rapid response following the earthquake. Cuban doctors were the first on the scene and the last to leave (and received little mainstream media attention in Canada), while Venezuela wrote off the considerable debt Haiti owed it. Unlike Cuba and Venezuela, however, the reconstruction vision promoted by Haiti's "Friends," including Canada, the U.S., World Bank and IMF, is a strict neoliberal one. The role of the free market and corporate investment is heavily stressed. They want Haiti to focus on building up its export-oriented sweated garment manufacturing industry, something Haiti has been doing for decades now with no benefit to the poor Haitians who toil in the factories at sub-poverty level wages. Harper was also the first head of state of a major donor country to visit Haiti after the earthquake, where he announced $12 million for the construction of a temporary government headquarters. That $12 million is not new money, though; it is coming out of Canada's previous aid commitments.[46]

Imperial Invasion and the Re-engineering of Afghanistan

With over 2,500 military personnel involved, the occupation of Afghanistan is Canada's biggest military engagement since the Gulf

War. It has become a centrepiece of Canadian foreign policy and Canada's War on Terror, and a key rationale for military expansion. Politicians, military leaders and media commentators sympathetic to the war commonly insist that the Afghanistan campaign is a fight for freedom, democracy and economic development against terrorism: the Canadian military is bringing democracy, security and stability to Afghans suffering from the Islamic fundamentalism of the Taliban, while protecting Canadians at home by stamping out terrorism before it reaches their shores. Afghans, we are told, need assistance from Canada (and the international community) to rebuild their state and economy after decades of violence and war, and this can only be achieved through the barrel of a gun.[47]

However, not only is Canada not close to defeating the insurgency led by the Taliban, but it appears that the military conflict is actually fuelling the insurgency, as foreign military occupations tend to do. At the same time, state rebuilding is mired in corruption and violence, and Canada's development policy, ranking well below the war in terms of importance to overall Canadian foreign policy in the country, has failed the Afghan people. What the occupation has accomplished, though, is a neoliberal remaking of the country and the increased regional strengthen of the U.S.-led transatlantic imperial alliance via NATO.

Imposing "Democracy"

Canada participated in the initial invasion of Afghanistan in 2001, which was conducted in outright violation of international law since neither the United States nor any of its allies were under attack, or faced the imminent threat of attack, from Afghanistan. Two thousand soldiers, JTF2 members and sixteen warships participated in the U.S.-led campaign to overthrow the Taliban. Canadian forces also operated in Kabul protecting the new government of Hamid Karzai from 2003 to 2005 as part of the International Security Assistance Force (ISAF), which was established by the United Nations following the Bonn Agreement in 2001 and came under NATO command in November, 2003. In 2005, Paul Martin's Liberal government moved the majority of Canadian forces from Kabul to Kandahar to engage in the counter-insurgency campaign against the Taliban-led resistance to the Karzai government and foreign backers.[48]

The Taliban, as is widely known, had a horrendous human rights record and is virulently misogynistic. Sadly, the Karzai government, which is diplomatically and militarily supported by the foreign powers, has itself a very poor record on human rights and democracy. Without that foreign support, it is unlikely Karzai would have won power to begin with or would be able to hold on to it.

Led by the United States, the foreign powers, including Canada, have had a hand in all the major developments in the process of rebuilding the Afghan state following the defeat of the Taliban—rendering absurd any claims that Afghanistan is a genuinely sovereign nation. From the beginning, they have tied their efforts to supporting the Northern Alliance and other Western-friendly politicians.

When the Soviet-backed regime of Najibullah was defeated in 1992 by the U.S.-backed Mujahideen, fighting broke out between Mujahideen factions for control of Kabul. When the Taliban came out on top in 1996, a number of armed groups united under the umbrella of the Northern Alliance (NA) and carried out a war against the Taliban government in the few areas of the country outside Kabul that were under its control. Although they fought against the Taliban, the warlords leading the NA had a well-documented terrible human rights record, including murder and intimidation of opponents and civilians living in the areas it controlled and enforcement of an extremely misogynistic interpretation of Islamic law, including forcing women to wear burqas in some parts of the country, violence and a vice squad and violence against women for un-Islamic behaviour in public.[49] Nevertheless, the U.S. and its allies worked closely with the NA (with the former spending tens of millions of dollars arming them) to topple the Taliban after 9/11. Not surprisingly, while the Taliban's defeat was warmly received by Afghans, the ascendance of the NA was not. The Revolutionary Association of Afghan Women (RAWA), an organization which courageously documented the Taliban's crimes against women, had this to say when the NA entered Kabul on the heels of the Taliban's retreat: "The retreat of the terrorist Taliban from Kabul is a positive development, but [the] entering of the rapist and looter NA in the city is nothing but a dreadful [sic] and shocking news for about two million residents of Kabul whose wounds of the years 1992–96 have not healed yet."[50]

Following the Taliban's defeat, the U.S. and UN organized a conference in Bonn, Germany, in late November 2001 to establish an interim government. Political parties openly promoting a secular, democratic and sovereign Afghanistan were denied official status, while the largest group represented was the NA. The foreign powers' pick for interim president was Hamid Karzai, a one-time supporter of the Mujahideen and the Taliban with ties to the U.S. going back to the 1980s. Karzai is the kind of weak and compliant leader the U.S. and foreign powers could rely on to ensure the rebuilding of Afghanistan is done in the manner they wish. Although Karzai initially had little support from delegates, he eventually won the leadership thanks entirely to U.S. and UN backroom pressure. Karzai subsequently named NA warlords to key ministerial positions. Troops loyal to one of those warlords, Rashid Dostum, are implicated in the deaths of thousands of Taliban prisoners from gunfire and asphyxiation while being transferred to a prison in Sheberghan not long after the Bonn meeting. In Canada, Karzai's selection was praised by then Minister of Foreign Affairs Bill Graham.[51]

The body convened to create a representative transitional authority leading to elections following Bonn, the Emergency Loya Jirga, was again notable for the strong representation of warlords and their favoured delegates, despite the rules coming out of Bonn declaring that war criminals were to be excluded from the process. Although Afghan provinces expected to select their own delegates, in many instances local independent candidates were beaten or detained by warlords and subsequently forced out of contention. With pressure from the foreign powers, Karzai was again selected as transitional president until elections could be held, and he again named warlords to his cabinet.[52]

Following his selection as interim president by the Emergency Loya Jirga, Karzai set about creating the country's new constitution. Written by a committee handpicked by Karzai and eventually approved by the Loya Jirga, the constitution vests a great deal of power in the president. The president has significant powers of appointment, including for most political offices, the courts, officers of the army and the police, one-third of the seats in one of the legislatures, provincial governors and mayors of cities. It is often close friends and family members who are the benefactors of Karzai's authority. Meanwhile, although it contains basic liberal democratic rights, the role of these rights in Afghan society is potentially threatened by the constitution's first principle, which states that no laws can violate "the sacred religion of Islam."[53] This is not a faint possibility, given that Karzai's appointment to the Chief Justice of the Supreme Court is Fazil Hadi Shinwari, an ultra-fundamentalist cleric who has subsequently expanded the power in the judiciary of individuals who favour a fundamentalist interpretation of Sharia law. According to Canadian ambassador to Afghanistan Chris Alexander, Canada played an important supporting role in the creation of the constitution.[54]

Presidential and parliamentary elections were eventually held on October 9, 2004, and September 18, 2005, respectively. Hailed as a victory for democracy in Afghanistan, both elections were nevertheless mired in controversy. The registration process for the presidential election was widely criticized, with observers reporting that across the country many people registered more than once. There were also not enough voting stations or people to staff them; nor did the Afghan independent monitoring body have the resources to monitor more than a mere twelve percent of the stations. Poor monitoring was especially problematic since local warlords throughout the country were accused of bribery, threats, confiscation of voter registration cards and arbitrary detentions of opponents in order to ensure a favourable outcome. Thirteen of eighteen candidates complained of interference from America's top man on the scene, Special Envoy Zalmay Khalilzad (see endnote 126). He was accused of bribing people to drop out of the race to guarantee a Karzai win, including NA candidates who had the temerity to challenge Karzai. In the end, an estimated seventy percent of eligible voters turned out, and Karzai won with fifty percent of the vote. While the turnout is indeed impressive, a number of observers suggest that support for Karzai represented a best-of-the-worst choice for many Afghans, who hoped he would represent a vote for peace. After the election, Karzai again appointed NA warlords to several key ministry portfolios.[55]

Similar problems beset the parliamentary elections. Warlords were again present, despite election regulations nominally banning candidates linked to armed militias. Human Rights Watch reported that intimidation of voters and candidates was widespread, as was stuffing of ballot boxes and discrimination against women trying to vote. As a result, more than eighty percent of winning candidates in the provinces and sixty percent in Kabul have links to armed groups. Voter turnout this time, however, was much lower at forty percent.[56]

As in Haiti, CIDA funded, and Elections Canada helped to run this sordid electoral process, obviously using a far different measure for what constitutes a fair and democratic election for Afghans (and Haitians) than it does for Canadians. Ignoring the obvious problems with Afghan democracy on display in the elections, Allan Rock, Canadian ambassador to the UN, proudly declared after Karzai's triumph that "Afghanistan is now at a stage where democracy has taken root and is paying dividends."[57] Afghanistan's new "democracy" may be "paying dividends," but not for average Afghans.

The situation for most Afghans is extremely bleak, especially for women. Despite pronouncements from Canadian officials and politicians that women have been liberated from the horrors of the Taliban, women's rights have improved little since 2001. In many parts of the country, according to Kolhatkar and Ingalls, "the warlords have actually targeted women in a manner similar to the Taliban, and sometimes even worse. Only months after the Taliban's fall, there were cases of rape and mistreatment of women."[58] In 2006, Karzai's cabinet approved the re-establishment of the Department for the Promotion of Virtue and Prevention of Vice, which was created by Mujahideen forces and gained international notoriety under the Taliban. It targets women for un-Islamic behaviour, including in Kabul. In the province of Herat, Taliban strictures on women's appearance have returned: women have been forced to wear the burqa or chador (a full-length veil with only the face uncovered) when outside; proper dress is enforced by police, employers and school officials; and religious police have reportedly subjected women and girls to gynecological chastity checks to ensure they are virgins.[59] On top of this, in April 2009 the Afghanistan parliament passed what became known as the "rape law," legislation for the country's Shia minority that legalizes marital rape. Karzai signed the legislation. While the Canadian government expressed outrage when news of the legislation got out after it had been passed, Canadian diplomats and CIDA officials in Afghanistan apparently knew of the law well before it was passed. In response to the international and domestic outcry, Karzai suspended the law's enforcement so that it could be reformed. The reformed law was ratified in August, 2009; it allows husbands to withdraw food from their wives if they refuse their husband's sexual demands and stipulates that wives need to receive permission from their husbands to work. It also enables rapists to avoid prosecution by paying "blood money" to the victim.[60]

It is true that twenty-five percent of the seats in Afghanistan's lower house (the House of the People) are reserved for women. Yet the cost for speaking out against anti-democratic practices and misogynistic laws and policies can be very high. Warlords have regularly threatened women who have challenged them. In one case, courageous and outspoken legislator Malalai Joya became the target of death threats leading the UN to provide her with bodyguards. She subsequently withdrew from electoral politics.[61]

Another major problem plaguing Afghans under the Karzai government is widespread corruption. Investigations by human rights organizations and journalists have uncovered a deeply entrenched system of graft and abuse by government officials, army officers and police—and the latter two groups are being trained in part by the Canadian military. So bad is the situation that one international survey ranked Afghanistan as the second most corrupt country in the world behind only Somalia. A study by several mainstream Afghan and international NGOs found that Afghans blame corruption and poverty more than the Taliban for the war. Bus and taxi drivers are hijacked by police and soldiers for not paying bribes to use provincial roads; political opponents face death threats; individuals have been arrested on trumped-up charges of being members of the Taliban and forced to pay to get out of custody; government positions, such as the position of district police chief in areas in Kandahar, where Canadian soldiers are stationed, are commonly bought by people with means (in Kandahar individuals have paid upwards of $150,000 to secure the position of district police chief); government officials regularly steal land, taxes and foreign aid; and government officials have been implicated in heroin trafficking. Hamid Karzai's younger brother Ahmad Wali Karzai, a member of the Kandahar provincial council who owes his career to his brother's influence and is reputed to be the most feared and powerful man in the province, is well known to be one of the richest drug barons in the country.[62] The profoundly corrupt nature of the Canadian-backed Afghan government gained widespread international attention with the August 20, 2009, presidential election. Karzai "won" with more than the fifty percent of the vote required to avoid a second round. According to international and independent Afghan observers, vote rigging in Karzai's favour was commonplace. Irregularities included polling stations where the turnout exceeded 100 percent; as many as 800 fake polling stations where no one voted, but Karzai received hundreds of thousands of votes; the denial of observer status at polling stations to representatives of Karzai's main challenger and former Foreign Affairs minister, Abdullah Abdullah; and intimidation of voters. Because of the negative attention the election was receiving internationally, the Electoral Complaints Commission (ECC) had to investigate. But Maulavi Mustafa Barakzai, one of two Afghans on the ECC, raised concerns about the Commission's commitment to the investigation. He quit because the Commission's international members, including Canadian Grant Kippen, allegedly ignored input from its Afghan representatives. The Commission, however, had little choice but to call a second round because of the extent of corruption in the first, but no guarantees were offered Afghans that the second round would be any fairer. Abdullah eventually withdrew from the run-off. Given the importance it has invested in the Karzai government as part of its occupation strategy, Canada chose to downplay the electoral irregularities and to accept the legitimacy of the election. Stockwell Day, chair of the Harper government's cabinet committee on Afghanistan, even went so far as to compare the allegations of fraud made against Karzai with allegations of fraud in any other country's elections.[63]

While average Afghans struggle to get by in a country where unemployment is over fifty percent in some areas and access to clean water and basic health care is non-existent for many, a small number of political leaders and government officials have grown immensely wealthy through bribery, pilfering aid money and drug dealing. The problem has become so bad that UN Secretary General Ban Ki-moon publicly rebuked the Karzai government for corruption, weak governance and losing public confidence. One

British official has gone so far as to suggest that government corruption—sowing the seeds of anger and hostility toward the state across the country—is now a worse problem than the Taliban. Canada acknowledged the extent of the problem when it decided to sidestep the government and begin paying Afghan police in Kandahar directly in cash after Canadian money earmarked for the police began disappearing into the pockets of government officials before it reached the intended destination. But as corruption increases, the space for dissent appears to be shrinking. Both Afghan and foreign observers report increasing violence and threats against journalists who criticize the government, while one newspaper's offices were regularly raided before it shut down. A U.S. State Department human rights report found torture and rape to be endemic to the police and prison system, and the country is plagued by restrictions on freedom of the press, official impunity and abuse of workers rights.[64]

This is what the Canadian military is fighting to protect— a thuggish, misogynistic and profoundly corrupt government, many of whose members are war criminals, that is making a small elite quite wealthy at the expense of the poor majority. This is imperialist democracy—the best people in the Global South can expect from foreign powers of the North.

In reality Canada's role goes beyond merely protecting the Afghan government; it is far more deeply implicated than that. I have noted that Canada played a direct role in organizing the constitution and the problematic elections. Canadian officials—including personnel from Foreign Affairs, CIDA and DND—also act as policy advisers to cabinet ministers. Canadians not only shape the government's security strategy in its war against insurgents, they are also helping develop its familiar neoliberal framework for state rebuilding and economic development. Despite the poverty most Afghans live in, public assets are being privatized, regressive tax reforms implemented and the natural resources sector is being liberalized for foreign investors. But Canadian influence appears to go beyond an advisory role to government officials. In April 2008 loose-lipped comments by Foreign Affairs Minister Maxime Bernier inadvertently exposed Canadian meddling behind the scenes to quietly remove the governor of Kandahar from his post. No doubt the governor was an unsavoury figure, with accusations of torture and corruption swirling around him. But the incident forces one to question both the genuine sovereignty of the Afghan state and the self-interested role Canada is playing in it. Canada is using its weight to selectively push certain government officials out of office because their dirty secret of human rights abuse has been publicly exposed. Yet other government officials with equally unsavoury records that Canada surely deals with on a regular basis remain in place with at least tacit Canadian approval.[65]

Losing the War, Strengthening the Taliban
The most visible Canadian presence in Afghanistan is the military war against the Taliban-led insurgency. Since 2005, Canadian troops have been leading the fight against the insurgency in Kandahar. The insurgency can no doubt be brutal, and has targeted civilians. But far from the image of foreign troops as liberators presented by Canadian and NATO leaders, the occupation has been devastating for Afghan civilians. This sadly is no surprise, as civilians typically suffer under foreign occupations that face guerrilla resistance. Foreign troops typically do not distinguish between civilians and insurgents, and actively punish civilians they suspect of harbouring sympathies for the resistance. This is a story that repeats itself time and again throughout the history of the European and American empires. Afghanistan is no different.

Thus stories of civilian casualties and human rights abuses against the local population committed by foreign troops inevitably emerge despite the government's propaganda effort to manage the news coming out of occupied Afghanistan. Reports surface of rape, indiscriminate bombing of villages and violent house-to-house searches for insurgent sympathizers by NATO forces. We learn of Canadian soldiers firing what appears to be indiscriminately in a vengeful manner on a street after facing a bomb attack, killing a homeless beggar and an Afghan police officer (shooting him in the back) standing on a rooftop post in the process. Afghan witnesses to this particular event claim a half an hour passed between the time of the attack on the Canadian soldiers and their subsequent shooting rampage. We also hear about civilians being killed at Canadian military roadblocks when they do not slow down quickly enough for soldiers or on public roads when they get too close to Canadian military convoys; the military calls these incidents "an escalation of force." In the wake of a number of these shootings, it came to light that Canadian soldiers open fire almost weekly on Afghans getting too close to their convoys or approaching roadblocks. In one roadblock incident near the Pashmul area twenty-five kilometres west of Kandahar city, Canadian soldiers shot into a vehicle they felt did not slow down quickly enough. They maintained that no one was injured, but shortly afterwards civilians showed up at the Mirawis hospital complaining of being shot by Canadians, and relatives of one of the victims report that he later died from his wounds. In another incident in July 2008, a four-year-old girl and two-year-old boy sitting in the back of a car travelling on the main highway in Panjwai district in Kandahar were riddled with bullets fired by Canadian soldiers at a checkpoint. The military claimed the soldiers acted appropriately in the face of a potential suicide bomber threat, although suicide bombers usually are alone in a car. In yet another incident, two teenagers riding a motorcycle were gunned by startled Canadian soldiers in Zangabad.[66]

The killings of civilians reported in the mainstream press and acknowledged by Canadian forces are likely just the tip of the iceberg. Neither Canada nor NATO collect data on civilian deaths, likely because this would force them to acknowledge the widescale violence civilians are experiencing at the hands of the foreign powers. This does not stop them from condemning every civilian death caused by insurgents. And to be sure, civilians suffer at the hands of insurgents as well. But despite the image presented to us by NATO and the mainstream media, most civilian deaths are caused by foreign militaries and not the Taliban. The UN publishes data on civilian deaths caused by foreign militaries, and reports that they increased from 2007 to 2008. However, according to Marc Herold, the UN almost certainly underestimates civilian deaths and does not publicly disaggregate its figures so that others can double-check them. Herold, a development economics professor at the University of New Hampshire, created the "Afghan Memorial Project," in which he collects data on the killings of civilians by U.S. and NATO troops from newspapers and other publicly available sources. Every civilian death in Afghanistan since 2001 reported in public sources is presented on his website. By his estimate, at least 7,714 civilians have been killed by U.S. or NATO forces between October 7, 2001, and September 1, 2009, and possibly as many as 9,169—a staggering figure that is more than triple the number of people killed on 9/11.[67] The Canadian military has also been implicated in the beating of prisoners. Canadian soldiers allegedly beat and abused Afghan soldiers in the spring of 2006 while military police turned a blind eye. The abuse became public when Amir Attaran, a University of Ottawa law professor, uncovered unexplained patterns of injuries among Canadian detainees in documents received under an Access to Information request. An investigation was undertaken by the Canadian Forces National Investigation Service. However, by the end of 2009 the investigation is still incomplete and no charges have been laid. Military records for the detainees from the period in which the abuse allegedly took place have also mysteriously gone missing.[68]

Meanwhile, the Canadian military was handing prisoners over to the Afghan prison system where they routinely faced torture. The former governor of Kandahar, Asadullah Khalid, was accused by at least one prisoner of beating and electrically shocking him. Former Chief of Defence Staff General Rick Hillier initially responded to the accusations with praise for the governor, asserting that he is doing "phenomenal work." It turns out the Tories knew about Khalid's involvement in the torture of detainees but tried to keep it secret while Foreign Affairs officials quietly worked to remove him from power before the incident became public knowledge.[69]

In February 2007 the Military Police Complaints Commission (MPCC) began investigating the treatment of Afghan detainees after the allegations of abuse became public. Stephen Harper dismissed the concerns because, according to him, they were made by Taliban. Yet one of the victims was able to correctly tell Canadian investigators where the rubber hose and electrical cable used by the torturers were kept. The military also acknowledged that it cannot account for at least fifty prisoners it turned over to Afghan authorities. No record of them exists. As public criticism of detainee transfers grew, the military quietly stopped transferring prisoners into Afghan authority in November 2007, although it is unclear where they transferred them instead, since DND has no prison in Afghanistan. However, the military subsequently resumed transferring detainees into Afghan custody in April 2008, claiming it had assurances from the Afghan government that prisoners transferred from Canada would not be tortured. Leaked memos indicate, however, that the military suspended the transfers at least one more time.[70] That has not stopped the Tory government from trying to clamp down on the MPCC so that the true extent of abuse of detainees, and knowledge of the abuse among political and military leaders, is not exposed. It has stalled the MPCC's inquiry by challenging its mandate in the courts; made clear to the Commissioner that his term will not be renewed when it is finished well before the inquiry is complete; refused to provide documents to the inquiry and heavily redacted others even though the MPCC's investigators have the highest level of national security clearance; and it threatened the former director of the Kandahar Provincial Reconstruction team until 2007, Richard Colvin, with charges under Canada's Anti-Terrorism Act if he testified at the Inquiry. In response to the threats against Colvin, the parliamentary committee on the Afghan mission subpoenaed him in November 2009, where he testified that the military had been regularly and knowingly transferring Afghan civilians, most having never been a part of the insurgency, to Afghan authorities where they were subsequently tortured, and that he had been warning military and Foreign Affairs officials as far back as May 2006. Harper, Tory cabinet ministers and military leaders have all denied Colvin's claims, attacked his credibility and even, in the case of Hillier, suggested that violence in prisons is commonplace everywhere—despite leaked memos that back up Colvin's testimony that his warnings were in fact received at the highest levels, including McKay's office, and reports from several human rights organizations, including the Canadian-funded Afghanistan Independent Human Rights Commission, that torture in Afghan prisons was routine.[71]

The violence and abuse committed by Canadian and NATO forces—combined with the widespread government corruption—is undermining whatever legitimacy the Karzai government and foreign powers may have garnered from their role in removing the Taliban from power, and is increasing support for the insurgency. An ABC TV poll conducted in October 2007 found that only forty-five percent of Kandahar residents support the presence of NATO forces, while others have found that even those who do support their presence are critical of their treatment of civilians.[72] According to the Senlis Council, a mainstream security and development think tank that has conducted several field investigations in Afghanistan, the foreign powers' military campaign:

> has provided Afghanistan's insurgency movements with a broad recruitment base, and enabled insurgents to establish themselves as substantial power holders in a number of regions. This power-holding now allows the insurgency movements to successfully compete with the weak Kabul government for legitimacy and the support of the impoverished local communities.[73]

As Tariq Ali argues, "The repression leaves people with no option but to back those trying to resist ... If a second-generation Taliban is now growing and creating new alliances it is not because its sectarian religious practices have become popular, but because it is the only available umbrella for national liberation."[74] In the face of government and foreign military violence, Afghans are seeking out those options available to them for self-defence and a political alternative. For their part, the Taliban claim that best sources for new recruits are families forced into refugee camps by indiscriminate NATO bombings of their villages. It has been reported that some Canadian military leaders, such as Brigadier General Jonathon Vance, have scolded local Afghans (after a convoy he was riding in was attacked) for not taking security seriously enough. But he clearly refuses to accept what growing numbers of Afghans understand: the biggest fuel to the resistance's fire is not a lack of concern for security, but growing resentment of Canada's and NATO's disregard for Afghans' security.[75]

Emboldened by increased support from ordinary Afghans, insurgency attacks on the foreign occupiers and Afghan army have been steadily increasing. Canadian politicians and military leaders claim semi-regularly that the insurgents are in retreat, or that a new wave of attacks is only a seasonal uptick caused by warming weather. Although an analysis for the top levels of the Canadian state by the International Assessment Staff of the Privy Council concluded that the security situation in Afghanistan is worsening and the Karzai government is losing credibility, Canadian political leaders are loathe to acknowledge this. But even a 2008 Pentagon report publicly admitted that the Taliban and its supporters have grown stronger and more effective. Indeed, in June 2008 the

Taliban managed to successfully break into the Kandahar prison and free thousands of prisoners, including several hundred of their members. They gave local shopkeepers an advance warning of the attack, yet Canadian intelligence had no idea it was coming. In August 2008, the Canadian military acknowledged that the Taliban are growing in strength and rebounding quickly, and in large numbers, after defeats. According to Afghan and international officials, furthermore, insurgent attacks averaged 400 a month in 2006 (a four fold increase from 2005) and 500 a month in 2007. A UN report published in 2007 finds that suicide attacks, once nonexistent in Afghanistan, escalated from seventeen in 2005 to 123 in 2006, and seventy-seven in the first half of 2007. The southern region, which includes Kandahar, has seen the most attacks—ninety, or forty-five percent of the countrywide total for 2006–2007. Attacks on occupation forces continued to rise in 2009: the number of incidents from improvised explosive devices alone, for instance, rose to 828 in July 2009 (that highest number since the invasion) double the number from a year earlier, while deaths from roadside and suicide bombs increased six fold from July 2008 to July 2009. Perhaps not surprisingly, by the fall of 2009 it was reported that Canada was shifting its focus away from engaging the Taliban in the entire province of Kandahar to trying to maintain stability in and around Kandahar city. What was not reported by the Canadian military or government at that time, but was subsequently revealed in military documents made public through Access to Information in 2010, the Taliban nearly retook Kandahar in the spring of 2009, leading most provincial council members to leave the region.[76]

While Canadian leaders can claim all is well in Afghanistan from the safety of the House of Commons or fundraising dinners with well-heeled corporate benefactors, it is a different matter for the Canadians sent overseas as warm bodies to do the fighting. By the end of February 2010, 140 Canadian soldiers have died as result of the conflict in Afghanistan, the third highest number of casualties behind the U.S. and U.K. However, when measured for the size of troop commitment, a Canadian soldier is almost three times more likely to be killed than a British soldier and four-and-a-half times more likely than an American soldier in Afghanistan, and nearly six times more likely than an American soldier in Iraq.[77]

Aid: Rhetoric vs. Reality
Canadian leaders also like to boast about their contribution to Afghanistan's development. The truth of the matter, however, is that spending on aid pales in comparison to military spending. Since 2001, Canada has spent approximately $1 billion a year on the war. But its costs are escalating beyond that, and according to the parliamentary budget officer, they will reach as high as $18 billion by 2011. Meanwhile Canada spends approximately $100 million a year on aid—just over one-twentieth of what it spends on the military. In 2008, CIDA announced an extra $550 million for development spending until 2011, which is still a paltry sum compared to what Canada spends on the war. Canada is actually eleventh among donor countries in aid spent on Afghanistan as a percentage of Gross Domestic Product.[78]

Field investigators from the International Council on Security and Development (formerly the Senlis Council), an international NGO, wrote a damning report of CIDA's work in Afghanistan. According to the report, there is, for example, no evidence of CIDA work or CIDA-funded work at the Kandahar hospital that corresponds to CIDA claims. For instance, they were unable to find the Maternal Waiting Home project listed by CIDA as one of its efforts. Nor could they find evidence that funds CIDA claims it has given to the hospital have actually been received. They describe the situation at the hospital as "desperate": the ward for starving children is extremely overcrowded, basic medical equipment is needed and no air conditioning, heating or ventilation is in place. CIDA claims to have distributed thousands of tons of food aid for starving people in Kandahar, but Senlis investigators were unable to get information on any specific distribution points to validate the claim. Investigators also could only find evidence of $5 million in infrastructural development funds having been spent out of the $18.5 million CIDA claims. There is also no evidence of a program CIDA says it established to assist civilian casualties of the war. Finally, there is no evidence, according to the Senlis report, that the largest refugees camps for people displaced by war received food aid between March 2006 and August 2007 when the report was written. Another Senlis report sums up Canada's attitude toward development: "The failure to demonstrably address the extreme poverty, widespread hunger, and appalling child and maternal mortality rates in Afghanistan—let alone boost economic development—is decreasing local Afghan support for Canada's mission and increasing support for the insurgency."[79] Canada's so-called "model village" strategy is also plagued with similar problems. This strategy involves a specific rebuilding focus, with money provided through CIDA, in villages in which the Canadian military has pushed out the Taliban. The idea was to win "hearts and minds" by demonstrating Canada's role in establishing security and basic infrastructure to poor communities. However, officials in both Afghanistan and Ottawa have acknowledged that the program is failing because CIDA has not issued the contracts and funds for it.[80]

Making matters worse, Canadian aid is heavily politicized. It is used as a weapon to force compliance from communities that do not support the government. Communities that aren't sufficiently compliant are being denied reconstruction projects and kept out of government positions by Canada, which has further increased hostility toward Canadians in some regions of Kandahar.[81]

Corruption, foreign pressure, military violence and worsening living conditions are leading increasing numbers of Afghans to see the NATO mission, as Tariq Ali observes, "as a fully fledged imperial occupation."[82] The adoption of the Manley Report in early 2008, which calls for an extension of the mission but with more attention to diplomacy to get more countries involved, a commitment by NATO of 1,000 more troops and more focus on reconstruction, will not change a thing. The Manley Commission was made up of four political and corporate leaders who support the war, and not surprisingly they do not seriously interrogate why the occupation is failing and losing support. It ignores how corrupt to the core the Afghan government is and how the war by its very nature is strengthening rather than weakening the insurgency. More troops and more unfulfilled promises of aid will do little to endear the foreign powers and the Karzai government to ordinary Afghans. What the report did accomplish was the consolidation of Canadian ruling class consensus for continuing the mission until at least 2011, providing cover for reluctant Liberals concerned by a public backlash at home if the war continues to go badly by calling for more troops and attention to development. So Canadian support for the occupation will continue while Afghans face little prospect for improvement in their daily lives.[83]

Why Canada is in Afghanistan

Despite the reality on the ground in Afghanistan, and the war's unpopularity amongst Canadians (at least half or more of the public consistently opposes the war in opinion surveys), Canada's political and military leaders continue to promote the conflict. Following the Manley Report, in the winter of 2008 the governing Tories and the Liberals voted to extend the mission to 2011. In fact, Foreign Affairs officials have plans to keep a "reconstruction" base (staffed by Foreign Affairs, CIDA and RCMP personnel and protected by the Canadian military) open until 2015. Both Tory and Liberal senators have stated that Canadian soldiers will likely be in Afghanistan past the 2011 deadline, and Defence Minister Peter McKay has acknowledged that Canada is considering different options for keeping Canadian soldiers beyond 2011. So why the stubborn support for the occupation from Canada's leaders despite its military failure and the strong opposition at home?[84]

It is common to hear from critics of the war that Canada has participated in the Afghanistan occupation to appease the Americans and show its support for the War on Terror following 9/11. No doubt this was a factor in the decision-making process of political and military leaders and foreign policy officials. The United States, Canada's closest ally, had been attacked and was bent on demonstrating its strength to the world. As the superpower, the U.S. had to act in order to maintain its credibility. While Iraq had been discussed as a military target by Bush's inner circle before he was even elected, the case for taking out Saddam Hussein still had to be made to the American public. Afghanistan, ruled mercilessly by the Islamic fundamentalist Taliban, which has ties to Al-Qaeda, was an easier opening salvo in the War on Terror. The U.S. wanted Canadian support in Afghanistan, particularly after 2003 when the U.S. started to get bogged down in its Iraqi venture. Canada acquiesced. Although there was American pressure on Canada to participate in the invasion and subsequent occupation of Afghanistan, it is a mistake to see that as the only reason behind Canada's decision to join the war. This line of argument, while not without its insights, simplifies Canada's security and foreign policy interests, and places far too much responsibility for Canada's imperial recklessness on the U.S. American pressure may have played a role, but that does not mean the interests of Canada's ruling class can be strictly reduced to relations with the U.S.[85]

The Canadian intervention in Afghanistan serves a number of Canadian ruling class interests. As with the intervention in Haiti, it provides Canada with another opportunity to signal to both friend and potential foe, as well as to the Canadian public, that Canada's non-peacekeeping combat role in the world today is not mere rhetoric but reality. The political and military establishment is willing to send Canadian troops halfway around the world to enforce its and its allies' interests, and to sacrifice the lives of its soldiers and civilians in the conflict zones in the process (Afghan civilians are being sacrificed in much greater numbers than Canadian soldiers) Hillier's "our job is to be able to kill people" line was actually made during a discussion of Canada's new combat role in Kandahar, and the occupation of Afghanistan has made that case quite bluntly. It is increasingly hard to maintain that Canada is a peacekeeping nation in the face of all the evidence to the contrary, which undercuts one of the main anti-war positions of left nationalists, including the New Democratic Party (NDP) (that is, that Canada is a peacekeeping, not a war-making, nation). As Colonel D. Craig Hilton argues, "[W]hile the clear articulation of military roles and missions defined in both the International Policy Statement 2005 and its Defence counterpart put a formal end to any suggestion of a peacekeeping *raison d'être* for Canada's military, it is the evolution of Canada's mission in Afghanistan ... that has utterly shattered the widely accepted myth of Canada as benign peacekeeper."[86]

A similar position to that of Hilton was expressed by Bill Graham during his tenure as Liberal Defence Minister when he argued that:

Canada's military commitment to Afghanistan has marked a watershed moment for the Canadian Forces ... it has been a transformational mission, representing a new type of operation, against a new type of enemy, requiring new skills, new capabilities, and, frankly, a new way of thinking for our military and our government ... Afghanistan has many of the characteristics of the new type of mission that the Canadian Forces will be called on to perform in the years to come.[87]

l The Afghanistan war marks a clear determination by Canada to project its power abroad. At the same time, it is a new mission for a revamped Canadian military—a mission against the archetypal threat of the post-Cold War period: a relatively well-armed asymmetric enemy located in the Global South using guerrilla tactics. Afghanistan is thus a key part of the strategy of building a military that, in the words of Tory Defence Minister Peter MacKay, "will help Canada assume a leadership role in the world."[8] Of course, leaving Afghanistan without at least the appearance of victory will not help Canada's reputation in this regard.

Like the intervention in Haiti, Afghanistan offers Canada the opportunity to marry development and military policy, transforming military engagement into a matter of humanitarian concern (and aid into a military issue at the same time). As I have shown, the reality of Canadian aid policy in Afghanistan nowhere near matches the rhetoric. Nevertheless, CIDA, Foreign Affairs and DND officials have all contributed to the increased integration of aid and military practice, where they are treated as symbiotic elements of Canadian foreign policy in the failed states of the Third World. We are led to believe that the only way the poor can be saved—that development policy can be realized—is by military force. In Kandahar, development policy is managed by several Provincial Reconstruction Teams (PRT), which consist not only of CIDA and Foreign Affairs personnel, but also of DND and RCMP staff. This is clearly an important foreign policy direction—a frightening proposition given what little development has taken place in the Afghan example, and the number of civilians who have been killed in the occupation.

Many critics of the war have suggested that the initial invasion and the ongoing occupation is motivated by America's interest in building the Trans-Afghan Pipeline (TAP), which will transport natural gas from Turkmenistan (which contains the fourth largest reserves of natural gas in the world according to the International Energy Agency) through Afghanistan to Pakistan and India. In the late 1990s the Taliban visited Texas energy giant Unocal's headquarters in order to discuss a contract for the TAP, though the deal was never concluded. Kolhatkar and Ingalls caution, however, that there is no evidence to suggest that the U.S. invaded and occupied Afghanistan specifically because it wanted to reap the profits off of the proposed TAP. Instead, they argue that the invasion was initially planned for several reasons: to recover America's imperial prestige, gain experience in establishing "democratic" imperialist regime change and because more time was needed to build the case against Iraq. It has provided the U.S. with an excellent opportunity to position itself and gain influence in a strategic region that is rich in natural gas and surrounded by potential rival powers (i.e., Russia, China and Iran). Military bases and pipelines become important tools in the region's new Great Game. The U.S. has expanded its major military bases in the region to Afghanistan, Kyrgyzstan and Uzbekistan, giving it a much strengthened security presence near its rivals. At the same time, the U.S. is concerned about Russian energy influence in the region, including a potential Russian-led energy alliance, and thus it has encouraged pipeline deals such as the TAP, which compete with Russian projects for control over the supply and transport of natural gas in the area, and which bypass both Russian and Iranian territory.[89]

As Kolhatkar and Ingalls and Tariq Ali point out, though, this is not just a matter of American strategic interests. NATO has been centrally involved in the Afghanistan campaign from the beginning, supporting the U.S. invasion and eventually leading a military mission. This is the first time NATO has been involved in Asia, and marks an ongoing effort to recast itself as an alliance with not only the ability but the right to project the collective military power of its members. In the view of some NATO supporters, developments in the "Asia-Pacific region" are a security matter for NATO nations. According to security analyst Julian Lindley-French, writing in NATO Review:

> The centre of gravity of power on this planet is moving inexorably eastward … the Asia-Pacific region brings much that is dynamic and positive to this world, but as yet the rapid change therein is neither stable nor embedded in stable institutions. Until this is achieved, it is the strategic responsibility of Europeans and North Americans, and the institutions they have built to lead the way.[90]

Some American officials, Kolhatkar and Ingalls argue, likewise see NATO as playing a role in building and defending transatlantic unity against the rise of rival powers in the East bidding for global capitalist dominance. Canadian support for NATO and participation in Afghanistan should be situated within the context of these developments shaping the alliance. The Canadian ruling class's ongoing commitment to the war may therefore also be seen as a strategic decision to support the collective geopolitical interests of the transatlantic imperialist countries, and not just as an attempt to appease the U.S. This is not to suggest that there aren't serious tensions between NATO nations, that individual NATO nations do not have specific imperialist interests, or that the alliance's efforts to revamp itself in this manner will be successful in the long term. But these current developments in NATO vis-à-vis Russia and China do help us to make sense of the involvement of Canada and other imperialist nations in the Afghanistan war.[91]

While access to natural resources such as natural gas may not have been the reason Canada chose to join the war effort in Afghanistan, it may nevertheless factor into its decision-making in conducting the occupation and determining the length of the mission. Before Canada had become more heavily involved in the occupation with its decision to take the lead role in Kandahar, Canadian energy companies had travelled to Turkmenistan to discuss investments in the hydrocarbons sector. The Canadian companies were accompanied by recently retired Prime Minister Jean Chrétien, who was reportedly acting as an adviser to Calgary law firm Bennet Jones, which specializes in energy issues, and Calgary-based PetroKazakhstan Inc. The Canadian delegation would have been well aware that the Turkmenistan gas would most likely be transported through Afghanistan to reach the Pakistani and Indian markets. It would also have been aware of Turkmenistan's extremely poor human rights record, which includes arbitrary detention and persecution of the regime's political opponents. Foreign Affairs' own website notes that opposition parties are outlawed in Turkmenistan.[92]

In February, 2008 Chrétien returned to Turkmenistan, this time with Calgary-based Buried Hill Energy, which won a license to explore and develop a gas field in the country. The rush by foreign suitors to exploit Turkmenistan's gas deposits was finally followed not long after by the signing of formal agreements in April 2008 between the four participating countries in the TAP project. The 1,680 kilometre pipeline will start in the Turkmen city of Dauletabad and pass through the Afghan cities of Herat and Kandahar, where Canadian forces are heavily concentrated, before entering Pakistan and India. The pipeline is estimated to export thirty-three billion cubic metres of gas from Turkmenistan annually. It is unclear at this point when construction will be finished, given the instability in Kandahar. According to some estimates the pipeline will not be completed before 2018. But given that the Canadian military is responsible for security in Kandahar, the successful completion of the TAP now rests heavily on its shoulders. And even though the completion date is still up in the air, that has not stopped DND officials from announcing that they will help to protect the pipeline.[93]

Canadian mining companies may also become direct beneficiaries of the occupation and Canadian military-imposed "stability." The Karzai government has been courting Canadian and other foreign companies to develop Afghanistan's mining industry. Afghan officials claim only five percent of the country's potential mineral deposits have been explored because of decades of war, and like the rest of the Afghan economy, the natural resources sector has been subject to neoliberal restructuring creating a strong pro-foreign investment legal climate. Karzai's Minister of Mines Ibrahim Adel has become a regular attendee at the Prospectors and Developers Association of Canada's annual gatherings. He has been supported by Foreign Affairs and International Trade, which has set up round tables between Adel and Canadian mining executives at the meetings. The Afghanistan Investment Support Agency, a government agency established to promote foreign investment, declares that: "Afghanistan offers a pro-business minded environment with legislation favourable to private investments." It stresses that Afghanistan "is rich in natural resources," but adds that it is also "keen on establishing a low-cost, labor-intensive manufacturing sector which absorbs the many unemployed Afghans."[94]

Canadian investment in the surrounding region is considerable, and the Canadian state's increased presence in the region — diplomatic, aid and military—as a result of the Afghan occupation could serve to encourage Canadian capital to seek out new opportunities there. With an active military and diplomatic presence that may well extend beyond 2011, Canadian capital can count on greater support from its state. FAIT is in fact providing information to Canadian companies to assist their participation in the First Afghan Hydrocarbon Bidding Round in which oil and gas resources are being auctioned off by the Afghan state] Meanwhile, Alhambra Resources proudly declared on its website that beside its CEO, John Komarnicki, in the Kazakhstan Supreme Court when the company finally won a long-standing dispute with the Kazakhstan state, allowing it to proceed with a gold mining investment, was a "senior representative of the Canadian ambassador to Kazakhstan."[95]

So there are a number of likely reasons why Canada joined the war in Afghanistan and why political leaders and policy-makers are planning to maintain some form of presence for the next several years if not longer. And while U.S. pressure to be a good ally in the War on Terror no doubt informs Canadian decision-making, it is not the only thing weighing on the minds of Canadian leaders. Canada is also there as part of a broader NATO mission, defending the collective interests of North American and European imperialism. Meanwhile, military, political and economic self-interest cannot be discounted as reasons for Canada's intervention] Afghanistan could represent, despite all the failures on the ground, a key historical moment in which Canadian imperialism became more brazen.

A Region of Strategic Interest:
Toward a Latin American Security Policy

As we saw in chapter three, Canada has become a dominant economic player in Latin America. Together with the Caribbean, it is the region of the world where Canadian capitalist expansion is the most pronounced. This puts greater responsibility on the Canadian state with respect to its Latin American foreign policy, including in the realm of security matters. For Canadian capital has not always had an easy go of securing its investments in the region, facing hostile local populations defending their natural resources and labour rights and now anti-neoliberal governments in some countries. It is likely, then, that we will see a greater security focus on the Americas in the years to come, as the state seeks to ensure the stability, predictability and certainty in this zone of interest for Canadian investors.

These are the considerations informing the thinking of former Foreign Affairs Minister Maxime Bernier when he asserted that

"Canada has the influence, the capacity and the responsibility to play a leadership role in the Americas" and that with its allies it "must strengthen hemispheric security, and build a safer and more secure neighbourhood"; or Stephen Harper when he declares that "Canada is committed to playing a bigger role in the Americas," including being prepared to "meet new security challenges."[96]

A more aggressive security stance becomes an important option, as we saw with Haiti. Canadian officials may not always be explicit about the role of economic interests in driving their Latin American security agenda, but there is little evidence of a serious security challenge to Canada. Thus when Harper cites "security challenges," Bernier calls for a "more secure neighbourhood," or a CSIS intelligence report notes that instability in Latin America could "develop into security concerns," what is really at stake is the security of Canadian capital, the investments of which dominate Canada's relationship with countries in the Americas.[97]

Aligning With State Terror: Canada's Rapprochement With Colombia

One of the more significant developments in Canada's Latin American foreign policy in recent years is its increasingly close relationship with Colombia, including the Free Trade Agreement enacted in June 2009. Canada's orientation to Colombia speaks not only to its relationship with that country in particular, however; it is also indicative of its attitude toward the progressive left-wing governments in Venezuela, Ecuador and Bolivia. In a region where workers' and indigenous movements have grown in power and influence in the last decade, and where governments have moved to the left and implemented anti-neoliberal policies, Canada has opted to clearly align itself with Colombia—a country with an aggressive neoliberal agenda and an atrocious human rights record.

Four members of the federal Tory cabinet travelled to the Andean country to meet with high-ranking Colombian politicians and discuss political and economic ties between July, 2007 and February 2008. Prime Minister Stephen Harper met with President Uribe in July 2007; Jean-Pierre Blackburn, Minister for Labour, met with Uribe and his vice president in November 2007; Beverly Oda, Minister for International Cooperation, met with Colombia's Minister of Foreign Affairs in January 2008; and Maxime Bernier, while Minister of Foreign Affairs, met with Uribe in February, 2008. Colombia's vice president also visited Canada in May 2008. Aside from the U.S. (Canada's neighbour and closest ally) and Afghanistan (where Canada is at war), few other countries have received this kind of attention from high ranking Canadian political leaders in recent years.

During Harper's visit to Colombia and Chile (where he opened a Scotiabank branch and met with Barrick officials) in the summer of 2007, he made the point of distinguishing those countries that pursue strong free markets from the "economic nationalism, political authoritarianism and class warfare" taking hold in other parts of the Andes.[98] Colombian political and economic policy, in other words, is being presented by Canadian political leaders as an alternative to that of Venezuela, Ecuador and Bolivia. Harper's position on the growing political and economic divide in the region was applauded by Canadian business leaders. Richard Waugh, president of Scotiabank, joyously declared: "I think it is just great that Canada's showing some leadership in Latin America ... We have in Latin America two major forces, free markets in some countries, and some other forces in other countries ... Canada is a good role model (in Latin America) for principles like free markets and good governance."[99]

The Harper government defends its move to deepen relations with Colombia—and to be clear, Liberal governments of the 1990s and early 2000s also supported Canadian investment there—by playing down the profound human rights issues plaguing the country. Harper took the occasion of his visit to the country to laud the president, declaring that "President Uribe and his government have made tremendous progress against the vicious cycle of conflict, violence and under-development that has plagued Colombia for decades."[100] Harper's praise for Uribe was actually parroted word-for-word by Bernier during his trip to the war-torn country in February 2008, as if by saying it enough it may actually become true.[101] After announcing a free trade deal to be near at hand in May 2008, Emerson too eschewed concerns about Colombia's and Uribe's rights record: "Unless we were presented with overwhelming and solid evidence that the government is somehow behind some of the killings of labour leaders, I just do not think it is right to simply ... hold them back and to penalize them when they are trying very hard to make progress." Instead, the problem rests with the critics' ideological blinkers: "There are people who, for dogmatic reasons candidly, do not want us to do a free trade deal with Colombia."[102] The Conservatives continued their agenda of minimizing the reality of repression in Colombia in the parliamentary debates on the deal. Stockwell Day, then Minister of International Trade, offers one notable example of the depths to which the Tories were willing to sink to defend the agreement, comparing Colombia to Canada. Noting that kidnappings have decreased in Colombia, he asks: "Do they still happen?" "Yes, they do," he answers, but "They still happen in Canada, too." "Are people still murdered in that country" he continues. "Yes, they are. They are still being murdered in Canada also."[103]

Shortly after Bernier's comments, and just two months before Emerson's, at least six trade unionists who participated in or helped to organize countrywide demonstrations against state and paramilitary violence on March 6, 2008, were assassinated. Four were killed within a week of the demonstration. Observers argue that the assassinations and death threats were encouraged by the comments of Uribe's close political ally and adviser José Obdulio Gavaria, who called the protest organizers FARC guerrillas in the media. Such accusations are tantamount to placing a bounty on a person's head. It is well known that labelling government opponents as FARC members or supporters—and therefore as terrorists—is an excuse used to exterminate them, given the government and the paramilitaries are at war with the FARC and thus consider its members and supporters to be legitimate targets. Indigenous peoples opposing resource development or union activists are commonly denounced by the government and paramilitaries as guerrillas or complicit with guerrillas, and then arrested or assassinated.[104]

But these murders, most likely done by paramilitaries, are not anomalous under Uribe. The rate of paramilitary murders each year, according to the Colombian Commission of Jurists, is between 800 and 900 people, and has been essentially unchanged since 2003 when the Uribe government supposedly began "demobilizing" paramilitaries. Moreover, the Uribe government is facing a corruption scandal in which seventy-seven political leaders, most of whom have strong relations with Uribe, and some of whom are family members, are under investigation for ties to paramilitaries. Is it simply dogmatic, then, to point out that violence against government opponents is taking place as Canada strengthens its ties to the Colombian government and negotiates a free trade agreement, or that political leaders to whom Harper et al. are cozying up are connected to the paramilitaries responsible for much of that violence?[105]

Violence and corruption are deeply entrenched in Colombian political life. Colombian elections regularly feature assassinations of candidates, threats against candidates and voters, vote buying, illegal campaign financing, fraud and disenfranchisement of the country's significant displaced population. Following the October 28, 2007, elections for governors, mayors and municipal posts, OAS election observers noted that these election irregularities, some of which they witnessed first-hand, undermine democracy in the country. One observer declared that "Colombia has the most backward electoral system in Latin America."[106]

Contrast that observation with those of international observers who found the recall referendum and presidential elections of Venezuela's Hugo Chávez to be fair and legitimate. But according to Canadian political leaders and foreign affairs officials, Chávez's Venezuela, despite having a far superior human rights and electoral record than Colombia, and despite making some efforts to redistribute wealth to poorer communities, is authoritarian. Uribe's Colombia, on the other hand, is a beacon of freedom and democracy. In a speech to the Council on Foreign Relations on Canada's orientation to Latin America, Harper praised the Colombian government and presented it (and Chile, which he also visited in summer of 2007 tour) as an alternative to left-wing governments in the Andean region: "While many nations are pursuing market reform and democratic development, others [read *Venezuela, Ecuador and Bolivia*] are falling back to economic nationalism and protectionism, to political populism and authoritarianism."[107]

Yet the evidence for Colombia's dismal rights record is there for Canadian political and business leaders and Foreign Affairs officials to see—if they wished to. Their portrayal of the region, and their cozying up to the Colombian government despite Uribe's support for state and paramilitary violence, is not an accident. Colombia is not only rich in natural resources but its political leaders are proudly compliant with imperial interests in the region while governments around them increasingly are not. It is a reliable imperial ally in the midst of political and economic uncertainty represented by strong social movements and left-wing governments. As Harper told the *Wall Street Journal,* Colombia is an important "ally" in a region with "serious enemies and opponents."[108] It is worth noting here too that this view is not lost on the Liberals. During the debate in the House of Commons on the Canada-Colombia FTA, Liberal trade critic and FTA supporter (which is the position of his party), Scott Brison, consistently referred to the importance of supporting Colombia against the (unexplained, because non-existent) threats it faces from Chávez.[109]

Thus the United States and Canada have chosen to promote Colombia as an aggressive and heavily militarized bulwark against anti-imperialism in the region—an Israel of the Andes. Like Israel, Colombia receives strong diplomatic support from its imperial allies despite its terrible rights record and because of its role in policing and destabilizing its neighbours. And like Israel, it has also been the beneficiary of American military largesse, most notably via Plan Colombia. Plan Colombia was initiated by Bill Clinton, nominally for the eradication of coca in the Andean country. It has involved US$4 billion in aid, eighty percent of which was directed to the Colombian police and military. But as critics have pointed out, Plan Colombia has led to an increase in violence and displacement in regions where foreign companies are hoping to exploit natural resources. Despite this, Foreign Affairs supports the plan.[110]

Canada has also contributed directly to Colombia's military buildup, if in a small way compared to the U.S. At least forty-five helicopters have been sold from Canada by the military and private companies—thirty-three by DND—to the Colombian military since 1995. DND sold the Bell CH135 choppers to the U.S. State Department, which retrofitted them with machine guns and sent them to Colombia. DND knew where the helicopters were headed when it made the sale. Even though the Canadian government requires export permits for military hardware and says it is opposed to the sale of weapons to countries in conflict and with a record of human rights abuses, no export permit was required for DND's sale because the helicopters were originally sold to the U.S. Another Canadian company, Vector Aerospace, was contracted in 2001 by the Colombian military for helicopter maintenance and servicing. No government permit was required for this contract either.[111] In a tell-all book called *Nous étions invincibles* (We were invincible) an ex-Joint Task Force 2 member (Canada's highly secretive commando unit) alleges that Canadian commandos battled the FARC in the late 1990s. If true—and it is hard to independently verify given the secretive nature of JTF2, although there is no good reason for the author to make up stories about fighting the FARC in particular—it is an astonishing revelation that the Canadian military has been actively (and secretly) intervening in Colombia.[112]

Colombia's policing role in the region was bluntly demonstrated on March 1, 2008, when its military violated Ecuadorean sovereignty and bombed a FARC camp located just inside the Ecuadorean border with Colombia. Colombian ground soldiers then crossed into Ecuador to secure the camp. Twenty-three people were killed in the attack, including the FARC's second in command, Raul Reyes. Ecuador and Venezuela (which has been threatened by Colombia in the recent past) responded to this violation of international law by cutting off diplomatic ties and sending troops, tanks and planes to their respective Colombian borders.

While Colombia and the international mainstream media reported widely that those killed were FARC guerrillas, it turns out that one was an Ecuadorean citizen and four were Mexican graduate students interviewing FARC members for their research on the country's peace process. Uribe also claims, as was widely reported in the media, that Reyes's computer, found by Colombian soldiers (despite the camp being turned to rubble), contained direct evidence linking Hugo Chávez and Venezuelan money to the FARC. This claim has not been independently verified. According to Interpol, the volume of data on the computer corresponds to 39.5 million pages in Microsoft Word. Yet Colombian officials somehow managed to read it in less than two days. The fact is, no illicit relations between Chávez and the FARC have ever been documented. Uribe also alleged that a picture of Reyes with Ecuador's Security minister was on the FARC leader's laptop. The photo was printed on the front page of the Colombian daily El Tiempo before it was revealed that the person with Reyes was in fact the secretary of the Argentine Communist Party.[113]

The raid follows Chávez's successful negotiations with the FARC that led to the release of six of the guerrilla group's hostages in January and February 2008. Uribe, who maintains an extremely hardline position in which he constantly makes recourse to security threats which provide a pretext for the continued militarization of Colombian society, and argues that the only solution to the country's conflict is a military one, did not look favourably upon the successful negotiations. Adding to Uribe's frustrations, Chávez, whose government as noted offers a dramatically different political and economic development model to Colombia, garnered international praise for his success, while the FARC's willingness to negotiate the hostages' release (and Reyes played a leading role here for the FARC) is aimed at strengthening the group's diplomatic relations in Europe. Thus the attack targeted the FARC's lead negotiator and diplomatic contact person in Europe, while serving as a provocation to Colombia's populist neighbours.[114]

Uribe steadfastly refuses to guarantee that Colombia will not violate its neighbours' sovereignty again. Instead, he maintains Colombia's right to pre-emptive intervention in the region as a supposed defence against terrorism. The intervention in Ecuador and the threat to do it again is a clear warning from Colombia to its left-leaning neighbours that it will not hesitate to throw its military might around should they get out of line. Chávez actually claimed well before the March 1 raid that Colombia was trying to provoke Venezuela into a military conflict. In the last few years, the Colombian government covertly recruited Venezuelan military and security officers for the kidnapping of a Colombian leftist leader; Colombian paramilitaries infiltrated Venezuela to violently support would-be anti-Chávez plotters; and paramilitaries routinely crossed into Venezuelan to hunt down people fleeing them. Just a couple of months after the violation of Ecuadorean sovereignty, four men—three Colombians and one Ecuadorean—were arrested in an alleged plot to kill Correa. Some reports suggested the plotters were tied to Colombian paramilitaries, while the Colombian government responded that they were tied to the FARC, which does not have any reasons for assassinating Correa. While not all the details have come out at the time of writing, the arrests cast a further pall over Ecuador's relations with Colombia.[115]

Canada supports Colombia's violation of Ecuadorean sovereignty, if not as bluntly as does the United States. Despite Colombia's role as the aggressor, the serious nature of its actions and the potential instability it could cause the region, Canada's intervention at the OAS debate on the incident was a mere one minute and ten seconds. Canada's representative at the OAS, Graeme Clarke, made a brief and general call for a respect for sovereignty, without naming Colombia as the violator of international law or criticizing it for threatening to do so again. It is not a stretch to read his remarks as directed not only at Colombia but also at Venezuela and Ecuador for supposedly supporting terrorism and for sending troops to their borders with Colombia in response to the latter's aggression. Clarke then urged dialogue between the three countries and proposed mediation if necessary, as if they are all equally at fault or Uribe has ever showed any serious interest in mediation in the past. Combine these remarks with the efforts of Canadian political leaders to strengthen ties with Colombia, and it is clear where Canada's interests in the Andes lie.[116]

FOCAL analyst Vladimir Torres defends Colombia's actions in Ecuador quite sharply in a *Globe and Mail* op-ed piece: "One could argue that if Israel were right to bomb Hezbollah in southern Lebanon, then Colombia was right to act in self-defence in Ecuador." The real danger in the region, according to Torres, is Venezuela, Ecuador and Nicaragua (whose president, Daniel Ortega, they claim is moving closer to Chávez), which are anti-democratic and support "terrorism." Despite its human rights record, then, Colombia is again presented as the defender of freedom in the Andes.

The Israel analogy is indeed apt, if not for quite the same reasons as Torres might think. Colombia, as I noted above, is clearly positioned as the regional bulwark against democracy and progressive economic policy for imperialist powers like the United States and Canada. While a direct invasion by the U.S. and Canada to defend their interests in the region is unlikely at this point, a well-armed, aggressive and compliant Colombia may help to strengthen the imperial hand in the Andes. This is what lies behind Canadian foreign policy toward Colombia.[117]

However, Canadian security policy in the region extends beyond support for Colombia. Through the Canada Fund for Local Initiatives (administered through the Caracas embassy with financial support from CIDA), Canada also funded up until 2005 at least two Venezuelan civil society organizations that have been working to destabilize the Chávez government, including support for the failed 2002 coup. These groups are Súmate A.C. and Fundacion Justicia de Paz Monagas. Foreign Affairs and International Trade has funded the Justice and Development Consortium, another far right-wing organization. Each of these groups work to organize the opposition and disseminate anti-Chávez propaganda. Foreign Affairs and International Trade actually brought Maria Corina Machado from Súmate to Ottawa where she spoke with government officials and politicians about political rights in Venezuela. Funding for these organizations is part of the Canadian state's agenda of democracy promotion and human rights in the Andes, which the Harper government has declared as a key element of Canadian foreign policy. Fenton notes how Canada's efforts in this regard intersect with the U.S., which has put a lot of money into democracy promotion in the region, including in Venezuela (the budget for this has increased under Obama to an astounding US$1.7 billion for 2009). FOCAL has received money from the NED to carry out democracy promotion work in Venezuela. In a 2007 communiqué to CIDA, FAIT and DND officials in Ottawa, the Caracas embassy notes that the Chávez government has blocked the American embassy from spending development and human rights funds (the Americans were funding coup plotters). With less political baggage than the Americans, Canada has an "opportunity ... [comments redacted] ... to fill the gap created by this reality. As far as Canadian funds are concerned, we will continue to be supportive of NGOs that work on human rights and for the preservation of civil society space." All efforts to find out who Canada has been funding since 2005, however, have been blocked by CIDA on the grounds that releasing the information would threaten the security of those organizations.[118]

What is clear, however, is that the Harper Conservatives are planning on increasing funding to democracy promotion initiatives, while centralizing their efforts and focusing more on political parties and organizations as the NED does. This is the strategy advocated by Conservative Senator and strategist Hugh Segal, who has argued for removing democracy promotion initiatives from CIDA and concentrating them in a new democracy promotion centre. A foreign affairs parliamentary committee report on democracy promotion raised the idea for such a centre in July, 2007, and the Conservative Minister of State for Democratic Reform, Steven Fletcher, tabled a report laying out a blueprint for a democracy promotion centre that would fund political parties in the Third World in December 2009. In October of 2009, furthermore, FAIT established a democracy promotion centre in Lima, Peru, the Andean Unit for Democratic Governance, which will have a specific focus on all countries in the Andean region. Given the clearly reactionary recent history of Canadian democracy promotion efforts in the Americas (going back at least to Aristide's 2000 election in Haiti) these new developments are extremely alarming, to say the least.[119]

Supporting a Coup in Honduras

On June 28, 2009, Honduran President Manuel "Mel" Zelaya was overthrown in a military coup and forced into exile. Zelaya had raised the minimum wage, announced a moratorium on new mining concessions, sought to nationalize energy-generating plants and the telephone system, entered the Venezuelan-initiated Bolivarian Alternative for the Americas, a political and economic formation that seeks to counter imperialist influence in the region, and called a vote for June 28 (the day of the coup) to test if Hondurans wanted a referendum in November on whether or not to call a constitutional assembly (Honduras's inflexible constitution was adopted by a U.S.-backed military dictatorship in 1982).

As one of the largest foreign investors in the country, Canada had a lot to potentially lose if Honduras kept tilting leftwards. Thus when the first rumblings of a potential coup were heard two days before it eventually took place, Canada said nothing. Foreign Affairs and International Trade issued no press release on the 26 or the 27 condemning the clear threat to Honduran democracy. By contrast it issued three press releases in a two-week span earlier in the month condemning the Iranian government's clampdown on protests following that country's controversial presidential elections. The Organization of American States (OAS) did pass a resolution on Friday, June 26, that called for the maintenance of democracy and the rule of law. Yet, at the same time, in the special session of the OAS Permanent Council on the situation in Honduras held that same day, the Canadian representative remained silent.[120] A press release was finally issued by Peter Kent, Minister of State for the Americas, very late in the evening of June 28, more than twelve hours after the coup became known outside of Honduras. While Kent condemns the coup d'état, he "calls on all parties to show restraint and to seek a peaceful resolution" to the crisis, as if all parties, including Zelaya and his supporters, are responsible for the military-orchestrated coup or are equally unrestrained in their actions.[121] This position is echoed in the Canadian representative's statement to the OAS Permanent Council following the coup on the 28th. Kent argued later, as the OAS was planning a trip to Honduras to press the interim government to allow Zelaya to return, that the international community has been too one-sided in its approach to the coup, noting that "The coup was certainly an affront to the region, but there is a context in which these events happened ... There has to be an appreciation of the events that led up to the coup."[122] The Canadian government was signalling to Zelaya that, should he return to power, he is expected to moderate his policies.[123] At the same time, along with the U.S., Canada sought to weaken the OAS's position on the military-backed Honduran government by pushing it not to pursue sanctions and to merely review diplomatic relations.[124]

When U.S.-brokered mediation between Zelaya and coup leader, Roberto Micheletti, broke down several weeks later, Kent responded by declaring that Zelaya should return to Honduras only after a negotiated settlement had been achieved and the risk of violence had passed.[125] The violence following the coup, Kent failed to mention, was perpetrated by the military, not Zelaya's supporters; and making Zelaya's return conditional on the coup leader negotiating a settlement with him lent credibility to an undemocratic government that should not have been involved in negotiations to begin with, while putting pressure on Zelaya to make major concessions to Micheletti. It is clear in all this that, while Canada on the surface did not openly support the coup, in practice it did little to challenge the coup government's legitimacy and worked instead to undermine Zelaya's strength.

Canada's silence about the systematic repression meted out against coup opponents is quite striking, given how prominent a role the repression played in sustaining the coup government, particularly as the anti-coup movement gained in strength. Canada was quick to condemn government repression in Iran and Guinea during the same period.[126] A clear message was sent to opponents following the coup, for example, when Fernando "Billy" Joya, a notorious Honduran Cold War death squad leader (Battalion 3-16), was made special security advisor to Micheletti. By the time of the November 29 elections, five months after the coup, thousands of human rights violations had been registered according to human rights organizations working on the ground in Honduras. According to the Committee of Family Members of the Disappeared of Honduras (COFADEH), a leading Honduran human rights organization, founded in the 1980s, at least twenty-six opponents to the dictatorship had been killed. Many more had been tortured, beaten, physically threatened and illegally detained. Protest marches have been dispersed by police and military with truncheons, tear gas and live ammunition, while the offices of anti-coup organizations have been attacked and anti-coup media outlets shut down. Women activists have also been targeted specifically by the repression, with the Women's Human Rights Week international delegation to Honduras documenting rapes, sexual harassment, assault and sexist insults against them.[127]

Not one press release from the Canadian government explicitly identifies or criticizes these repressive measures by the coup government. Instead, as I noted above, Kent would tersely, and very misleadingly, call on both sides to show restraint. When Zelaya initially tried to re-enter Honduras in July, his supporters went to the border to meet him and were greeted by the police and military with tear gas, rubber bullets, arbitrary detention and roadblocks. About this Kent said nothing, declaring instead on CBC Radio that the deposed president's "attempts to re-enter the country … [are] … very unhelpful to the situation."[128] When Zelaya did manage to return from his exile in September, the coup regime responded by stepping up its repression of coup opponents and laid siege to the Brazilian embassy where Zelaya was holed up. Initially Micheletti suspended constitutional civil rights for forty-five days, though he backed down quickly in the face of internal and external opposition (which did not come from Canada). However, that did not stop the increase in arbitrary arrests of coup opponents and the violent dispersals of protests, or the documented chemical and auditory (pain-inducing high-pitched sounds) attacks on the Brazilian embassy that followed Zelaya's return.[129] All Kent could muster in response was that Canada is "concerned with the violence that erupted in the aftermath of President Zelaya's sudden return to Honduras," which is followed by his extremely misleading call "on all parties to show restraint."[130] No acknowledgement of the attacks on the Brazilian embassy or of the suspension of the constitution is made. Kent released another statement three days later again calling "for all parties to refrain from any incitement to violence and provocation, and to respect the inviolability of the Brazilian embassy."[131] While alluding to the stand-off at the embassy, Kent fails to explicitly identify the attacks and bizarrely suggests the anti-coup forces are not respecting its "inviolability," demonstrating the lengths Canada would go to avoid meaningful criticism of the Micheletti dictatorship.

In the face of a growing anti-coup movement at home and international pressure (from the OAS, the European Union and the United States) Micheletti finally signed the San José-Tegucigalpa Accord with Zelaya on October 29. The Accord was initially heralded by many observers as a breakthrough, though in reality it was a victory for pro-coup forces inside and outside of Honduras. For instance, it did not ensure Zelaya's reinstatement but referred it back to Congress (which subsequently did not reinstate him before the elections); a power-sharing government of Zelaya and coup supporters was called for; appeals for the convening of a Constituent Assembly were ruled out; and, of course, the settlement came five months after the coup and with only two months left in Zelaya's term (had he actually been reinstated).

Canada was quick to support the Accord, pushing as it had been for an agreement that would effectively end the stand-off without empowering Zelaya and the opposition. Kent responded to it by noting, "I am pleased that negotiators for Honduran president Manuel Zelaya and interim leader Roberto Micheletti were able to reach an agreement on a way out of the political impasse affecting their country."[132] The fact that Zelaya's presidency was effectively nullified by it and the possibility of a democratically organized Constituent Assembly process foreclosed is ignored. Canada, furthermore, remained silent about the ongoing imprisonment of Zelaya in the Brazilian embassy long after the Accord was signed. Nor did Canada withdraw its support for the elections that took place under the Micheletti dictatorship, in spite of the fact that anti-coup forces and politicians called for a boycott. Kent instead simply expressed Canada's "disappointment" that the Accord was not implemented in time and announced that Canada's election observers would not participate.[133]

According to human rights observers on the ground in Honduras, the election process witnessed, in fact, another increase in repression against coup opponents, including a declaration of a state of emergency, the massive deployment of the military to "guard" polling stations, the closing of anti-coup media outlets, raids on the offices of anti-coup organizations, the illegal detention of regime opponents and the violent dispersal of a protest in San Pedro Sula.[134] The election was won by the conservative Porfirio Lobo of the National Party. Lobo was defeated by Zelaya in the 2005 election. While Honduras's Supreme Electoral Tribunal announced a 61.3 percent voter turnout (greater than the 2005 figure of fifty-five percent) following the election, it did not provide any breakdown of the vote to back up its numbers; and, unlike for previous elections, it decided not to include the 1.2 million Hondurans living outside the country when calculating the total number of possible voters, dropping the number from 4.6 to 3.4 million voters. After an initial count based on its observations of a selection of polling stations and including Hondurans outside the country, independent election monitor Hagamos Democracia suggested the turnout was 47.6 percent (below the 2005 turnout). Some international human rights observers, reporters and resistance members suggest the turnout was in fact lower still, based on their observations of polling stations and the empty streets of poor neighbourhoods. Honduran daily El Tiempo, which encouraged people to vote, estimated the abstention rate to actually be as high as sixty-five to seventy percent.[135]

Undeterred by the controversies surrounding it, Kent wasted little time in announcing Canada's recognition of the election—in contrast to most countries in the region—astoundingly declaring that "Canada congratulates the Honduran people for the relatively peaceful and orderly manner in which the country's elections were conducted. While Sunday's elections were not monitored by international organizations ... we are encouraged by reports from civil society organizations that there was a strong turnout for the elections, that they appear to have been run freely and fairly, and that there was no major violence."[136]

Kent has made the normalization of Honduras's relations with the rest of the hemisphere, including its return to the OAS fold, a primary diplomatic focus. Following Lobo's inauguration on January 27, 2010, Kent announced that Canada will "support President Lobo's efforts as he moves to fully reintegrate Honduras into the international and hemispheric community, including in the Organization of American States."[137] Less than a month later Kent visited Honduras, where he met with Lobo and three of his cabinet ministers. This included Micheletti's spokesperson, Minister of Planning and Cooperation Arturo Corrales, and Foreign Minister Mario Canahuati. Corrales supported the Micheletti government's refusal to implement the San José-Tegucigalpa Accord. Canahuati is the son of one of Honduras's most powerful capitalists, the maquila magnate Juan Canahuati. His brother, Jesus, is the president of the Honduran Manufacturers' Association. Mario, meanwhile, was Lobo's vice-presidential candidate in the 2005 election and is the past president of the Honduran National Business Council, a pro-coup organization. Kent also met with Canadian business leaders in the country, and toured the mining operations of Aura Minerals and Breakwater Resources.[138]

Kent's meeting with Lobo was followed up by Ambassador Neil Reeder, who met with Lobo on April 6. Reeder's visit lays bare the reason for Canada's support for the coup and Lobo (if it was not clear already): Reeder brought with him a selection of Canadian capitalists, including from Aura Minerals, talked about Canada's hope to expand its mining and maquila investments, and urged Honduras to implement new mining regulations. With the new Lobo government barely into its second month, Canada was already looking to cash in on the support it has provided, showing its solidarity with Canadian business rather than the Honduran people. Gildan Activewear—no stranger to operating in countries run by coup governments—had already announced that it is considering $200 million in new investments if Lobo's government can ensure its legal security. The same day Reeder met with Lobo it was also announced that Canadian diplomat Michael Kergin would join the Lobo-initiated Truth Commission, to round out

Canada's efforts to present Honduras as an upstanding democracy and normalize its relations with the rest of the hemisphere. The problem, of course, is that the truth commission, which is supposed to investigate events surrounding the coup, will take place, unlike other truth commissions that have taken place in South Africa or Central America, while repression is still occurring. It is farcical to suggest that the truth can be learned or genuine closure or healing achieved under such circumstances. The real aim of the commission is to provide a fig leaf of democracy to the repressive Lobo government. The resistance, not surprisingly, is boycotting it. As for Kergin, he has no expertise in the field of human rights, and is currently a member of Bennett Jones, a major corporate law firm which specializes in, among other things, international trade and investment matters and representing mining companies.[139]

During his visit to Honduras in February 2010, Kent declared that Lobo is "healing the wounds created by the recent political impasse."[140] The reality, however, is quite different, as surely Kent is aware. The resistance continues to organize, arguing that the Lobo government is not a break from the coup but represents its consolidation with the veneer of democratic legitimacy. And they continue to pay the price for their resistance: by April five activists with the Resistance Front had been assassinated since Lobo's inauguration, one two days before Kent's arrival and another four days after his departure. On top of this, eight journalists, some with connections to the Resistance Front, have been assassinated since January, and several campesinos fighting land expropriation by rich landholders in Aguan have been assassinated. COFADEH confirms that a total of forty-two Resistance members have been assassinated since the coup, though the real number, they acknowledge, are likely much higher as many family members are afraid to come forward for fear of reprisal, while many politically motivated killings are reported in the media as gang-related.[141] Anti-coup activists continue to face illegal detention, assault and threats for their activities. COFADEH itself was the target of threats in February.[142] The repression occurs, moreover, as Lobo plans to swing the country sharply back to the right. The day after his inauguration, he declared Honduras was in a state of financial emergency, and warned the country that it is entering a period of fiscal austerity.[143] This fiscal crisis will undoubtedly be used to justify opening the country up further to foreign capital, no doubt pleasing its Canadian supporters.

A More Bellicose Canada

Canada's foreign policy is becoming more aggressive and bellicose. This is certainly the case in countries where Canada is directly intervening, such as in Afghanistan and Haiti, or in regions where it has strong economic interests, such as Latin America. But Canada is also taking increasingly belligerent positions on other key international issues as part of its general foreign policy orientation.

One area in which this has become quite pronounced is the Israeli occupation of Palestine. While Canada has always supported Israel's occupation of Palestine, it used to be slightly more tempered about it. This strategy began to shift under the Paul Martin Liberal government in 2005, when Canada started voting with the small minority of the UN's Israel supporters against General Assembly resolutions criticizing Israel's occupation of the Palestinian territories and its military targeting of civilians. The decisively pro-Israel shift was followed up by the Harper Tories when they uncritically supported Israel's bloody war against Lebanon in the summer of 2006, in which over 1,000 people were killed, most of whom were Lebanese civilians. Among the non-combatants killed by Israel was a Canadian peacekeeper stationed at a UN post in the town of Khiam in south Lebanon. Israel claimed it did not know the peacekeepers were located there, but the UN insists Israel was notified several times of the peacekeepers' position. It is hard to believe that Israel was not sending a warning to UN forces to not interfere. Despite this, the Tories continued to uncritically support Israel, going so far as to work with the United States and Britain to undermine the efforts of European and Arab leaders to broker a ceasefire in order to allow Israel's attack on Lebanon and Hezbollah positions to continue.[144]

Canada was also the first state to withdraw funding from the Palestinian Authority after the democratic election of Hamas in 2006, in an effort to punish the Palestinians for electing a party that is less than compliant toward imperialism in the Middle East. Canada subsequently announced in the fall of 2007 that it is negotiating a counter-terrorism and homeland security agreement with Israel. The agreement promotes greater cooperation on technology, counterterrorism efforts, border-crossing security and biometric identification among other things.[145]

Canada's stance toward Israel should be situated within its overall security agenda. As Canadian capital continues its domestic and international expansion we can expect the aggressive security policy developments to continue, both with foreign partners and unilaterally where necessary. Militarism goes hand in hand with imperialist ambitions. Whether it is defending investments, challenging rogue states or intervening in failed states, the Canadian ruling class is preparing for ongoing asymmetric conflicts in the Global South and indigenous territories at home. Coups, military invasions and occupations, pacification programs against people who do not acquiesce with the imperialist order, and political support for compliant countries with wretched human rights records are now key ingredients of Canadian foreign policy.

And this cannot be blamed on the U.S., however happy it may be that Canada is taking this foreign policy course, and regardless of how often Canada works in concert with the U.S. Canada's policy is in the interests of Canadian capital. We do the struggle for a more socially just and peaceful foreign policy no service by sticking to the illusion that Canada is not imperialist or that it merely holds the bully's coat. Canada's a bully too that likes to throw it is weight around, even if it is not as heavy as the U.S. And unless Canadians, in solidarity with indigenous peoples at home and social movements in other regions of the world, organize to stop this security agenda, there is no reason to expect it will not continue well into the future.

1   P. Hallward, *Damming the Flood: Haiti, Aristide, and the Politics of Containment* (London: Verso, 2008); Y. Engler and A. Fenton, *Canada in Haiti: Waging War on the Poor Majority* (Halifax: Fernwood, 2005).

2   I took the idea of working with the U.S. as a self-interested imperialist insurance policy from O'Lincoln's work on Australia's alliance with American imperialism. I discuss it in the first chapter. See T. O'Lincoln, "Australia's imperialist insurance policy," Class and struggle in Australia seminar series, Australia National University (October, 2004), <dspace.anu.edu.au/bitstream/1885/42698/1/Australian_imperialism.pdf>, retrieved June 2008.

3   Hallward, *Damming the Flood*, xxx.

4   Hallward, *Damming the Flood*, 132-135; Engler and Fenton, Canada in Haiti, 97–100.

5   Hallward, *Damming the Flood*, 75.

6   Hallward, *Damming the Flood*, 75.

7   Fenton "'Legalized Imperialism': 'Responsibility to Protect' and the Dubious Case of Haiti," *Briarpatch* (December, 2005/January, 2006) <briarpatchmagazine.com/legalized-imperialism-responsibility-to-protect-and-the-dubious-case-of-haiti>, retrieved November 2007, 18.

8   Hallward, *Damming the Flood*, 106; Engler and Fenton, *Canada in Haiti*, 41–43.

9   Hallward, *Damming the Flood*, 78.

10 Hallward, *Damming the Flood*, 84–101.

11 Engler and Fenton, *Canada in Haiti*, 50.

12 Engler and Fenton, *Canada in Haiti*, 50–56. K. Skerret, "Faking Genocide in Haiti: Canada's Role in the Persecution of Prime Minister Yvon Neptune," *Press for Conversion* (September, 2007), 23-28. NCHR-H has been heavily criticized by a number of groups that sent investigative teams to Haiti shortly after the coup, including the Institute for Justice and Democracy in Haiti, National Lawyers Guild, Ecumenical Program on Central America and the Caribbean and the Centre for the Study of Human Rights. See R. Sanders, "How CIDA's NCHR-Haiti Cleverly Promoted and Then Covered Up Atrocities," *Press for Conversion* (September, 2007), 3–19.

13 Rights and Democracy is quoted in Engler and Fenton, *Canada in Haiti*, 51.

14 CPH is quoted in Engler and Fenton, *Canada in Haiti*, 52.

15 Engler and Fenton, *Canada in Haiti*, 52-53.

16 W. Robinson, "Promoting Polyarchy in Latin America: The Oxymoron of 'Market Democracy,'" in E. Hershberg and F. Rosen, eds., *Latin America After Neoliberalism: Turning the Tide in the 21st Century* (New York: The New Press, 2006), 96-119.

17 Hallward, *Damming the Flood*, 84–101.

18 Hallward, *Damming the Flood*, 120.

19 Hallward, *Damming the Flood*, 119–125.

20 Hallward, *Damming the Flood*, 124, 127–129.

21 Hallward, *Damming the Flood*, 147. The independent human rights reports cited by Hallward include one written in the British medical journal, *The Lancet* and the Harvard Law Student Advocates for Human Rights.

22 Hallward, *Damming the Flood*, 200–215

23 Hallward, *Damming the Flood*, 243–246; Engler and Fenton, *Canada in Haiti*, 19. While the activities of Canadian special forces are not publicly disclosed, pictures of Canadian special forces guarding the airport in Port-au-Prince can in fact be found on the internet.

24 Hallward, *Damming the Flood*, 234–238.

25 Fenton, "'Legalized Imperialism,'" 18.

26 Hallward, *Damming the Flood*, 249.

27 Hallward, *Damming the Flood*, 253–254, 271.

28 Ribeiro quoted in Engler and Fenton, *Canada in Haiti*, 69.

29 Hallward, *Damming the Flood*, 154; Engler and Fenton, *Canada in Haiti*, 63-68; R. Lindsay, "Peace Despite the Peacekeepers in Haiti," *NACLA Report on the Americas* (May/June, 2006), 32. A UN "peacekeeping" mission would be sent a few months later, including Brazilian, Chilean, Argentinean and Jordanian soldiers. A draft of the DND's *Counter-Insurgency Manual* (chapter six, "Army Operations in Counter-Insurgency") discusses actions by Canadian soldiers in Haitian slums. These included targeting "insurgent gangs" that were allegedly conducting surveillance on Canadian soldiers. "Observant soldiers in OPs and clearing patrols quickly identified and eliminated watchers." The accused were detained by the Canadians, their cell phones were confiscated and their names recorded. "This info was passed to UMSC regimental and Canadian intelligence staff that used it to identify the insurgent organization and command." The manual also discusses forced searches done by Canadian soldiers on a store they incorrectly thought was a weapons cache. Owners of the store were told they could get broken locks reimbursed at the Canadian military base. When they did so, they were detained because they turned out to be on the HNP's most-wanted list. The military handed them over to the police. Department of National Defense, *Counter-Insurgency Manual* (date not provided), retrieved under Access to Information Act, file n. A2007-00564.

30 Both Canada quotes are from Canada, "Government Response to the Fourth Report of the Standing Committee on Foreign Affairs and International Development," (2006), <cmte.parl.gc.ca/cmte/CommitteePublication.aspx?COM=10475&Lang=1&SourceId=201205>, retrieved February 2006.

31 Engler and Fenton, *Canada in Haiti*, 66. Both quotes are from CIDA, "Canada-Haiti Cooperation—Interim Cooperation Framework—Result Summary," (2006), <www.acdi-cida.gc.ca/CIDAWEB/acdicida.nsf?En/JUD-61414295-PP8?OpenDocument>, retrieved June 2008.

32 A. Fenton, "'Legalized Imperialism,'" 18; Hallward, *Damming the Flood*, 261

33 Canada, "Government Response to the Fourth Report of the Standing Committee on Foreign Affairs and International Development," (2006).

34 CIDA is quoted in CIDA, "Canada-Haiti Cooperation."

35 R. Saunders, "Helping Business Profit from Poverty and the Coup," *Press For Conversion*, n. 60 (March, 2007), <coat.ncf.ca/our_magazine/links/60/60-10.pdf>, retrieved November 2007; Y. Shamsie, "Export Pro-

cessing Zones: The Purported Glimmer in Haiti's Development Murk," *Review of International Political Economy* (vol. 16, n. 4, 2009), 649-672.

36 FOCAL, "The Role for Canada in Post-Aristide Haiti: Structures, Options and Leadership," (date not provided), <www.focal.ca/pdf/haiti_post_aristide.pdf>, retrieved January 2008. For more on FOCAL, including an investigation of its employees and associates, see A. Fenton, "Canada's Contribution to 'Democracy Promotion' in Latin America and the Caribbean," (October 29, 2006), <canadiandimension.ca/articles/2006/10/28/709>, retrieved January 2008.

37 Hallward, *Damming the Flood*, 297.

38 Hallward, *Damming the Flood*, 297–301.

39 Hallward, *Damming the Flood*, 297–301; R. Lindsay, "Peace Despite the Peacekeepers in Haiti," 31–32.

40 CIDA, "Canada-Haiti Cooperation."

41 Canada, "Government Response to the Fourth Report of the Standing Committee on Foreign Affairs and International Development," (2006).

42 Associated Press, "UN raids Haitian slum, igniting gun battle," *Globe and Mail* (February 10, 2007) A22; K. Ives, "Préval's Friend and Aristide's Foe Bob Manuel," (May 31, 2008), <www.haitiaction.net/News/KI/5_31_8. html>, retrieved June 2008; Haiti Action News, "One protester killed as demonstrations grow in Haiti," (April 4, 2008), <www.haitiaction.net/ News/HIP/4_4_8/4_4_8.html>, retrieved June 2008; J. Khan, "Riots expose Canada's Haiti adventure as sham," (May 21, 2008), <www.rabble. ca/news_full_story.shtml?sh_itm=6b0b02cf1872680dd6a85636467a65b 4&rXn=1>, retrieved May 2008.

43 S. Harper, "Statement by the PM on his visit to Haiti," (July 20, 2007), <www.pm.gc.ca/eng/media.asp?id=1766>, retrieved February 2008.

44 K. Pina, "Two-faced Democracy in Haiti," (November 28, 2009), <upsidedownworld.org/main/content/view/2227/1>, retrieved December 2009; W. Pierre, "Haiti's Electoral Farce Continues," (May 1, 2009), <www.dominionpaper.ca/weblogs/%Buser%5D/2636>, retrieved December 2009; Toronto Star, "Politicians vote against restoring ousted leader," Toronto Star (December 3, 2009), A28.

45 L. Cannon, "Minister Cannon Welcomes Haitian Prime Minister to Canada," (December 15, 2009), <www.international.gc.ca/media/aff/ news-communiques/2009/385.aspx>, retrieved December 2009; R. Sanders, "Lovinsky Pierre-Antoine has Disappeared!" *Press for Conversion* (September, 2007), 6–7.

46 A. Chung, "PM praises Canada's 'hard power,'" *Toronto Star* (February 17, 2010), A8; A. Chung, "PM delivers boost for Haiti," *Toronto Star* (February 16, 2010), A1; T. Fawthrop, "Cuba's Aid to Haiti Ignored by the US Media?" (February 15, 2010) <english.aljazeera.net/focus/2010/01/201013195514870782.

html>, retrieved February 2010; I. MacDonald, "'New Haiti,' Same Corporate Interests," (January 29, 2010), <www.thenation.com/doc/20100215/macdonald>, retrieved January 2010.

47 See Department of National Defence, "Canadian Forces Operations in Afghanistan—Why we are there?" (August 14, 2007), <www.forces.gc.ca/site/newsroom/view_news_e.asp?id=1703#athena>, retrieved June 2008. Curiously, Canada does not refer to R2P with respect to Afghanistan.

48 See Mandel, *How America Gets Away With Murder*, 29ff for an analysis of the Afghan war in the context of international law.

49 S. Kolhatkar and J. Ingalls, *Bleeding Afghanistan: Washington, Warlords and the Propaganda of Silence* (New York: Seven Stories Press, 2006), 103–108; 112-116.

50 RAWA quoted in Kolhatkar and Ingalls, *Bleeding Afghanistan*, 96.

51 Kolhatkar and Ingalls, *Bleeding Afghanistan*, 97–104; J. Warnock, *Creating a Failed State: The US and Canada in Afghanistan* (Halifax: Fernwood, 2008), 112-114. Many Afghan critics, including RAWA, argued that the person really in charge of their country, who played a key role at Bonn and after, is U.S. Special Envoy Zalmay Khalilzad. Khalilzad urged the U.S. to support the Mujahideen in the 1980s as director of the latter's support group "Friends of Afghanistan." He went on to work in the Reagan and Bush Sr. administrations, co-wrote the Pentagon's 1992 "Defence Planning Guidance" with the likes of Dick Cheney and Paul Wolfowitz (which argued, among other things, that U.S. security policy following the fall of the Soviet Union should be aimed at keeping a new rival power from emerging), and was a founding member, along with several other people in Bush Jr.'s inner circle, of the Project for a New American Century. Khalilzad also worked with Cambridge Energy Research Associates when it contracted to Unocal Corp while the latter was in discussions with the Taliban for a pipeline contract in Afghanistan. Kolhatkar and Ingalls, *Bleeding Afghanistan*, 127–128.

52 Kolhatkar and Ingalls, *Bleeding Afghanistan*, 135–137.

53 Warnock, *Creating a Failed State*, 119.

54 Kolhatkar and Ingalls, *Bleeding Afghanistan*, 139–145; Warnock, *Creating a Failed State*, 119.

55 Kolhatkar and Ingalls, *Bleeding Afghanistan*, 149–154; Warnock, *Creating a Failed State*, 121-123.

56 Warnock, *Creating a Failed State*, 123-125.

57 Rock quoted in Warnock, *Creating a Failed State*, 123. Political leaders commonly cite with pride Canada's support for the Afghan elections. For example, see P. MacKay's speech "Why We Are There: Canadian Leadership in Afghanistan," given as Minister of Foreign Affairs (October 19, 2006), <w01.international.gc.ca/minpub/Publication.aspx?isRedirect=True&

publication_id=384611&Language=E&docnumber=2006/21>,   retrieved
January 2008.

58   Kolhatkar and Ingalls, *Bleeding Afghanistan*, 113.

59   Warnock, *Creating a Failed State*, 144–146; Kolhatkar and Ingalls, *Bleeding Afghanistan*, 114-115.

60   J. Burch, "Karzai accused of chosing votes over women's rights," *Globe and Mail* (August 15, 2009), A15; M. Brewster, "Canadians failed to ring alarm bells on 'rape law'," *Toronto Star* (June 30, 2009), A10.

61   Kolhatkar and Ingalls, *Bleeding Afghanistan*, 140.

62   O. Ward, "'For Afghans, there is no refuge,'" *Toronto Star* (November 18, 2009), A21; K. Grieshaber, "Afghan corruption is on the rise," *Toronto Star* (November 18, 2009), A23; T. Ali, "Afghanistan: Mirage of the Good War," *New Left Review* (March/April, 2008), 12; Kolhatkar and Ingalls, *Bleeding Afghanistan*, 106; D. Saunders, "Corruption eats away at Afghan Government," *Globe and Mail* (May 3, 2008), A1. The organization that conducted the corruption survey is Transparency International.

63   G. Galloway, "Abdullah backers feel 'betrayal, shame, disbelief'," *Globe and Mail* (October 8, 2009), A15; G. Galloway, "Afghan quits team determining vote fraud," (October 13, 2009), A14; G. Galloway, "Hopes still high for deal to avert vote," (October 22, 2009), A16.

64   Ali, "Afghanistan," 12; Saunders, "Corruption eats away at Afghan Government," A16; Agence France-Presse, "Karzai's leadership challenged in UN report," *Globe and Mail* (September 27, 2007), A22; G. Smith, "Troops pay police to bolster security," *Globe and Mail* (October 9, 2007), A1; R. Westhead, "Kabul slaps muzzle on dissenting voices," *Toronto Star* (June 22, 2009), A8; P. Koring, "U.S. report offers damning picture of human rights abuses in Afghanistan," *Globe and Mail* (March 12, 2010), A4.

65   Warnock, *Creating a Failed State*, 162, 169; G. Smith, "Officials racing to salvage plan to quietly replace Kandahar governor after minister undercuts him personally," *Globe and Mail* (April 15, 2008), A1.

66   G. Galloway, "Canadian troops fatally shoot two teens," *Globe and Mail* (October 3, 2009), A22; O. El Akkad, "Afghan child likely killed by Canadian warning shot," *Globe and Mail* (July 23, 2009), A10; Ali, "Afghanistan," 15; G. Smith, "Investigators to probe shooting by Canadian troops," *Globe and Mail* (January 31, 2008), A14; Canadian Press, "Civilian dead, another shot by Canadians in Kandahar," *Toronto Star* (November 17, 2007), AA10; P. Koring, "Fingers on triggers, then split-second decisions," *Globe and Mail* (November 15, 2007), A22; G. Smith, "Afghans' anger muted in fatal shooting by troops," *Globe and Mail* (October 3, 2007), A17; G. Smith, "Canadian actions questioned in killings," *Globe and Mail* (February 20, 2007), A15; G. Smith, "Grieving father decries troops' judgement," *Globe and Mail* (July 29, 2008), A9.

67   Marc Herold, Personal Communication (December 18, 2009). His website address is <pubpages.unh/edu~mwherold/memorial.htm>.

68   P. Koring, "Military probe into alleged Canadian abuse hits brick wall," *Globe and Mail* (February 18, 2008), A1.

69   M. Brewster, "Canada 'defended' torture," *Toronto Star* (December 14, 2009), A1; B. Campion-Smith, "Tories accused of cover-up," *Toronto Star* (February 2, 2008), A20. The Hillier quote is from the Campion-Smith article.

70   P. Koring, "Canada quietly halts prisoner transfers," *Globe and Mail* (January 24, 2008), A1.

71   P. Koring, "Heavy blackouts hamper detainee probe," *Globe and Mail* (December 1, 2009), A1; S. Chase, "Afghan detainee warnings were e-mailed to Mackay's office," *Globe and Mail* (November 26, 2009), A1; M. Brewster, "Evidence of torture mounts," *Toronto Star* (November 23, 2009), A1; S. Chase and C. Clark, "Soldiers detained farmers, not Taliban, diplomat revealed," *Globe and Mail* (November 21, 2009), A4; S. Chase, "All detainees were tortured, all warnings were ignored," *Globe and Mail* (November 19, 2009), A1; S. Chase, "Ottawa warned detainees faced risk of abuse when Afghan mission began," *Globe and Mail* (October 15, 2009), A1; T. Thanh Ha, "Terror law used to harass witness at detainees probe, lawyer says," *Globe and Mail* (October 7, 2009), A13.

72   Warnock, *Creating a Failed State*, 168.

73   Senlis Council, *Losing Hearts and Minds in Afghanistan: Canada's Leadership to Break the Cycle of Violence in Southern Afghanistan* (Ottawa, October, 2006), 4.

74   Ali "Afghanistan," 15–16.

75   Ali "Afghanistan," 16; G. Galloway, "Top general lambastes locals after Canadian convoy hit by blasts," *Globe and Mail* (September 29, 2009), A12.

76   J. Straziuso, "US, NATO deaths from Afghan bombings spike 6-fold," *Associated Press* (August 12, 2009), <www.heraldstandard.com/news_detail/article/1220/2009/august/12/us-nato-deaths-from-afghan-bombings-spike-1.html>, retrieved August 2009; A. Mehler Paperny, "Mission becoming impossible task," *Globe and Mail* (September 16, 2009), A13; Warnock, *Creating a Failed State*, 168; S. Chase, "PM too bullish on Afghan challenge, critics warn," *Globe and Mail* (July 10, 2008), A11; G. Smith, "Afghan tribes plan manifesto of dissent," Globe and Mail (February 19, 2008), A14; G. Smith, "Inside the Taliban Jailbreak," Globe and Mail (July 2, 2008), A12; G. Smith and P. Koring, "The weight of war," *Globe and Mail* (March 1, 2008), A20; A. Freeman, "'Dramatic' Taliban resurgence detailed," *Globe and Mail* (June 14, 2007), A1; C. Fair, "Suicide Attacks in Afghanistan," (Kabul: United Nations Assistance Mission in Afghanistan, 2007), 38, 57; M. Brewster, "Taliban fielded battalion-size force only 10 months after rout, reports say," *Globe and Mail* (August

21, 2008), A13; M. Brewster, "Taliban came close to retaking Kandahar," *Toronto Star* (March 18, 2010), A6.

77 S. Staples and B. Robinson, "Canada's Fallen: Understanding Canadian Military Deaths in Afghanistan," *Foreign Policy Series* (vol. 1, n. 1, 2006), <www.policyalternatives.ca/documents/National_Office_Pubs/2006/Canadas_Fallen.pdf>, retrieved June 2008. DND's website has a chronological list of Canadians killed in Afghanistan. Not surprisingly, it has no list of Afghans killed in the conflict.

78 Warnock, *Creating a Failed State*, 165; M. Blanchfield, "Canada ups aid to Afghanistan," *National Post* (June 11, 2008); Globe and Mail, "Aid to Afghanistan," *Globe and Mail* (January 23, 2008); C. Clark, "Afghan mission's cost much higher than billed," *Globe and Mail* (October 10, 2008), A1.

79 Senlis Council, "Canada in Afghanistan: Charting a New Course to Complete the Mission," (May, 2007), 8. The CIDA study is Senlis Council, "The Canadian International Development Agency in Kandahar: Unanswered Questions," (August, 2007).

80 A. Woods, "Trouble in the 'model village'," *Globe and Mail* (November 24, 2009), A6.

81 G. Smith, "Canada defends policy on Afghan clans," *Globe and Mail* (September 28, 2007), A18.

82 Ali, "Afghanistan," 15.

83 J. Klassen, "Things Worth Killing For?" *Development Forum* (vol. 1, n. 1, 2008), 18-20. Canada's military and aid failure, expressed in a growing insurgency with support in Kandahar and worsening living conditions for average Afghans, is also behind the Canadian military's adoption of a psychological warfare (or "psychops") program intended to build support for its mission among locals. The strategy includes the creation of a DND-run, Pashtun radio station. Such a project is delusional, however; DND can tell the local populace all the great things it is doing all it wants, but unlike the broadcasters, who are sitting in a studio in Canada, the radio targets are actually in Afghanistan. They know the difference between rhetoric and reality—they live it. On Canada's psychops, R. Westhead, "Can Toronto woman win propaganda war in Kabul," *Toronto Star* (June 15, 2009), A4.

84 Toronto Star, "Defence minister hints at post-2011 Afghan role," *Toronto Star* (September 30, 2009), A12; M. Brewster, "Canada plans to keep a base in Kandahar until 2015," *Globe and Mail* (December 13, 2007), A21; S. Chase, "Senators forecast military deployment past 2011," *Globe and Mail* (June 12, 2008), A4.

85 The appease-the-Americans argument is pretty commonplace in anti-war writings of Canadians. Among other places, it can be found in McQuaig's *Holding the Bully's Coat* and J. Warnock, *Creating a Failed State.*

The Project for a New American Century, involving many people in Bush's inner circle, called for an invasion of Iraq before he was elected. A number of them also declared their support for an invasion in an open letter to president Bill Clinton.

86   Colonel D. Craig Hilton, "Shaping Commitment: Resolving Canada's Strategy Gap in Afghanistan and Abroad," (July, 2007), 3, <www.StrategicStudiesInstitute.army.mil/>, retrieved June 2008.

87   B. Graham, "Speaking Notes for the Honourable Bill Graham, P.C., M.P., Minister of National Defence at a conference on 'Canada in Afghanistan: Assessing the 3-D Approach," (May 13, 2005), <www.forces.gc.ca/site/newsroom/viwe_news_e.asp?id=1664>, retrieved January 2008.

88   Mackay, "Speaking Notes for the Honourable Peter G. MacKay, P.C., M.P., Minister of National Defence, for the Diplomatic Forum."

89   Kolhatkar and Ingalls, *Bleeding Afghanistan*, 225ff.

90   Lindley-French is quoted in Ali, "Afghanistan," 20.

91   Kolhatkar and Ingalls, *Bleeding Afghanistan*, 238–240; Ali, "Afghanistan," 20. Tensions within NATO have been fostered by efforts of France and Germany to establish an independent EU security policy, which the U.S. opposes. Tensions obviously increased when Germany and France refused to participate in the Iraq war of 2003. Public opinion in Europe was much more strongly against the Iraq war than it ever was toward Afghanistan, though even now France is balking at sending troops into the latter's more volatile regions.

92   Pipeline and Gas Journal, "Canadians Eye Pipeline Work in Turkmenistan," *Pipeline and Gas Journal* (October, 2004), 10; Amnesty International, "Turkmenistan," <thereport.amnesty.org/eng/regions/europe-and-central-asia/Turkmenistan>, retrieved June 2008; Foreign Affairs and International Trade, "Fact Sheet: Turkmenistan," <geo.international.gc.ca/cip-pic/geo/turkmenistan-fs-en.aspx>, retrieved June 2008.

93   J. Foster, "Countries vie for access to Turkmenistan's huge gas deposits," *Canadian Centre for Policy Alternatives Monitor* (June, 2008), 10–11; B. Pannier, "Trans-Afghan Pipeline Discussions Open in Islamabad," (April 23, 2008), <www.refrl.org/content/article/1109618.html>, retrieved June 2008; S. McCarthy, "Would help protect pipeline, Canada says," *Globe and Mail* (June 20, 2008) A18.

94   S. Chernos, "One gem of a mission," Now (March 20-26, 2008), 16; A. Hoffman, "Afghan copper lode a key to renewal?" *Globe and Mail* (March 9, 2007), B1; <www.aisa.org.af/>, retrieved August 2009.

95   A. Fenton, "The maple leaf needs to be there," (October 8, 2009), <www.vueweekly.com/article.php?id=13294>, retrieved October 2009; <alhambraresources.com/news/releases/nr_2009_08_12.html>, retrieved October 2009.

96 M. Bernier, "The Americas as a Priority—Notes for an Address to the House of Commons," (October 19, 2007), <w01.international.gc.ca/minpub/ Publication.aspx?isRedirect=True&publication_id=385527&language= E&docnumber=2007/32>, retrieved February 2008. Harper is quoted in CIDA, "Americas—Overview," <www.acdi-cida.gc.ca/CIDAWEB/acdicida. nsf/En/JUD-12911557-LVS>, retrieved June 2008.

97 CSIS is quoted in S. Bell, "Canada is a terrorist haven: CSIS," *National Post* (March 1, 2004), A1.

98 A. Freeman, "PM sells Canada as third market option," *Globe and Mail* (July 18, 2007), A1.

99 Waugh quoted in R. Foot, "Harper wins praise for focus on Latin America," (July 18, 2007), <www.canada.com/topics/news/story.html?id= 0df7b3ab-ae-3b-40d2-96bo-792b6be9d30b>, retrieved February 2008.

100 S. Harper, "Statement by Prime Minister Harper on his visit to Colombia following meetings with President Uribe," (July 16, 2007), <www.pm.gc. ca/eng/media.asp?id=1755>, retrieved May 2008.

101 Foreign Affairs and International Trade, "Minister Bernier Concludes Successful Trip to Colombia," (February 19, 2008), <w01.international. gc.ca/minpub/Publication.aspx?isRedirect=True&publication_id=38586 3&Language=E&docnumber=38>, retrieved May 2008.

102 The first Emerson quote is from M. Blanchfield, "Colombia's V-P dismisses rights criticisms as left-wing bias," (May 9, 2008), <www.canada.com/montrealgazette/story.html?id=505299ae-0779-47f3-83b3-bd1fa278696e>, retrieved May 2008; the second Emerson quote is from Reuters, "Canada says close to trade deal with Colombia," (May 5, 2008), <ca.reuters.com/ article/domesticNews/idCAN0541066720080505>, retrieved May, 2008.

103 S. Day, "Canada-Colombia Free Trade Implementation Act," 40th Parliament, 2nd Session, Number 080 (September 14, 2009).

104 A. Isaacson, "Human Rights Takes a Beating in Colombia," (March 21, 2008), <www.counterpunch.org/isaacson03212008.html>, retrieved May, 2008.

105 Kairos, "A missed opportunity for a new vision," (July 20, 2007), <www. kairoscanada.org/e/countries/colombia/HarperLatinTripCommentary. asp>, retrieved February 2008; Blanchfield, "Colombia's V-P dismisses rights criticisms as left-wing bias," F. Hylton, "Colombia's Cornered President Raises the Stakes," (March 5, 2008), <news.nacla.org/2008/03/05>, retrieved May 2008.

106 Election observer quoted in G. Leech, "Colombia's Elections Highlight Democratic Shortcomings," (November 5, 2007), <www.colombiajournal. org/colombia266.htm>, retrieved May 2008.

107 The Harper quote is from Harper, "Canada's Prime Minister Stephen Harper," (October 1, 2008), <www.latinbusinesschronicle.com/app/

article.aspx?id=1670>, retrieved May 2008. We should be careful not to overstate the radicalism of Ecuadorean President, Rafeal Correa. While he has put restrictions on mining (as discussed in the case studies chapter), refused to pay back international debt and is an ally of Hugo Chávez, he has also clashed with the radical indigenous organization CONAIE over mining and supported a watered-down version, pushed by Canada, of a new mining law that initially had high royalty rates for foreign investors.

108 Harper is quoted in M.A. O'Grady, "A Resolute Ally in the War on Terror," *Wall Street Journal* (February 28, 2009), <www.wsj.com/article/SB123578347494598289.html>, retrieved March 2009.

109 Scott Brison, "Canada-Colombia Free Trade Implementation Act," 40th Parliament, 2nd Session, Number 080 (September 14, 2009).

110 F. Hylton, *Evil Hour in Colombia* (London: Verso, 2006), 97; P. Knox, "New approach to Colombia urged," *Globe and Mail* (May 28, 2001), A9.

111 G. McGregor, "Colombian military now using surplus Canadian choppers," *Montreal Gazette* (March 21, 2001), A12.

112 D. Morrisset and C. Coulombe, *Nous étions invincible: Témoignage d'un ex-commando* (Chicoutimi: JCL Inc. Editions, 2008).

113 J. Ross, "Colombia Kills Four Mexican Students in Ecuador Bombing," (April 5, 2008), <www.counterpunch.org/ross/04052008.html>, retrieved May 2008.

114 Hylton, "Colombia's Cornered President Raises the Stakes."

115 J. Petras, "The US/Colombia Plot Against Venezuela," (January 25, 2005), <www.counterpunch.org/petras01252005.html>, retrieved May 2008. The kidnapping referred to here is the so-called Granda affair, which was uncovered by Venezuela's Ministry of the Interior and reports from journalists. When Venezuela demanded a public apology the Uribe government responded by defending its right to violate the former's sovereignty in order to defend itself against acts of terrorist aggression. On the plot against Correa, Associated Press, "Ecuador Arrests 4 In Alleged Plot Against Correa," <www.cbsnews.com/stories/2008/06/13/ap/latinamerica/main4177909.shtml>, retrieved June 2008; Press TV, "Colombians arrested in Correa plot," (June 14, 2008), <www.presstv.ir/detail.aspx?id=59878&sectionid=351020706>, retrieved June, 2008.

116 G. Clarke, "Address to the OAS General Assembly," (March 4, 2008), <www.oas.org/OASpage/videosondemand/home_eng/videos_query.asp?sCodigo=08-0064>, retrieved March 2008.

117 Torres quote is from V. Torres, "The root of the Andes crisis: Hugo Chávez," *Globe and Mail* (March 8, 2008), A25.

118 A. Fenton, "The Revolution Will Not Be Destabilized," (April 3, 2009), <www.dominionpaper.ca/articles/2557>, retrieved May 2009. The names of groups receiving money through the Canada Funds for Lo-

cal Initiatives up to 2005 is from Canadian International Development Agency, Access to Information, file number A-2007-00124, released November 23, 2007. The quote from the Caracas embassy communiqué is from the Department of National Defence, Access to Information, file number 2007-01004, document 5008, released September 17, 2009. For an exposé of the opposition groups the U.S. government is financing in Venezuela, see E. Golinger, *The Chávez Code: Cracking US Intervention in Venezuela* (London: Pluto Press, 2007).

119 H. Segal, "Time for New Beginnings on Foreign Aid," *Embassy Mag*, <embassymag.ca/page/view/segal-10-16-2008>, retrieved March 2010; L. Berthiaume, "Democracy promotion centre inching forward," *Embassy Mag*, <embassymag.ca/page/view/democracy-02-03-2010>, retrieved March 2010; A. Gurzu, "Canada-Peru: Co-operation, not supervision," *Embassy Mag*, <embassymag.ca/page/view/dipcirc-05-12-2010>, retrieved May 2010. Thanks to Anthony Fenton for drawing my attention to the Andean Unit.

120 Organization of American States, Special Meeting of the Permanent Council to receive information from the Permanent Mission of Honduras regarding the risk to the democratic institutional political process and/or the legitimate exercise of political power in the Republic of Honduras (June 26, 2009), <www.oas.org/OASpage/videosondemand/show/video.asp?nCode=09-0168&nCodeDet=2>.

121 P. Kent, "Statement by Minister Kent on the Situation in Honduras," (June 28, 2009) <w01.international.gc.ca/MinPub/Publication.aspx?lang=eng&publication_id=387343&docnum=184>, retrieved June 2009.

122 Kent quoted in M. Lacey and G. Thompson, "Envoy prepares to visit Honduras, warning of obstacles," *New York Times* (July 3, 2009), <www.nytimes.com/2009/07/03/world/americas/03honduras.html>, retrieved July 2009.

123 For a comparison of the different responses by Canada to repression in Iran, on the one hand, and repression in Honduras and Peru, on the other, see my "Acceptable versus Unacceptable Repression: A Lesson in Canadian Imperial Hypocrisy," (June 30, 2009), <www.counterpunch.org/gordon06302009.html>.

124 P. Markey and M. Rosenberg, "Honduran airport bars president's flight home after deadly day of riots," *Globe and Mail* (July 6, 2009), A1.

125 P. Kent, "Statement by Minister Kent on the Situation in Honduras," (July 19, 2009), <w01. international.gc.ca/MinPub/Publication.aspx?lang=eng&publication_id=3873405&docnum=200>, retrieved July 2009.

126 L. Cannon, "Canada Condemns Political Violence in Guinea," (September 29, 2009), <w01.international.gc.ca/MinPub/Publication.aspx?lang=eng&publication_id=387637&docnum=281>, retrieved September 2009.

127 G. Grandin, "Honduran Coup Regime in Crisis," *The Nation* (October 8, 2009); B. Oliva, "Statistics and Faces of the Repression—Violations of Human Rights in the Context of the Coup D'état in Honduras," (October, 22, 2009) Rights Action, Alert 85; Laura Carlsen, "Coup Catalyzes Honduran Women's Movement," *Americas Program* (August 20, 2009), <americas.irc-online.org/am/6369>, retrieved August 2009. Human rights abuses have also been documented by Human Rights Watch, <www.hrw.org/americas/Honduras>, retrieved October 2009 and Amnesty International, <www.amnesty.org/en/news-and-updates/several-reported-dead-honduras-turmoil-20090925>, retrieved September 2009. On March 1, 2010, COFADEH released a summary of all the assassinations since the coup, "Reigstry of Politically Motivated Violent Killings in Honduras, June 2009-February 2010." A translated version can be found at <www.rightsaction.org/Alerts/Honduran_resistance_030110.html>.

128 Kent quoted in Rights Action, Alert 41 (August 2, 2009).

129 M. Stevenson, "Desperate Honduran leaders vow to restore freedoms," *Associated Press* (September 28, 2009); L. Carlsen, "The sound and fury of the Honduran coup: acoustic and chemical attacks on Brazilian embassy," Rights Action, Alert 74 (September 27, 2009); L. Beyerstein, "Honduran labor organizer dead after tear gas attack," (September 28, 2009), <inthesetimes.com/working/entry/4962/honduran_labor_organizer_dead_after_tear_gas_attack/>, retrieved September 2009.

130 P. Kent, "Canada Calls for Restraint and a Negotiated Solution in Honduras," (September 22, 2009), <w01.international.gc.ca/MinPub/Publication.aspx?lang=eng&publication_id=385796&docnum=268>, retrieved September 2009.

131 P. Kent, "Canada Continues Engagement to Support Peaceful Resolution to Situation in Honduras," (September 25, 2009), <w01.international.gc.ca/MinPub/Publication.aspx?lang=eng&publication_id=387628&docnum=277>, retrieved September 2009.

132 P. Kent, "Canada Welcomes Agreement in Honduran Negotiations," (October 30, 2009), <www.international.gc.ca/media/state-etat/news-communiques/2009/326.aspx>, retrieved October 2009.

133 P. Kent, "Minister of State Kent Calls for Peaceful Elections in Honduras," (November 27, 2009), <www.international.gc.ca/media/state-etat/news-communique/2009/360.aspx>, retrieved November 2009.

134 A. Giordano, "Honduras Coup Regime Declares New State of Emergency Prior to Sunday 'Election'," (November 24, 2009), <narcosphere.narconews.com/thefield/3626/honduras-coup-regime-declares-new-state-emergency-prior-sunday-%E2%80%9Celection%E2%80%9D>, retrieved November 2009; Rights Action, "Honduras: More Candidates Join Election Boycott," (November 15, 2009) Rights Action Alert 92; Rights Action,

"Honduran Military Asks for Names and Phone Numbers of Community Leaders, In All Municipalities of Honduras," Rights Action Alert 93; L. Carlsen, "Honduran military raids campesino organization day before the elections," Rights Action, Alert 99 (November 29, 2009); T. Brannan, "Honduran military shoots man on eve of 'free and fair' elections," Rights Action, Alert 98 (November 28, 2009); Amnesty International, "Honduras: Stock pile of tear gas grenades triggers fears of human rights abuses," (November 30, 2009), <www.amnestyusa.org/document.php?id=ENGPR E200911301429&lang=e>, retrieved December 2009.

135 El Tiempo, "Veredicto Electoral," *El Tiempo* (November 20, 2009); D. Altschuler, "Winner is Clear, But Turnout Questions Remain," (November 30, 2009), <www.americasquarterly.org/node/1091>, retrieved December 2009; D. Altschuler, "From Tegucigalpa: Preliminary Election Analysis, Part Two," (December 9, 2009) <www.americasquarterly.org/node/1105>, retrieved December 2009; J. McVicar, "The People Say 'We Didn't Vote!'," (December 2, 2009), <upsidedownworld.org/main/content/view/2235/1>, retrieved December 2009.

136 P. Kent, "Canada Congratulates Honduran People on Elections," (December 1, 2009), <www.international.gc.ca/media/state-etat/news-communiques/2009/364.aspx>, retrieved December 2009. Costa Rica, Colombia, Peru and the U.S. also recognized the elections immediately.

137 P. Kent, "Statement by Minister of State Kent on Inauguration of Honduran President," (January 28, 2010), <www.international.gc.ca/media/aff/news-communiques/2010/048.aspx>, retrieved January 28, 2010.

138 The names of the Canadian companies with which Kent met could only be obtained through an Access to Information and Privacy request to DFAIT, file A-2009-02141.

139 Honduras Weekly, "Canada Seeks to Expand Mining and Maquila Investments in Honduras," (April 7, 2010), <hondurasweekly.com/money/2520-canada-seeks-to-expand-mining-and-maquila-investments-in-honduras>, retrieved April 2010; El Heraldo, "Diplomático canadiense acepta integrar Comisión," (April 7, 2010), <www.elheraldo.hn/País/Ediciones/2010/04/08/Noticias/Diplmatico-canadiense-acepta-integrar-Comision>, retrieved April 2010; <www.bennettjones.coma/areas_practices_item.aspx>, retrieved April 2010; M. Cameron and J. Tockman, "A Diplomatic Theater of the Absurd: Canada, the OAS, and the Honduran Coup," *NACLA Report on the Americas* (May/June 2010), 18–22.

140 P. Kent, "Minister of State Kent Concludes Successful Visit to Honduras," (February 22, 2010), <www.international.gc.ca/media/state-etat/news-communiques/2010/076.aspx>, retrieved February 22, 2010.

141 COFADEH, "Reigstry of Politically Motivated Violent Killings in Honduras, June 2009-February 2010." See also <hondurashumanrights.

wordpress.com/category/targeted-assassinations> and Associated Free Press, "Los periodistas Hondureños, en total indefensión; 8 asesinados en 3 meses," *La Jornada* (April 24, 2010), 21.

142 On kidnappings, see, for example, El Tiempo, "Raptan y torturan a dos camarógrafos de Globo TV," *El Tiempo* (February 4, 2010), <www.tiempo. hn/secciones/sucesos/10351-raptan-y-torturan-a-dos-camarografos-de-globo-tv>, retrieved February 2010. It is worth noting that El Tiempo is a mainstream corporate newspaper. Globo, on the other hand, is one of the key anti-coup media sources in Honduras and has been the target of repeated repression. On threats against COFADEH, see COFADEH, "COFADEH denounces threats against its members," (February 7, 2010), <www.hondurassolidarity.wordpress.com/2010/02/14/en-cofadeh-denounces-threats-against-its-members>, retrieved February 8, 2010.

143 J. Kryt, "A Lobo in Sheep's Clothing?" *In These Times* (February 4, 2010), <www.inthesetimes.com/article/5509/a-lobo-in-sheeps-clothing>, retrieved February 2010.

144 L. Whittington, "No deal on truce at Rome Meeting," *Toronto Star* (July 27, 2006), A8; BBC, "Israel troops 'ignored' UN plea," *BBC News* (July 26, 2006), <news.bbc.co.uk/1/hi/world/middle_east/5217176.stm>, retrieved May 2008. See also D. Maloy, "AIPAC North," (June 26, 2006), <www.zmag.org/znet/viewArticle/3659>, retrieved May 2008.

145 A. Freeman, "Ottawa negotiating pact with Israel," *Globe and Mail* (November 4, 2007), A4.

CONCLUSION:
Challenging Canadian Imperialism

It seeks to dispossess indigenous peoples of their land and resources. It aggressively pursues the penetration of Third World
markets. It works with other rich nations to impose market liberalization and debt obligations on the world's poor. It drains several billions of dollars a year in wealth from the Global South while
contributing nothing positive to the living standards of people in
the region. It systematically engages in conflict with communities
resisting its foreign investments. It builds up its military to ensure
its version of order and stability in the world is maintained by
force if necessary. This is Canada in the global order, and these are
some of the hallmarks of an imperialist power.

We can continue to cling to the belief that Canada is fundamentally different from the other major capitalist powers only
by ignoring all the overwhelming evidence to the contrary. This
belief unravels quickly when we look honestly at what Canada is
actually doing both at home and around the world. This is what
Imperialist Canada has done, and in so doing it has exposed Canada's imperialist character. But the conclusion cannot simply be
that Canada is imperialist—that it does bad things at home and
abroad that must be condemned. As important as that observation is, it is nonetheless insufficient if we want to be able to mobilize a challenge to Canadian imperialism. We need to understand
what drives it; to get at the heart of why Canada is an imperial-

ist country. There are several key points about the nature of Canadian imperialism that I have sought to emphasize throughout this book that need to be stressed here, which should deepen our understanding of the problem and our capacity to respond to it.

First, Canadian direct investment in the Global South is not confined to a few atypical Canadian companies. The reality is that since the early 1990s Canadian corporations have gained an increasingly strong foothold in the Third World. The desire to aggressively penetrate Third World markets is in fact a dominant preoccupation of Canadian capital and the state today, and it has been fairly successful. Canada can boast of some of the leading corporate players in the world in a number of industries, with a pattern of penetration of Global South markets rivalling all the major powers. But if Canadian investment in the Third World is not restricted to a few corporations, neither are the human rights abuses and ecological destruction caused by the investment. They follow Canadian capital wherever it goes with often quite tragic consequences. As a result, resistance from workers and communities to Canadian investment in the Global South is commonplace. Wherever Canadian capital goes, people are mobilizing against it to defend their labour rights, environment and access to land. In short, the dialectic of expansion and resistance is systemic to Canadian capitalism.

Second, expansion is systemic to Canadian capitalism because capitalism itself is driven by an expansionary logic. The expansionary impulses are rooted in the competitive and unplanned nature of capitalism, which underpins its cycles of overaccumulation and decline in profit rates that force capital to seek out spatial fixes, or new areas for the accumulation of wealth, to resolve its crisis tendencies. Canadian capitalists, in their quest to grow and increase their international competitiveness in the world market's game of survival of the fittest, cannot simply opt out of the search for those new areas of accumulation of wealth with cheap labour, weak regulatory regimes for natural resources and high returns on investment. Canadian capitalists are driven by the same imperatives as their counterparts in the rest of the imperialist world. This means that reforms to the rules of Canadian foreign investment, such as stronger human rights standards, while helpful, are insufficient to challenging the increasingly destructive power of Canadian capital and the state in the Third World. In its insatiable thirst for more profit, Canadian capital, supported by the state, will constantly be seeking out new and more efficient ways to exploit the people and resources of the Third World and circumvent whatever regulatory hurdles are placed before them. This does not mean we should let individual capitalists off the hook for their avarice; it is simply to stress that the problem of the global expansion of Canadian corporations is at its core a problem of capitalism and its imperialist dynamic.

Third, the demands of Canadian capital clearly shape Canadian foreign and military policy. A primary role of the state is to ensure the reproduction of capitalist relations. As the success of Canadian capitalism requires that companies be able to expand both within and beyond Canada, the state must put its energies into creating the conditions for this. These include financing investment, pursuing trade and investment agreements, deepening diplomatic ties with some countries and isolating others, weakening regulatory regimes, undermining aboriginal title and military action. It follows that while elected politicians obviously steer state policy, the roots of that policy, and the political and economic imperatives framing it, go much deeper than particular political leaders. The Stephen Harper Conservatives have in many respects been more ambitious and blunt in their goals than previous Liberal governments, particularly with respect to Latin America, but the Liberals oversaw the initial neoliberal wave of corporate expansion into the Third World, began the hunt for trade and investment agreements, sent troops into Afghanistan and supported the coup in Haiti. Both governments, with the advice and direction from state policy-makers and corporate leaders, have sought to advance the interests of Canadian capitalism as they see fit. Imperialism and capitalist state power cannot be reduced to politicians or political parties and therefore will not disappear with the passing of this or that government.

The projection of military power, it needs to be emphasized, has become increasingly important to Canadian policy-making in the neoliberal period as capital faces increasing resistance to its interests. The Canadian ruling class has plans for building a bigger and more technologically sophisticated military, while the occupations in Haiti and Afghanistan have provided important experiences in counter-insurgency and participation in economic rebuilding. Canada's military is being built as a war-fighting machine, and its most recent military engagements have been imperial conflicts. Putting aside for the moment its extremely problematic history, there is nevertheless no meaningful evidence that peacekeeping has any substantive bearing on Canadian foreign policy today. The mainstream left, such as the NDP and NGOs like the Council of Canadians, do the opposition to the war in Afghanistan a disservice by continuously repeating the unsustainable assertion that Canada is a peacekeeping nation with a history as a benign international force to which it should return.

Fourth, Canadian imperialism has a domestic component to it, and cannot be properly understood without consideration of the state and capital's efforts to expropriate indigenous land and resources. Indeed the same logic of capitalist expansion underlies both domestic and international imperialism: indigenous lands at home and Third World markets are prized assets—not yet fully penetrated by Canadian capital—seen as key to the global successes of Canadian companies. In some cases, in fact, the same company is embroiled in environmental or human rights controversies both at home and abroad. And just as Canadian corporations face resistance wherever they go in the Third World, resistance is also a condition of corporate practices in indigenous territories at home. In both cases Canadian companies and the state respond to resistance by racializing indigenous and Third World peoples as inferior and incapable of understanding their interests or caring for themselves. Canadian imperialism is a racist process.

Fifth, Canadian imperialism is not the product of American interests or demands. Whatever lead role the U.S. plays in the global imperialist system, and even though Canada is often (though not always) aligned with U.S. foreign policy, we simply cannot find solace in the idea that Canada's role in this system is merely the result of American pressures. Canada is imperialist in its own right, with extensive international interests that regularly come into conflict with communities in the Third World. There is, furthermore, nothing inherently progressive about Canada that is being warped by American influence, as nationalists still claim. Pretending that this is the case misdirects our energies and anger away from where it should be focused—the capitalist system of imperialism and the ruling elite in Canada who lead it (in terms of Canadian interests) and benefit most directly from it. Whatever progressive political gains that have been won at the domestic or international level—such as health care, union rights, specific instances of indigenous land reclamations, and even, nominally, international aid—are not the product of some abstract thing we call Canada that is unique from America and exists independent of class or national divisions. They are the product of class and anti-colonial struggle from below, in which workers and First Nation peoples forced concessions from a reluctant Canadian capital and the state. The ruling elite never offered these things to people on a silver platter because they are Canadian and these were good Canadian things to do. Canadian capitalists are, after all … capitalists. The fact that they are Canadian, and not quite as powerful as their American counterparts, does not alter that basic fact of their existence as a capitalist class. Thus while opposition to American imperialism is important, it cannot be seen as a substitute for opposition to Canadian imperialism and the privileged forces that lead it. Anti-imperialist struggle in Canada is also a class struggle.

Lastly, as imperialism is the product of the contradictory dynamics of capitalist accumulation, it will not disappear of its own accord. *We must build an anti-imperialist resistance.* Canadian capitalists will not relent unless forced to do so. It will take a mass movement, shaped by an anti-imperialist perspective that understands the limits of mere regulatory reforms on corporate behaviour, to mount a challenge to the power of Canadian capital and the state. Capital and the state need to know that we see them for what they are, and that we will not acquiesce any longer to their pillaging of the Third World and indigenous resources at home. Their pressure points need to be identified, and the stakes for them must be raised. Canada's ruling class understands no other language except that of force, as in fact resistance movements in the Global South (and indeed progressive domestic social movements) have demonstrated. Meaningful social change never comes without a struggle. Anti-imperialist transformation of course will not be easy, victories will not be achieved overnight. Such movements require time, patience and commitment to be built properly. But the payoff is that they can change the course of events, as, for example, the worldwide anti-Vietnam War movement did in the 1960s and 70s or the international anti-South African apartheid movement did in the 1970s and 80s.

Canadians must also take the lead in fostering genuine bonds of solidarity with the communities affected by, and resisting, imperialism. It should not be the responsibility of indigenous people in Colombia, for example, to actively build networks of solidarity with Canadians when it is Canadian companies invading their communities, and especially when resistance in places like Colombia entails considerable risks to people's lives. But while it is the responsibility of Canadians to build solidarity with people in the Global South and indigenous peoples at home, it is important to recognize that it is not about teaching them their rights or providing them with the tools to defend themselves against the predatory activities of Canadian capital. When it comes to challenging the power of Canadian capitalism and imperialism, communities in the Third World and indigenous nations at home are far more advanced and experienced than Canadians. Against great odds, including the repression that is visited upon those Davids who defy the Canadian Goliath, indigenous peoples at home and Global South activists have built militant mass movements against Canadian intervention in their communities. They have forced Canadian political and business leaders to take notice, and in some cases forced them to turn tail and retreat. Canadians would do well, then, to respect and learn from the leadership and examples set by these groups. This is especially the case within Canadian borders, for how can we possibly fight Canadian imperialism if we do not put front and centre the fight against the ongoing dispossession of indigenous land and the denial of indigenous self-determination.

The resistance in the Third World and in indigenous communities in Canada should be sources of inspiration. At a time when movements for social justice in Canada are at a very low ebb politically, Third World movements and indigenous struggles at home continue to fight back. Their determination reminds us that resistance is possible, that hope for a better world is not anachronistic. Their struggles, particularly those of indigenous peoples, also offer a different vision of how we can better manage our world. Like their rich world counterparts, Canadian leaders and their apologists paint indigenous peoples as backward and uncivilized, unable to take care of themselves. But the truth is radically different from this racist caricature. It is on the basis of indigeneity that the spirit and will of resistance of many defiant communities is mobilized, and that a future transcendent of unmanaged growth, environmental irresponsibility and callous greed is envisioned. For capital and its apologists, that may be a sign of backwardness; for the rest of us, it should be an inspiration.

Anti-imperialist organizing has some way to go in Canada toward the realization of its potential. This political outlook has historically been a minority position in Canada, and nationalism remains a pole of attraction for many and arguably still holds sway over some of the largest left institutions outside of Québec and First Nation communities. I hope Imperialist Canada will encourage people to rethink traditional Canadian views of Canada's role in the world, and serve as a resource for those who have already moved beyond them. But the ranks of the latter are growing, as Canada's active role in the imperial order becomes increasingly difficult to ignore. These are some of the people who can be found in such places as the various Haiti Action groups across the country, organizing against Canada's reactionary role in the impoverished Caribbean country. They can also be found organizing against the war in Afghanistan and Canadian support for Israel, raising awareness about Canadian mining and sweatshop manufacturing, working in international solidarity committees in unions, challenging racist immigration policy and building support for First Nation struggles. These are some of the early rumblings of a new Canadian anti-imperialist politics.

The challenges faced in the fight against Canadian imperialism are significant, but so are the consequences if it continues with little resistance at home. As I have shown throughout *Imperialist Canada*, Canadian imperialism is driving the Third World and indigenous communities at home ever deeper into poverty and destroying ecosystems at alarming rates, while making a few Canadians grotesquely wealthy. The targets of imperialism cannot continue to wait for Canadians to catch up politically to what their ruling class is doing. The call is being made now. They await our response.

INDEX

Todd Gordon teaches political science at York University in Toronto and is the author of Cops, Crime and Capitalism: The Law-and-Order Agenda in Canada. His articles on Canadian imperialism have appeared on *Znet, Counterpunch, Rabble,* and in *The Bullet* and *New Socialist.*